A REPORT ON UBUNTU

Thinking Africa is a series produced by the Department of Political and International Studies at Rhodes University and University of KwaZulu-Natal Press. For more information on the project, visit http://www.ru.ac.za/politics/thinkingafrica/ or write to:

Leonhard Praeg: Series Editor
Thinking Africa
Political and International Studies
Rhodes University
Private Bag 94
Grahamstown 6139
South Africa

Email: L.Praeg@ru.ac.za

Previous series titles:
The Return of Makhanda: Exploring the Legend by Julia C. Wells (2012)
On African Fault Lines: Meditations on Alterity Politics by V-Y Mudimbe (2013)

A REPORT ON UBUNTU

Leonhard Praeg

Published in 2014 by University of KwaZulu-Natal Press
Private Bag X01
Scottsville, 3209
Pietermaritzburg
South Africa
Email: books@ukzn.ac.za
Website: www.ukznpress.co.za

© 2014 Leonard Praeg

Reprinted 2017

All rights reserved. No part of this publication may be reproduced or transmitted in any form or by any means, electronic or mechanical, including photocopying, recording, or any information storage and retrieval system, without prior permission in writing from University of KwaZulu-Natal Press.

ISBN: 978-1-86914-256-8

Managing editor: Sally Hines
Editor: Alison Lockhart
Typesetter: Patricia Comrie
Indexer: Ethné Clarke
Cover design: MDesign
Cover artwork: *The Becoming Child* by Tanya Poole

Printed and bound in South Africa by Paarl Media Paarl

CONTENTS

Acknowledgements   viii

Preface   x

Introduction: Three Fragments   1

Part I   31
1   A Political Economy of Obligation   33
2   African Modes of Writing and Being   83

Part II   133
3   African Socialism   135
4   The Law: First *Epoché*   179
5   The Law: Second *Epoché*   224

Coda: In Itself   275

Select Bibliography   278

Index   288

To

Maria, for your courage; Juanita, for your care; and Jacques – or is it Jack, or is it Jakes? – for your late night SMS: 'I am so in the wrong place at the wrong time. But is that repetition not beautiful, and does it not also have a place?'

We wish to contribute to Man's development if we can, but we do not claim to have any 'solution'; our only claim is that we intend to grope forward in the dark, towards a goal so distant that even the real understanding of it is beyond us . . .
— Julius Nyerere, *Freedom and Unity*

I think that all genuine questioning is summoned by a certain type of eschatology, though it is impossible to define this eschatology in philosophical terms.
— Jacques Derrida, in *Dialogues with Contemporary Continental Thinkers* by Richard Kearney

ACKNOWLEDGEMENTS

This book was born of a failure to make myself understood. In 2008, I published an article – 'An Answer to the Question, "What is [Ubuntu]?"' in the *South African Journal of Philosophy* (27[4]) – intended as the first instalment of a two-part essay on the topic. It provoked much incomprehension: too dense, too complicated, too wilfully obscure, I was told. From a colleague at another university, I heard that it had been referred to as 'spectacularly incomprehensible'. I wasn't really surprised because most people tend to think that it is obvious *what* Ubuntu is. Like pornography, we know it when we see it. But as with pornography, things get difficult as soon as people try to explain what they see. What troubled me even more at the time, however, was a failure of a different kind, for what does it mean to write an article about our shared humanity that remains incomprehensible to most of humanity? And so I set out to rewrite the essence of that article in book form. Along the way, a wise friend cautioned, 'There is no such thing as a rewrite' and, of course, he was quite correct. My exploration soon took me in a number of directions that I could never have anticipated – particularly with regard to the question about Ubuntu in relation to the law, the subject of the last two chapters. The journey has been exhausting and rewarding in equal measure and my first acknowledgement of gratitude goes to the people who found the original exploration incomprehensible.

In the course of drafting the outline of this book, I started to teach a postgraduate course on Ubuntu as part of Thinking Africa – a project launched by a number of colleagues and myself in the Department of Political and International Studies at Rhodes University. I am very grateful to all the students who have taken this course over the last four years and who, in the words of Julius Nyerere quoted in the epigraph to this book, took on the challenge of groping 'forward in the dark, towards a goal so distant that even the real understanding of it is beyond us'. To my colleagues in this project – Sally Matthews, George Barrett, Siphokazi Magadla, Phumlani Majavu and Richard Pithouse: I deeply appreciate your enthusiasm for and hard work on the project in general, the spirit of collective responsibility and your help in organising the 2012 colloquium, Ubuntu: Curating the Archive. A special word of gratitude goes to Rhodes University's vice-chancellor, Dr Saleem Badat, for sharing the vision of this project and for helping us to find an answer to the even more obscure question: Where is the funding going to come from?

I am also very grateful to my three assistants – Danielle Bowler, Mbali Baduza and Jocelyn Coldrey – for all their hard work in hunting down references, copying, scanning and assisting me in 'personifying' the archive.

Colleagues who became friends through their generous involvement in Thinking Africa have commented on various chapters of this book: Lewis Gordon, Grant Farred, V-Y Mudimbe, Nigel Gibson, Drucilla Cornell – I am humbled by your wisdom, patience and willingness to engage me on this topic. Where I have ignored your advice or decided not to heed your caution, the responsibility is, of course, all mine.

A heartfelt word of gratitude to the team at UKZN Press: Debra Primo, Louis Gaigher and Sally Hines – without their professionalism and dedication, this book series would not have seen the light of day. In particular, I would like to thank my editor Alison Lockhart for her outstanding work on this manuscript.

Lastly, to Hannes and Jaime for allowing me to stay on their beautiful farm for ten days in December 2012 when I needed to rethink the whole enterprise: an embarrassing number of insights could only have matured in the quiet of the Karoo. That in itself says a lot about many things, but there it is.

PREFACE

> If in that second – that is to say, at the last conscious moment before the fit – he had time to say to himself, consciously and clearly, 'Yes, I could give my whole life for this moment,' then this moment by itself was, of course, worth the whole of life. However, he did not insist on the dialectical part of his argument: stupor, spiritual darkness, idiocy stood before him as the plain consequence of those 'highest moments'.
> — Fyodor Dostoyevsky, *The Idiot*

The process of preparing for publication the two volumes that mark the culmination of the Thinking Africa project of 2012 – the *Report on Ubuntu* and the proceedings of its annual colloquium, *Ubuntu: Curating the Archive* – commenced in the week that marked the first commemoration of the Marikana massacre. Though the place and meaning of this event in a future South African historiography is already (and always will remain) hotly contested, one thing is already abundantly clear today. The African National Congress's (ANC's) claim to have founded the new South Africa on the *nomos*, or spirit of law, of an extraordinary humanism has bottomed out. After Marikana, no such claim can plausibly be made or sustained. Just as its so-called human-rights-inspired foreign policy revealed itself as a myth soon after it was named as such, any claim by the ANC government to have founded our democratic politico-juridical order on the idea of a shared humanity will and indeed *must* in future be met with derision.

For this reason alone, it would be the most obvious thing in the world to denote and dismiss, or perhaps embrace, this as the dawn of our post-humanist present, to abandon talk of Ubuntu altogether, to dismiss it as historical artefact or as a passing infatuation with an already exhausted nationalism. In that case, projects such as this *Report* or *Ubuntu: Curating the Archive* would amount to little more than a silly intellectual and economic gamble because they would be a memorial to a history-just-past, the history that was betrayed; testament to a lasting traumatic melancholy that would do no more than make visible, through its very engagement with the topic, the absence of Ubuntu in the postcolony, a sign of a shared recognition of the absence of a shared humanity and the vacuity of any claim to a founding humanist *nomos*.

From another more resilient perspective, however, it seems that what has passed is not the possibility of a humanist *nomos*, per se, as much as its conception in the narrow nationalist terms of an *African nomos*, one that was always driven, less by a concern with our shared humanity than with the violent politics of identity claims, premised on an infatuation with an equally violent logic of cultural and political sovereignty, which historically manifested nowhere so clearly as in the beloved myth of South Africa's so-called miraculous transition – always a function, it was claimed, of something as lasting, because essential, as Africa's exceptional humanism. Of course, this is not to say that there have not always been theorists who contested this Ubuntu-driven nationalism, this nationalist, reductive violation of Ubuntu. There have been many excellent critiques, but even they were always articulated within the confines of a nationalist matrix: a binary juxtapositioning of the old South Africa with the new South Africa, of apartheid with democracy, Eurocentrism with Africanity and so on. Within this matrix, the claims of those who posited Ubuntu as the founding value of a new politico-juridical order were contested by anti-nationalists, who saw in such claims nothing but the vacuous identitarian claims of a bourgeois politics, largely unconcerned with mobilising the radically expansive understanding of justice implicit in Ubuntu as a potent critique of neoliberal constitutionalism. This is to say that the problem was never with Ubuntu as such, but with the politics of Ubuntu, the domestication of humanism to do the necessary, but not therefore less dirty, work of the politics of the day; the tendency to reduce a humanist emphasis on our shared humanity to an ideology, a human*ism* narrowly conceived in terms of the nationalist project, always premised on the identitarian assumption of a miraculous African subjectivity and its exceptional humanism – in short, the violent reduction of humanism to the logic of identity politics. If, for nationalists, Ubuntu was always simply *present* as a founding *nomos* of a potentially humanist order, it was only ever considered either as *vacuous* by those who, through the seductions of neo-racist dismissals of things African, trivialised its potential to found a new order, or as *absent* by those who could see no need to found a politico-juridical order on anything other than the contractarian axiomatic, the Law of laws, of liberal constitutionalism.

In retrospect, it was to be expected that this nationalist matrix, inspired as it was by the transition as our 'highest moment', should have delivered us onto this post-humanist moment of spiritual darkness and idiocy, that it should have culminated in this paradox of a humanism exhausted by its incarnation as nationalism, the moment at which we suddenly find ourselves disillusioned by the very idea of nationalism and everything that was invoked in order to make it plausible and executable as political project, a moment that will always predetermine as irredeemably apocalyptic the meaning of Marikana in our collective imagination. Marikana was an apocalyptic moment (*apocalypse*: from the Greek 'unveiling') precisely because it revealed with incontestable clarity the horror of a politico-juridical order that had come adrift from the 'highest moment' of its founding promise. Marikana is a sign of the drift of political Will, of a juridico-political order that has lost its moorings, become detached from its own founding as a political event, excluded from the very promisorial structure that would make of Marikana a *political* event. There can be few experiences as horrifying as this collective sense of being adrift from the origin for, implicit in the founding, is always a sense of purpose, of direction and intent immemorially captured by the claim, 'We the people . . .' commit to or believe in this or that, so that for a society to find itself severed from and, as a consequence, adrift from its founding, amounts to recognising the horror of no longer existing with a sense of purpose premised on a founding intent. Existence is reduced to the random outcome of the calculation of fleeting interests. Of course, there is a real sense in which the political is always precisely such a calculation, but what keeps political orders from imploding under the weight of random calculations has always been nothing but a conception of themselves as a lasting iteration of the founding intent, a determination to remain anchored to the sense of purpose that first unified the collective as a 'We'.

But a different response to the present is possible, one that will have to proceed from a temporary suspension (*epoché*) of the nationalist matrix and all the dead-end questions that have resulted from it (what is *African* about this communitarianism, this humanism, this socialism? What does *African* mean?), in order to reposition Ubuntu in the more cosmopolitan terms of a critical humanism that must always remain irreducible to the politics of the day, a project that has to return to, in order to retrace, the founding claim that a politics premised on shared humanity is, after all, perhaps, possible. Such an endeavour will demand of us nothing less than a return to the origin that ushered in our contemporary, postcolonial discourse on Ubuntu, in order to reinterpret its meaning and place, no longer in the narrow binary terms of the nationalist matrix, but in the more universal terms of a pre-nationalist undecidability that was reduced to simple presence by a nationalist claim to speak on its behalf. If Ubuntu is to be reinvented, yet again, but this time beyond the easygoing seductions of a belated nationalism and its discontents, it is to the inescapable ambivalence of the founding that we have to return, in order to appropriate it as founding trope that was always necessarily going to be both present *and* absent.

There is therefore an argument to be made that as a critical project Ubuntu needs to be rethought, or at the very least, that the question of how it interrogates us, and not just us, 'it', must be thought all over again.

We at Thinking Africa can only hope that these two volumes will do some of the urgent conceptual work needed to give discussions on Ubuntu a new philosophical and political life, one in which we may one day, yet again, return to the idea and the possible viability of claiming that contemporary political life is, indeed, the constant iteration of a founding commitment to our shared humanity.

INTRODUCTION

Three Fragments

> We have always been consigned to responding from the place where we ought not to have been standing.
> — Ato Quayson, 'Obverse Denominations: Africa?'

Fragment I: Responsibility

Perhaps the most appropriate way to introduce this book is to offer a brief explanation of its curiously officious title, *A Report on Ubuntu*. The notion of a 'report' carries a variety of associations, meanings and pompous appeals to authority and their legitimation. One may well imagine a monarch or a minister of cultural affairs commissioning a 'report' on Ubuntu, which could end up bearing a subtitle such as this. Of course, we know that whoever commissions a report always has a vested interest in what will be reported, which means that it is very difficult to imagine a report that truly asserts its freedom to report whatever its findings may be. Consider an extreme example: A report is commissioned and includes among its findings, perhaps even listing as one of its major 'recommendations', that the governing body or person who commissioned the report lacked the necessary authority to do so. A curious outcome, indeed. In what sense would such a report still be an official report? Perhaps only in the rather complicated sense that by questioning or denying the authority of the commissioning body or person, the report will implicitly or explicitly appeal to some other authority as the true source of its legitimation – the 'discipline of philosophy', for instance, or perhaps more romantically, the 'people'. The report may even elaborate on its subversion of the commissioning authority: 'It is not within the purview of the minister's power to canonise the issue under investigation by appointing consultants and researchers to define, circumscribe and legitimise certain voices while marginalising others – which, in the experience of the writer of this report, is always the invariable outcome of official reports . . .' and so on and so on.

I imagine it was something along these lines that the French philosopher Jacques Derrida had in mind when, in one of his lesser-known writings, 'Mochlos; or: The

Conflict of the Faculties' (1992b), he commented on an idea that was emerging in higher education discourse at the time, namely that universities and the intellectuals who work in them must be 'accountable' to society for the vast amounts of money spent on them. Does the very notion of accountability not imply the logic of the 'report', of 'giving an account of oneself', of 'reporting back' to those who pay the bills? Of course it does. Just as the twin terms 'accountability' and 'report' also imply a third, namely 'responsibility'. But as Derrida and a host of other scholars have consistently argued over the last couple of decades, the financial logic of 'accounting' is inappropriate when it comes to assessing the value of knowledge-production and the institutions tasked with generating such knowledge (see Readings 1996). 'Accounting' too readily slips into a logic of balancing the books, which, in turn, suggests that the value of studying at tertiary institutions, in fact the whole experience of being a student and an academic, can be quantified in a currency of sorts that somehow will enable universities to balance their running costs with what society gains from having them. The easiest and laziest way to forge a currency out of what is essentially unquantifiable is to argue that a developing society (are all societies not developing societies?) needs productive citizens with real skills and that the usefulness of the university lies in producing such skilled and productive citizens. As banal as it may seem, this is not a completely wrong-headed argument. In fact, articulated more carefully, it almost seems obvious: 'Being an academic is justified only if it serves humanity in some way or other, and society is justified in requiring this of us. If philosophy is a worthwhile activity it must prove its worth in the human context that supports it and makes it possible' (Shutte 1993: 6).

The problem here is not usefulness per se, but the reduction to usefulness – as if an important part of any university's identity has not always consisted in being somewhat useless to society. The space of the 'somewhat useless' is essential because it enables scholars and students to explore ideas that may either end up in the trash or revolutionise the world. This brings me to the question of responsibility and Derrida's early intervention in this debate:

> Today the minimal and in any case the most interesting, most novel and strongest responsibility, for someone attached to a research or teaching institution, is perhaps to make this [politics], its system and its aporias as clear and thematic as possible. In speaking of clarity and thematization . . . I still appeal to the most classical of norms, but I doubt that anyone could omit to do so without, yet again, putting into question every thought of responsibility . . . (1992b: 22).

What does it mean to suggest that responsibility consists in making this politics, 'its system and its aporias as clear and thematic as possible'? I shall take Derrida to mean that our first responsibility as academics and intellectuals consists in making visible the fundamental tensions and contradictions that are constantly reproduced in the act of knowledge-production and in the institutions tasked with this process. This sounds complicated, but it is really no more than an intellectually specific way of saying that the first responsibility of students and scholars alike consists, not in 'giving an account of themselves' or even 'reporting back' to the state or society, with the intention of demonstrating usefulness, but rather in articulating and making visible the politics that is constantly reproduced in and through our institutions of higher learning.

Elsewhere (Praeg 2010b) I have responded to this demand to be 'as clear and thematic as possible' by listing eight first principles that could assist us in thinking through this responsibility. Four of these are particularly pertinent here:

1. The university is independent, not autonomous. There is a world of difference between the claim to autonomy and the claim to independence. The claim to autonomy prioritises freedom, while acknowledging *some accountability*, while the claim to independence does the exact opposite: it implies a recognition of accountability and responsibility, while asserting *some freedom* (Praeg 2010b: 9). In a developing society such as South Africa, it is only to be expected that this difference, as subtle and complex as it may appear, will become pivotal in a debate on institutional (and academic) freedom, responsibility and so on. How we interpret this difference is of the utmost importance. What some may interpret as a clear instance of the erosion of intellectual and institutional autonomy, others may well defend as the need to balance the desire for autonomy with the responsibility implicit in the recognition of independence. At a meta-level this may translate into a contestation of values, an interrogation of Western-style autonomy (which prioritises entities over relations) by a (postcolonial) African insistence on independence (which prioritises relations over entities).
2. Some knowlege must be recognised as an end in itself. In other words, not all knowledge produced by scholars and students has to be useful to society. Universities do not only train citizens to *do*, they also educate them to *be* (Vale 2010). The claim that a certain amount of freedom is indispensable to exploring, recognising and embracing alternative ways of being as an end in itself is the existential (and epistemological) equivalent of the claim to institutional independence.

3. Apparently contradicting this principle is a third, which asserts that there is no such thing as knowledge 'as an end in itself' because all knowledge constructs, irrespective of which discipline, has a sociological and therefore a political base. Everything is political, particularly the claim not to be political. There is no such thing as *apolitical* knowledge and every claim to be pursuing knowledge as 'an end in itself' is first and foremost a political statement or claim that seeks to conceal from itself and everyone else the simple fact that all forms of knowledge work to sustain what one could call their implicit socio-epistemic communities and the institutions that such communities have created to perpetuate and sustain their interests.
4. From the tension generated between the third and fourth principles, it seems to follow that one of the central aims of higher education should consist in making visible to students the political fact of their belonging to certain socio-epistemic communities, so that they can understand the extent to which such membership both determines and limits their perceptions of the world.

An example may better illustrate what I am trying to articulate here. Few South African students – of any cultural and/or class background – are aware of the extent to which the post-apartheid economy and politico-juridical system congeals into, or finds structural coherence in, the basic assumption that the autonomous, rational individual is prior to (in the sense of being more fundamental than) social relations, interdependence and the kind of obligations (moral, political, social) that would follow from holding these relations as more fundamental. Of course, there is nothing particularly South African about this. It merely reflects what it means to describe a modern society in Western, liberal, democratic terms. In such a society, the basic assumption or axiomatic is that the individual is an autonomous entity who enters into relations with others solely on the basis of a rational and voluntary calculation of self-interest. This assumption is reflected as much in a neoliberal economic emphasis on the pursuit of self-interest as it is in a juridico-political order premised on the protection of individual rights or in educational institutions that, through a complex combination of curriculum choices and institutional arrangements (the solitary research project, assessment practices and so on), prepare students for a life consonant with such a notion of personhood and its implicit values.[1] To raise the question of Ubuntu as African philosophy or as a cornerstone of an African

---

1. See, for instance, Beets and Le Grange (2005).

philosophical practice in such a context, with the assumption that whatever it means it may be useful and relevant to us, is indeed a very complex business. It demands of us not only to ask and answer a philosophical question, but also, in the spirit of our responsibility, to interrogate philosophy itself, to make 'its system and its aporias as clear and thematic as possible'.

A vast number of writers have interrogated the complicity of Western philosophy in the reproduction of racist, Western modernity. In fact, doing so is one *raison d'être* of Africana philosophy (which includes African philosophy and diaspora studies). This is not the explicit aim of this report. In fact, I shall address the issue of the racialisation of knowledge-production only obliquely and in the process of pursuing a much more specific question, namely, What are the historical conditions for the possibility of asking questions such as: What is Ubuntu? What does Ubuntu mean? What is or should be the place of Ubuntu in a modern South Africa? To readers unfamiliar with the way philosophers approach questions, this may sound like a complex way of going about things and indeed it is. What it really amounts to is an attempt to make visible the background – historical, political, social – against which questions about Ubuntu appear as meaningful, urgent and, above all, as 'simple'. Formulated differently, we can say that in order to address the question 'What is Ubuntu?' it may be useful to suspend, through a temporary bracketing (or *epoché*), the question itself in order to ask a number of other questions, such as: Why are we asking this question now? Why not 300 years ago? What difference does the *when* (we ask the question) make to the *what* (we give as an answer)? Further, why do the majority of attempts aimed at defining Ubuntu remain blind to their most basic assumption, namely that there is something significant or particular about Ubuntu? Is it not possible that Ubuntu is so over-determined by identity politics – by postcolonial questions about what it means to be African, the demand to be unique, to be authentic and so on – that every engagement with Ubuntu is never simply an intellectual investigation, a way of *saying* things, but first and foremost a way of conducting identity politics, of *doing* things? The moment we acknowledge this, we have already temporarily suspended the question of Ubuntu by insisting that there are more fundamental, political questions that need to be addressed in order to understand how we have come to think about Ubuntu in the way that we have. A simpler way to articulate all of this is to say that to speak of Ubuntu is first and foremost a political act and that our responsibility lies precisely in recognising this priority of the political.

But what does it mean to say that a question about something is first and foremost a political act, a way not of saying something, but a way of doing something, of doing politics? How are we to understand this 'first and foremost'? Readers who are familiar with philosophical practice will already have recognised in this phrase the claim that the political is 'First Philosophy'. That claim is central to this report. More than that, it is a claim that I think every humanities student in the postcolony should understand and appreciate. Because not all such students (nor all readers) will be familiar with the philosophical notion of First Philosophy, I want to summarise something of its meaning, not in the form of an abstract philosophical argument (which would beg the question), but rather in a more practical, perhaps prosaic manner, namely through philosophy's oldest conceit, the conversation.[2]

Fragment II: The political
The conceit of the philosophical conversation is admittedly a bit thin and makeshift, hardly the sort of thing that nowadays invites suspension of disbelief. Nonetheless, I imagine a conversation between a (white) philosophy lecturer and a (black) postgraduate law student, who is considering doing a second master's degree in philosophy. The student I imagine may as yet know very little about philosophy as such but, for a variety of reasons that all intersect with the fact of her blackness, she nonetheless has a lived experience of being oppressed and of what it will require to be recognised as an equal, not in any complicated theoretical sense of the word, but simply as an equal in a conversation with somebody who is not black. So the lecturer asks:
– Why don't you try philosophy?
– What is philosophy?
– Simply put, it is the subject in which we ask the most abstract or fundamental kinds of questions. This means that when physicists or biologists get to a point where they ask very abstract and fundamental questions about the origin and purpose of life, they invariably meander into philosophy.
– What do you mean by 'fundamental questions'? Can you give me an example?
– Well, for a long time it was thought that the most fundamental questions we can ask are *epistemological*; that is, questions concerned with how we know the world and how we can be sure that our knowledge about the world is correct . . .

---

2. For more substantial, theoretical, representations of the argument that the political is First Philosophy, see Praeg (2008a), reprinted in *Au-delà des lignes: Fabien Eboussi Boulaga, une pratique philosophique*, edited by L. Procesi and K. Kavwahirehi. See also Gordon (2007).

– You say 'for a long time'. Sounds like philosophers have since changed their minds?
– Well, in a sense, yes. The German philosopher Martin Heidegger argued that we don't only exist as creatures that want to have knowledge about the world. He insisted that 'knowing' is only one kind of relationship we have with the world. There are many others and our existence is much more multifaceted . . .
– Can you give me an example of another kind of relationship we have with the world?
– Well, Heidegger argued that long before we set out to know the world, we already have certain knowledge. At some level we already know, for instance, that we *live in the world*, that we live in the world *with other people* and so on. These he called 'modes of existence' and, much in the same way that the categories of 'space' and 'time' structure our perceptions of the physical world, these modes make all our experiences in and of the world possible – even the experience of knowing something. Understanding these modes is the foundation of all philosophy. Because they are what we call *ontological* questions, concerned with how we exist at all, it must be that these ontological questions are the most fundamental questions we can ask.
– Very interesting. I get a sense of what you're after. It's a bit like saying, 'Understand what it means to exist as a human being before you try to know the world.'
– I suppose so. But it did not end there. Things soon took another turn. Not long after Heidegger, Emmanuel Lévinas came along and pointed out that this whole project of understanding modes of existence is all very 'me': *me* understanding *my* existence, *me* grappling with the modes of existence that make *me* aware of what being a human being means to *me* and so on. What if, he argued, the most fundamental questions are not ontological, but rather *ethical*? What if all these modes of existence Heidegger talked about were, in some sense, a function of a deep ethical confrontation with an Other, whom I should never, if I were to allow them to remain Other or different from me, simply reduce to one element in a 'mode of existence'? What if my first obligation consisted, not in knowing the world or even in understanding what it means to be human, but rather in figuring out how to respond to this other person who is standing right in front of me? Are the most fundamental questions not perhaps ethical?
– I like that, but I'm not quite convinced . . .
– Think of it this way: Lévinas suggested that the most fundamental questions relate to this Other whom I need to understand, but whom I constantly threaten to

violate by imposing on him or her all sorts of ideas, prejudices and so on. I recognise this Other, but my very recognition always threatens to make of the Other something more like me, something . . .

– Oh, I get it; it sounds a bit like what the American jurisprudence scholar Duncan Kennedy had in mind when he said that other people present me with a 'fundamental contradiction' in the sense that they are both necessary *for* and a threat *to* my freedom; without other people in the world I cannot meaningfully claim to be free, but as soon as they enter the world, they also invariably pose a threat to my freedom.[3]

– Yes, I can live with that comparison. For Lévinas this meant that the most fundamental questions are indeed *ethical*.

– Very interesting. This 'primacy of the ethical' of course resonates with being African because of Ubuntu and all that. But I am also an African whose family as recently as one generation ago suffered the most outrageous form of racial oppression. Of course, we're technically free now and the fact that I am standing here having this conversation about what I should continue to study at this formerly white university seems to demonstrate that fact. But it's not that simple. And while I think this Lévinas was onto something, I think there may be a kind of question that is even more fundamental than ethical questions.

– Such as?

– Well, think back twenty years or so. During apartheid we would not have been able to have this conversation – not here anyway because I would not have been allowed on campus. I would have been excluded from conversations like this on the basis of the colour of my skin.

– Your point being?

– Well, it seems obvious to me then that the most fundamental starting point for any philosophical conversation should be questioning the mechanisms that decide who is included and who is excluded from that conversation and whose traditions of thought will or will not be invoked in that conversation. Perhaps the most fundamental questions, the questions that every conversation should start with are *political*, questions such as: How is the difference between the included and

---

3. In Chapter 5, I explore the work of Duncan Kennedy – 'Form and Substance in Private Law Adjudication' (1976), 'The Structure of Blackstone's Commentaries' (1979) and, to a lesser extent, 'Freedom and Constraint in Adjudication: A Critical Phenomenology' (1986) – as well Johan van der Walt's discussion of these texts in *Law and Sacrifice: Towards a Post-Apartheid Theory of Law* (2005).

excluded legitimised and what kind of institutional arrangements exist to safeguard and perpetuate certain kinds of knowledge at the exclusion of others?
– Oh, but that's an easy example. We're, what, almost twenty years down the line and here we are having a conversation, so obviously . . .
– Obviously it's all fine now and we can just get on with it? I don't think so. The only thing that has changed is that the filtering mechanisms that determine who gets in and who stays outside, as well as *what* we study once we're on the inside, have become more subtle and nuanced.
– I suppose you're right. Every conversation is a function of a political background that determines who participates in the conversation, what gets talked about – in the case of the university, what gets taught – and what institutional arrangements will be adopted.
– Surely these questions are the most fundamental? In terms of your Lévinas, the implication would then be this: by insisting on the fact that the most fundamental questions are political, I am also insisting that the ethical is political. I mean, whose ethics are you going to invoke in order to deal with this Other?
– Makes sense. In philosophical terms, one would perhaps sum this up by saying that all philosophies are historically peculiar to the societies that produce them, 'all philosophy is ethnophilosophy', the philosophy of an *ethnos* or a people and that the political therefore is First Philosophy.
– Which brings us right back to where we're standing because everything around us, everything in this so-called new South Africa, from its neoliberal economics to its liberal constitutionalism, exists by virtue of the marginalisation of what perhaps the majority of the population still accept as a given, namely the simple fact that we are interdependent, that *I am because we are.* Is this insight as well represented in law, politics and economics as individualism and the pursuit or defence of self-interest? Obviously it isn't and that is what I mean by institutionalised marginalisation, by stating that *everything is political.*
– This is beginning to feel a bit like we have to reinvent the world before we can have a conversation about it.
– Well, there is a sense in which criticism always means going back to the beginning, returning to the origin of things in order to reinvent how they hang together. Ask any conscious black person about this stuff and he or she will tell you that if we're going to have a conversation about anything that affects all of us, a discussion of the political is the most fundamental or, as you put it, the First Philosophical question.

– That does seem to turn everything on its head, doesn't it?
– I suppose it does.
– Thanks for making that so clear to me. For a brief moment our roles were reversed and you became the teacher . . .
– That's okay. It was a thin conceit to begin with . . .

Fragment III: Critical humanism

> You try to draw everything into the net of your faith, father, but you can't steal all the virtues. Gentleness isn't Christian, self-sacrifice isn't Christian, charity isn't, remorse isn't. I expect the caveman wept to see another's tears. Haven't you even seen a dog weep? In the last cooling of the world, when the emptiness of your belief is finally exposed, there'll always be some bemused fool who'll cover another's body with his own to give it warmth for an hour more of life.
>
> — Graham Greene, *A Burnt-Out Case*

I do not think it would be an exaggeration to say that the most fundamental political matrix that structures our thinking about Ubuntu and that needs to be made visible *from the start* is the tension between the local and the global, a tension that is truly 'supercomplex' (see Barnett 2000). New democracies such as South Africa have to renegotiate what we may loosely refer to as the 'social contract'. They have to rearticulate citizenship in terms of a new understanding of duties, rights and obligations – which in a context of radical pluralism is a complex business. This becomes a supercomplex business when we realise that all of this has to be done in the context of globalisation, marked by the systematic erosion of the power of states and local cultures, in order to meaningfully contribute to our understanding of what these concepts mean. In other words, new or emerging democracies have to enter a global fitness landscape of competitive knowledge economies through 'an intelligent use of the opportunities made possible by globalization whilst at the same time facing up to the various challenges that are posed by globalisation to their national identiy and resources' (Jucevièienë and Vaitkus 2007: 43).

Like the university, states, nations and cultures are enmeshed in complicated local and global networks of interdependence; they are structured by a fundamental relationality within which they must fight for and maintain their political independence as well as their cultural specificity. From a postcolonial perspective, the most important characteristic of these networks is the asymmetrical nature of their power (small countries contribute little, if anything, to the meaning of goods, styles and ideas that circulate as 'global'). This *external* assymetry is almost always replicted as an *internal* asymmetry between elites and the poor, between those who historically were and continue to be disadvantaged and those who have become superadvantaged, either as a result of having obtained the political power to dominate local networks or as a result of having managed to capitalise on the interfaces between local and global networks that globalisation everywhere makes possible.

Ubuntu, whose reinvention more or less coincided with South Africa's reinvention of itself as an African country and its readmittance to the global community of states, was never going to escape this asymmetrical pull and push of globalisation. In fact, as Wim van Binsbergen (2001) has convincingly argued, the reason why Ubuntu is so very difficult to define is exactly because it is what some complexity theorists would call a *glocal* phenomenon; that is, a phenomenon about which it is impossible to to say whether its content derives exclusively from either a local or a global *imaginaire*. The reason why Ubuntu has been and will remain impossible to define is precisely because it is an interstitial concept whose meaning has always been and will continue to be a function of the combination of local needs and global expectations. I have argued before and continue to do so in this report that the meaning of African humanism – what we call Ubuntu in southern Africa – is constantly reproduced in the complex space between the local need for cultural identity and a global demand for the expansion (and naturalisation) of human rights, by essentially infusing the meaning of these rights with local understandings, through a process that V-Y Mudimbe has described as 'retrodiction' (1991a: 13).[4] Suffice it to say that since the start of decolonisation in Africa, these local and global *imaginaires* have constantly intersected in order to reproduce very different meanings of and for African humanism – at first a form of humanism, then an African kind of socialism and, more recently, a quasi-Christianised theology of reconciliation and forgiveness. It is simply symptomatic of the asymmetrical relations constitutive of the relationship between African postcolonial societies and the West that African humanism in general and Ubuntu in particular will

---

4. To be more linguistically inclusive, ubuntu is sometimes called 'ubuntu-botho'. However, in this report 'ubuntu' is used to refer to the living practice and 'Ubuntu' to refer to the abstract postcolonial articulation of that practice as philosophy.

always be framed *as* a form of humanism, *as* an African communitarianism, *as* an Aristotelian virtue ethic, *as* an African Socialism and so forth. In this regard, there are two questions that we must always remain sensitive to: When is what frame adopted and for what purpose? And what do we gain/lose by encoding African humanism in general and Ubuntu in particular in any one of these frames?

The way I want to frame Ubuntu for the purposes of this report is as critical humanism. Within this frame, the word 'critical' refers to the primacy of the political as elaborated above. In this sense, the critical humanism I have in mind differs from traditional, Western humanism in at least one very important respect: the central focus of critical humanism is not simply the human – the human capacity for science, beauty and knowledge in a world that no longer defers meaning to a transcendental source. In critical humanism, the 'human' is a secondary concept; true to the logic outlined in the conversation above, a more fundamental or primary concern is with the relations of power that systematically exclude certain people from being considered human in the first instance. Lewis Gordon has argued that this concern accounts for the fact that 'there is no black philosophical text . . . that lacks an appeal to some kind of humanism or to the humanity of black people, often defended in the form of a philosophical anthropology' (2008: 123). In a similar vein, Mogobe B. Ramose has commented that Africans 'are an injured and conquered people' and that this is 'the pre-eminent starting-point of African philosophy in its proper and fundamental signification' (1999: 44).

To do African philosophy, to posit, ask and address the question of Ubuntu is therefore always, inescapably first and foremost, a political question. When we advance Ubuntu as a different or counter-hegemonic (because African) philosophical anthropology, we have to keep this meta-reflective nature of the question as a political activity in mind. How we do so; that is, how we go about talking about Ubuntu, all the while remaining conscious of the political contestations involved in doing so, requires something like a theoretical model that will enable us to contain, in a more or less coherent fashion, the various registers in which the discoure on Ubuntu operates. In order to start working in the direction of such a theoretical model, let me outline what I think of as the three main features of critical humanism as used in this report.

The political as First Philosophy
The first feature of critical humanism was explored above and concerns the primacy of the political, the political as First Philosophy. The claim is not simply that politics is important or even only that it is inescapable, but rather that, in the Aristotelian

sense, it should be considered First Philosophy – that which 'indicates [the] scientific discipline of a beginning' (Farber 1963: 315). Ever since Aristotle, philosophers in the Western tradition have argued that philosophy requires a fundamental, grounding discipline that is closed in itself, with its own problems. This discipline, 'with inner necessity', would precede all other philosophical disciplines and would ground them methodologically and theoretically. Whatever this discipline is, its status would be that of First Philosophy.

In 'Concern with Politics in Recent European Philosophical Thought', Hannah Arendt reminds us that the Western articulation of philosophy started with the Greeks, for whom the activity of philosophising was rooted in a sense of wonder. She also points out that the Greeks 'had refused to accept [this sense of wonder also] as the preliminary condition for *political* philosophy' (1994: 430, emphasis added). Philosophy, she notes, 'has shown an unhappy inclination to treat this one of her many children as though it were a stepchild'. This disavowal of political philosophy was premised on a binary distinction between thought and action, reflection *on* and participation *in* public affairs, according to which the former was always considered superior. The reason that political philosophy was considered a second-class citizen in the pantheon of human sciences was due to its proximity to praxis – doing, acting. This means that when my imaginary black, postgraduate law student posits the political as First Philosophy, she is doing so in violation of any *Western philosophical* conception of what may legitimately be posited as First Philosophy. In short, to insist on the political as First Philosophy is to relativise philosophy itself as a specific context, culture or civilisation and *therefore a political* endeavour. A hegemonic philosophical tradition, such as that of the West, is very good at concealing from itself the simple fact of this historical contingency, the fact that it is an ethno-philosophy in the sense of belonging to a people or a civilisation that we roughly and obscurely refer to as the 'West'. Historically marginalised traditions, on the other hand, have no choice but to depart from this recognition of thought as ethno-specific because that is the very condition, the sine qua non, upon which a conversation between equals who are not yet equal, must be premised. I think of this as the first feature, the ground zero of critical humanism. At the risk of labouring the point, let me illustrate this notion specifically in relation to the question of Ubuntu.

Ubuntu is about power. More accurately, to write about Ubuntu is to engage in a struggle for power. By all accounts, power is the last thing we should associate with Ubuntu because it has become a synecdoche for a whole range of non-violent political praxes, such as forgiveness and reconciliation. But the reduction of Ubuntu to a synecdoche of the apolitical, sometimes even anti-political, is at best naive and at worst sinister. Not recognising that the founding assumption of postcolonial Ubuntu discourse, namely that it is a unique philosophy and a sign of African authenticity, as well as not acknowledging the process through which Ubuntu has been inducted into service in the name of a struggle for recognition, has resulted in Ubuntu becoming complicit in a particular kind of violence that we have come to associate with a Western, modernist understanding (and its contestations) of identity politics in terms of personal and cultural autonomy and/or sovereignty. Contrary to this naivety, we should recognise as our point of departure that every attempt to speak about Ubuntu is an exercise in power, a primordial attempt to get the fact and meaning of blackness, black values, traditions and concepts recognised as of equal value to the people for whom they matter. It is an attempt to put this on the agenda, to have it understood and taken seriously. As Drucilla Cornell comments in 'Ubuntu and Subaltern Legality': 'To even take Ubuntu seriously, or more precisely, to demand that Ubuntu be taken seriously, is to challenge the racist assertion that somehow or another this African value, because it is so contested in its meaning, is too vague to have any moral, let alone legal purchase' (2014). But it is not only about recognising the fact that to speak about Ubuntu is to engage in a political struggle for recognition. It is much more complicated than that because we also have to recognise that this struggle will change the way we think about Ubuntu. We do not only struggle to get Ubuntu recognised; the struggle for recognition also determines how we come to think about Ubuntu. We do not speak of Ubuntu because it happens to be interesting; we speak of it, in part, *because we need to make a point* about being black in a white world and African in a Western-dominated world. At the same time that 'making a point about Ubuntu' is motivated by a desire to change the world, making that point also changes what it means to be black in that world. There can never be anything naive about speaking of blackness. For that, the Black – as Frantz Fanon would name them/us – was always too late. Blacks come to speak of our-/themselves as a struggle. They/we do not tell the world about lost, ancient African civilisations because they are interesting, but because every act of recollection is an act of struggle that seeks to make a point. It is a way of asserting blackness, of power asserting itself as memory.

To speak of Africa is to struggle for power, to assert power, to assert presence. This is why to say that 'Africans have Ubuntu' is never simply to make a disinterested observation about Africans, but a statement we should *feel, experience* and understand as a challenge, as an exercise of power, as an assertion of the right of Africans to be recognised, to be present, to be a part *of* (not apart *from*) the conversation. Only once we recognise the fundamental fact that Africans are putting blackness and its meanings on the table can we proceed to discuss *what* is being put on the table and how the prior political fact of having had to fight in order to get it on the table has already predetermined its meaning. We will get nowhere if we do not first recognise that to put Ubuntu on the table is to make a statement; it is a political act. We can play a little with this ambiguity and say that to make a statement about Ubuntu is *to make a statement* or say that asking, 'What is Ubuntu?' is not simply posing a question, but making a statement about power, representation, discursive dominance, subversion and so on. Simply put, 'What is Ubuntu?' is a statement before it becomes a question. Given that politics is always contextual, if putting Ubuntu on the table is firstly a political gesture, its content – what it is in addition to being a political gesture – will be contextual. Ubuntu – as a philosophy or an idea about our shared humanity – in its articulation as first and foremost a political act cannot but amount to or imply a confrontation with the measures and mechanisms that historically excluded it as sign of primitiveness, only to reappropriate it later as a messianic signifier of our shared humanity.

This confrontation of the philosophical with the political will always generate fascinatingly complex questions – as was demonstrated by the comment reportedly made by Aubrey Matshiqi in response to the Equality Court's ruling on Julius Malema's singing of *Dubul' ibhunu*:

> African National Congress (ANC) Youth League leader Julius Malema suffered yet another setback yesterday [12 September 2011] when the Equality Court ruled that his singing of the anti-apartheid struggle song *Dubul' ibhunu* (Shoot the boer) at a rally in 2009 amounted to hate speech ... Aubrey Matshiqi, research fellow at the Helen Suzman Foundation, said the ruling would deepen the perception that Mr Malema was under siege. 'He has suffered very serious reversals of political fortunes. Some may think this is a continuity of those political misfortunes.' Mr Matshiqi also said the judgment had serious implications for the country and race relations. '*There is a growing feeling in the African community that in this country, ubuntu is about black people giving up something ... the principle of ubuntu is being applied cynically*,' he said (Shoba 2011, emphasis added).

Matshiqi's comment referred to Lamont J.'s unusually elaborate reference to Ubuntu – alongside constitutional provisions, foreign and international law and international treaties – as 'providing the framework to be used to alleviate and overcome the friction resulting from change' (par. 13).[5] In delivering his judgment, Lamont J. argued:

> Pursuant to the agreements which established the modern, democratic South African nation and the laws which were promulgated pursuant to those agreements, the enemy has become the friend, the brother. Members of society are enjoined to embrace all citizens as their brothers... It must never be forgotten that in the spirit of ubuntu this new approach to each other must be fostered (par. 108).

He then concludes his judgment rather forcefully: 'Persons who are aware of the line which has been drawn by the Court are as a matter of both law and ubuntu obliged to obey it' (par. 111).

We have indeed come to a curious point when a white, male judge publicly reprimands a black revolutionary for not acting in the spirit of Ubuntu. Ironic as this may be, it is not race or even culture, their continuation, inversion and appropriation that fascinates, but rather the complicated relation between the ethical and the political that emerges from their political mobilisation. For what does it mean to tell a (admittedly self-styled and in many ways *faux*) revolutionary that his struggle for liberation against the continued oppression of the black majority after 1994 lacks Ubuntu? Is there not something deeply suspicious going on here? At stake, I think, are two issues related to ethics in a political context of colonialism and decolonisation. The first is that the ethical can be untimely and the second is that, in the process of decolonisation, the truly ethical can often only be brought about by and through a suspension of the ethical; that is, through the unethical. These two are closely related, but let me start with the first.

When Nelson Mandela emerged from 27 years of incarceration and almost immediately started demonstrating goodwill, reconciliation and forgiveness towards the white minority, there was an outcry from sections of the black population,

---

5. See *Afri-Forum and Another v. Malema and Others* (http://www.saflii.org/za/cases/ZAEQC/2011/2).

particularly the ANC Youth League, which argued that Mandela's gestures of reconciliation were too early; that ordinary black South Africans needed space and time to vent their anger and express their hurt; that white South Africans had first to acknowledge the wrongs of the past and *ask* for forgiveness, before it could be offered to them. At the heart of this objection lies a simple truth: forgiveness is an important moment of the political and not a substitute for it. To extend forgiveness in anticipation of a process that *may* culminate in an act of forgiveness can and often does add to the oppression of the very people from whom forgiveness ought to be sought. It is an untimely forgiveness and, as such, may contribute to the continuation of the very asymmetrical power relations whose subversion it ostensibly celebrates.[6]

This leads directly to the second issue, namely that, in a context of decolonisation, the ethical can often only proceed through a temporary suspension of the ethical – a suspension Gordon has referred to as the 'tragedy of the colonial condition' (2007: 126). This tragedy consists in the fact that often, but not always, freedom fighters cannot remain ethical while fighting for freedom from oppression. At some point, the ethical often has to be suspended and the violence of the armed struggle embraced in order to bring to an end the violence inflicted upon the oppressed. The oppressor's lack of ethics cannot be rectified by the ethical conduct of the oppressed and this motivated Fanon's often-misunderstood embrace of the necessity of anti-colonial violence. As Gordon puts it:

> When Fanon argues that we need to set humanity into its proper place, he means by this that this ethical problem has a political cause. In other words, unlike the modern liberal paradigm, which seeks an ethics on which to build its politics, Fanon argues that colonialism has created a situation in which a politics is needed on which to build an ethics (2008: 126).

The twin dilemmas of the untimely and the suspension of the ethical intersect in the Equality Court's appeal to Ubuntu in order to justify its conclusion that the singing of *Dubul' ibhunu* constitutes a form of hate speech. As in most cases where

---

6. For Van Binsbergen, untimely invocations of Ubuntu may result in the term sinking back into the semantic field of other 'pejorative expressions for financially robbed, easily exploitable, legally unprotected, socially excluded and mentally broken Black subject-hood' (2001: 78).

it is invoked, Ubuntu does not play a pivotal role in this judgment. Nonetheless, the fact that a white judge appeals to Ubuntu in order to judge – not simply in the legal sense of applying rules, but in the moral sense of invoking standards – the conduct of a (populist) freedom fighter, at the very least, opens a door that leads directly back into this complex relationship between the ethical and the political. Is it not untimely to invoke notions of our shared humanity (a 'brotherhood' of former enemies) as long as we live in a society where there is still no real sharing of resources? At what point does the demand to honour the spirit of Ubuntu turn into an instrument of oppression, rather than a liberating act of humanism, because it has been used to maintain the status quo? Should all talk of Ubuntu not be temporarily suspended in order to create the necessary space for the agitation of political and economic change that, while temporarily at odds with Ubuntu-style notions of brotherhood, will nonetheless create the necessary socio-economic conditions for bringing about the truly ethical, a world of true Ubuntu in which we can meaningfully substantiate talk of shared humanity with the fact of a more equitable sharing of resources? Such would be Fanon's response. But we no longer have the luxury of Fanon's perhaps simplistic linearity in which colonialism provokes the violence that brings about a counter-reaction that will culminate in the freedom that can create the possibility for a truly inclusive humanism. South Africa has had its legitimately sustained moment of ethical suspense, political revolution or so-called first transition, which culminated in the adoption of an inclusive Constitution. It would be difficult to still argue for a legitimate suspension of the ethical in order to reinvent the political as a condition for bringing about the *truly* ethical – as necessary and urgent as such a continuation of the quest for meaningful liberation may be.

Such were the complexities at stake in *Afri-Forum and Another v. Malema and Others*. Exactly how matters are more complex for us than for Fanon will be investigated in more detail in the last two chapters of this report, where I consider the implications of what it means to live in a world where the ethical cannot be announced through its own temporary suspension, but where it must present itself as a deconstructive force for the expansion, and not the negation or suspension, of the juridico-political order. This continuation of Ubuntu as a deconstructive force is in some sense the continuation of what I have been referring to as the founding premise or axiomatic of Ubuntu discourse, namely the political as First Philosophy. In a wider, more general sense, it also suggests what I think of as the second feature of critical humanism.

Humanism as mode of critique

The second feature of critical humanism is that no humanism, including the critical, political variety advanced here, should ever aspire to become an ideology. Humanism is a *mode of critique*. This does not mean that attempts have not been made to codify humanism into full-blown ideology. We need only recall how the first generation of post-independence African leaders, such as Kwame Nkrumah and Julius Nyerere, attempted to systematise and formalise traditional African humanism either as humanism or as socialism *avant la lettre*. If anything, these attempts demonstrated something of the realistic and difficult-to-hear answer to the question 'What is Ubuntu?', namely that Ubuntu, considered as an emergent phenomenon of what Patrick Chabal (2009) calls a 'political economy of obligation', should not and never will find articulation as an autonomous ideology or philosophy to rival Western political and philosophical forms. The tension between the local and global referred to earlier has already illuminated why it will not, so let me briefly explain with reference to the 'should not' why this is not all bad news. Perhaps Gordon provides the clearest entry into this point when he asks:

> Why such a focus on the human in a postcolonial phenomenology? On one hand, the answer is historical. Colonialism, slavery and racism have degraded humankind. The reassertion of humankind requires the assertion of the humanity of the degraded. But such an assertion is . . . not as simple as it appears, for there was not, and continues not to be, a coherent notion of the human subject on which emanicipation can be supported (2007: 135).

In other words those who are asserting their humanity in response to the dehumanising reality and continuing legacy of colonialism do not necessarily have, nor should they be expected to have, a coherent and universally acceptable definition of what it means to be human. The question of the human must be raised again and again, not in the hope of settling it once and for all, but in order for it to remain open as a horizon for the critique of unrealised potentialities. In his *Hope and Memory: Lessons from the Twentieth Century*, Tzvetan Todorov comments:

> A . . . 'critical humanist' is a philosopher of democracy, and therefore a pragmatist. Humanists know that no knowledge can ever be claimed as final and definitive, and therefore no '-ism' . . . is going to yield final answers

and bring heaven to earth. Instead, humanism promotes an attitude towards humanity premised on the principle that all people have the same rights, and the same claim to respect, no matter whether or not they live in the same ways as each other (2003: 24).

I take this to mean that there is no human*ism*, but only the sustained praxis of humanising – which is why the structure of this report in general and the last two chapters in particular place much emphasis on the fact that, contrary to the seductions of identity politics, what is unique about Ubuntu is not any epistemological, ontological or even axiological specificity, but simply the fact of its being an actualised communitarian praxis of the humanising. This shift in understanding its specificity resonates well with Nikolas Kompridis's articulation of the urgent contemporary need for critical theory:

> A critical theory prepared to fully embrace its romantic self-understanding, would be a critical theory more capable of responding to its own time, and more attuned to the needs of its time. Is there anything more urgent today than to resist the sense that our possibilities are contracting or that they are exhausted? And is there anything more important for critical theory to do, any way to be more receptive to its calling, than to once again take on the task of disclosing alternative possibilities, possibilities through which we might recapture the promise of the future – through which we might recapture the future as promise (2006: 280)?

Critical humanism, then, is not a discipline 'closed in on itself' as its description as First Philosophy suggests. Neither is it an '-ism'; it is *a mode of critique*. Here a complex question arises, for if Ubuntu will never blossom into an ideology or autonomous philosophical construct, what happens to the problem that Fanon grappled with so extensively, echoed in Matshiqi's comment quoted earlier? How do we deploy Ubuntu as a mode of critique to effect real changes in the world? More precisely, how do we conceive of the relation between humanism and a praxis of emancipation if the former cannot be conceived as coherent, autonomous construct? These questions must be addressed in relation to a third feature of critical humanism.

Philosophical anthropology, meta-critique and emancipatory praxis

The third feature of critical humanism is that, considered a mode of critique, it proceeds by simultaneously making three distinct, but closely related moves, which Gordon in 'Problematic People and Epistemic Decolonization: Toward the Postcolonial in Africana Political Thought' (2007) refers to as: philosophical anthropology, emancipatory praxis and a meta-critique of reason. Advancing Ubuntu as critical humanism requires us to synchronise the liberation or decolonisation of our understanding of *what it means to be human*, while secondly, reflecting *self-critically* on all the paradoxes and aporias that shadow our attempts at thinking both within and against dominant intellectual traditions and thirdly, exploring what it would mean to deploy this critical anthropology as *emancipatory praxis*. Achille Mbembe, too, has suggested something along these lines: 'Postcolonial thought, the critique of European humanism and imperial forms of universalism, is not an end in itself. It is carried out with the aim of paving the way for an enquiry into the possibility of a politics of the future, of mutuality and of the common' (2009: 35).

The chapter divisions of this report reflect this threefold distinction. In Chapter 1, I engage with the question of philosophical anthropology. What kind of anthropology is implied by the concept of Ubuntu? What conception does it advance of what it means to *be* human and to *belong*? A philosophical, rather than empirical, anthropology takes us in the direction of the abstract for, while an empirical anthropology concentrates on empirical studies and the methods used to conduct them, philosophical anthropology 'explores the concepts by and through which any understanding of the human being is both possible and makes sense' (Gordon 2007: 133). In this respect, this report is very limited. I am not addressing or even raising questions related to a general philosophical anthropology, nor do I discuss how answers generated in Africana thought have challenged Western philosophical anthropology in general. Instead, with reference to Chabal's *Africa: The Politics of Suffering and Smiling* (2009), I articulate Ubuntu in terms of a praxis conceived as a 'political economy of obligation'.

Chapter 2 proceeds as a meta-critique of the manner in which Ubuntu theorists present this philosophical anthropology in philosophical and political discourse. It is a critical chapter in the precise sense that it invites readers not only to think about Ubuntu, but also to reflect on *the way* we think about it. I map some of the different kinds of politics implicit in various attempts at reinventing the political economy of ubuntu as abstract, theoretical Ubuntu. In his '*Ubuntu* and the

Globalisation of Southern African Thought and Society', Van Binsbergen states, quite correctly I believe and in line with the recognition of the political as First Philosophy, that 'it is pointless to study the contents of a philosophy (such as *ubuntu*) in isolation – *in vitro* – without constant reference to the particular sociology of knowledge by which it came into being and by which it is perpetuated' (2001: 59). In this chapter I articulate perhaps not a sociology as much as a politics of knowledge, through which various conceptions of Ubuntu appear as the result of combining certain assumptions about what thinking means with certain other assumptions about what it means to be an African, a combination of assumptions regarding *thinking* and *being* that produces an array of different political stances on the question of Ubuntu. Following Gilles Deleuze and Félix Guattari (2004), I describe and categorise these according to their implied 'conceptual personae'. I distinguish between the Prophetic, with a subsidiary division between the Revolutionary and the Saviour, the Archivist, the Cosmopolitan and the Conformist. This chapter brings to a tentative conclusion the main emphasis on a meta-critical, philosophical anthropology. The three remaining chapters explore Ubuntu in terms of the third and last dimension of Gordon's threefold division, namely as emancipatory praxis. In Chapter 3, I exlore this question by looking at one historical attempt to convert African humanism into an ideology – Nyerere's Ujamaa project – while the last two chapters consider the emancipatory potential of Ubuntu in South African law.

A central theme that appears in Chapter 3 and which continues to inform the last two chapters will no doubt be somewhat contentious. It is the suggestion that Ubuntu must always be understood in terms of its constitutive violence – a violence that is either visible or invisible, depending on how the Ubuntu question is framed and presented. When we present Ubuntu as a form of humanism, the question of violence seems entirely foreign, even heterogenous to it. Ubuntu is equated with reconciliation, shared humanity, forgiveness, harmony and so on. On the other hand, if we describe Ubuntu as African communitarianism, the question of violence or coercion is simply par for the course, a standard element of the objection raised by liberals to any form of communitarianism. From the perspective of African Studies, the interesting and challenging question becomes: How do we conceptualise and articulate this violence? To simply interpret it as an instance of the violence associated with any and all forms of communitarianism seems problematic on at least two counts: First, because I have always thought that the debate between liberalism and communitarianism is haunted by an incoherence that is a function of the deep structure or axiomatic of Western modernity itself. There is no liberalism that is not always already a form of communitarianism. Every political liberal thinks of him- or herself first and foremost and inescapably in terms of a constitutive attachment to liberalism *qua* tradition. Tradition, history, community: these things precede us even (especially) where they are denied as fundamental starting points for various forms of political and philosophical individualism. In the case of liberalism, its constitutive attachment to liberalism as a tradition and the community of liberals who share an apophatic assumption about our interdependence becomes the unthought of liberalism, or that which makes it possible, while remaining invisible. That we should be presented with a 'debate' between liberalism and communitarianism is a function of a Western binary axiomatic that forces us to choose between two mutually exclusive metaphysics: that the individual is prior to society *or* that society is prior to the individual – a Trojan Horse that is then wheeled into the African polis, where it contaminates thinking with a belief in two supposedly irreconcilable ontologies – Western individualist and African communitarian.[7] In this way, every attempt African subjects make to think their place in the world is structured in advance by the projection, into their very place of thinking, of a binary that is neither sustainable, nor of their own making. I deal with this troubling binary and its various racist manifestations throughout this report. Suffice it here to say that to read Ubuntu as a form of communitarianism is already to frame and predetermine in important ways how we present and position ourselves in relation to the question of its constitutive violence.

The same is true for a second, equally problematic approach that interprets Nyerere's Ujamaa project within a Marxist framework as a form of totalitarian developmentalism, reminiscent of Joseph Stalin's (and Nkrumah's) five-year plans and in which Nyerere appears as little more than an authoritarian social engineer who introduced and imposed a vision of postcolonial communalism (*as* African Socialism) on his people, by creating a parastatal state-captialism, which, by suppressing class development allied with private property, encouraged another type of class development. I am sympathetic to both the communitarian and Marxist critiques of the violence of the Ujamaa project. What I try to avoid is the reduction of an African *problematique* to a mere example of a greater, universal (where

---

7. There are various ways of resisting this reduction. See, for instance, Eze (2008) and Christians (2004).

'universal' is, of course, shorthand for 'Western') *problematique*, which would leave the Ujamaa project wholly subsumed under or within communitarian and Marxist debates. Of course, there is nothing wrong with going about things in this way – in fact, given the arguments presented in Chapters 2 and 3, it is actually inescapable. But it implies a political stance that, *in this particular instance*, I do not wish to adopt, one represented by the Cosmopolitan conceptual persona, for whom thinking is always a matter of comparison and of articulating the universal in the particular. I want to stay on this side of the particular, just before it gets historically *aufgehoben* or conceptually subsumed into general debates on communitarianism and Marxism. I have thus chosen to pursue the question of Ujamaa's (and Ubuntu's) constitutive violence in a more contextual way – first, by articulating it as a constitutive element of the political economy of obligation and second, by asking the question: What happened to this constitutive violence when Nyerere translated ujamaa into Ujamaa; that is, when he took the family writ small as the ideological basis for the projection of the family writ large, ujamaa *as* African Socialism (Ujamaa)? The advantage of proceeding in this way is that it generates questions that may otherwise have remained obscured: What does it mean to suggest that African humanism or Ubuntu is also constituted by violence, *as* violence; that Ubuntu is not simply the antithesis to violence, heterogenous to its very logic? Does posing this question not already make visible certain aspects of the process that account for the relentless and systematic sentimentalising of Ubuntu that has left it empty of all content and emancipatory potential?

In every epoch since independence, African humanism has spoken through a different, contextually relevant master trope: socialism, humanism, communitarianism and in South Africa's case, a Christianised or at least *spiritualised* understanding of forgiveness and reconciliation – an almost apophatic humanism that in its seeming limitlessness enabled forgiveness where none was thought possible. In such an understanding of humanism (and forgiveness) as limitless, possible only where unimaginable, we run the risk of emptying Ubuntu of all content. For, what is a humanism that can imagine no limit where people and actions become inhuman? What is a forgiveness that fails to recognise and institute against what is unforgivable? The inhumane and the unforgivable are necessary limits that make humanism and forgiveness possible. But an acknowledgement of the necessity of limits implies an acknowledgement of the inescapability of violence, for where there is a limit, there is policing, control and coercion – benevolent control, policing and coercion, perhaps, but nonetheless, an exercise of violence that draws, thereby instituting, the very limit that makes a community possible and the meaning of belonging imaginable. Now, it may well be that true humanism and true forgiveness only start at the very limit where and when their meaning is in jeopardy – as Derrida (2001) has indeed argued – but this does not mean that there is no limit or that the limit is not a necessary or constitutive element of what it means to be human, to act in consort with human expectations and of what it means to forgive those who act in violation of those limits.

Drawing out the logic of African humanism's constitutive violence in relation to the discourse on Ubuntu is the objective of Chapter 3. It is a forceful reading of Nyerere that some will disagree with. Naturally, such forcefulness is problematic because in its very force it imitates the violence under discussion. Nothing calls forth violence more readily than violence itself. Is it possible to engage with the question of violence, to think about it, read about it, write about it, without in the process being even a little bit contaminated by it? Or did the contamination precede the analysis in the form of a prejudice that only seeks in the analysis a justification for its own existence? These are question I cannot answer. What I also do not make explicit in this chapter are the two sources that motivated my forceful interpretation of Nyerere: first, the sentimentalising of Ubuntu that needs to be resisted with all our might in order that it may reappear as a sign of the possibility of the humane that recognises itself as a function of the limit; second, the aporias that I see everywhere in this discourse: the aporia of the *untimely*, the aporetic structure of *hypermodernity*, the aporia of the *founding* and so on.

We know that there is no way out of an aporia, that it is an unresolvable paradox that nonetheless haunts us with an imperative urge to resolve it. Nothing better describes an aporia than this urge to make possible what we recognise as impossible. We do not resolve an aporia; we merely find a way around the impasse we are presented with. But that was not my intention in this chapter. Rather, I pursued what I think of as the vanishing point of the aporetic tension between African Socialists and scientific socialists: between two equally valid, but mutually exclusive interpretations of precolonial African communalism (ubuntu praxis) – as socialism *avant la lettre* and the way of the future (African Socialism) or as outdated and primitive mode of production and being (scientific socialism). In the tension between these two political performances of emancipation, a difference stretches out before us like the vanishing point in a perspectival painting. Of course, the difference has no ground and no origin; it vanishes at exactly the same point where we give up on Zeno's paradox of infinite divisibility. But before we can attempt a way beyond the impasse of the aporia, our obligation consists, first and foremost, in pursuing this path to trace the tension before us as if it were possible to find the source, the grounding, the origin of difference itself. In pursuing this vanishing point, there is no doubt a certain violence of thought at work, an exaggerated difference, a violent juxtapositioning that finds its sole legitimation in the possibility that it will make clearly visible what is at stake in that very difference. Ultimately, the aim of my interpretation is not to make the violence of Nyerere's Ujamaa project problematic in principle and/or exceptional, but rather to make it *visible* in a very specific way that will relate back to our discourse on Ubuntu. By pointing to its constitutive violence, we restore that violence to its proper place in the question: What does it mean to think the human (and society) in relation to a limit? Of course, this does not make the violence unproblematic, but it does make it visible so that, in future, we can deal with violence *as political choice* in those instances where more than the protection of individual rights is called for.

That contemporary South Africa is such a place – and by 'such a place' I mean a juridico-political order premised on the axiomatic of contractual individualism – is as true as it is problematic. The question I pursue in the last two chapters on Ubuntu and the law is essentially this: How do we conceive the emancipatory potential of Ubuntu in relation to that axiomatic and its limitations? This is a surprisingly complex question. In the context of a study such as this, concerned as it is not only with knowledge-production about things African, but also meta-reflectively with the politics at play in that knowledge-production, the problem approaches what complexity theorists refer to as a 'wicked problem' or a problem of infinite complexity. In responding to this complexity, I argue that any meaningful engagement with Ubuntu in relation to the modern juridical must respond, at the very least, to the implied difference between the universal and the particular, between a *general* and a *particular problematique*, between the general problems of modernity the question raises and the particular challenges of postcolonial modernity we are presented with. In other words, I argue that the particularity of the postcolonial challenge must be understood also, or perhaps firstly, as grappling with the promises and limitations of modernity in a general sense. But understanding this generality or universality is only the first step, for an engagement with Ubuntu and the particularity of postcolonial modernity also suggests a response to or a 'talking back' to the general narrative of liberal democratic modernity. To balance the universal and the particular in such a way is what it means to understand Ubuntu both as a product *of* and a response *to* modernity.

In both Chapter 4 and Chapter 5, I start by distinguishing between the universal problematic of modernity and the particular problematic of postcolonial modernity, through a suspension or bracketing (*epoché*) of what seems most particular about the Ubuntu question. In both cases, the *epoché* reveals a general or universal logic at work in the question that, once articulated, allows us to return to the contextual particularity of the question, not only with a better understanding of its often-underestimated complexity but also, I hope, with a better understanding of what we can expect from Ubuntu as emancipatory praxis in the domain of the juridical.

My choice to address the supercomplexity of the problem in this manner is premised on a particular philosophical assumption. This assumption is presented in the form of a definition of modernity as *the moment when belonging becomes, first and foremost, a problem for thought*. The first *epoché* demonstrates that what separates the work of the young G.W.F. Hegel from the work of the later, mature Hegel was exactly his eventual acceptance of such an understanding of modernity. His *Phenomenology of Spirit* (first published in 1807) occupies the place it does in the Western imagination because only in this text does Hegel reconcile himself with the passing of time, with the fact of history, with the fact that the communitarian praxes of his youth are irredeemably lost and that the very possibility of a new community of moderns would need to be embraced, first and foremost, as a problem for thought, what it means to *think* of ourselves as a community of rights-bearing individuals (legitimated, in his case, by a theory of history that locked both the loss of the old and the possibilities of the new into a teleology). What this first *epoché* reveals is that Ubuntu discourse is essentially a similar attempt to think through postcolonial modernity as that moment when past communitarian praxes, because they have been lost or substantially fragmented, can only return to the imagination as a problem for thought that, as for Hegel, requires of us a fundamental engagement with our historicity, with how we reconcile the fact of having lost ubuntu praxis with what it means to hold out a philosophical reimagining of Ubuntu as master trope of/for a future community.

The second *epoché* of Chapter 5 reveals as universal another feature of the debate we assume to be particular, namely that Ubuntu represents some kind of communitarian or altruistic logic over and against the liberal, individualist axiomatic of the Constitution. I argue that, in a very important sense, this kind of thinking must be recognised as the racialisation of what Kennedy calls the 'fundamental contradiction'. As indicated earlier in my imaginary dialogue between the law student and lecturer, the fundamental contradiction suggests a tension so profound and terrifying at the heart of our thinking about belonging that we will do anything in our power to either keep it invisible or to escape from it. The tension emerges as a result of recognising that the Other is both necessary *for* and a threat *to* my freedom. I want to be free from other people at the same time that I recognise them as indispensable for my continued existence and freedom. In a sense, all political arrangements of modernity – and not only the law, as Kennedy claims – are devised to work out solutions to this contradiction. One immediately suspects that constitutionalism is better at protecting me from the threat posed by the Other's existence than it is at facilitating the kind of obligations that logically follow from my recognising my dependence on them. But this is not entirely true. In the context of adjudication in the United States, Kennedy identifies two political geographies in adjudication, two general tendencies in the interpretation of the law: an individualist and altruist. The former often represents the positive legacy of classical legal individualism (formalism), which insists on applying legal rules both for the protection of rights and their limitation – a view that threatens to reduce society to no more than an emergent phenomenon of the limitation of individual rights. The positive legacy of the altruistic tradition of interpreting the law, on the other hand, is its insistence that such a view of the social is not enough. Community is not only the leftovers of restrained individual freedom, but is a good in itself that should be actively pursued. To this end, we need to draw on social standards that will inform the ultimate purpose of law, or the Law of law. The argument in Chapter 5 is that this tension between individualism and altruism, which we confusedly reduce to a tension between Western individualism and African communalism, is constitutive of the legal cultures of modern societies as such; that it is an integral part of what it means to put in place institutions tasked with negotiating the fundamental contradiction that visibly comes to haunt us when modernity presents belonging as, first and foremost, a problem for thought.

For many scholars who have written on Ubuntu in relation to the law or justices who have invoked Ubuntu in their adjudication, it has the status of a norm or social standard that we can sometimes invoke to prioritise collective good over individual rights. I am critical of this manner of conceiving Ubuntu in relation to the law. I find it contradictory, limiting and presupposing of a normative consensus that is doubtful in a context of radical pluralism such as South Africa. The last two chapters advance an alternative way of conceiving of Ubuntu in relation to the law. I argue that a combination of the first and second *epochés* leaves us with a greater appreciation of the particularity of the question about Ubuntu in relation to the law: what is specific about postcolonial modernity is a bifurcation (between two contesting notions of belonging) that will remain unredeemed by any Hegelian grand teleology of development; that this unredeemed double structure reflects not only two different understandings of belonging, but also two very different understandings of justice; that this double structure is the ambivalent founding or *aporia-archē* of the Constitution and that this very founding marks the culmination of an original injustice that it alone can address. Lastly, I argue that this ambivalence haunts the Constitution and will continue to do so in the form of a question that exceeds the logic of the contractual axiomatic itself, namely: what is a *just* justice? Ubuntu encourages us – no, insists – that we constantly ask this question, perpetually return to it, in order to respond to the original injustice that our constitutional order is founded on.

Part I

The unification of the planet's history, that humanist dream which God has spitefully allowed to come true, has been accompanied by a process of dizzying reduction. True, the termites of reduction have always gnawed away at life: even the greatest love ends up as a skeleton of feeble memories. But the character of modern society hideously exacerbates this curse: it reduces man's life to its social function; the history of a people to a small set of events that are themselves reduced to a tendentious interpretation; social life is reduced to a political struggle, and that in turn to the confrontation of . . . global powers. Man is caught in a veritable *whirlpool of reduction* where Husserl's 'world of life' is fatally obscured and being is forgotten.

— Milan Kundera, *The Art of the Novel*

CHAPTER 1

A Political Economy of Obligation

> To be realistic, however, one must recognise that these are only partial manifestations, and that even they are threatened by powerful opposing forces. There is work to be done to find forms in which the spirit of Ubuntu can be embodied in some permanent and all-pervasive way in our contemporary world.
> — Augustine Shutte, *Ubuntu: An Ethic for a New South Africa*

The analysis in this first chapter will be guided by three questions: one, what is the nature of the philosophical anthropology implicit in ubuntu? Formulated differently, what understanding of being and belonging does ubuntu offer us? Two, what historical conditions have made it possible for us to talk and think about Ubuntu in the way that we have come to do? Three, how are we to understand or interpret those dimensions of ubuntu that seem at odds with a neoliberal, democratic order? These are all big and complex questions and this chapter is divided into three parts dedicated to exploring these questions.

Part 1 makes use of the work of Patrick Chabal (2009) to flesh out the kind of philosophical anthropology implicit in ubuntu. He describes the precolonial African understanding of being and belonging in terms of a 'political economy of obligation', which I appropriate as the basis for understanding ubuntu as living praxis. Part 2 traces the manner in which various historical conditions or historic a prioris can be invoked to account for the reinvention of ubuntu praxis as abstract Ubuntu philosophy. My concern here is with understanding how these historic a prioris made a certain kind of Ubuntu possible by excluding certain dimensions of ubuntu praxis from our contemporary understanding of Ubuntu. The argument is that two of these excluded dimensions – one, a constitutive violence or logic of coercion and two, the unity of idealist (love) and materialist (labour) dimensions of ubuntu praxis – have left us, at worst, with a rather vacuous and sentimental understanding of ubuntu and, at best, with a profound challenge to deploy this reinvented Ubuntu effectively to emancipatory ends. Part 3 formalises the reinvention of ubuntu as Ubuntu by attributing to it the status of *glocal* phenomenon; that is, a phenomenon of which the content is mostly 'retrodicted' (Mudimbe 1991a: 13) through dominant discourses such as Christianity and human rights.

Perhaps another useful point of entry into this chapter is the question that informs the last two chapters of this book: what is modernity? In an essay titled 'Philosophy and Sociology' – an elaboration on her earlier review of Karl Mannheim's *Ideology and Utopia* – Hannah Arendt quotes Karl Mannheim:

> Groups of pre-capitalist origin, in which the communal element prevails, may be held together by traditions or by common sentiments alone . . . In such a group, theoretical reflection is of entirely secondary importance. On the other hand, in groups which are not welded together primarily by such organic bonds of community life, but which merely occupy similar positions in the social-economic system, rigorous theorizing is a prerequisite of cohesion (in Arendt 1994: 41).

Arendt continues this line of thought, adding:

> Only when people no longer see their existence in community as given, only when, as by means of economic advancement, the individual suddenly finds himself belonging to a completely different community does something like ideology arise as a justification of one's position against the position of others. Only at this point does the question of *meaning* arise, a question born of the questionableness of one's own situation. Only when the individual's place in the world is determined by economic status and not by tradition does he become homeless.

We may well put this differently and say: Only when we become homeless, do we start theorising about what it means to belong. Or only when we stop taking belonging for granted, does belonging become a problem for thought. Or, lastly and with reference to our investigation, only when we no longer live ubuntu, does Ubuntu become a problem for thought. Modernity is that moment when belonging becomes, first and foremost, a problem for thought. This, I think, is the historical locus of our contemporary concern with the question of Ubuntu.

In the first two chapters of *Africa: The Politics of Suffering and Smiling* – a title borrowed from Fela Kuti's 1978 song 'Shuffering and Shmiling' – Chabal offers us an illuminating description of the 'web of meaning within which [African] individuals and groups act in the world' (2009: 86). In effect, what he offers is a philosophical anthropology along two axes of what being African can be said to have meant in precolonial societies. These relate to what it meant *to be* a person and what it meant *to belong* to a community. The distinction between being and belonging is by no means obvious or natural. In fact, the very idea that existence can be understood in terms of a conceptual separation between *being* and *belonging* already presupposes an epistemological framework in which it makes sense to separate being (individual) and belonging (community). It implies the possibility of understanding *being* outside of or apart from *belonging*. In much of the Western philosophical tradition, this is indeed the assumption: we start by thinking the individual and then proceed to work out how best to conceive the coming together of individuals to form a society or community; that is, what it means to *belong*. From the manner in which this coming together is imagined and theoretically or ideologically constructed, various concepts of the political and juridical then become either possible or impossible. In the first part of this chapter, I follow Chabal in his analysis, while recognising from the start that this distinction may well be a good example of what it means for the Ubuntu theorist to work and think both *within* and *against* dominant intellectual traditions.

To engage with the idea of Ubuntu means answering the question of what being and belonging meant in precolonial Africa and to represent this meaning as its implicit philosophical anthropology. This is effectively what Chabal offers us: a philosophical anthropology as a baseline or point of departure indispensable to any discourse on Ubuntu. This baseline takes the form of a conceptual or formalist abstraction (derived from empirical anthropology), on which there seems to be a workable consensus among Africanists, and which Chabal calls a 'political economy of obligation'. As already indicated, the relationship between the political economy of obligation as praxis and Chabal's formalist analysis of it remains somewhat strained because what is most clear at a formal level – a distinction between being and belonging – is less clear, perhaps even absent, at the level of praxis where people live being *as* belonging. It is ultimately the latter, namely an understanding of the praxis of living being *as* belonging that we must return to as starting point, for as Kwame Gyekye reminds us: 'Moral or normative matters may be expressed in sophisticated and elaborate conceptual formulation; but as practical matters they have their best and unambiguous articulation or translation in the actual way of life of a people – in the way individuals are expected or not expected to respond to one another' (2002: 297).

But the strain in Chabal's analysis between a praxis in which being *is* belonging and the formalist expression of that praxis as a political economy that distinguishes between being *and* belonging, although problematic, can also be generative. It compels us to keep returning to the praxis in order to question our expression of it in modes of knowledge-production alien to it; alternatively, it allows for the praxis to perpetually deconstruct our formal expressions of it *as*, in this case, formalist philosophical anthropology, *as* ideology (African Socialism), *as* philosophy (Ubuntu) and so on. For this reason, it is important to constantly keep in mind the movement of *translation* or *codification* of praxis in various abstract forms. To this end, I want to introduce another term that will assist us in keeping a distance from this movement of translation in order to keep visible the politics at play in every translation of the praxis of ubuntu as abstraction, of ubuntu as Ubuntu. The term is the 'logic of interdependence' (Praeg 2008a: 369) and it has none or very few of the normative presuppositions embedded in various contemporary, abstract translations and codifications of the historical praxis in which ubuntu was embedded. The usefulness of this phrase will hopefully become clearer in Part 2 of this chapter, but it basically derives from the fact that it offers an example of the kind of strategy we can deploy to allow for the perpetual deconstruction of the conceptual apparatus we bring to bear on our thinking about ubuntu – of which the presupposed difference between being and belonging is but one example.

The general aim of this chapter is relatively simple: to argue that much of the confusion and heated disagreements in the discourse about Ubuntu is a function of the failure to distinguish clearly between praxis and the philosophical expression of praxis, between the political economy of obligation in which ubuntu praxis is/was embedded and the decontextualised expression of that praxis in the abstract form of Ubuntu – in short, a failure to distinguish between, what I shall write about in the remainder of this report, the difference between ubuntu and Ubuntu.[1] This difference is crucial because while the praxis of ubuntu is endogenous to Africa, its articulation as a philosophical expression (Ubuntu) is not, for the simple

---

1. For an example of disagreement in the discourse of Ubuntu, see Van Binsbergen (2001) and Bewaji and Ramose's response (2003).

reason that, through the paradoxical logic of globalisation, the latter is fundamentally constituted as modern, contemporary philosophy; that is, as glocal philosophy. To call Ubuntu a glocal phenomenon means recognising that global discourses (Christianity, human rights and so on) give a particular expression to the meaning of local traditions such as ubuntu, but in a way that also allows the resulting Ubuntu to feed back into the global discourse as a locally based critique and expansion of those very discourses. The result, as I argue, is that Ubuntu is neither here nor there, neither simply from 'over here' nor reducible to what is from 'over there'. It is at once here and there. To argue the case for this distinction between ubuntu and Ubuntu, I want to start with the local or endogenous praxis of which ubuntu is/was a function, the praxis or political economy of obligation in which ubuntu historically was and, in many complicated, overlapping and fragmented ways, continues to be embedded.

Part 1: Being and belonging

According to Chabal (2009), we come to understand the meaning of *being* in Africa by looking at three aspects that define it: origin, identity and locality. These categories would probably be useful for understanding *being* anywhere in the world, but they generate specific meanings in Africa. The aim is not to come up with a single, essentialised description of African subjectivity, but to use these key aspects to unlock – thus allowing us to understand – the way in which they continue to determine what happens at various political levels in modern, post-apartheid South Africa.

Origin

In colonialist literature on Africa, 'origin' was mostly understood in relation to ethnicity; that is, in so far as it assisted colonial authorities in working out answers to instrumental questions, such as 'Who comes from where and who was here first?', questions that were often driven by the need to classify superior and inferior African 'tribes' for the purposes of indirect rule. If we want to be more precise about the meaning of origin in relation to African subjectivity, we should distinguish between location (place of birth or family origin) and the importance attributed that location. In Africa, not only is much importance attached to the geography of origin – evident in the link maintained between the place of origin and burial – but origin is also 'a marker of community' (Chabal 2009: 27). This social or communal nature of the origin can be dissected in terms of three further dimensions: land, the living-dead and belief systems. *Land* signifies not only a symbiotic relationship between people and their land, reflected in creation myths and oral traditions, but also 'provides the context within which people define and organise themselves in socio-political terms' (28) – as, say, agriculturalists, pastoralists – so that 'identity is derived as much from sociological as from ethnic factors'. The *living-dead* are inseparably part of the land an individual hails from. If community in Africa is understood to include both the living and the living-dead, 'land' refers to both a geographical space where this extended notion of the living community is physically located, as well as to a metaphysical locale where the interface between the living and living-dead occurs. Land is the locale for the continuity from the visible to the invisible, from the living to the living-dead. As a result, 'burial is important not just because it is a key moment in the cycle of life but also because it makes manifest and keeps alive the concrete link between the individual, the community and the land with which it is identified' (29). In other words, 'there can be no complete sense of being that is not embodied in a physical place, which marks the link between the world of the living and the dead. Life itself is defined by that long chain.' This connection between land and the living-dead forms the structural base for *belief system* or religion and, argues Chabal, its continuing ramifications for postcolonial African societies are clear:

> The belief system upon which ethical and socio-political values are erected draws intimately from the actual place of origin, the location and the roots of the self-acknowledged individual-within-the-community. This matters greatly for politics, in at least two important ways. One is that politics and politicians cannot be dissociated from their link to a concrete physical location, a place of origin to which they belong. The other is that the local remains central to the identity and action of all political actors, even if they operate primarily at the national level (2009: 30).

Identity
If one had to define the two most salient characteristics of colonialism, one could do a lot worse than listing them as transformative, in the dual sense of rearranging local territories into the self-image of the colonial territory (Mudimbe 1988: 1) and transforming fluid ethnic identities into rigid, inflexible tribal identities. Much of the violence we have witnessed in postcolonial Africa – such as the Rwanda genocide of 1994 – can be traced back to and articulated as a direct result of the

manner in which colonial powers managed successfully to convert a system of fluid ethnic differences into a metaphysics of difference (Said 1986) – often through the introduction of mythological but politically devastating constructs, such as the Hamitic hypothesis (Mamdani 2002: 76–87). That colonial powers could have succeeded in this suggests that there may be a difference between those determinants of African subjectivity or identity that have always been considered negotiable or historical – that is, malleable, changeable – and those that are not. The centrality, hence the meaning and importance, of *origin* is non-negotiable. One can neither change the place of origin nor the importance attached to that fact. Depending on changing circumstances, everything other than origin – including ethnicity and religion – is much more fluid and open to reinvention. Prior to colonialism, Africans moved in and out of their ethnic groups; the geographical boundaries of these groups were vague and different ethic groups often shared, as they still do today, the same language and culture. As 'a scheme of identification' (Bayart 1993: 50), the meaning of ethnicity was contextual. Colonialism changed both the meaning and the status of these differences and instrumentalised their use (Chabal 2009: 33). In the process, ethnicity was politicised and transformed into political tribalism. After independence, elites would find this new language of petrified ethnicity useful as a channel for patrimonial distribution and consumption, while ordinary people very often continued to think of their identity in more historically fluid, overlapping terms. But it is the fluidity of religion as identity marker that is perhaps most relevant for our attempts to understand the changing meaning of Ubuntu.

Chabal points out that in Africa conversion to a different religion had always been quite 'languid' and 'functional' (2009: 34). He argues that such conversion was very often not driven by deep conviction, nor did it necessarily mean the abandonment of traditional, precolonial beliefs. From a dogmatic perspective, 'African religions have always been highly adaptable and did not find it difficult to accommodate the strange dogma and rituals of the foreigner's creeds'. Second, and at a deeper level, when the quasi-spiritual humanism we call Ubuntu so easily presents as ubuntufied Christianity (or UbunTutu), when it so readily presents as a spiritualised socialism or humanism or even as a local understanding of what is sacred about human dignity, it is not simply because there are significant overlaps in values between ubuntu and Christianity (compassion, mercy, forgiveness) or between ubuntu and Western humanism (the priority of harmony) or between ubuntu and human rights (a quasi-sacred understanding of dignity), but also because of a specific dynamic at work in the logic of ubuntu itself, a logic according to which what we sometimes refer to as 'the spirit of ubuntu' is always first and foremost a *praxis*, a way of doing things and harmonising difference. As praxis, ubuntu is 'more concerned with sharing humanity than with what such sharing is understood to mean' (Praeg 2008a: 375). I think of this willingness to translate or codify the self in terms of the language of the Other, to conceive of the Other (belonging) as a condition for the possibility of existence (being), as the originary gift of ubuntu, or simply *the work of ubuntu*.² The *work of ubuntu* or *ubuntu praxis* is the originary or *archē* 'reconciliation', of which discourses on 'reconciliation' and phenomena such as 'languid' and 'functional forms of religious conversion' are but symptomatic.

Locality
Origin and identity come together in the notion of community or locality. Crucial to any consideration of the importance of community in Africa are three matrixes – gender, age and authority. In terms of gender, Chabal comments:

> Women and men are not autonomous sexualised individuals but female and male members of specific groupings, the ethos and values of which impinge strongly on their identity. Within such a context the way in which one behaves and belongs as wo/man is inscribed in a long history. Changes both in the definition of female/male identity and in the ways 'traditions' affect political behaviour are slow and incremental. For this reason, it is necessary to pay particular attention to what are sometimes called the informal aspects of political roles and political action (2009: 38).

This means that the actions of both male and female politicians must often be understood to unfold against a backdrop of ethical codes that are 'only fully intelligible against the norms and values of particular localities' (Chabal 2009: 38). Similarly, age

> is not merely a numerical marker in a continuous chronological series; rather, human beings are defined in part by their age and their position

---

2. Note that I do not mean 'original', as in first, but 'originary' as that which originates things, generating them, making them possible, *archē*.

within the relevant age grouping. Even where rites of initiation no longer take place or carry much less conviction, the notion that male and female members of a community belong to a particular age group is of significance (39).³

Like gender and age, authority is a function of loyalty – but in intricate ways. In African studies, it is very useful to take seriously how often and to what extent power and authority do *not* overlap. One instance where this difference becomes visible is through the lens of the traditional/modern binary, according to which traditional leaders claim *authority* over their (ethnic) subjects, leaving presidents with a sense of merely exerting *power* over these subjects considered as citizens. These two claims are interlocked in a complex conflict that often cannot be easily resolved. What we need to remain sensitive to, Chabal argues, is not their binary difference, but the many nuanced and complex ways in which these forms of power/authority overlap (2009: 41). When African politicians embrace and visibly partake in the reinvention of tradition and custom, it is not only because of expedient electioneering or for the sake of simplistic populist politics, but also 'because politicians [remain] part of their grouping of origin as defined above and their own identity [rests] in part on their ability to propitiate the keepers of their locality' (42).⁴

Let us now consider the second axis in the philosophical anthropology of African subjectivity proposed by Chabal. If the first considered *being* in terms of origin, identity and locality, the second axis invites us to consider what all this means in terms of *belonging* to a community. As I pointed out in the introduction, the markers used to describe *being* above (origin, identity, locality) are themselves already social or, at least, only meaningful in relation to the social or communal. Each of the markers deployed by Chabal to describe (individual) *being* is at the same time already a first circumscription of living with others, of social *belonging*. To further elaborate, we should note the interaction between kin (reciprocity) and how this spills over into the socio-political and politico-juridical domains. When and where

---

3. Elsewhere (Praeg 2007), I have described the intimate way in which locality is structured in terms of a gender and seniority bias (patriarchy/primogeniture) as phallo-primocentric. In postcolonial Africa this phalo-primocentric logic and its de-differentiating unravelling sometimes plays out in what appears to be nothing short of a war on women and children.
4. For a concise description, see Mann (2013).

the spillover occurs is a function of the fact that kin cuts across the socio-economic and political stratifications of modernity. To understand the logic according to which it does so, it is useful to disentangle *association* and *obligation*. In terms of 'association', Chabal basically offers a communitarian description of the dictum, which, as Christian Gade (2011) rightly points out, only very recently appeared as an accepted synecdoche of Ubuntu, 'I am because we are'. One's existence is recognised as a function of the existence of others or, in terms of Chabal's analysis of *being*:

> Since the attributes of the person are inherently linked to the identity of the locality, one is only 'human' in so far as one is part of a kin network. It is for this reason that those who break from that bond or are cast away become non-persons, socially 'dead' as it were (2009: 47).

The 'because' is the lynchpin of existence in the dictum 'I exist *because* of others'. Where the understanding of 'us' is ontologically or metaphysically grounded with reference to a meaning of locality that includes the reality of the sacred (in the form of the living-dead), a violation of the 'because' motivated by the pursuit of self-interest would not only be considered an act of disloyalty, but indeed present as an all-destroying act of ontological betrayal, a threat to existence as such – a logic which, given the extension of the political economy of obligation as living praxis into postcolonial politics, often manifests as a politics fraught with the understanding of difference as violence: too much of a difference always threatens the assumption of interdependence (the priority of 'unity') so that 'difference' is always more than simply a difference of opinion.

In order to sustain the existence of the 'we' and to give reality to what it means, one needs to recognise and honour certain obligations. This effectively means that 'one's responsibilities as an individual are . . . the mirror image of those features that contribute to one's identity as a human being' (Chabal 2009: 47). Alternatively, obligations are the currency of associations (48); they make the association real, visible, manifest:

> To have no obligation is not to belong; it is not to be fully and socially human. Obligations therefore, are not seen – as the western concept seems to imply – as impositions, claims on one's otherwise better used time and energy, but as a means of sustaining one's place in a network of belonging:

that most vital attribute of humanity, socialibility and, ultimately, being-in-the-world (48).

From this ontological understanding of association as a form of strong or deep communitarianism and its manifestation in reciprocal obligations follows a clear understanding of what constitutes morally good and bad behaviour. In a world where 'morality is indistinguishable from the rest of African social life' (Richardson 2009: 131) or where 'the life of the community, with its conscientious observance of rituals and traditions, is its own ethic' (135), in a world where 'religious beliefs were fused with moral values to form a single whole' (Prozesky 2009: 5), those actions will be considered good that sustain the association and those that threaten it will be considered bad. In the memorable formulation of Placide Tempels, we have to imagine a world in which '[morality] depends on things ontologically understood' (1969: 121). In terms of this report, recognising this reciprocity and honouring its implicit obligations is a condition for being referred to as someone who 'has ubuntu' since it 'refers to one's diligence as a member of society to accept the duties the community imposes on its members' (Coertze 2001: 113).

Naturally this understanding of belonging is not simply something of the past. In fact, the continuation of this political economy of obligation into modern or post-apartheid South Africa defines its postcoloniality and issues the politician with the specific challenge 'to fashion political space above and beyond such worlds of kinship' (Chabal 2009: 50). But therein lies the rub. At its simplest, postcoloniality presents as the tension between a national domain of politics, imagined in terms of a *contractual* understanding of association – which views obligation mostly in terms of negative restraints on the autonomy of the individual – and a local domain of politics that, spilling over and overlapping with the national, expresses being and belonging visibly and tangibly in terms of kinship, reciprocity and a political economy of obligation. The *contractual* understanding of association is the *imaginaire* of a 'post-industrial revolution South Africa' (Bayart 1993: 35), its self-conception as a modern, constitutional state in which the basic axiom or a priori is that entities are prior to relations. The master trope here is *difference*: how to conceive it, manage it, encourage it and institutionalise it, in order to facilitate, guarantee and promote it, but also to contain it. In the political economy of obligation, on the other hand, the axiom or a priori is that relations are prior to entities. The master trope here is *unity*: how to sustain it, protect it, reimagine or reconstitute it in political as opposed to sacred terms, how to negotiate the fragmentation of kinship-based unity conceived in terms of origin and locality into quasi-deontologised versions of it as the kind of 'network society' pivoting around shared political and economical interests. In short, the problem here is how to square the logic of *unity* with a neoliberal modernity that promotes the relentless pursuit of interests conceived in terms of its *individualist* a priori, while criminalising, delegitimising or struggling to reduce to mere *difference* any pursuit of interests articulated, formally or informally, as attempts to honour, recognise and sustain the value of *unity*. Of course these domains do not overlap with any geographical demarcation (rural, urban), neither are they reducible to race or even the binary Western/Africans. Better to think of them as two *imaginaires* that mark the outer or most extreme logic of each set of assumptions, with membership fluid in the sense that individuals may, under various circumstances, participate in or encourage either logic with varying degrees of commitment and permanence, in order to obtain rewards associated with one *imaginaire*, but not encouraged or more difficult to obtain or even simply not available in the logic of the other (see Kemahlioglu 2011).

The task of tracing the fluidity and overlapping nature of these *imaginaires* is perhaps better left to political sociologists. My aim in this section has been twofold: first, through a description of the political economy of obligation, to raise as a formal principle of that political economy what I shall be referring to as a 'logic of interdependence'. As indicated in the introduction, this phrase will enable us, where and whenever necessary, temporarily to suspend the normative evaluation of the recognition of our interdependence as either good, useful or desirable, or bad, treacherous and problematic. Of course, in precolonial Africa, this question seems to have been relatively (not absolutely) straightforward: recognising and adhering to the logic of interdependence was not only good, but good *because* constitutive of the meaning of *being* and *belonging*. In fact, so constitutive of their meaning was it that the very logic of interdependence must be recognised to describe, first and foremost, the relationship between the concepts of *being* and *belonging* themselves. My second aim in this section has been to introduce, however obliquely, the question of values: historically, what it meant for someone to recognise and adhere to the logic of interdependence, what it meant for someone *to be recognised* as one 'who has ubuntu', was inescapably constituted as a value-laden or normative recognition. Two things are at work in this description: first, that the recognition of me as one 'who has ubuntu' was a function of, or presupposed as a condition of sorts, *my prior recognition* of the logic of interdependence, of the fact that I lived being *as* belonging, that *my* being is *our* belonging and so on; second, that this prior recognition was never a recognition of interdependence in the abstract, as idea or philosophy or even as principle, but in *praxis* or in the *act* of living the reality and actuality of that interdependence. The recognition of 'having ubuntu' meant not only the actualisation of our interdependence, but also the actualisation of that interdependence in terms of the values that gave interdependence content and made it meaningful. In other words, to become the embodiment of ubuntu meant to have become the embodiment of the values presupposed by it. Combined, these two dimensions (prior recognition and the affirmation of values) suggest that the condition for recognising me as one who 'has ubuntu' resulted from my prior re-en*act*ment of (my) being as belonging, of the self (*being*) recognising being as a function of *belonging*, understood or decoded in terms of the values that make *belonging* meaningful. This further suggests that ubuntu cannot meaningfully be construed as either adjective or predicate. One cannot have ubuntu, firstly and obviously because it is not something one can *have*, but secondly and more importantly, because it is not something *one* can have. The statement is directed at 'one' who has demonstrated that s/he is primarily not one. To say, then, that 'you have ubuntu' is not to recognise a personal attribute, but rather, already the *return* of recognition, the return of a compliment (as response to your prior recognition, in praxis, of the fact that I exist, that I matter and so on). Strictly speaking, then, the statement 'you have ubuntu' is really a logic of interdependence reflecting itself, articulating itself, naming itself – not 'self' as in auto-nomination (from the Greek *autos*, 'self') but the mutuality of self, a mutual-nomination, the cultural iteration of praxis as speech or an isomorphic doubling up of culture and speech, perhaps even the tautological reiteration of praxis *as* speech.

We have a good sense of the constellation of values that are articulated as the re-enactment of ubuntu in their historical context from Chabal's analysis of the political economy of obligation. Much else has been written on the tension between this historic constellation of phallo-primocentric values (Praeg 2007: 141) and the postcolonial, liberal, democratic constellation of equality and rights (see, for instance, Keevy 2009a, 2009b, 2009c). The question I want to keep circumscribing in this report is the narrower and more focused question about the relationship between historical values and contemporary philosophical practices, between ubuntu as cultural praxis and Ubuntu as philosophical practice. Crudely put, I am intrigued by the question of whether or not a contemporary Ubuntu, shorn of its phallo-primocentric values, still constitutes a meaningful political, social and/or philosophical practice. What difference does it make? What difference *can* it make?

It seems to me that there are at least two ways of approaching this question and the distinction between them is premised on a dangerously arbitrary distinction between local and global, between thinking from the 'inside' and thinking from the 'outside'. First, we can take as point of departure the global or the exterior – Western ideologies and philosophies, such as humanism, communitarianism, virtue ethics, socialism and so on – and effectively sidestep the question of values by allowing these pre-existing ideologies and philosophies to filter in and out certain aspects of ubuntu praxis, in order to leave us with an *African* humanism, *African* communitarianism, *African* Socialism and so on. But this route is fraught with contradictions and circularities – some of which are addressed throughout this report, but particularly in the following chapter – in addition to which, it is fundamentally premised on the dead end of a politics of recognition and the violence of sovereignty associated with it (*we* also have communitarian traditions, *ours* is the original socialism, *our* humanism is more extreme and profound).[5] Alternatively, we can start on the 'inside' – and this is a very loose and fuzzy notion of the 'inside' that perhaps denotes more of an intention than a location – and proceed by way of a critique that will trace in the broadest and most abstract of outlines the historical processes, the interplay between local aspirations and global expectations, which will explain how the ubuntu praxis became reconstituted as decontextualised and abstract Ubuntu. While the first route is predominantly epistemological (what is the difference between socialism and African Socialism?), the second route is predominantly political (how did we come to talk about Ubuntu the way we do?). The reason I am opting for the second route is because I think it will better equip us to ask the kind of questions that are likely to get sidelined by the first approach, such as: What are the Western, modernist assumptions at play in this quest for an authentically African Ubuntu? How does the politics of recognition predetermine the thinking through which we try to describe the nature and emancipatory potential of Ubuntu? What forms of racism and exoticism are at work in the gaze that so eagerly appropriates Ubuntu as 'exceptional' (as a *form of* humanism, exceptional *to* Africa) and so on.

---

5. This amounts to what Hountondji (1983: 67) calls a form of 'cultural exhibitionism which compels the "Third World" intellectual to "defend and illustrate" the peculiarities of his tradition for the benefit of a Western public'.

Part 2: Migrant thinking; Four a prioris

> The majority of the population of Southern Africa today cannot be properly said to know and to live *ubuntu* by virtue of any continuity with village life. They have to be educated to pursue (under the name of *ubuntu* [Ubuntu]) a global and urban reformulation of village values.
> — Wim van Binsbergen, '*Ubuntu* and the Globalisation of Southern African Thought and Society'

The political economy of obligation and its constitutive formal principle, the logic of interdependence, would be shattered by a number of events and outcomes that can be considered historical conditions of the possibility of talking about Ubuntu in the manner we have come to do. Certain things happened that effectively removed or, in the words of Gilles Deleuze and Félix Guattari (2004), *de-territorialised* ubuntu from the domain or territory of cultural praxis and reinserted or *re-territorialised* it in a different context as a trope or philosophy, an abstract idea or perhaps a set of ideas, in a way that sometimes (and under certain conditions and in specific contexts) allows Ubuntu to function as legitimate sign for 'us all'. That Ubuntu can signify or speak to 'all South Africans'; that is, beyond the territory of a political economy of obligation, is the basic assumption of every Ubuntu theorist who believes not only in the recovery or reappropriation of ubuntu as unifying sign for an African image of thought and a mode of being, but also in the possibility of formalising it as, say, African humanism in such a way that other people, far removed from its originating territory may benefit from it or learn from it or, at the very least, use it as a point of entry to understanding 'the African mind'. There are two assumptions at work in this belief: one, that Ubuntu can be abstracted from the values implicit in ubuntu praxis and two, the assumption that this abstracted Ubuntu will remain at once specific enough to be African *and* general enough to be understood and applied outside the context of its originating values.

I think four historical conditions – two global and two local – have made it possible to think about Ubuntu in this way. These conditions are only analytically distinct and to present them as subtle and complex interfaces between global and local conditions or a prioris, one ideally needs a three-dimensional text or any representation with spatial depth in which to posit the two global conditions as vast background determinants over which, and interacting with which, we find the local conditions or a prioris. Without such a medium at hand, we can proceed with the next best alternative and that is to splice the global and local a prioris into an elliptical unity of sorts. And that is what I do below, to splice – which literally means to join or connect ropes by interweaving strands – these two global and local a prioris that have made postcolonial Ubuntu possible.

First global a priori: Colonialism

Historically, the different normative evaluations of the logic of interdependence that came to be associated with Africa(ns) were a function of two different a prioris. By historic a priori I mean, following Michel Foucault, that which

> in a given period, delimits in the totality of experience a field of knowledge, defines the mode of being of the objects that appear in that field, provides man's everyday perception with theoretical powers, and defines the condition in which he can sustain a discourse about things that is recognized to be true (1982: 158).

To simplify, we can also think of this a priori as a historic predisposition to fragment reality in a way that would render it digestible by the disciplinary subjects (anthropology, philosophy, etc.) invented for the study of reality, while keeping in mind the manner in which those very disciplinary structures in turn determine how we see reality, what they allow us to consider as serious objects of study and what procedures are considered legitimate for the analysis and discussion of the objects of study so defined. The two main historic a prioris that, over the last 300 years, would give normative content to the logic of interdependence were, first, a *historicist* and second, a *relativist* a priori.

The *historicist* a priori – of which the whole colonialist project was a function – considered the logic of interdependence as a mere reminder or 'symbol of Western prehistorical experience' (Mudimbe 1991a: 11). By historicist I mean the assumption, embedded in disciplines of the time, that there is but one path of social evolution or development, that the West was further down this road of development than Africa and that the pre-eminence of a logic of interdependence in Africa was proof of the underdeveloped nature of African societies. From the perspective of this historicist a priori, the logic of interdependence was considered both necessary and potentially negative: *necessary* because it was a stage of development that all societies had to go through, *potentially negative* because undue adherence to it would become a stumbling block to future development (modernity). This negativity was reflected in the terms used to describe it: tribe, ethnicity, collectivism, clan and so on. The legitimation of the colonialist project derived entirely from this historicist a priori and amounted to an attempt to transform Africa in the image of a West considered further down the path of development.[6]

Informing the very logic of colonialism was the desire to transform African nature (in the dual sense of the word) to reflect the more advanced, Western nature. On the one hand, colonialists transformed physical nature into a reflection of European spaces by recreating the West in African cities, landscapes and nation-states. On the other hand, they set out, through 'civilisation', education and Christianisation, to transform the very nature of colonised people into a reflection of the Western self. The *implicit legitimacy* of this transformation (implicit, for the West did not need to explicitly legitimise itself) derived from the racialised belief that primitive societies (much like children) are in the process of re-enacting or recapitulating stages of development that the more civilised West (*qua* adults) had already gone through.

However, 'by the 1940s, a new *a priori* detached itself from the very experience of the normative language, and it became accepted that all languages, all civilizations, are arbitrary' (Mudimbe 1991a: 11). This *relativist* a priori was the historic condition for the political processes that, over the next twenty years, would culminate in the independence of African states from colonial rule. The resulting discourse on African self-determination was a function of this relativist a priori. Through the struggle for liberation and post-independence attempts to give content to what liberty meant, a different normative evaluation of the logic of interdependence emerged, premised on a rejection of the historicism of the colonialist project. The logic of interdependence was hence celebrated, not merely as a passing stage of development, but as a mark of cultural authenticity, of what is most unique about Africans and the African state and that should therefore be saved and appropriated as a sine qua non of the future development of these states. Of this desire to found the African state on a reappropriation of the logic of interdependence as an authentic mode of being, the African Socialism project was probably the most coherent and ambitious example. Closer to home, the suggestion by Drucilla Cornell and others that Ubuntu should be considered foundational to the Constitution, the Law of law or meta-purpose that should inform our interpretation of the law, is another example, to which I return in Chapter 4.

---

6. See Praeg (2008a: 369) and Mudimbe (1991a).

First local a priori: Urbanisation

R.D. Coertze (2001) distinguishes between '*Ubuntu/botho* the original concept' and two semantic shifts that the concept has undergone in the process of becoming what we now refer to as Ubuntu or the 'philosophy of *ubuntu*'. Of the original concept, he notes the following:

- the terms *ubuntu/botho* referred to the essence of being human, but that this 'theoretically included both the positive and negative qualities found in [humanity]' (113);
- in the Nguni languages, derogatory terms such as *abelungu* or *makgowa* were used to refer to white people, suggesting that '*ubuntu* and *botho* refer only to the essence of humankind from Africa';
- the logic of interdependence was actualised in kinship-based cultural practices and rituals, which meant that reciprocal duties and obligations were perpetuated or sustained through a 'process of enculturation within the extended family [which] ensured that the members of a new generation accept the preferred conduct and the duties expected of them' (114);
- in this very enculturation we find at work a certain constitutive violence, the ambivalent interplay of solidarity and coercion we have come to recognise in all forms of communitarianism: 'Within... peer groups the individual could not only call on support but was through the pressure of co-members compelled to conform and perform according to the example and expectation of the majority';
- for this very reason, 'it becomes very difficult for the individual to subscribe to absolute standards of kindness, morality or goodwill that are not endorsed by specific examples of such sentiments within the societal framework of every-day existence';
- and lastly, his research suggests:

> There are no proverbs or sayings... in which either *ubuntu* or *botho* were explained or praised as abstract concepts [but the] observance of the abstract qualities of kindness, goodwill and high moral standards ... were all extolled in concrete situations between relatives, friends or persons having common interests or speaking the same language (115).

Wim van Binsbergen concurs: 'I have never witnessed the technical terms *ubuntu* (or local morphological equivalents) or *Zambian humanism* to be used as a matter of course, of accepted parlance, in these concrete situations of the village and the family' (2001: 69). I do not interpret these authors to mean that there was no abstract recognition of our interdependence, such as suggested by the Venda proverb, '*Muthu u bebelwa munwe*' (a person is born for the other) (Murove 2009b: 30) or in the recognition that 'so-and-so has ubuntu', but rather that in these situational invocations, 'utterances invoking principles of sociability . . . are set in a context of elaborate rhetorical acts . . . [and] that the socio-ritual events in which they feature produce *implied* meaning . . . much more than that they articulate *explicit and codifiable* meaning' (Van Binsbergen 2001: 68) and that this implied meaning was understood, historically, as the actualisation of culturally specific values. The idea that ubuntu could make sense beyond the immediate context of values 'belongs to a later stage than the original or traditional life style' (Coertze 2001: 115). In fact, as I argue below, this codification would come about first as a result of colonialism and, second, through resistance to colonialism.

Colonialism and the processes of industrialisation and urbanisation that produced South Africa's industrial revolution brought about a sustained reorganisation of the socio-economic substratum of people's lives (Munyaka and Motlhabi 2009: 79–83). In the townships and cities of industrialising South Africa, Africans encountered the solitariness of life associated with modernity in a context where it is expected of individuals not always to rely on community networks, but to learn to 'fend for themselves amidst strangers in a strange and hostile environment' (Coertze 2001: 115). The impact of these socio-economic changes on a traditional political economy of obligation was far-reaching because, as Ncedile Saule comments, not only were the 'traditional religious forms of worship and customs of which kings and chiefs were custodians . . . destroyed [but by implication also] the very roots of *ubuntu*' (in Munyaka and Motlhabi 2009: 79) – to the extent that Jacobus Hendrik Smit, Moya Deacon and Augustine Shutte can claim that ubuntu currently exists 'mainly in South African rural areas, it being a value [that was] lost through the process of urbanisation' (80).

But I think we should be careful here. What colonialism and urbanisation brought about was the destruction of a coherent ubuntu praxis. Carried forth alongside emerging forms of individualism was a very political version of that praxis – and by political I mean a political strategy centred on the master trope of 'solidarity' deployed, sometimes consciously and sometimes unconsciously, to great effect in the struggle for liberation. To put this somewhat bluntly, with urbanisation and the anti-apartheid struggle, came the expansion or secularisation of the formal principle of ubuntu praxis, so that it no longer referred to local, kinship-based and visible communities of metaphysical locality, but rather to larger, imagined communities of political practice. This expansion into secular, modern politics of a principle historically associated with an ontological praxis was merely symptomatic of a greater widening or expansion. In this regard, Coertze notes that 'the reciprocity inherent in the [practice of] *ubuntu* or *botho* was under these circumstances understandably extended to include those working together or to include those living in the same neighbourhood of a specific urban township' (2001: 115).[7] Beyond this, 'contact with others than one's relatives or tribe-members [sic] or those having the same life style eventually necessitated the extension of *ubuntu* or *botho* to include the entire amorphous total of humanity'. The importance of this shift derives from the fact that Ubuntu became an abstract concept, the meaning no longer simply derived from an implicit agreement about what was meant or understood by one's diligence as a member of society to accept the duties imposed by a community on its members. Rather, as an idea or concept abstracted from historical praxes, the meaning of Ubuntu increasingly became articulated in confluence with the very discourses through which Western modernity articulated its imposition on Africa, namely Christianity and a liberal discourse of individual human rights. Ubuntu, once severed from the historical praxes of a visible community, had to speak a language that would be understood by everyone who derived a sense of purpose from acknowledging their imagined shared humanity and who, through such acknowledgement, came to constitute the *we* of the 'I am because we are' in the imaginary terms of various political communities – the local, struggle/township community, 'Africans' as opposed to Westerners, and later the 'nation' itself.[8] This process explains Van Binsbergen's comment that Ubuntu, once decoupled from the ubuntu praxis, came to have 'a very wide and internally richly textured semantic field, a vast area of possibilities and implications, out of which in concrete contexts a specific selection is being made, triggered by the juxtapositions which accompany the root *–ntu* . . . in that context' (2001: 54).

---

7. There is evidence that this change in the socio-economic base from rural to urban or even semi-urban also reflects shifts in the understood meaning of ubuntu. In her study, Marta Bonn reports that ubuntu 'meant "cooperation, sharing and interdependence" to the rural children much more often (30%) than to the urban children (6%), or to the semi-urban children (17%)' (2007: 871).
8. There is some resonance here with Kwasi Wiredu's (2008: 335) distinction between communalism (the kinship-based social formation) and communitarianism (the representation of that communalism as theory).

Context and circumstance so favoured Christianity and human rights as two discourses most suitable to retrodict a meaning of Ubuntu that it was now assumed ubuntu had always already been their articulation (much like Julius Nyerere, for whom traditional African societies were socialist long before the invention of socialism). In this regard, Coertze notes: 'From the demands of Christianity as well as the precepts of Western philosophy the African individual was now called upon to profess a personal commitment to abstract standards of morality, kindness, charity and even benevolence as well as mercifulness' (2001: 115). But here a paradox emerges as the result of a clash between the identity-based claim (Ubuntu is unique) and the circularity through which a meaning is derived from the present, only to be retrodicted as a voice of the past. In both cases – Christianity and human rights – the borrowing of an abstract language is accompanied by the paradoxical claim, on the one hand, that ubuntu always already articulated or represented the insights contained in these discourses and, on the other hand, a conflation of its meaning with that of Christianity and human rights so that they become virtually indistinct.[9] In other words, a paradox emerges as a result of asserting that these external influences tell us nothing we do not already know and, on the other hand, only ever being able to articulate what it is that we already knew in and through these discourses. This paradox registers a tension between identity politics and dogmatism that plays out in claims that are either strange: 'No one who does not have Ubuntu should be called a Christian' (Mqhayi in Bonn 2007: 865), perplexing:

> It is this very principle [of sharing] whose spirit as well as application is similar to the message of Christ. Accordingly, while Jesus Christ might have been necessary for those segments of humanity who have readily accepted Christianity, it may not be inferred that he was therefore necessary for most traditional societies in Africa (Ramose 1999: 34).

or problematically identitarian: 'It also outlines the five stages of the peacemaking process found among ubuntu societies: acknowledging guilt; showing remorse and repenting; asking for and giving forgiveness; and paying compensation or reparations as a prelude to reconciliation' (Murithi 2009: 221).

---

9. For example, 'Kaunda's Humanism stems from the Christian concept of the brotherhood of mankind' (Babu 1981: 65).

The simple equivalence of Ubuntu with a regime of rights is particularly glib, not because the concept of Ubuntu is heterogenous to the concept of law – on the contrary, it is the very embodiment of a specific *nomos* or spirit of Law (as per Montesquieu) – but because Ubuntu is in very useful ways the complete antithesis of the law as represented by the a priori of constitutionalism – from which the status of Ubuntu as both function and critique of Western modernity derives. To present Ubuntu as a representation of such rights *avant la lettre* is to forget that ubuntu does not substantiate notions of individual or even collective rights as much as it does duties and obligations. As Coertze reminds us: 'Neither the traditional nor the acculturative formulation of *ubuntu* or *botho* imbued the individual with specific rights as a human being. To be human, as of old, meant to shoulder the concomitant duties and thus to be judged an example to others' (2001: 115). In this regard, Bede Onuoha notes that the traditional African 'thought more of his duties to his community than of his rights' (1965: 41) and Coertze concludes that the shift towards human rights discourse 'ended with a concept granting inherent rights to all human beings without a concomitant stress on duties. This is completely different from the emphasis placed in the past on the necessity to accept the duties entailed by the membership of various societal cohesions' (2001: 117).

It is possible that the putative tension between a regime of obligations and a regime of rights, evident in much of the Ubuntu discourse, merely reproduces the basic binary of African communitarianism versus Western individualism. In this case, it would be as problematic to read Ubuntu as an exemplification of the former regime as it would be to appropriate it as an expansion of the latter. Ubuntu *qua* glocal, retrodicted phenomenon can illuminate and enrich our understanding of both regimes exactly because it can be interpreted to represent an 'interplay between rights and obligations' (Wiredu 2008: 333) premised on the contemporaneity of the individual and the social (Eze 2008). This said, much of the relevance and potential power of Ubuntu lies in the idea that membership of imagined communities entails duties and obligations. Whether or not it would be useful to think of citizenship along the lines of membership suggested here and what the implications of doing so would be for a political system premised on the priority of individual rights is another question.[10] Some of these questions are explored in the last two chapters of this book.

---

10. For a critical exploration of this question, see Enslin and Horsthemke (2004) and, for a response, see Letseka (2012).

Second global a priori: The dialectic of recognition

The struggle against colonialism presented in two registers that Paget Henry (in Gordon 2008) has called the historicists and the poeticists.[11] Lewis Gordon summarises the difference between these two traditions as follows: 'The former [the historicists] are primarily concerned with problems of social change and political economy. The latter [the poeticists] celebrate the imagination with a focus on the conceptions of the self as represented by literature and poetry' (175). Historicists respond to colonialism by disputing the historicism of colonialism, while poeticists are concerned with restoring the dignity of the African self through an analysis of the inner life, past, present and future. The difference can be illustrated with reference to two forms of secular humanism that emerged in twentieth-century Africa. The work of Cheikh Anta Diop (1923–86) represents the historicist dimension, in as much as he was concerned with showing not only that Africa indeed had a history, but also that its history was foundational to human civilisation as such. Léopold Sédar Senghor (1906–2001) is the father of Africa's poeticist tradition (191). He wanted to demonstrate that Africans had their own distinct ways of knowing and being. He argued that whereas the West valorized being rational and analytic, the African's emotional and passionate nature was not only equally valuable, but also an equally valid way of being in and knowing the world. Senghor forms part of a tradition of African philosophy known as ethnophilosophy, of which the three main principles – the temporal, existential and epistemological – remain relevant for the contemporary discourse on Ubuntu.

In terms of its temporal dimension, ethnophilosophers consider colonialism as a fundamental rupture pivoting around the binary opposition of pre- and postcolonial. This binary, in turn, produces two radically different and incompatible conceptions of a Western way of being (individualist) and an African way of being (communalist) that typically are taken to represent two irreconcilable ideas about the nature of human existence (ontologies). The temporal and existential beliefs are closely related in the sense that the radically different time of precolonial Africa corresponds to a radically different way of being. And this is where the third principle – the epistemological – comes in. Ethnophilosophers believe in the possibility of recovering the logic of interdependence as a cornerstone of a politics of identity that will confirm the essential authenticity of Africans, while also serving as the

---

11. For a detailed discussion, see Gordon (2008).

ideological foundation for the sovereign, postcolonial state. Historically this project – essentially one of liberation as self-recognition – replicated the historicism at the root of colonialism in a number of problematic ways that will be discussed in more detail in Chapter 2. Suffice it here to delimit some of the most obvious consequences of appropriating the logic of interdependence in this way. These become visible the moment we remember that, just as Africans did not know they were black before Westerners told them they were not white, Africans did not celebrate their 'communalism' before colonialists told them they lacked a sense of individualism. The categories of 'being black' and 'having communalist traditions' are functions of a global a priori, first of colonialism (their negative denotation) and subsequently of postcoloniality and self-determination (their positive denotation). Succinctly placing this in historical context, V-Y Mudimbe writes:

> Eboussi-Boulaga aptly wrote that *at least for Africans*, the emergence of an African 'We-Subject' was the major human phenomenon of the second half of [the last] century . . . [Thus] emerged . . . a strong emphasis on history and a new anthropology as a means for better understanding of both African tradition and identity (1988: 60).

This has obvious resonance with the notion of double consciousness as theorised in critical race theory as far back as W.E.B. Du Bois and which found some of its most poignant expressions in the work of Frantz Fanon. According to Gordon, when Fanon stated that blackness is 'a white construction', he meant that

> the people who have become known as black people are descendants of people who had no reason to have regarded themselves as such. As a consequence, the history of black people has the constant motif of such people encountering their blackness from the 'outside,' as it were, and then developing, in dialectical fashion, a form of blackness that transcends the initial, negative series of events (2008: 158).

Fanon famously summarised this insight in 'Algeria Unveiled' when he stated: 'It is the white man who creates the Negro. But it is the Negro who creates negritude' (1980: 25). The creation of Negritude (or Black Consciousness, for that matter) 'originates in the need to respond to the negations of blackness embedded in Western philosophical discourse . . . [It] becomes a means of overloading the denominating structure with precisely that which the latter names as negative' (Quayson 2002: 586). In other words, a system that nominates the fact of blackness as negative will engender in the various forms of resistance to it, dialectical oppositions aimed at 'overloading the denominating structure with precisely that which the latter names as negative'.

The reinvention of Ubuntu was never going to escape the logic of double consciousness and the power struggle implicit in offering counter-representations of Africa's 'primitive communalism' that would 'overload the denominating structure' of colonialism with precisely that which the latter always named as negative (by re-presenting Ubuntu as a messianic, even salvific humanism, for instance). Following the logic of double consciousness, African communalism in general and Ubuntu in particular is a 'white construction' in the precise sense meant by Fanon, namely that Africans encounter it from the outside as a result of being told that they lack not only whiteness, but also a concept of the individual. Just as black people have set out in dialectical fashion to develop a meaning of blackness that would overcome its initial postulate as lack, so they/we have set out in dialectical fashion to develop a meaning of communalism aimed at transcending the initial colonialist insistence that a lack of individualism equates a lack of humanity.

The problem here is the dialectic itself, for to conceive of the self in the binary logic presented by it, to accept the idea that the most significant fact about the African self is its communal (as opposed to its individualist) nature, is to affirm the very violence of Western thought through the act of contesting it *on its own terms*. Whether it is indeed possible to proceed in a non-dialectical manner is, of course, another question and one that Fanon grappled with all his life. All I am pointing out here is that to accept Ubuntu as a signifying fact of blackness or Africanness is already to constitute its relevance and meaning in predetermined ways and to commit oneself to proceeding in a binary fashion that will necessarily conflate 'Western' with 'individualist' – thereby rendering impossible any rigorous comparison of Ubuntu with, say, a feminist ethics of care (see, for instance, Friedman 1989) – while in the process denying the reality of ascendant forms of individualism in Africa that *pre-dated* colonialism. A non-dialectical response to racist modernity may be difficult to imagine, but the very least we can do is to remain conscious of the violence we perpetuate as part of the liberating performativity of dialectic opposition – in this instance, the violence necessarily inflicted both on the Western Other and African self as a prerequisite for talking about Ubuntu as exceptional or as a 'solution to Western individualism' and so on.

Second local a priori: Constitutionalism as 'liberation'

> Whenever a phenomenological concept is drawn from primordial sources, there is a possibility that it may degenerate if communicated in the form of an assertion. It gets understood in an empty way and is thus passed on, losing its indigenous character, and becoming a free-floating thesis.
> — Martin Heidegger, *Being and Time*

In 'Person and Community in African Traditional Thought', Ifeanyi Menkiti stirred up a controversy when he suggested three features of the traditional African world view that distinguish it from 'most Western views' of humanity (1984: 171). Two of these – that 'the reality of the communal world takes precedence over the reality of individual life' and that the moral community includes the living-dead – will for the moment be accepted as unproblematic facts of being and belonging in the political economy of obligation. The third feature has had a more complicated reception and is related to the notion of 'processual personhood' or the idea that in precolonial African societies, 'full personhood is not perceived as simply given at the very beginning of one's life, but is attained after one is well along in society' (173). There is ample evidence in contemporary literature of what such a processual understanding of personhood would mean in practical terms. In Thando Mgqolozana's *A Man Who is Not a Man*, the male narrator speaks about his depraved youth in Cape Town and how the soccer coach reprimanded him and his friends for wasting their lives:

> That is why Ta-Diski, the coach, called us into his kamer and treated us to a long belting session when he heard of our wayward actions outside the kasi. He was the first to suggest that what we needed was uKwaluswa – to be circumcised. Among traditional people, uKwaluswa is commonly held to be the remedy for mischievous behaviour like ours (2009: 16–17).

The reason for this remedy is explained a little later in the novel:

> According to the elders, if a boy reached a stage where he was problematic in society, there was only one way to curb this, and that was 'the obvious'. The boy's mischief was considered to be an indication of wanting a rite of passage into manhood. The things that were done at the mountain were held to be so powerful that they could root out any foolish notions from a

boy's stubborn head, sending him back with a clear sense of right and wrong (29).

But initiation is not only about morality; it is about morality embedded in a greater genderised conception of personhood and humanness. In addition, non-participation or failed participation in such rituals leaves the individual a non-person, inhuman, 'ostracised from humanity' (182). The narrator's friend warns him before he leaves to undergo his initiation:

> Finally, he told me the things I was to avoid. Above all the cautions, Mcsquared emphasised that I should avoid landing up in hospital at all costs. 'It is better to die than to go to hospital. It would be the end of you anyway,' he warned me. 'There's no living space for failed men in our society. Either you become a man the expected way, or you are not one at all' (65).

This is no empty threat because the warning prefigures exactly how the narrator is treated by one of the nurses when he eventually ends up in hospital as a result of a botched circumcision:

> She was openly insulting us for having landed up at the hospital – we cowards! She was bringing home to us the disgrace of our being survived by our empty huts at the mountain, impressing on us our invalidity, the manhood rejects that we had become by fleeing to the hospital and the sub-human status that we were about to assume in society as a result. Her reaction might seem extreme, but it was typical of the mockery and censure that we could expect to encounter outside (122).

The fate of the narrator's girlfriend articulates the connection between ritualised becoming and personhood even more clearly:

> She started doing sex with strangers she met at the beachfront. She'd disappear from home for days and come back looking like the fifteen-year-old junkie she'd become. It was after the incident when she and Tracey were caught by the police in possession of drugs that her mother decided to send her to the villages to learn humanness anew (55).[12]

---

12. On this, see also Van Binsbergen (2001: 63).

The point here is that this processual dimension of ubuntu may be a function or epiphenomenon of ubuntu *praxis*, but it will for obvious reasons generate complex tensions in a context of equality and inalienable rights – as scholars such as Ezra Chitando (2008: 45) have indeed argued. One way out of this dilemma is to argue along with Kwasi Wiredu (2002) that what is at stake in the process of becoming is not personhood, but social status – an interpretation I find unconvincing because it underestimates the fact that in a political economy of obligation to have no social status (in terms of gender, to not be reckoned a 'man') is, for all intents and purposes, indistinct from not being recognised as person or human being. This follows from the fact that in the philosophical anthropology outlined by Chabal (2009), the category 'man' – both in the sense of hu*man* and the gendered man – is a functional concept which, as Alasdair MacIntyre argues in *After Virtue*, is rooted in the form of social life in which 'to be a man is to fill a set of roles each of which has its own point and purpose: member of a family, citizen, soldier' and so on (1982: 16–17). In a world where there is such an inextricable link between morality and function, between being and purpose, to accuse a man of not being able to fulfil his function *as man*, is per (functional) definition to suggest that he is subhu*man*. The debate on this issue of processual personhood remains open.[13] What interests me is not whether or not this conclusion is justified or correct, but rather what is at stake in the debate. For it seems to me that in order for ubuntu praxis to be reappropriated as Ubuntu, a certain circumcision is called for, one through which the *ontic* orientation of ubuntu, the fact that 'having ubuntu' is a function of ritualised becoming-through-other people, will need to be deontologised or reinvented in order to retain its relevance in a postfunctionalist context, where our humanity or personhood as rights-bearing individuals is accepted as an existential and ontological bottom line, not subject to the vagaries of communitarian

---

13. See Bewaji (2003: 395), Murove (2009: 71–2, 260, 323) and Shutte (2009: 92). This debate is, for obvious reasons, highly charged. What seems indisputable to me is that in a precolonial African cosmology, the failure 'to become a proper member of a community of persons [as] a processual, evolutionary, developmental, intellectual maturation kind of thing' (Bewaji 2003: 395) will carry ontological implications very different and far more serious from those faced by an individual living in a society understood as the reciprocal recognition of inalienable human rights. Further, as argued here, this functionalism can be a useful way of framing or bringing into focus the implications of adhering to a processual understanding of personhood in the context of contractual modernity.

consensus or ritualised processes of belonging. I spent some time on the example from Mgqolozana's novel in order to demonstrate something of the arrow of time at work in the process that saw, first, the adoption of the 1996 Constitution as a culmination of the struggle for liberation and second, the formalising, through the Constitution, of the principle that tradition will be actively and passively developed in line with constitutional values.

Colonialism was in many ways the beginning of the end of the political economy of obligation as a sustained and coherent praxis. The struggle for liberation conceived in terms of a Western a priori – that entities precede relations and hence that individual rights are more fundamental than social obligations – continued this movement away from that praxis and is sustained in the idea that tradition and custom should be actively and passively developed in line with constitutional values. In Part 3 of this chapter, I consider the implications for Ubuntu discourse of this double negation or movement away from Africa. I argue that the meaning of Ubuntu reproduced in and through this interface with constitutionalism is neither one in which Ubuntu is simply reducible to human rights discourse nor one that can simply be dismissed as a traditional form of communitarianism at odds with a constitutional regime of rights. Instead, Ubuntu should be considered a glocal phenomenon that must be understood both as a product *of* and a critical response *to* Western modernity. What I am interested in outlining in this second local a priori is the role of constitutionalism in the reproduction of such a glocal Ubuntu. To start delimiting this role, we have to bear two things in mind: (1) The movement from ubuntu praxis to Ubuntu philosophy always involves a process or movement of *translation* or *codification* and (2) the formal principle distilled from Chabal's analysis, namely the logic of interdependence, by virtue of its normative neutrality, allows us to bring into sharper focus the politics involved in every such act of translation or codification. In this specific case, it will allow us to understand how an ubuntu praxis is refracted through constitutionalism in order to produce a rather shallow, because very carefully delimited and circumscribed, glocal meaning of Ubuntu.

We can retrace this refraction by making two moves that seem relatively unproblematic to me: one, by positing the logic of interdependence as a conceptual or formal a priori of the political economy of obligation; two, by recognising the adoption of the 1996 Constitution as a pivotal moment of modernity, which, through the very logic it represents (a Western-modern axiomatic of the individual as conceptual and, now, historical a priori of the political) stands as a clear separation between a now *historical* praxis or political economy of obligation and a *contemporary* or *future* political economy of individual freedom or republican constitutionalism (Kant 1970: 99) premised on three principles: the *freedom* of the members of a society (as human beings), the *dependence* of all on a single, common legislation (as subjects) and the law as guarantor of the *equality* of all (as *citizens of the state*).

These two moves allow us to image the Constitution as a point of refraction through which the post-apartheid political domain is reconstituted. Much like a prism refracts a beam of light, the Constitution refracts the logic of interdependence into various forms or manifestations of that interdependence in a political order at odds with the totality of its expression. What used to be a singular and unified or coherent whole – an ubuntu praxis of interdependence – is refracted into a multiplicity or manifold manifestations of interdependence, each of which, from this pivotal point of refraction onwards, cannot but appear prejudged in a constellation of philosophical and political traditions of thought peculiar to the domain in which it manifests (law, economics, culture, etc.). In each of these domains, a whole matrix unified around the assumption of an individualist a priori is brought to bear on any particular manifestation of the logic of interdependence in that domain, which renders it either as subversive of that a priori or as a salvific alternative to it: *juridically* (restorative justice can subvert the rule of law *and* appear as a salvific alternative to retribution); *economically* (the destructive pursuit of individual interest is good, tenderpreneurship is not); *politically* (ruthless personal ambition is good, nepotism is not). In most constellations, the logic of interdependence creates a certain undesirable 'white noise' that needs to be named, condemned and filtered out, eliminated in order for these domains to retain their chosen (although always contested) (neo)liberal integrity. In the economic constellation, for instance, nepotism is prejudged as unacceptable economic manifestations of that interdependence, while those economic activities that represent the logic of interdependence within the confines of the capitalist system (for example, the *stokvel*) are encouraged, even legitimised.[14] But the refraction of the logic of interdependence does not always give us the equivalence of separate colours suggested by the refraction metaphor. We also find judgements that bleed

---

14. 'A *stokvel* is a very popular example of informal social security. This is where, for instance, a group of five friends make monthly contributions to a *stokvel* or pool. Each member will have a turn (every fifth month) to use the total of the pool, enabling them to buy goods such as furniture and school clothes' (Tshoose 2009: 15).

across the colour bar, for instance those that are both normative and juridical (depending on the context, restorative justice is sometimes *better* than retributive justice) or *moral-economic* (at the macro-level of ideology, socialism is problematic in a way that the micro-level, economic, quasi-socialist praxis of the *stokvel* is not) and so on. Relevant to our purposes is how the process of refraction seems to have managed to carefully hedge Ubuntu – formerly epiphenomenon of the totality of a praxis of interdependence – into the constellation of 'culture' in a manner that leaves it impotent to challenge or contest two discursive and materialist conditionalities of neoliberalism: one, shared humanity is not to be confused with shared resources, much less should the materialist dimension of sharing be considered an inextricable condition for shared humanity; two, even this dematerialised Ubuntu should be interpreted solely as a unifying sign of everything positive about these refractions. In a sense, this second condition is a function of the first: Ubuntu becomes associated with forgiveness, reconciliation, restorative justice and the *stokvel* in a way that dissociates it from any implication in vengeance, tenderpreneurship, nepotism, socialism and so on. In God's rainbow nation, cultural entrepreneurs and the proxies of constitutionalism have successfully colluded in the production of a conception of Ubuntu that is mostly vacuous because it really functions as shorthand for 'being nice', a kitsch Afro-chic artefact that in many ways resembles the sort of thing late capitalism exists to produce.

Be that as it may and, considered as a totality, all these judgements of the manifestation of the logic of interdependence within and against the neoliberal order pivot around an emotive distinction between *empathetic* and *antipathetic* manifestations of the logic of interdependence in post-apartheid South Africa. And while there appears to be no *über*-sign or master trope that unifies all antipathetic manifestations, other than predictable neo-racist liberal tropes such as 'banana republic', 'return of the state of nature', 'traditionalism' and 'culture', it seems that Ubuntu does function as *über*-sign for the unification of all the empathetic manifestations of the logic of interdependence across the various constellations – be they juridical, economic, social or cultural.

The empathetic nature of Ubuntu as master sign derives from the fact that it taps into what we may think of as the unthought of neoliberalism – which is more than simply its opposite (although it often appears as that). Rather, under the notion of 'unthought', I mean to gather everything that a system premised on the axiomatic that 'entities are prior to relations' necessarily needs to repress and forget in order to construct itself as viable *imaginaire*. In such an order, Ubuntu becomes not only a glocal sign that unifies elements of endogenous praxis with global discourses on law, the political and the spiritual, but also an uncanny sign of the very relationality that needed to be suspended, destroyed or repressed in each of these domains in order for Western modernity to violently reinvent itself as the postcolony *qua* politico-juridico-economic system or Constellation of constellations. Those manifestations of the logic of interdependence will be empathetic; that is, celebrated as manifestations of Ubuntu, which either deliver a profound and necessary critique of this violence or concretely and practically manifest a world-disclosing humility as an alternative to it through a praxis that resurfaces forgotten relations (the Truth and Reconciliation Commission [TRC], the *stokvel* and so on). It seems, then, that the logic of interdependence is refracted to produce a figure or sign, 'Ubuntu', through a process of reification that proscribes, through a logic resembling that of the ban, a range of elements that historically were a condition for the very possibility of ubuntu, but which now appear as troublesome or destructive within a liberal democratic order.

In the third and last part of this chapter, I want to do two things: first, to consider the troubled relationship this reified Ubuntu has with three tropes – violence, justice and solidarity. The first has been so successfully proscribed that it appears completely irreconcilable with or heterogenous to the very meaning of Ubuntu, while justice and solidarity require a constant renegotiation according to context. Second, I want to conclude by substantiating the notion of Ubuntu as a glocal phenomenon. The two global and two local a prioris discussed here have effected a difference between ubuntu as historic *ethnic* morality and Ubuntu as contemporary abstract *ethic*. This abstract ethic is given substance through a process we can either describe as a principle of transformation (Cornell) or as retrodiction.

Part 3: Reification, refraction, retrodiction and transformation

> If ubuntu is to be Africa's great gift to the global world of thought, it is primarily not th e African villagers' gift, but that of the academic and managerial codifiers who allowed themselves to be distantly and selectively inspired by village life: ignoring the ubiquitous conflicts and contradictions, the oppressive immanence of the world-view, the witchcraft beliefs and accusations, the constant oscillation between trust and distrust, and merely appropriating and representing the bright side.
>
> — Wim van Binsbergen, '*Ubuntu* and the Globalisation of Southern African Thought and Society'

Violence, justice and solidarity: The collateral damage of retrodiction

Nothing seems more obvious than that Ubuntu represents shared humanity, non-violence and an image of the sublime because of its implicit non-retributive understanding of justice and reconciliation. But I would argue that nothing better demonstrates the refraction of local ubuntu into a sanitised and inoffensive glocal Ubuntu. This suggestion elicits at least two questions: one, what about the residual dimensions of ubuntu praxis that do not make it into this reinvented Ubuntu? Two, how do we formally or theoretically account for or explain this process of refraction?

Violence and the just

Precolonial African societies as an 'ideal type' (as per Max Weber) were characterised by a subsistence economy of interdependence that manifested in the sharing of resources and the reciprocity of obligations and duties, a political economy of obligation, the reproduction of which depended on the successful enculturation of the individual. This reproduction occurred not only through rites and rituals, but also through cultural or idealist expressions or articulations transmitted 'from one generation to the next by means of oral genres such as fables, proverbs, myths, riddles and storytelling' (Kwamwangamalu in Bonn 2007: 866). As Saule puts it: 'Ubuntu could be viewed as a sum total of human behaviours inculcated in the individual by society through established traditional institutions over a period of time' (in Mnyaka 2003: 144). This, comments Mluleki Mnyaka, is 'how ubuntu is attained'. At work here is a form of benevolent coercion, indoctrination, inculcation or perhaps simply cultural strategies of discipline, aimed at the reproduction of certain modes of being and belonging we have come to associate with Ubuntu. What is relevant here is the contradiction or tension between Ubuntu theorists who routinely ignore this constitutive violence and African politicians who routinely appeal to that very violence in the name of discipline or as a strategy for sustaining the coherence of various imagined political formations – either as conscious ideological constructs (as I illustrate in Chapter 3 on African Socialism) or unconsciously as political praxis – the anti-apartheid struggle and its most notorious sign, the 'necklace murder', but also, beyond that, the African National Congress (ANC) as movement and political party – as a recent comment by an ANC member demonstrated: 'The ANC tradition is to cure the illness to save the patient . . . The tradition of ubuntu is to try to help the individual overcome misconduct and, in branches, sometimes a great deal of effort goes into dealing with it' (in Molele 2011).

In Ubuntu literature, it is fascinating to witness how theorists struggle to reconcile Ubuntu's ecstatic humanism with the often-brutal nature of the technologies of discipline required for its manifestation. In the case of necklace murders, the phrase often used was that these sacrificial technologies of discipline were the 'shadow side of Ubuntu', the dark side of the *muntu*, as it were, while Allister Sparks comments that in a situation involving necklacing, Ubuntu took 'a back seat as more aggressive and abrasive competition for survival emerged' (in Munyaka and Motlhabi 2009: 81). Christoph Marx simply notes that 'the other side of Ubuntu is ostracism and compulsory conformity. This comes to the fore as soon as a strategy for survival is transformed into a nationalist ideology' (2002: 52),[15] while M. Munyaka and M. Motlhabi hope that it 'is more appropriate to say that *Ubuntu* was at that time not in play at all but set aside in the interest of expediency' (2009: 81).

This discomfort is wholly a function of the refusal to appreciate the extent to which Ubuntu has become refracted into, or as Van Binsbergen would have it *conflated with*, the 'good news', to the exclusion of those cultural praxes or benevolent technologies of discipline and coercion that were always deployed in order to reproduce certain moral ideals which, when embodied in a person, allowed that person to be described as being human, as having ubuntu. There is no racist conspiracy here, no perplexing opposition between Ubuntu and strategies of coercion. These are simply flip sides of the same coin of interdependence – something liberals never tire of criticising communitarians for. The point I am making is that the conversion of ubuntu into Ubuntu was characterised from the start by a process that sought to sanitise ubuntu, either by presenting its constitutive violence in the socially acceptable language of desirable outcomes (patriotism in the case of nationalist discourse, compulsory reconciliation in the case of *S. v. AZAPO*, 1996) or by expelling from the very meaning of Ubuntu any allusion, implication or manifestation of the coercive and/or ambivalent strategies historically deployed to indoctrinate the individual or inculcate the values associated with what 'being human' was understood to mean.[16]

---

15. A similar position is taken by Swartz (2006).
16. In *S. v. AZAPO*, 1996, along with others, Steve Biko's family challenged Act 34 of 1995 that established the Truth and Reconciliation Commission, specifically the constitutionality of the clause that provided for conditional amnesty for those who would disclose their part in apartheid violence. This, they argued, violated their right to justice. Mohamed D.P. upheld the

But if the main result of this codification has been to proscribe, ban or expel the very idea of benevolent coercion, the second most salient feature of that process has been the absolute manner in which talk about *shared humanity* has been quarantined from all talk about *shared resources*. Who ever dares to publicly advocate that Ubuntu conjoins the materialist and idealist dimensions of our existence in the totality of what Nyerere called the principles of love, sharing and work? Perhaps it is a sign of the failure of African Socialism, but where are the Ubuntu theorists who have insisted on an African *nomos* as condition for the possibility of a development programme that, even in our post-ideological age, can strive for some unity of the collective experience beyond the theme-park intellectualism of an African Renaissance? Was that our best stab at a post-apartheid *nomos*?[17] Perhaps more daring, who would justify what is otherwise dismissed as nepotism as the logical implication of Ubuntu?[18] I am not necessarily advocating the latter view. What I am pointing out is that the extent of our dis-ease with these

---

constitutionality of the clause on the grounds that the transition to democracy required prioritising reconciliation over justice. I analyse this judgment at length towards the end of the final chapter of this book.
17. For two radically divergent answers to this question, see Farred (2003) and Bongmba (2004).
18. Here, Thaddeus Metz's application (2009) of his African moral theory (2007) is not very helpful for four related reasons: one, the meaning attributed to 'friendship' as abstract synecdoche is astoundingly naive, sentimental and self-servingly teleological; naive because it is deployed to argue that 'for government to coordinate its behaviour with that of the general public, it must be forthright about its policies' (347), in addition to suggesting, contrary to the postcolonial legacy, that the one-party state 'would not be altogether bad' (348); sentimental because it justifies the state's preferential treatment of certain individuals 'from whom it demanded unjust sacrifices in the past' on the basis that 'a person's first duty should be to mend any discordant relationships *before forging new ones*' (349, emphasis added). This violent sentimentality aside – you have to make up with Peter before you can be friends with Susan – the *raison d'être* of the suggested theory begs exactly what is at stake here, namely that the 'We' of the national imaginary is not as compelling a moral community of interdependence as the kinship-based community constituted as political economy of obligation. To assume the opposite simply amounts to responding to the challenges of Africa's modernity with wishful thinking. Thirdly, the theory radically misinterprets the nature of nepotism, which is not simply a matter of preferential giving, but also of honouring obligations (Chabal 2009; Ekeh 1975; De Maria 2009), which firmly locates the phenomenon in the realm of identity praxis and not rational/moral choice. This is but one instance where the theory auto-deconstructs into a Western episteme in which 'family, village, history and ethnicity are pushed aside in the search for culprits that stand alone' (De Maria 2009: 362).

suggestions is the exact measure of the success with which a neoliberal order has managed successfully to quarantine the very logic of our shared humanity within the domain of ideas – that is, within the parameters of the division that the ANC government has made and institutionalised between the ideal and material, the political and the economic, between the priority of political freedom (first transition) and the realisation of the material conditions for the meaningful exercise of that freedom (second transition). But, of course, this is what capitalism has always done. It quarantines the economic, political and cultural domains because only on the basis of such a separation can the supremacy of the economic imperative be sustained. Abdulrahman Babu vividly describes the manner in which capitalism, at the moment of its inception, first granted workers the right to organise based on economic interests, while simultaneously preventing that right from assuming a political form:

> Although capitalism brought about enormous development of the productive forces, particularly in those parts of the world where it first emerged as a system (i.e. Europe), this development was in contradiction with the *social relations of production*. Working-class movements struggled for the right to organize themselves in order to strengthen their bargaining position, and the bourgeois grudgingly conceded to them here and there, but not without making certain that *the concessions were confined to industrial demands (e.g. wages) and insisted that they be separated from any political activity*. That is to say, the workers must never resort to industrial action for political ends (1981: 27, emphasis added).

In the case of post-apartheid South Africa, the mismatch between the logic of neoliberalism and the social relations of the majority of its workforce is even more acute. The value system that could conceivably present a more or less coherent picture of these social relations has effectively been separated from both the political *and* economic domains, confined to – no, quarantined within – the domain of culture, leading David McDonald to speculate on why 'the South African Communist Party (SACP) laments the "new values of individualism and accumulation that have robbed [South African] society of its noble value system of ubuntu and communalism" but does not attempt to redevelop or reinvigorate ubuntu concepts in any systematic way in its publications or practices' (2010: 148).

Of the three principles Nyerere identified as constitutive of the ujamaa/ubuntu praxis – love, sharing and work – and which he tried to codify into his vision of an African Socialism, only 'love' has made it into the refraction of ubuntu praxis as Ubuntu philosophy. The result has been a plethora of vacuous claims to which we have become inured, such as:

> Ubuntu is unique in the following respects: it emphasizes respect for the non-material order that exists in us and among us; it fosters man's respect for himself, for others, and for the environment; it has spirituality; it has remained non-racial; it accommodates other cultures and it is the invisible force uniting Africans worldwide (Makgoba in Enslin and Horsthemke 2004: 547).

Gone are any references to the rootedness of shared humanity in shared resources and the socially generative function of labour.

Juridico-politically, the fundamental proscription at work here is one that *individualises justice* in line with a Western, Enlightenment understanding of the subject, such as presupposed by Immanuel Kant's republican constitutionalism referred to earlier. While the well-contained constellation of Law does, under certain conditions (this judge and not that one), insist on changes in socio-economic conditions as a sine qua non of meaningful talk about justice, there is very little room even here for militating in favour of a conception of justice premised on the inseparable unity of love, sharing and work – or, in more contemporary terms, the unity of dignity (being), community (sharing) and work (material conditions) – as any critical humanist *qua* philosopher of true democracy would. Should we be surprised that we have ended up with a conception of Ubuntu as vacuous as the promise that it can play an emancipatory function in contemporary politics?

I will not elaborate any further here on the proscriptions relating to violence and justice. I return to the question of violence in Chapter 3 and to the question of justice in the two final chapters. Suffice it here to say that both violence and justice offer us ways of enriching our understanding of Ubuntu. Regarding the former, it enables us to recognise that all decisions imply a certain measure of violence – particularly those made in the name of a collective 'We'. The problem is not violence, coercion or technologies of discipline as such. Violence becomes destructive only when its generative function is capitalised on without being acknowledged and articulated; that is, when violence is naturalised as something that exists beyond the political. Similarly, we can and I believe *should* draw on Ubuntu to enrich our understanding of justice as the unity of being, belonging and having in a way that will take us beyond the dead end of the tired opposition between guaranteed first-generation rights and nice-to-have, second-generation or aspirational rights. I hope that the last two chapters will develop the dialogue between political philosophy and post-apartheid jurisprudence in that direction.

Solidarity

In Damon Galgut's novel *The Good Doctor*, Dr Ngema, superintendent of the hospital in which the 'good' (white) doctor works, is apparently refusing to deal 'appropriately' with the theft of hospital equipment by one of her employees, Tehogo, despite the fact that the 'good doctor' himself, here the representative of liberal anonymity and equality before the law, has pointed it out and brought facts to her attention to prove that Tehogo is guilty of theft and absenteeism. Their heated exchange over how to proceed in dealing with Tehogo – a difference about what to prioritise, the law and/or private property or our humane understanding of the difficult life somebody may have led – eventually comes to a head:

> 'I know who Tehogo was. He was a thief, I saw what he did. I was disappointed in you, that you protected him.' . . .
> 'That young man,' she said, 'that young man had a very hard life. A very difficult life. Much more difficult than yours. None of your chances, none of your advantages. Doesn't that count with you?'
> 'Not in this case. No.'
> 'No. I can see it doesn't . . . I can see you have no idea of what it means to be a black person in this country. Only your own life is real to you.'
> 'That's true of everybody. You can only live one life.'
> 'Black people live many lives.'
> 'What rubbish.'
> 'Yes, to you it is rubbish. To me it is real' (2003: 210).

The statement that 'black people live many lives' recognises a simple fact about solidarity: it is not entirely of our choosing. What it means to recognise, much less *live*, this recognition in a world that prizes being solitary over belonging in solidarity is a complex question that we can only approach obliquely here by tracing the refraction of solidarity into its *empathetic* and *antipathetic* manifestations. Of course, how to cleave the one from the other, under what conditions and to what end, these are the difficult questions – as one participant at the founding conference of African Socialism in Dakar was reported by Aristide Zolberg to have said:

> After having demonstrated the role of traditional values in African Socialism, one participant continued: 'We also hear that this perpetuates nepotism, bribery, and corruption – this may be so, but our objective is to expunge all these imperfections from our way of life without destroying the *sense of community* which sometimes gave rise to them' (1964: 123).

Indeed – how to save from a complex matrix of measures, rituals, technologies of discipline and power a sense of community or solidarity that historically was a function of these? And, following on from this, how to understand and define that sense of solidarity so that it can enrich (rather than subvert) the liberal democratic order?[19] The refraction and subsequent containment of ubuntu as Ubuntu seems to have generated a simple principle that derives from its nationalist mandate: those subversions of the Law committed in the name of solidarity that will guarantee the continued existence of the sovereign 'We', as imagined by the Constitution's preamble, will be tolerated and accommodated as productive or *empathetic subversions*, as exceptions that guarantee the rule. Anything short of that will be reduced to *antipathetic solidarity*, to be tolerated only within the limitations of individual liberty. This difference is demonstrated by two examples. In neither case was there any explicit appeal to Ubuntu, even though both represented clear examples of the continuation of the ubuntu praxis into the post-apartheid domain:

1. *Antipathetic solidarity*: That the individual lives many lives is a belief that united a number of democratic South Africa's founding fathers in a scene I never tire of contemplating. Of course, there have been many incidents since then that would equally well demonstrate the point I want to make

---

19. 'The concept of *ubuntu* shares important characteristics with the concept of solidarity, both the modern social democratic and the Christian democratic variants of the European ideas of solidarity. First, all concepts of solidarity and *ubuntu* imply a demarcation against unfettered individualism and economic liberalism. Second, today, these concepts tend to emphasize that human beings are interdependent. All ideas of solidarity imply that the government shall have the responsibility for social protection against the hazards of life for its people, although the extent of that responsibility may vary' (Tshoose 2009: 19).

here, but this event was special because it not only involved Allan Boesak, Dullah Omar (then minister of justice) and Nelson Mandela, but it also occurred at the dawn of the new South Africa in a manner that prefigured many of its future discursive fault lines. A liberation theologian and leader in the anti-apartheid struggle, Allan Boesak returned to South Africa on 16 March 1997 to stand trial on 21 counts of theft and 9 counts of fraud, involving almost R2 million that he had allegedly misappropriated from the Foundation for Peace and Justice. For a brief spell, the scandal of a liberation theologian defrauding the oppressed of millions of donor money was eclipsed by the fact that Boesak was welcomed with open arms at the airport by an estimated 3 000 ANC supporters led by the minister of justice – at the behest of President Mandela himself. In the ensuing media frenzy over the scandalous behaviour of the minister of justice, some very predictable and some not-so-predictable statements surfaced. Marking the outer extremes of the predictable and unpredictable respectively were warnings of a self-fulfilling apocalypse by liberals, who already then sensed a return to a 'state of nature' in the form of a banana republic and Boesak's own peculiar opening gambit in which he proclaimed: 'When I go on trial, the struggle for freedom will be on trial and all of my people will be on trial. If I am guilty then the struggle will stand condemned' (Praeg 2000: 124).[20] But it is really in between these two extremes that the spectre of ubuntu emerged. In response to the media outcry, Omar claimed:

> We salute Dr. Boesak as a great comrade in arms in the struggle against apartheid . . . We say to Dr. Boesak in his hour of tribulation: 'You have been one of us. You remain one of us. We will not turn our backs on you. You enjoy our support and solidarity and we stand by you' (125).

The spokesperson for Mandela's office similarly responded: 'Dr. Boesak is a human being who does not deserve to be hounded in this way . . . He is a citizen who is entitled to be supported by friends and those who know him.' The statement concluded that the president wished 'to look at Dr. Boesak not only as citizen, but also as his son'. Lastly, Tony Yengeni

---

20. This is analysed at length in Praeg 2000: 124–9, 293–300.

contributed the reinvention of the ontological 'I am because we are' as the cavalier political 'one for all and all for one' when he claimed: 'In the ANC we always subscribed to the idea of an injury to one being an injury to all. That is why we give each other strength and support at all times, not only the good but also the hard times' (Praeg 2000: 125). Bearing in mind the context of this incident as one in which two competing conceptions of political transitions – one founded on retribution, the other on reconciliation – were being weighed up, we can understand why the philosopher Tony Holiday felt it necessary to seriously weight the claims to solidarity against the master-conception of the young Constitution, indebted as it is to the European Enlightenment in general and the thought of Kant in particular. This philosopher, Holiday wrote,

> left us a brilliant, but bloodless, picture of the free agent ... In pursuing the 'categorical imperative' to treat all other individuals as ends in themselves and never as means to its own end, the Kantian individual relies on none of the warmth 'solidarity' confers, is indifferent to the trappings of worldly office and wants no thanks for doing what morality requires (in Praeg 2000: 126).

Against this backdrop, Boesak's peculiar claim, 'When I go on trial, the struggle for freedom will be on trial and ... if I am guilty then the struggle will stand condemned' is intriguing. It is clear that what Boesak aimed to establish in that moment was a defence as all-encompassing as it would be absolute: that his entire life *was* the struggle, no more and no less; that, as a part reflects the whole, his entire existence was but a mere reflection of the struggle for freedom and that to condemn one would be to condemn the other. Less obviously at work in his claim is not only a lame appeal to the rhetorical power of synecdoche, but also the very logic of transubstantiation, the belief that the substance of one entity (bread or wine) can miraculously be transformed into the substance of another (flesh or blood) without changing its appearance (bread will be bread). Boesak knew that the most reliable way out of this confrontation with the law consisted in mobilising the very antithesis of the law, human solidarity, not as defence *against* the law – which would still leave him inside and therefore subject to the law – but in defence *of* the law, which would place him outside and against the law, as the foundation of law itself. In order for this to be effective, however, he had for one miraculous moment to become more than only a solitary individual subject to the rule of law. He had to become the very antithesis of the law, the logic and the movement of solidarity itself; more specifically, he had to identify his person and plight with the movement of the solidarity that culminated in the founding moment of Constitution-making. Allan Boesak, the individual subject, had to be transubstantiated into Boesak, the collective subject. Only through such a miraculous transubstantiation would he become the Collective Subject contemplating itself and, through that conflation, find himself beyond the law derived from the will of the collective subject. If he could transubstantiate into the Collective Subject responsible for making the Constitution, how could he also be subjected to it? Simply put, Boesak tried to place himself beyond the reach of the law by escaping through the mystical foundations of its origin. Many, many freedom fighters would subsequently follow Boesak down this road of political transubstantiation that sees an individual citizen – until then, subject to the rule of law – miraculously transubstantiated into solidarity vigilante, Legislator of the Law.

2. *Transcendent solidarity*: More than 40 years before the TRC, Fanon admonished colonialist doctors who refused to recognise the humanity of African patients who appeared before them:

> If YOU do not reclaim the man who is before you, how can I assume that you reclaim the man that is in you? If YOU do not want the man who is before you, how can I believe the man that is perhaps in you? If YOU do not demand the man, if YOU do not sacrifice the man that is in you so that the man who is on this earth shall be more than a body . . . by what conjurer's trick will I have to acquire the certainty that you, too, are worthy of my love (1969: 16)?

Many years later, Cynthia Ngewu made a statement that hauntingly placed Fanon before the TRC when, appearing to face the murderer of her son, Christopher Piet, she stated:

> This thing called reconciliation . . . if I am understanding it correctly . . . if it means this perpetrator, this man who has killed Christopher Piet, if it means he becomes human again, this man, so that I, so

that all of us, get our humanity back . . . then I agree, then I support it all (in Praeg 2000: 275).

Her statement has in many ways become a synecdoche of the transcendent humanism we have come to associate with Ubuntu and of the Ubuntu moment of the TRC, of what it would mean to rebirth the self through care of the Other. Part of the fascination with her statement derives from the fact that she can be interpreted to have succeeded where Boesak so spectacularly failed: her embodiment of a praxis of being-as-belonging can be hypostasized into a collective yearning to understand being-as-belonging. Only on the basis of the possibility of such a hypostasizing could Ubuntu have become the master trope of a new nationalism. It is as if in this founding moment, Ubuntu as precolonial praxis and postcolonial trope for being-as-belonging was briefly allowed to play the part that Fanon had envisaged for such an ethic.

In a general and complex sense, the transitional moment – represented by the adoption of the Constitution, the TRC and the first number of judgments by the new Constitutional Court (particularly *S. v. Makwanyane* and *S. v. AZAPO*) – amounted to a suspension of the political; more precisely, a suspension of the liberal democratic project in order to prioritise, not juridical vengeance but forgiveness, not individual rights but reconciliation and not the state as monopoly of the means of violence, but the inalienable right to life.[21] In other words, the liberal democratic order was founded on a temporary suspension of the liberal democratic order itself – a temporary suspension without which the constitutional order could not have been birthed. A new vision of the juridico-political was ushered in through a temporary suspension of its own conception of the political; that is, through a state of constitutional exceptionalism, in which a nebulous

---

21. This is perhaps also what Mbembe has in mind when he comments that the 'Constitution's underlying principle is *ubuntu* or *human mutuality*. It promises a transcendence of the old politics of racial difference and an affirmation of a *shared humanity*' (2011: 6). I disagree with the use of the phrase 'underlying principle' here because first, if there were such a bedrock norm (*Gründnorm*), it would surely be dignity and, second, because I think the relationship between ubuntu and the Constitution is infinitely more complex – as I argue in the last two chapters of this book. For a useful introduction to and summary of these and other Ubuntu-engaged judgments, see Cornell and Muvangua (2011).

ethic loosely configured around an ubuntufied Christianity and/or Christianised UbunTutu and shadowed by a quasi-purposive or teleological, but always secular, nationalist ethic of messianic 'togetherness', congealed into something of an ethic adequate to the foundation of the political.

In retrospect, however, this transitional discourse appears as little more than a monument to these expectations of a political founded on the ethical, a monument that commemorates the real political possibilities of communitarian praxis as an alternative vision of the political, as well as a memorial that marks the disappearance of that very possibility, its almost instantaneous passing into obscurity and irrelevance. The fact of the matter is that we wanted Ubuntu to do all the work for us, the reconciliation and forgiveness, the unification and the transcendence of guilt, complicity and suffering *so that we could get on with the business of living*, but we wanted none of the obligations that came with such an ethical understanding of the political. Most of what has happened since then marks a fundamental retreat away from this *nomos* and its foundational commitment to ground the political in the ethical – to the extent that nothing better characterises contemporary South Africa as the visible fault line between a political system in search of ethical legitimation and an ethics in search of political representation.

I have argued that there is a meaningful difference between ubuntu praxis and abstract Ubuntu. The former is a function of a local political economy of obligation, while the latter is a glocal phenomenon. The point is neither that there is no such thing as Ubuntu, nor that it is vacuous or wholly reducible to its global interfaces. Rather, *Ubuntu has no final origin*, no essence that precedes or overflows the discourses that speak its name. Abstracted from ubuntu praxis, Ubuntu is largely, but never totally, dependent for its content on the socio-political context and the philosophies and ideologies invoked to articulate it. One of the limiting binaries at work in Ubuntu discourse is the opposition between the naive and the nihilist, between the Revolutionary who believes in its spectacular uniqueness and the jaded Archivists for whom it offers nothing new.[22] Contrary to the univocity of these positions, I am arguing for Ubuntu's plurivocity, the kind of plurivocity that suggests

---

22. The Revolutionary and the Archivist are two of the conceptual personae of Deleuze and Guattari (1994), which I discuss in some detail in Chapter 2.

we think of Ubuntu as a 'polysemous ideological concept which conjoins human rights, reconciliation and nation-building in the populist terms of a relatively benign African nationalism' (Wilson in Coertze 2001: 116). This plurivocity is also irreducible to relativism for the simple reason that Ubuntu is never a purely intellectual construct, given content by theorists and intellectuals alone. Every attempt to articulate the meaning of Ubuntu will always have to take as one of its points of reference the praxis of ubuntu, what one could also call living ubuntu, *that unification of being as belonging, which will always precede and remain irreducible to any translation or codification of ubuntu as Ubuntu*. There is, therefore, a sense in which academics, theorists, ideologues and intellectuals will always trail behind ubuntu, trying to make sense of a praxis that preceded and always will, in this precise sense of the word only, exceed discourses about it.

In the following subsection, I want to conclude by advancing the concepts *refraction*, *glocality* and *retrodiction* as useful ways of understanding the subtlety of the interplay between gain and loss that accompanies every translation and codification of ubuntu as Ubuntu.

Refraction, glocality and retrodiction

> In its preoccupation with Eurocentrism, postcolonial criticism has also refused to confront an increasingly audible revival of traditions that – while perhaps serving as antidotes to Eurocentrism – nevertheless present serious problems of their own, as the values they espouse are neither necessarily progressive nor to the benefit of the peoples they purportedly represent.
> — Arif Dirlik, 'Historical Colonialism in Contemporary Perspective'

As a first step, we can cast the distinction that has emerged so far between ubuntu and Ubuntu in terms of the more familiar distinction between morality and ethics, as explained by Harold Titus:

> Morality derives from the Latin word *mos* (plural *mores*), meaning 'custom or way of life'. *Ethics* is derived from Greek, *ethos*, which also means 'custom' or 'character'. Both terms refer to types of behaviour which become customary because of the approval or practices of the group (as in communitarian practice). The term *morals* and *ethics* are thus synonymous. However, *morals* and *morality* ordinarily refer to the conduct itself, while

ethics and *ethical* suggest the study of moral conduct or the system or the code followed. For example, we usually speak of an ethical system or code and of a moral act or a moral man. Ethics attempts to determine what conduct is good and what is bad, or what ought to be approved and what disapproved. It undertakes to furnish a standard for distinguishing between a better character and a worse one. Ethics is a normative study of the principles underlying the desirable types of human conduct (in Tomaselli 2009: 585).

We can thus distinguish between ubuntu as 'ethnic morality' (Prozesky 2009: 5) and Ubuntu as abstract ethic. As ethnic morality, ubuntu is a function of the absence of a distinction between morality and religion; it refers to what Martin Prozesky describes as 'the moral traditions embedded in the many and various cultures of sub-Saharan Africa, the moral traditions of Black African cultures' (4) and which, in the words of Saule quoted earlier, represents the kind of human behaviour 'inculcated in the individual by society through established traditional institutions over a period of time' (in Mnyaka 2003: 144). This difference perhaps explains why Neville Richardson comments that 'to set out to discover and understand African ethics via abstract moral principles is to embark on a journey of frustration. Instead, one has to observe and reflect upon the social life of the people – their rituals, customs, practices, events and relationships' (2009: 131). In fact, Prozesky limits the meaning of the word *ethics* solely to refer to this ethnic morality, to 'lived and practiced beliefs about right and wrong, good and evil', while consciously excluding 'the other meaning of the word, namely the academic study of ethics, mostly undertaken by philosophers and theologians' (2009: 4). This is ubuntu as a function of a deeply ontologically rooted ethnic morality, in which 'infringements are seen as damaging not only to community relations but also to the delicate harmony of the whole deeply religious order of the universe' (Richardson 2009: 136).

I would argue that the rearticulation of an ethnic mortality in the form of an abstract ethic, the transition from ubuntu ethnic morality to a generalised, abstract Ubuntu ethic is marked by two related, but conceptually distinct movements. Far from simply *abstracting* Ubuntu from ubuntu, it always involves the *translation* of an ethnic morality into an abstract ethic, a translation that always gets refracted through the historical demands of the time – in our case, the pivot of constitutional values. We can also imagine this abstraction and translation in spatial terms: vertically, we decode the lived reality of praxis into the abstraction of an ethic; horizontally, we move from ubuntu as a function of the historical political economy of obligation of a visible community to an Ubuntu refracted and projected into a contemporary community in search of a metaphor through which to express an expanded, but now imagined sense of belonging. We see this dual process clearly at work in the grand, institutional background choices that made Cynthia Ngewu's statement about reconciliation and shared humanity possible. To the extent that Ubuntu was appropriated as master trope of the ethical in the TRC as a founding moment, it could only have happened on the back of a profound refraction that, through the local and global a prioris outlined in this chapter, produced a particularly decontextualised, glocal understanding of both forgiveness and reconciliation, in which the 'semantic field' of *ubuntu* came to include *'the perpetrator's restored personhood as granted by the very individual they wronged'* – a concept of reconciliation that is 'profoundly Christian' (Van Binsbergen 2001: 76). Totally absent from this refraction of ubuntu praxis as Ubuntu was any appreciation of the way in which ubuntu praxis never conceived of belonging in infinite terms; that, historically, ubuntu praxis not only conceived the possibility of shared humanity (a positive definition), but also, through the very violence constitutive of its inculcation of the values that made it possible, also articulated the limitation or conditions of community (a negative delimitation). The TRC was instrumental in refracting an Ubuntu that made belonging imaginable in its infinitude by suspending every trace of the apophatic, negative or conditional. Comments Van Binsbergen:

> It can be no accident that no traditional diviner-priest (guardians of the ancestral world-view) participated in the TRC context, where they could have articulated historic Southern African viewpoints on evil, sin, i.e. not only the possibility *but also the limitations* of expiation. In the absence of such experts, the concept of *ubuntu* was to supply what little traditional guidance was allowed to inform the situation (2001: 76).[23]

The net result of this combined vertical abstraction and horizontal translation is a movement that sees Ubuntu discourse rearticulating the master trope or essence

---

23. For a very interesting exploration of this question, see Masoga (1999).

of a range of global discourses as the quintessence of ubuntu praxis: from Christianity is borrowed a spiritualised notion of an almost infinite *forgiveness*; from human rights, a quasi-sacred notion of *dignity* and from nationalist discourse, an emotive appeal to reconciliation as condition for imagined *belonging*. Small wonder that one of the standard responses to Ubuntu is that it seems to be all things to all people, or that its meaning is stretched to the point of collapse (Kroeze 2002: 260).

However, such an interpretation would be an ungenerous reading, for what is at stake here is no simple one-way borrowing or imitation: every time Ubuntu articulates the essence of one of these discourses as its own, it returns that borrowing back to the global discourses, enriched with local understandings. In the last chapter of this book, I briefly discuss how Cornell has motivated for an Ubuntu-engaged interpretation of dignity that will take South African jurisprudence beyond an individualist, Kantian understanding of the concept. A further example of this two-way interface emerges from the difference between Coertze and Wiredu on the question of African conceptions of personhood. While Coertze (2001: 115) claims that urbanisation is one of the reasons that original African interpretations of personhood have been adapted to suit modern life, Wiredu (2002: 294) insists that an African understanding of personhood could be the solution to keeping the process of modernisation and urbanisation human-sensitive. At the heart of this difference – is Ubuntu a mere phenomenon of global discourses or it is a local counterweight against the globalising imperialism of these discourses? – lies a complex misunderstanding: Ubuntu is neither *here* nor *there*. It is a 'model of thought [which has had to] take on a globalised format in order to be acceptable to the majority of modern South Africans' (Van Binsbergen 2001: 64). When we say of Ubuntu that it is a glocal phenomenon, we mean that we can no longer meaningfully differentiate between its local and global content.[24] Considered as

---

24. This claim is really neither novel nor radical, for it really amounts to taking seriously what state theorists have been arguing for almost twenty years. Jean-François Bayart, in *The State in Africa: The Politics of the Belly*, writes that there is no distinction between the 'internal political life of States and the international environment to which they belong... The "external dynamics" are not really separable from the "internal," and the postcolonial State has come about at the point where they meet.' Also: 'It is now widely accepted that the structure of political arenas cannot be isolated from their articulation with related arenas and that "internal and eternal explanations are inextricably linked" as Braudel put it so simply' (1993: 31).

such, Coertze's and Wiredu's interpretations are profoundly complementary: a complex combination of the two global and local a prioris represents an Ubuntu that can be used to humanise modernity by introducing 'non-global, particularistic and intimate elements in the very heart of Southern African globalisation. *Ubuntu* can work precisely because it is novel, out of place there where it is most appealed to' (Van Binsbergen 2001: 74). Furthermore:

> Since most of the forces that have shaped the societies of contemporary Southern Africa can be subsumed under the heading of globalisation, it stands to reason that an intellectual product meant to overcome the negative effects of these forces has to be global in format, even though its content is largely inspired by the local intimacy of village and kin group. If in concrete situations of social transformation and conflict the appeal to *ubuntu* is going to make a positive difference, the global format lends recognition and respectability in ways the original, implicit normative orientation of contemporary Southern African village and kin situation could never claim in an urban, globalised context (72–3).

The formal process or principle through which a glocal Ubuntu emerges as both function and critique has been described by Mudimbe as one of 'retrodiction' – the opposite of 'prediction'. As defined by Mudimbe, in the context of the call to Africanise Christianity, retrodiction

> establishes an analogical parallel between the missionary performance under colonial rule and the future of Christianity under African initiative. It insists on the necessity of looking into traditional systems of beliefs for unanimous signs or harmonies which might be incorporated into Christianity in order to Africanize it without fundamentally modifying it (1991a: 13).

As a result, as Van Binsbergen argues: 'We could acknowledge the tension between ancestral and global formats and contents in *ubuntu*, without seeking to resolve that tension by opting for either of these complimentary poles and denying authenticity and legitimacy to the other pole' (2001: 67). Simply put, Ubuntu is simultaneously a function and a critique of Western modernity.

Conclusion

Ubuntu cannot and should not be located *over there* in the past and as fundamentally foreign to the constitutional order by virtue of its different ontological axiomatic. On the contrary, Ubuntu has a much more complex relationship with the present that derives from at least three factors: one, it represents the unthought of Western modernity. As the first global a priori suggests, African communalism became a problem for Western thought and a stereotype of backwardness at the precise moment when individualism became the point of departure for Western reflections on belonging as a problem for thought. Two, adopted by Africans as a significant fact of what being African means, Ubuntu has been reappropriated and reinvented by Africans both as a sign of authenticity and the building block for emancipation, however conceived. From this emerges a third dimension of Ubuntu's complex relationship with the present: once Africans appropriated this projection of the West's unthought as sign of our/their authenticity, Ubuntu could not but acquire the additional meaning of a return of the repressed that now continues to haunt our liberal democracy with the ambivalence of the *uncanny*: as that which both terrifies the project of this modernity with the spectre of incompleteness – the fear of inexecution and the end of individualism – as well as that which promises to save modernity from the dead end of an exhausted individualism. In other words, the status of Ubuntu as both a function and a critique of modernity has its source in the origin of Western modernity itself.

In the chapters that follow, I tease out some of the implications of what this means. In the following chapter I proceed very much in the spirit of a meta-critique of reason by considering this complexity in terms of the tension between local and global. With reference to Deleuze and Guatarri's *What is Philosophy?* (1994), I map the various political stances implicitly assumed by authors when they over-evaluate Ubuntu either as a predominantly global or as a predominantly local phenomenon.

CHAPTER 2

African Modes of Writing and Being

> We will not say of many books of philosophy that they are false, for that is to say nothing, but rather that they lack importance or interest, precisely because they do not create any concept or contribute an image of thought or beget a persona worth the effort.
> — Gilles Deleuze and Félix Guattari, *What is Philosophy?*

This chapter investigates the conditions under which different ways of talking about Ubuntu become possible. It considers some of the prominent modes of thinking through which the recovery of Ubuntu is conventionally understood and narrated. The idea of 'modes of thinking' is not unrelated to what Achille Mbembe (2002) has referred to as the different grand-narrative positions historically assumed to interpret Africa's history and give meaning to being Africa(n) in relation to the rest of the world.

In *Metahistory: The Historical Imagination in Nineteenth-Century Europe* (1973), Hayden White demonstrates how every historical account presents a mode of thinking that we can describe in terms of its narrative form. The politics of a historian shape the kind of history he or she is likely to present and this political stance or mode is the result of decisions (not necessarily conscious) made at two levels: chronicle and narrative structure. All historians have to make decisions about what facts to include from what is effectively a limitless chronicle of possibly relevant facts. A full account of anything is impossible and the choices made in order to construct a historical account are shaded by political empathies, understandings and imperatives. Less obviously, the way in which selected facts are then strung together is always structured by narrative assumptions implicit in the author's political stance. For instance, a historical account of the emergence of Afrikaner nationalism may include rebellions against British colonial rule in the Cape colony as relevant facts in a chronicle of events narrated as an epic (because Promethean) 'opening up of the dark continent'. But such a history may be contested by an alternative account that either dismisses and excludes the same originary events as 'mere criminal unrest' or relegates them to footnotes of little consequence, then proceeding to narrate the 'same' history as a *tragic* story of colonial domination. In other words, history writing is determined as much by what we choose to include as it is by the narrative structure used to convey the meaning of what we include.

Given that Ubuntu is a historical phenomenon and that any attempt to articulate its meaning will be based on certain presuppositions regarding what it means to tell the history of anything, it should come as no surprise that attempts to articulate its meaning can be usefully conceptualised in terms of the political modes or stances presupposed by them. This chapter proceeds by way of what Lewis Gordon calls a 'meta-critique of reason' (2007: 123); that is, by thinking about our thinking about Ubuntu in a way that will make visible the various political modes or stances presupposed by our thinking. That Ubuntu discourse can be subjected to such an analysis of its various implicit political stances is a direct consequence or implication of the *archē* distinction of this report – between ubuntu and Ubuntu.

In the previous chapter, I argued that ubuntu refers to the praxis of a political economy of obligation, while Ubuntu refers to the abstraction *of a certain dimension of that praxis* and its representation in abstract, decontextualised form. I also delimited in the most cursory manner what I think of as the historical conditions for the possibility of this transition from ubuntu to Ubuntu. These were presented as historic a prioris and they illuminate the historical processes that have culminated in the transformation of the 'we' in the dictum 'I am because we are' from referring to real, kinship-based communities to its aspirational application to much larger, imagined communities – the township community, the anti-apartheid struggle community and, post-1994, the nation as imagined community. In the process, the logic of interdependence was abstracted from its historical political economy of obligation (in which proper, ritualised participation was a condition for 'having ubuntu') to become an abstract idea applicable to imagined communities, which by definition could no longer provide any similar ontological grounding or justification for what proper participation in their communal structures meant.

I also argued that Ubuntu is reconstituted through this process as a glocal phenomenon, the meaning of which becomes an indeterminate fusion of memories of the endogenous praxis of ubuntu and of the exogenous globalising discourses that can be said to resonate with the affect of these memories. Depending on the context in which this fused understanding of Ubuntu is invoked, we can distinguish between those glocalised fusions that are predominantly religious (drawing on

Christian notions of reconciliation, forgiveness and so on), those that are more philosophical (drawing on humanism, virtue ethics, communitarianism and the like) and those that are ideological (drawing on the economy of obligation as quintessentially a socialist practice or paradigm of human rights). Cultural nationalists are likely to resist this interpretation of Ubuntu as a glocal phenomenon and there is little I can do to assuage their melancholy other than to reiterate that to call something a glocal phenomenon does not amount to suggesting that the local plays no part in its construction, or that the plurivocity of its articulation means Ubuntu has no voice or meaning, or that the whole notion is vacuous and not deserving of our attention. Quite the contrary, all these suspicions and reactions already represent what this chapter seeks to surface, namely some of the political stances we implicitly assume when we address the question of the meaning, uniqueness and place of Ubuntu or respond to those who make such claims.

The way in which I want to surface these political stances is through the notion of a conceptual persona, developed by Gilles Deleuze and Félix Guattari in *What is Philosophy?* (1994). These personae will reveal a variety of different modes of the political at work when scholars connect ideas about *knowing and writing* about Africa (the epistemological) with *modes of being* postcolonial African (the ontological). As a useful first step in the direction of such an analysis, I want to start with what Mbembe has controversially called 'African modes of self-writing' (2002).

African modes of self-writing

For Mbembe (2002: 240–2) the most significant obstacle to writing the African self meaningfully into the present with reference to the past and the future, has been historicism (see also Benégas 2006). Isaiah Berlin provides a useful analysis of historicism in his well-known essay 'Historical Inevitability' (1969), but Hannah Arendt has probably offered us the most devastating description of historicism as a form of explanation that effectively hypostasizes the explanatory concept of 'law' into a world-negating and self-abolishing reality. In her essay 'On the Nature of Totalitarianism', she writes:

> In the totalitarian interpretation, all laws become, instead, laws of movement. Nature and History are no longer stabilizing sources of authority for laws governing the actions of mortal men, but are themselves movements. Their laws, therefore, though one might need intelligence to

perceive or understand them, have nothing to do with reason or permanence. At the base of the Nazis' belief in race laws lies Darwin's idea of man as a more or less accidental product of natural development – a development which does not necessarily stop with the species of human beings such as we know it. At the base of the Bolsheviks' belief in class lies the Marxian notion of men as the product of a gigantic historical process racing towards the end of historical time – that is, a process that tends to abolish itself. The very term 'law' has changed in meaning; from denoting the framework of stability within which human actions were supposed to, and were permitted to, take place, it has become the very expression of these motions themselves (1994: 340–1).

Mbembe (2002) argues that two forms of historicism have led postcolonial African theorists into a conceptual (epistemological) and, if we take these things as seriously as we should, existential (ontological) dead end. Like all forms of historicism, they too present teleological accounts of what it means to think postcolonial Africa. The first of these, the Afro-radical narrative, uses a combination of Marxist and nationalist categories to construct an eschatological narrative of hope and redemption, in which the rhetoric of autonomy, resistance and emancipation functions as a conceptual filter for determining not only what may legitimately be said about Africa, but also what counts as useful knowledge about Africa. It typically offers an account of history that starts with colonialist oppression and leads through resistance to emancipation conceived, materially, in terms of the seizure of the state apparatus and, in idealist terms, as the recovery and re-establishment of an autonomous African self. The second form of historicism offers a nativist grand narrative that promises the articulation of an authentic definition of African identity on the basis of membership of the black race. In this division between the historical grand narrative concerned with material freedom and the existential narrative concerned with identity, we see a further reflection of the division discussed in the previous chapter between the historical and poeticist traditions of anti-colonial resistance.

Both teleological and nativist narratives depart from the experiences of existential alienation (loss of self), material exploitation (loss of resources) and psychological humiliation (loss of dignity) which, when combined, act as 'a unifying center of Africans' desire to know themselves, to recapture their destiny (*sovereignty*), and to belong to themselves in the world (*autonomy*)' (Mbembe

2002: 242). For Mbembe, the manner in which both narratives account for the unity of these experiences is hugely problematic because they do so in a manner that is essentially historicist – an accusation that will make more sense once we make explicit their various teleological assumptions.

First, these grand narratives reduce all knowledge and science, often retrospectively, to mere instruments in the struggle for liberation, which is assumed to have intrinsic moral significance; second, Africa's dilemma is attributed to the same set of mythical forces that return again and again to subjugate and destroy the continent, its people and their traditions, always preventing 'the blooming of African uniqueness' (Mbembe 2002: 243). Mbembe refers to this as a historiography of sorcery, in which unknown and impenetrable forces constantly manipulate the continent. This historiography ascribes 'the ultimate responsibility for what happens to the acts or behaviour of impersonal or "trans-personal" or "super-personal" entities or "forces" whose evolution is identified with human history'. Crucial for Mbembe about such an 'impersonal interpretation of historical change' (Berlin 1969: 45) is exactly this question of responsibility, for it makes it almost impossible to raise the question of precolonial disunity and fratricide that would otherwise account for Africa's own complicity in catastrophes such the transatlantic slave trade. The third problematic aspect of the Afro-radical grand narrative particularly is that it threatens to destroy tradition in the mistaken belief that only the class struggle, with the proletariat as the universal agent of all plausible action, matters. In the fourth and last instance, this victimology is countered by an exaggerated belief in the possibility of achieving independence, of which the clearest sign is the mythical notion of decolonisation and/or the promise of a final liberation *from*. If the West historically and consistently misrepresented Africans and exploited them on the basis of these misrepresentations then, so it is argued, it is necessary and indeed possible to liberate Africa(ns) once and for all from these *'repressentations'* (Praeg 2000: 264) in order for Africa to find a voice through which to 'narrate its own fables' (Mbembe 2002: 244) authentically and to establish intellectual autonomy and political sovereignty.

But here is the dead end reproduced by this grand narrative of tragic optimism, victimhood and autonomy: the idea of freedom, what it is and what it will look like when it is achieved, is conceived in the very terms of the oppression; that is, in terms of a racist, Western modernity. Differences between African people and peoples are glossed over in order to construct an African subject that coincides with a certain geography (on the borders of which Egypt consistently remains undecidable), on the basis of which the racialised native is created, who can then speak in his/her 'own voice'. In this conception of freedom, Africans have bought into and replicated a way of thinking about the difference between Africa and the West premised on exactly the same logic the West used to colonise the continent. By this I assume Mbembe to mean something like the following: African anti-colonial resistance accepted as axiomatic the Western notions that the difference between Africa and the West is so fundamental as to be ontological, that this difference can be accurately symbolised in racial terms, that this racialised difference, when explored, could produce knowledge of what is uniquely African and that Africans will only be free once they have employed the instruments of power to create the spaces in which to articulate and give real effect to their uniqueness or authentic way of being. This is essentially the Enlightenment project of autonomy and freedom turned on its head, except that here 'the neurosis of victimisation fosters a mode of thought that is at once xenophobic, racist, negative, and circular' (Mbembe 2002: 252).

The circularity hinted at by Mbembe becomes particularly evident in Ubuntu discourse where it manifests as a definitional circularity. The conventional or mainstream articulation of the meaning of Ubuntu often, but not necessarily, combines elements of the Afro-radical and nativist assumptions in order to posit Ubuntu as a lost African way of being that, once recovered, promises a reimagining of the founding of the postcolonial state on an authentically African understanding of being and belonging (autochthony/being from here) – of which Julius Nyerere's Ujamaa project (discussed in the following chapter on African Socialism) has probably been the clearest and most tragic example. In this view, liberation or decolonisation appears as the final moment of institutionalised self-recognition and self-becoming, of instituting what it means to re-member what had been dismembered by colonialism. Often in Ubuntu discourse, however, this act of re-membering is but a prelude to a further act of reversal that sees Africa offering its unique insight into the inseparableness of being and belonging as gift to the rest of the world, in order to save it from its morbid fascination with destructive individualism. The hope of decolonisation, of finally and absolutely liberating oneself from oppression – this 'mad dream of a world without Others' (Mbembe 2002: 252) – will only come to pass when Africa has succeeded, finally, in saving the erstwhile oppressor from himself (see also Marx 2002: 65). But this whole train of thought is premised on a definitional circularity that, in its crudest form, unfolds in three steps: First, an image of the West is constructed, from which is excluded all Western philosophies, traditions of thought and political praxes premised on a recognition of and commitment to our interdependence; that is, various Western forms of humanisms, socialisms, communitarianisms, phenomenologies and so on. Only through such an expulsion or ban can the 'West' be wholly conflated with 'individualism'. Second, this allows for a coterminus image of Africa to emerge as essentially the opposite; that is, a place and a people that recognise our profound interdependence. This structural interplay between the ban and the self-nomination as communal is the condition for talk about Ubuntu as a gift to become possible because Ubuntu can only be gifted to the rest of the world on the assumption that there is a need 'over there' for what we alone have 'over here'. But, and this is the crucial third point, when asked, 'But what is Ubuntu? What is this gift?' theorists who write in this mode can only explain what Ubuntu is with reference to, and in most cases by equating it with, one of the Western philosophies of interdependence initially banned from the construction of the image of the West – Ubuntu as African *humanism*, African *Socialism*, African *communitarianism*, etc. At the risk of labouring the point, we can say that it is assumed that the space in which to exist authentically 'over here' can only be created by forcefully removing from 'over there' all signs that trouble the desired distinction between 'here' and 'there'. After the clearing that made the 'here' visible, however, we can only interpret or give substance to what 'being from here' means with reference to the very signs that were cleared from 'over there' in order to make visible the difference between 'here' and 'there'.

The *locus classicus* of this definitional circularity and its attendant violence are those discursively dominant explanations of Ubuntu that depart from a juxtapositioning of what is taken to be its central tenet ('I am because we are') with the putative poverty of the Cartesian 'I think therefore I am' – as if subsequent to this 'Idiotic' utterance (Deleuze and Guattari 1994),[1] the Western conception of the self had not turned some fundamentally communitarian corners (as I argue with reference to Hegel in Chapter 4). The violence through which a difference between 'over here' and 'over there' is made consists in using a *contemporary* reinvention of traditional ethics to deliver a critique of a Western conception of subjectivity, for which a *historical* statement of modernity is taken as synecdoche. The reason for this has to do with more than sheer intellectual laziness. If pre- and

---

1. This notion from Deleuze and Guattari is discussed in more detail later in this chapter.

post-Cartesian Western traditions of communitarian thought were not from the outset expelled in order to invent a salvific role for Ubuntu, the whole Ubuntu discourse would face a dangerous apocalypse – which in its original Greek sense refers to an unveiling or a making visible (Bailie 1995: 15). What would become visible in this instance is not only the politics of sovereignty ('we have Ubuntu'), not only the violence necessary to sustain this sovereignty in its mode as identity claim ('unlike you'), but also the profound lack of shared humanity or Ubuntu that such a politics of sovereignty implies.

To proceed differently, without these easy and self-legitimating – although given the history of the continent, entirely understandable – attempts at repositioning the meaning of being African, requires a much more sophisticated account of Ubuntu's *raison d'être*, one that would have to depart from the difficult-to-hear recognition of Ubuntu as a glocal phenomenon that relies on Western intellectual forms and ethical practices for significant dimensions of its own articulation.

Much of this already relates to the nativist grand narrative, in which the 'defence of the humanity of Africans is almost always accompanied by the claim that their race, traditions, and customs have a specific character' (Mbembe 2002: 254), but without fundamentally challenging the validity or justness of the categories (race, progress, etc.) necessarily invoked in order to demonstrate the claim. Just as in the case of the teleological Afro-radical narrative, where liberation from Western modernity is conceived in the terms of that modernity itself so, here, the claims to specificity and uniqueness hardly ever subject to scrutiny the principle category upon which this discourse was based, namely race.[2] In other words, 'whether we look at *négritude* or the different versions of Pan-Africanism, in these discourses the revolt is not against Africans' belonging to a distinct race, but against the prejudice that assigns this race an inferior status' (254). As Marx argues, 'Pan Africanism fails to transcend the ideology it is reacting to, and remains captive within a simplistic discourse of race and colour' (2002: 65). Mbembe further clarifies:

---

2. Much of the controversy generated by Mbembe's analysis relates to the reductive violence of the text through which all African thought is collapsed into two grand-narrative modes. The way I appropriate his suggestion here is to consider these two modes along the line of what chaos theorists would call attractors or thoughtways, perhaps simply salient tendencies in the geography of postcolonial thought.

This urge to make Africa unique is presented as a moral and political problem, the reconquest of the power to narrate one's own story – and therefore identity – seeming to be necessarily constitutive of any subjectivity ... It is this alterity that must be preserved at all costs ... not as the symptom of a greater universality, but rather as the inspiration for determining principles and norms governing Africans' lives in full autonomy and, if necessary, in opposition to the world (2002: 255).

The combination of historical racism and contemporary identity politics has backed Africa into a corner: the colonial denial of the humanity of Africans has prompted African theorists to counter with the universalist claim that 'we are human beings like any others' (a claim to *sameness*), but identity politics demands the contrary, namely the substantiation of a particularist claim to *difference*, to the effect that 'we are not like everybody else'. The question then becomes: How to substantiate the former without forfeiting the identity claim embodied in the latter, or how to substantiate the latter in a way that will not amount to contradicting the former? The different ways in which African theorists have struggled to balance these two imperatives are complex and nuanced (Mbembe 2002: 255–6). In Ubuntu discourse, these twin ambitions are 'characterised by a tension between a universalizing move that claims shared membership within the human condition (*sameness*) and an opposing, particularistic move. This latter move emphasizes difference and specificity by accenting, not originality as such, but the principle of repetition (*tradition*) and the values of autochthony' (252–3). The result, as demonstrated above, is the contradictory deployment of Ubuntu to achieve both ends: *qua* currency of cultural sovereignty Ubuntu is used to articulate *difference* but, deployed and exported as a critique of the limitations of sovereignty (retributive models of justice or Afro-chic versions of international relations), it seeks recognition for its insistance on our shared humanity or *sameness*.

This generates a tension I have described elsewhere (Praeg 2008a) as a representational undecidability or paradox of differentiation. The paradox emerges when Ubuntu *qua* philosophy of our *interdependence* (our shared humanity) is used for the political ends of demonstrating *independence* or cultural sovereignty. In other words, a cultural philosophy of *interdependence* is used to purchase the political ends of (cultural) *sovereignty*. In suspending the relationality that makes it necessary and possible to think Ubuntu, we contradict the very meaning of Ubuntu. Formulated differently, what we set out to do with the value system (to conduct a form of identity politics) remains radically at odds with what is central to that value system itself. If there is a disappointment in Ubuntu discourse, it is the almost complete lack of critical awareness of how *what* Ubuntu is taken to mean remains fundamentally at odds with what we try to do with what it means.[3]

We can simplify this somewhat. In the introduction to *African Ethics: An Anthology of Comparative and Applied Ethics*, Munyaradzi Felix Murove notes that 'the African ethical tradition has been influenced by western philosophical, and Christian and Islamic, ethical traditions. This triad of influences has meant that African ethics discourse is sometimes *overwhelmingly dialogical instead of purely assertive*' (2009c: xv, emphasis added). This diagnosis is perfectly correct and merely a different way of calling Ubuntu a glocal phenomenon. But Murove's description is useful because the tension between the dialogical and the assertive reveals the complex meta-*problematique* regarding the politics of positioning an ethical system, such as Ubuntu (that is constitutively dialogical or interrelational), in a world where it needs to play a role that is not first and foremost dialogical but assertive; that is, where the politics of its insertion into the world requires an assertiveness that in turn presupposes a suspension of its dialogical or interrelational nature, in order for it to be branded and patented in terms of the logic of cultural and political sovereignty: as African, as being 'from here' and 'not there', a sign of the particular, of authentic African identity and so on.

In subsequent chapters I have more to say about this discourse on Ubuntu's so-called exceptionalism and the various forms and mutations of racism at work in it. I argue that it may be useful to think of postcoloniality as a form of hypermodernity. What exactly this means is discussed at some length in the chapters that follow. Suffice it to say that all modernities are premised on a certain blindness regarding their founding logic, of what they include and exclude in order to execute the project of modernity. Making its blind spots visible will always threaten a project of modernity with collapse, failure or inexecution. The paradox of differentiation is the blind spot of South Africa's hypermodernity. It is that which, although necessary, must remain invisible in order for the myth of cultural autonomy to

---

3. This may be familiar to complexity theorists as a paradox that comes into being when a value system, premised on the anteriority of relations to entities, needs to position itself in a world predominantly premised on the exact opposite belief, namely the anteriority of entities to relations. In terms of the line of argument pursued in the rest of this book, this paradox can also be appropriated as typical of the condition of hypermodernity.

contribute to the political work of executing political sovereignty. The profound contradiction involved in understanding the need for this paradox to remain invisible, *thereby making it visible*, directly relates to the condition of hyper-modernity.

Scholars who write on Ubuntu seem to negotiate this paradox in one of two ways – either by offering Ubuntu as sign of cultural sovereignty back to the world as a gift, in the spirit of the very shared humanity it violated in order to become the articulation of it; alternatively, by not committing the definitional circularity in the first instance and by recognising the similarity between Ubuntu and other humanisms or communitarianism (that is, by sacrificing the claim to radical particularity), but nonetheless insinuating or presupposing a meaningful difference, often masked as a claim to superiority over other forms of communitarianism. It seems therefore that both the teleological and nativist meta-narratives

> draw their fundamental categories from the myths they claim to oppose and reproduce their dichotomies: the racial difference between black and white; the cultural confrontation between civilized peoples and savages; the religious opposition between Christians and pagans; the very conviction that race exists and is at the foundation of morality and nationality (Mbembe 2002: 256).

Mbembe's analysis drew many responses at the time of its publication, some appreciative and, a great many, very critical.[4] I want to focus on one critical response in particular because it compels us to return, yet again, to the dialectic of recognition discussed in the previous chapter. In so doing, I also point to the locus where Mbembe's text auto-deconstructs – a deconstruction that, although relevant to his overarching claim, does not impact directly on his insights regarding historicism in postcolonial criticism.

According to Arif Dirlik, in analysing these two grand narratives, Mbembe 'focuses on their problematic assumptions, but largely *bypasses questions of historicity* – the circumstances, in other words, that rendered those assumptions plausible, and also made it possible to overlook their limitations' (2002: 611, emphasis added). In other words, what Mbembe glosses over in his critique is that

---

4. A number of these responses to Mbembe appeared in *Public Culture* 14(3), 2002.

at the time of adopting certain nationalist (teleological) and/or nativist positions, the criticism that in doing so liberation fighters were simply replicating colonial categories of nation, class and race 'would have been impossible to entertain . . . [because] a unified national entity [premised on the "myth" of race and Africanness] was the only conceivable agent capable of overthrowing colonialism and withstanding its ravages' (613).[5] This comment is valuable because it takes us to the heart of an issue regarding the political naivety of much Ubuntu discourse, namely that many texts read very much like outdated ethnophilosophy. How is it possible that after so many years the South African Ubuntu debate can in so many respects read like boring ethnophilosophy? How is it possible that, despite a whole reception history of critical engagement with ethnophilosophy in all its manifold manifestations, Tinyiko Maluleke can still write in 1994: 'The Négritude school of thought remains popular and is restated in a variety of ways even in our times . . . Today we see a resurgence of négritude in the popularity of the concept Ubuntu' (in Vervliet 2009: 29). There are no doubt many reasons for this – not least of which must be the intellectual isolation of South Africa from the rest of the continent during the formative years of what would emerge as the subdiscipline of African philosophy, which produced an undeniable degree of myopia among many South African intellectuals that still plays itself out in a kind of parochialism that refuses to read Ubuntu historically; that is, against the backdrop of a range of postcolonial attempts that have been made to translate African humanism into a viable postcolonial development ideology or emancipatory philosophy – a conversation in which Ubuntu discourse must be recognised as little more than an as yet underdeveloped and undertheorised latecomer. As Mamphela Ramphele put it in a slightly different context and with slightly different intent:

---

5. This, of course, raises a complex question about the inescapability, or not, of the dialectic and the assertion that racism calls forth a performative counterclaim that can and must (so the dialectic goes) temporarily present as racism itself or, in Jean-Paul Sartre's immortalised description of *négritude* as 'anti-racist racism'. I cannot engage with the inescapability, or not, of the dialectic here. More relevant for our purposes is the fact that Dirlik's criticism points to the locus of the text's auto-deconstruction. What Mbembe's text ultimately aims to demonstrate is what the epigraph attributed to Deleuze adroitly hints at, namely that 'the only subjectivity is time'. As Dirlik's criticism implies, by refusing to recognise or even engage with the performative necessity or dialectical inescapability of these two grand-narrative responses to colonialism, Mbembe denies the very historicity that is the subject (and, according to Deleuze, subjectivity) of his analysis.

> *Ubuntu* as a philosophical approach to social relationships must stand alongside other approaches and be judged on the value it can add to better human relations in our complex society... The refusal to acknowledge the similarity between *ubuntu* and other humanistic philosophical approaches is in part a reflection of the parochialism of South Africans and a refusal to learn from others... We have to have the humility to acknowledge that we are not inventing unique problems in this country, nor are we likely to invent entirely new solutions (in Enslin and Horsthemke 2004: 548).

To proceed with working in and against the naive discourse on Ubuntu and in order to consider the implications of doing so in an ever-globalising world, I want to retain the essence of Mbembe's critique, while at the same time expanding on it by bringing to the fore some of the political modes of being at work in the different ways the recovery of Ubuntu has been imagined and narrated. My suggestion is that the political stances of scholars working in this domain can usefully be made visible through what Deleuze and Guattari (1994) refer to as conceptual personae. It seems to me that there is a whole range of these personae at work in the Ubuntu discourse, each of which represents a particular conception of the possibilities and limitations of thinking Africa and how these embody specific ways of being.

The thinking self never remains uncontaminated or unaffected by the ideological position assumed. Ideological positions, such as that of the Saviour or Archivist, convey a specific way of thinking, through which the self imagines him- or herself to be in the world and what it means to live history in a particular way. It is on the basis of these conceptions of *what kind of thinking* we need and *what kind of being* is possible that we position ourselves, make claims and contest injustices. Perhaps one can say that these personae simplify by capturing what is meant by specific *imaginaires*; that is, 'complex systems of presumption... that enter subjective experience as the expectation that things will make sense generally' (Vogler 2002: 625). The discussion that follows of the conceptual personae at work in Ubuntu discourse does not pretend to be exhaustive. It may merely present the main characters. No doubt others may be waiting in the wings for their opportunity to make an appearance, to be heard and recognised as additional modes of being that capture something essential about the possibility of what it means to think, write and be African.

African modes of being

> It is possible that the conceptual persona only rarely or allusively appears for himself. Nevertheless, he is there, and however nameless and subterranean, he must always be reconstituted by the reader.
> — Gilles Deleuze and Félix Guattari, *What is Philosophy?*

Implicit in each of the personae is a conception of what it means to think Africa – in this case, the possibilities and limitations of thinking what Ubuntu means – as well as a postulate relating to what it means to be assertive and sovereign in a world that is in some ways quite post-sovereign. These personae not only reveal different understandings of thinking and ways of being, but also, considered together, present us with something like a coherent field of inquiry. Within this unified field, each persona represents a specific political stance on questions such as: What can we know and what not? What is the status of knowledge about Africa and what kind of agency is possible and impossible in terms of any specific conception of thinking and being Africa(n)? These different conceptions of the political play out as differences regarding the possibility of past recovery and future autonomy (the Revolutionary); or a messianic anticipation that a fully recovered self can be offered to the world, either as a contribution to a 'Civilisation of the Universal' (as per Léopold Sédar Senghor) or as privileged, uncanny reminder of a shared humanity (the Saviour); alternatively, as the impossibility of knowing Africa, given its invention by the West, and therefore of being unable to act in the world with any certainty (the Archivist) or, alongside this persona, a fatalistic and often racist emphasis on the coercive subtext or 'dark side' of Ubuntu that, so the story goes, merely represents a more virulent form of the coercive tendency represented by any form of communitarianisms (the Conformist). Lastly, a politics in which the specificity of Africa (conceived as an autonomous subject with sovereign politics) is considered less important than the embrace of a sense of belonging, in which Ubuntu represents no more than a local name for a universal phenomenon (the Cosmopolitan). In addition to these perhaps somewhat obvious personae, there is an additional one that embodies the recognition of the aporetic nature of postcoloniality as hypermodernity. This mode is not unrelated to calls to consider authenticity no longer in terms of the autonomy of the subject, but as an 'exploratory attitude' (Diagne 2002: 622), driven by the appreciation of the performative dimension of political discourse. I return to the persona of the Text Worker or Construction Worker at the end of the last chapter of this book.

It must be said that the purpose of foregrounding these different modes or stances of thinking and being as personae is not to suggest a debilitating relativism, but rather an attempt to show how different avenues are determined and complete *imaginaires* constructed on the basis of assumptions regarding the world and what we can know about it, how this positions the living subject in the world in certain ways, not in the abstract, but in the very real sense of what such assumptions make possible or foreclose as impossible.

Of characters and personae

In *After Virtue: A Study in Moral Theory*, Alasdair MacIntyre interrogates the failure of the Enlightenment to produce universal moral standards. He notes how the moral code of cultures is often best represented by a stock of characters specific to that culture:

> In the case of a *character* role and personality fuse in a more specific way than in general; in the case of a *character* the possibilities of action are defined in a more limited way than in general. One of the key differences between cultures is in the extent to which roles are *characters*; but what is specific to each culture is in large and central part what is specific to its stock of *characters*. So the culture of Victorian England was partially defined by the characters of the Public School Headmaster, the Explorer and the Engineer; and that of Wilhelmine Germany was similarly defined by such characters as those of the Prussian Officer, the Professor and the Social Democrat (1982: 26–7).

Characters become the stock-in-trade of cultures precisely because they embody different dimensions of the moral aspirations encoded in that culture. MacIntyre continues:

> Characters have one other notable dimension. They are, so to speak, the moral representatives of their culture and they are so because of the way in which moral and metaphysical ideas and theories assume through them an embodied existence in the social world. *Characters* are the masks worn by moral philosophies. Such theories, such philosophies, do of course enter into social life in numerous ways: most obviously perhaps as explicit ideas in books or sermons or conversations, or as symbolic themes in paintings or plays or dreams. But the distinctive way in which they inform the lives

of *characters* can be illuminated by considering how *characters* merge what usually is thought to belong to the individual man or woman and what is usually thought to belong to social roles. Both individuals and roles can, and do, like *characters*, embody moral beliefs, doctrines and theories, but each does so in its own way (1982: 27).

Although there would be some similarity between morality encoded as characters and personae as the embodiment of a certain position assumed on the nature of and the relation between thinking and being, my immediate concern here is not with morality or virtue. Rather, the personae I am concerned with illuminate something of an assumed relationship between knowing the world (epistemology) and being in it (ontology). Because Deleuze and Guattari's theorising on this matter is deeply embedded in a theory of the concept, this is where we have to start.

For Deleuze and Guattari (1994), every concept consists of components that, much like clustering atoms, group and overlap to form meaning, both within a concept (to give it substance) and in relation to other concepts, with which certain bridges or associations are formed. Concepts exist and function in what Deleuze and Guattari conceive of as the historical planes of philosophical thought. In many ways, their analysis reads like a complex physics of language, from which I want to extract just one idea, namely what they refer to in a very specific sense as the presuppositions of a concept. Presuppositions do not refer to the way one concept presupposes another (the concept of a rose presupposes the concept of flower). Rather, what Deleuze and Guattari mean is that every concept is premised, first, on a preconceptual 'image of thought' (61) that represents an implicit understanding of *what it means to think* and second, on a further supposition that relates this understanding of what thinking means to what it means to exist; that is, *a mode of being*. An example will clarify what they mean.

When Descartes stated, 'I think therefore I am', he articulated and thereby presented us with a very specific idea of *what thinking means*: it is an everyday activity, something we all do all the time, not something that needs to be explained to us, not anything particularly difficult: 'Everyone can think; everyone wants the truth' (Deleuze and Guattari 1994: 62). But in addition to this image of thought, there is something else at work in Descartes's claim, an assumption of another kind, one that relates the image of thought to the way the thinking person is assumed to exist in the world, to a certain *way of being*. This can best be described as the concept's persona. In Descartes's case, the conceptual persona is that of the Idiot, the private thinker; one who does not think or act with or alongside other people or a tradition as such:

> The idiot is the private thinker, in contrast to the public teacher (the schoolman): the teacher refers constantly to taught concepts... whereas the private thinker forms a concept with innate forces that everyone possesses on their own account by right ('I think'). Here is a very strange type of persona who wants to think, and who thinks for himself, by the 'natural light' (Deleuze and Guattari 1994: 62).

At work in Deleuze and Guattari's analysis is perhaps something that a whole range of contemporary theorists from an array of interdisciplinary fields of study, such as postcolonial studies and complexity theory, have all come to agree on, namely that there is and perhaps never was a clear distinction between knowing the world (epistemology) and understanding or projecting how we exist in the world (ontology). For Lesley Kuhn (2007), this means recognising that epistemology and ontology are mutually constitutive – a claim supported by Gregory Bateson, for whom we live 'bound within a net of epistemological and ontological premises which – regardless of ultimate truth or falsity – become partially self-validating' (1972: 314).

Deleuze and Guattari's notion of conceptual personae affords us not only a useful way of conceiving the unity of such nets of 'epistemologial and ontological premises', but it also opens the door for describing as a political stance every combination of *what thinking means* and its assumed *mode of being*. In other words, how any author unifies epistemology and ontology can be decoded to represent a persona with a certain politics. This is not only a matter of epistemology and ontology being mutually constitutive. The way in which they constitute each other *is* political or is a useful way of describing what we mean by the concept of the political.

Once we have been alerted to conceptual personae, we find that the history of Western philosophy is replete with them – in fact, Deleuze and Guattari argue, 'the history of philosophy must go through these personae, through their changes according to planes and through their variety according to concepts. Philosophy constantly brings conceptual personae to life; it gives life to them' (1994: 62). One philosopher alone may generate a whole range of personae in the process of an evolving *oeuvre*. Friedrich Nietzsche is a very good example of this. His work presents us with different personae, including Dionysus and Zarathustra, Christ, the Saviour, the Higher Men and even Socrates. In addition, according to Deleuze and Guattari, the range of personae can be divided into those that we instinctively warm to (sympathetic personae) and those that we find repulsive (antipathetic personae). Regardless of their mode, the function of all personae is to capture the dangers, perceptions, feelings and positive or negative moments that may be implicit in a specific philosophy or way of thinking (63).[6]

With this in mind, I want to proceed by advancing two ideas that seem relatively unproblematic to me. First, all talk about Ubuntu implies a stance on big questions such as: What can we know of (precolonial) Africa? What can we hope to achieve by re-membering this knowledge? What kind of freedom is possible on the basis of this knowledge? How do we go about re-membering modes of being and belonging in a way that both recognises the debt our thinking owes to the West and the urgency with which we need to think against Western dominance about what thinking means? Second, texts about Ubuntu represent a fascinating range of different nets of epistemological and ontological premises that can usefully be represented as conceptual personae. In mapping these, it is important to keep in mind that the personae seldom manifest as a univocal presence in any given text. In fact, only in extreme and rare cases do texts manifest one persona to the exclusion of all others. Rather, the text, like a conventional stage production, has a main persona and a support cast of lesser personae. Nonetheless, in every text, there is a main character or persona that captures something of an overriding and pervasive assumption about the relationship between thinking and being. The cast of personae I have assembled for the purpose of this report are the Prophet (with a subdivision into the Revolutionary and the Saviour), the Archivist, the Conformist, the Cosmopolitan and the Text Worker or Construction Worker.[7]

The matrix of classification

At its most fundamental level, the matrix – defined as the surrounding medium or structure – within which conceptual personae appear as political suppositions, can usefully be negotiated with the concept of agency. Personae distinguish themselves

---

6. The relationship between personae and psychosocial types, although complex and important within the framework of Deleuze and Guattari's analysis, is not immediately relevant here. On this point see their analysis (1994: 67–8).
7. In what follows, I am only concerned with a broad characterisation of each conceptual persona. In each case, I make reference only to a limited number of texts that best exemplify that persona.

from each other through the different answers they provide to two fundamental questions: How much freedom does the African subject have to give meaning to Ubuntu? And, what end will this meaning serve? – that is, what is Ubuntu and why bother with it?

The first question pivots on the extent to which the meaning of Ubuntu is seen either to derive from endogenous sources (the extent to which its content is considered, unproblematically, as African) or from exogenous influences (inextricably to some extent dependent on Western theories and ideologies for its articulation). As argued in the previous chapter, this difference can also be represented in terms of the opposition between the *local* and the *global* – a binary that I argued is not very useful because the meaning of Ubuntu is irreducible to this tension and is, as such, glocal. The difference remains useful in as much as it enables us to bring into focus the political suppositions of the various conceptual personae. In what follows, I discuss the personae that prioritise globalism; that is, the assumption that it is more or less impossible to speak meaningfully about Ubuntu as local, given either the generality or universality it represents or the historic discursive invention of Africa. I also consider the personae that emphasise the *local* nature and particularity of Ubuntu as a revolutionary force and an authentic ethic with emancipatory potential.

The global: Archivist and Cosmopolitan

> Urban consumptivism and cosmopolitanism form the other side of historic trauma.
> — Wim van Binsbergen, '*Ubuntu* and the Globalisation of Southern African Thought and Society'

In 'African Modes of Self-Writing', having critiqued as historicist the Afro-radical and nativist grand narratives of liberation, Mbembe briefly discusses, if only to dismiss, two attempts that have been made to go beyond historicism and 'to break with this empty dream, this exhausted mode of thought' (2000: 257). The first came from V-Y Mudimbe, who in *The Invention of Africa: Gnosis, Philosophy, and the Order of Knowledge*, writes: 'Western interpreters as well as African analysts have been using categories and conceptual systems which depend on a Western epistemological order. Even in the most explicitly "Afrocentric" descriptions, models of analysis explicitly or implicitly, knowingly or unknowingly, refer to the same order' (1988: x). Mudimbe's articulation of the implications of this was as devastating then as it is now: 'Is it possible to consider [a more authentic reflection of *la chose du texte*] outside of the very epistemological field which makes my question both possible and thinkable?' (86). The suggestion is that our knowledge of Africa is so indebted to Western historical discourses *on* Africa that the theories and paradigms we use to think, write and talk about Africa derive from a Western archive and that every move we make in the direction of speaking about Africa implicitly or explicitly reiterates the same order. Comments Mbembe:

> From this point of view, Africa as such exists only on the basis of the text that constructs it as the Other's fiction. This text is then accorded a structuring power, to the point that a self that claims to speak with its own, authentic voice always runs the risk of being condemned to express itself in a preestablished discourse that masks its own, censures it, or forces it to imitate. This is as much to say that Africa exists only on the basis of a preexisting library, one that intervenes and insinuates itself everywhere, even in the discourse that claims to refute it – to the point that with regard to African identity and tradition, it is now impossible to distinguish the 'original' from a copy (2002: 257).

The metaphor of the library is powerful. It suggests a depressing underground archive or one in which the curtains are drawn, so that we can no longer look through the window to compare the external reality with the internal image. The distinction between fact and copy has been eroded to the point where it can no longer be invoked to assert a meaningful difference. We can fight and argue endlessly, but we will never get to the truth about Ubuntu or precolonial Africa because ultimately all these arguments, positions and knowledges derive from the very archive they seem to contest.

For instance, in the case of Ubuntu, along with its description as African communitarianism comes a whole lot of conceptual and ideological baggage that sets the parameters of interpretation that keep referring our thinking back to the same order of things – liberalism, the history of communitarian thought and praxes – that predetermines the meaning of individualism in a way that makes it impossible for an African thought-complex to generate its own fault lines and questions. In this perpetual reiteration of the same order, the history of Africa is presented as, or reduced to, textual archive and the theorist to the role of mere Archivist. We can rummage through the collections as much as we like, but given the lack of written records by Africans themselves and the fact that those that do exist were all a function of a colonialist, historic a priori, whatever we come up with will only be more texts, so that, considered *in extremis*, all our work will really amount to little more than moving books around or playing Scrabble with a limited number of predetermined meanings or, less extremely, constantly reinventing the invention of Africa.

The point here is firstly epistemological. The image of thought implicit in what some would claim amounts to an ontological reduction of reality to textuality is one of *curating*: thinking is an act of curation, a gathering of thought in which originality or authenticity can never be much more than putting different collections in conversation with each other. We can commission more works, more thought and more writing on Africa, but ultimately the meaning of any text will always be but a memorial to an Africa that never got to speak its own name and which will, to a significant extent, always remain a function of prior exhibitions and collections that predetermine the possible matrix of what it could mean.

But the point is also political because this same order that perpetually gets affirmed is a very specific, Western, racist order of things. Seen in combination with the epistemological claim, the implication here is quite devastating: not only are we condemned to speaking within an archive constructed by the West, but we seem to be inescapably committed, not only to affirming the same epistemological order, but also to reiterating a racialised political order in which black people are eternally destined to play catch-up in a game of recognition they can never win. To contest race is to affirm the reality and meaningfulness of race and to do that always already means entering the conversation fighting back.

Almost three decades after it was published, I think of Mudimbe's *Invention of Africa* in more performative terms. A very necessary point needed to be made against the naivety and instrumentalism of Afro-radical and nativist accounts about what we realistically can expect from writing and rewriting Africa. In the subsequent decades, it is fair to say that while the notion of invention and reinvention will always recognise an inescapable indebtedness to the archive, many nuanced positions have subsequently emerged on what invention means and what the implications of that acknowledgement might entail – none of which amount to a complete reduction of reality to textuality.[8] One such position is that of Patrick Chabal who, in the introduction to *Africa: The Politics of Suffering and Smiling*, writes:

---

8. For a useful overview of these more nuanced positions, see Gordon (2008: 200–48).

> Indeed, that body of [colonialist] scholarship must be placed in its appropriate historical context and deconstructed accordingly. The early missionaries were certainly in Africa to save souls *but* they may also have thought carefully about the people they sought to convert and amongst whom they lived. The pioneers of African anthropology suffered little self-doubt about their methods and certainly believed in the superiority of the West *but* they may also have produced first-rate accounts of the societies in which they worked. Missionaries and anthropologists spoke the local language, which is more than today's social scientists can say... Just because they were the products of their colonial times does not mean that there is no merit to their work... The difficulty resides not in casting the anti-colonial stone but in determining the extent to which their work had value, both intrinsically and in terms of our own efforts to conceptualise politics in Africa (2009: 20–1).

Here is a sober reminder that while we may be confined to working in and against the archive, we can also take the elevator out of it. In so doing we will, of course, take with us all the knowledge we have accumulated from the archive and interpret the world in the light of that knowledge, but the experience of doing so will encourage the writing of new accounts, new books that will, in turn, find their place in the library. Every identity is always already only history in the making and Africa is perhaps only a politically acute instance of that. In fact, in a work that preceded his Foucauldian analysis of the discursive invention of Africa, *L'autre face du royaume*, Mudimbe speculated:

> Everything takes place as if the African intellectual were trapped in an elevator that perpetually goes up and down. In principle, a single gesture would be sufficient to stop the machine, get out, and rent an apartment or a room; in sum, live and experience the reality of the world. But apparently, he does not understand that the initiative to escape belongs to him (in Jules-Rosette 2002: 604).

The Archivist remains a relevant and present persona in general and in Ubuntu texts in particular if only because two of the most extreme political stances regarding the possibility and desirability of recovering Ubuntu pivot around it: in the first place, the nativist belief that it is not only possible to say what Ubuntu is, despite the archive, but also in the predetermination that it cannot but amount to something unique and culturally authentic – which, and this was Mudimbe's point, cannot but deconstruct in a reiteration of a Western, modernist order of things. Second is the political stance of a smug, mostly white, intellectual overdetermination of the logic of the archive that, thriving on an overvalued epistemological impotence, barely manages to conceal a virile, racist politics of developmentalism and Western superiority of thought.

Leaving aside for now the nativist optimism that I will discuss in relation to the Prophetic persona below, the latter stance manifests most clearly in those texts where the sophistication of Mudimbe's argument is made banal through a reduction of an epistemological conundrum to a conservatism that has radical epistemological, ontological and political implications. Here, Ubuntu is reduced to nothing more than a passing fad, just another politically correct philosophy or more African Renaissance mumbo-jumbo. Mudimbe's careful and considered understanding of our commitment (in both senses of the word) to the archive is trivialised by a racist politics that reduces everything to the surface, to the superficially political, to the merely political, the fashionable. In the politics of this racially expedient fatalism, Western societies can constantly produce theories and ideologies suitable *to* their time, *for* their time and as a function *of* their time, but when Africans do it, it is *merely* politics, *merely* ideology, *merely* what seems necessary for the time, a *mere* vacuous cornerstone of an even more vacuous, because mimetic, hope of a so-called Renaissance. Of course, what remains barely concealed behind this trivialising of the African academic project and its reduction to imitation and mere fashion is the racist belief that nothing new *can* come out of Africa. When it comes to Ubuntu, there is nothing real, nothing we need to investigate, account for or give an account of, nothing that interrogates us, because all is passing fancy, symptomatic of the politics of the day. Characteristic of these texts is often an almost complete lack of appreciation of the politics of knowledge-production, of recognising the political as *archē* of all intellectual traditions, including that of the West, and very little appreciation or comprehension of the difficulties encountered by African theorists engaged in knowledge-making within Northern-dominated theoretical discourses.

Ever so slightly to the left of this reactionary racism is the belief that there may perhaps be something to be said about Ubuntu, but whatever it is amounts to little more than a reiteration or recapitulation of insights already generated by Western intellectuals who, as original modernisers, first meandered down the path of self-discovery and enlightenment, which is really the same for everyone, so that Ubuntu now appears as little more than 'another way of trying to make sense of western ethical theories such as utilitarianism and Kantian deontology' (Murove 2009b: 16).

The Archivist, then – essentially an antipathetic persona – conjoins *curating* as an image of thought with a mode of being that is ghostly or *spectral* in order to produce a political stance commited to the belief that Africa does/not exist in and for itself, never has and never will.[9] Africans can/not aspire to the plenitude of being. Instead, they/we are condemned to living the frustration of potential being, of eternally coming to be. Condemned in this way to merely curate re-collections of ourselves, we supposedly pass our entire lives imitating those who embody the original plenitude of being, with ridiculous pomp and circumstance, fake Vaticans, motor cavalcades and long presidential titles.

The second alternative that Mbembe defines as having emerged in opposition to the historicism of Afro-radicalism and nativism presents itself in the persona of the Cosmopolitan. Here I distinguish between a historicist and a contemporary, non-historicist variety of cosmopolitanism. The former is particularly exemplified by the anti-nationalist, Marxist cosmopolitanism of scientific Marxists who, in their debate with African Socialists, were quite content to first reduce ujamaa or ubuntu to a function of a political economy of obligation and, second, to recast this political economy in developmentalist terms as a 'typical' mode of production, common to all precapitalist societies. It is this 'common to' that reveals the Cosmopolitan image of thought as one of *comparison*. Maluleke's comment below is a good example of this historicist cosmopolitanism:

> We forget that *ubuntu* must be understood within the context of a mainly feudal socio-economic system in which the chief, the chiefdom, the clan and the extended family, were crucial providers of wealth and values... Given the fact that the 'global village' is nothing like a 16th century 'African village' consisting of a network of extended families, what is the effect and wisdom of recommending ubuntu to blacks in 1999 (in Kroeze 2002: 261)?

---

9. Examples of texts dominated by the Archivist persona include Coertze (2001), Enslin and Horsthemke (2004) and Kroeze (2002).

Another good example is Abdulrahman Babu's description of African communalism:

> The qualities which our petty-bourgeois intellectuals describe as essentially African are really *human* qualities which find expression when a community is at a certain level of productive capacity. When a community does not have the capacity to produce social surplus, there is simply no means of becoming unequal. The sense of *brotherhood* which is common under such conditions is essential for the survival of a community which is permanently being threatened either by natural forces, which they cannot explain, or by hostile invasion (1981: 57).

In this mode of being, thought reveals itself as the constant iteration of itself: in a certain premodern or precapitalist mode of production, all societies will manifest a similar appreciation of reciprocity and obligation, at the root of which we always find a comparable understanding of being and belonging. Accordingly, what nativists confusingly understand as a sign of Africa's uniqueness is, at worst, no more than a forgotten praxis incongruously out of step with the requirements of life in the modern, increasingly corporatist state or, at best, the intellectual plaything of elitist statesmen who care more for the top-down imposition of nostalgia than for the bottom-up eradication of class differences and poverty.

For a more contemporary manifestation of this image of thought as iteration (viewed objectively) or comparison (viewed subjectively), 'the world is no longer conceived as a threat. On the contrary, it is imagined as a vast network of affinities. In contrast to unanimist mythologies, the essential message here is that everyone can imagine and choose what makes him or her an African' (Mbembe 2002: 257–8). In general Africana scholarship, this position is well represented by Kwame Anthony Appiah who, in 'Cosmopolitan Patriots' (1997) among other works, has argued against a nationalist intellectualism, celebrating instead the hybridity of our identities, the fact that in a sense no one is African any longer, so we should embrace the diversity of origin and purpose that seems to be part and parcel of the postcolonial condition. There are at least two problems with this position. The first returns us to Dirlik's criticism of Mbembe, in the sense that an untimely anti-nationalist embrace of the diversity and hybridity of our origins often makes the execution of nationalism as the emotive driving force of postcolonial state-building impossible. In the second instance, as Gordon (2007: 134–5) points out, it presupposes privileged access to the means necessary for recognising one's own hybridity as symptomatic of a greater, global human condition. In other words, cosmopolitanism so conceived presupposes a specific class position.[10]

For the Cosmopolitan persona, the image of thought is *comparative* in a dual sense. First, it suggests that all societies produce forms of communitarian thought and that the difference is really contingent or merely the context-specific outcome of a historical process that synchronises exogenous pressures with endogenous needs (identity, nation-building and so on). Second, it is comparative in the sense that thinking is about comparing the past with the present and matching what the past offers with what the present needs, by identifying those aspects of tradition that still have comparative usefulness in the present. What Cosmopolitans are after in a discourse on Ubuntu is simply the recognition that Africans are neither especially inhumane nor especially humane, neither demonically subhuman nor divinely superhuman, that peoples all over the world have communitarian traditions or philosophies and that Ubuntu is simply a local language in which to conduct universal politics.

In Ubuntu discourse, I associate this persona with a sizeable collection of texts that recognise the need for engaging with Ubuntu without exceptionalising it as unique, much less as Africa's gift to the world. Exemplary here is Ramphele's statement quoted earlier, which bears repeating here:

> The refusal to acknowledge the similarity between *ubuntu* and other humanistic philosophical approaches is in part a reflection of the parochialism of South Africans and a refusal to learn from others ... We have to have the humility to acknowledge that we are not inventing unique problems in this country, nor are we likely to invent entirely new solutions (in Enslin and Horsthemke 2004: 548).

---

10. According to Gordon: 'One can believe that one is a citizen of the world when most global institutions are already designed for one's benefit (as opposed to others). The folly of this position comes to the fore when one imagines how ridiculous it would be to deride a poor person for failing to be cosmopolitan. It is as ridiculous as applauding a rich person or a person of fair means for globetrotting. What is cosmopolitanism, then, in its concrete practice but the assertion of the values of the affluent as the standards for everyone – including the poor? After all, cosmopolitanism is advanced by cosmopolitanists as their claim to a universal logic, or at least a near-universal one. How could such a value-system be consistent without simply erasing those who contradict it or simply rendering them irrelevant' (2007: 134–5)?

Joe Teffo concurs:

> This philosophy is encapsulated in all the philosophies of the world, though it might be articulated and actualised differently. Effectively, therefore, it would be ethnocentric and, indeed, silly to suggest that the Botho ethic is uniquely African. The mere fact that the tenets that underpin this philosophy are intensely expressed by Africans, does not make those values exclusively African (in Munyaka and Motlhabi 2009: 67).

Lastly, Mvume Dandala writes:

> While *Ubuntu* finds most vocal expression, and is inherent, in African culture, it is not exclusively African. It is possible for an African not to have *Ubuntu*, whereupon people might say *asingomuntu lowo* (that one is not a person), and it is equally possible for a non-African to manifest *Ubuntu*. The law of averages, however, suggests that, from an African perspective, it is people of African origin who are most likely to have Ubuntu (2009: 261).[11]

The Archivist and Cosmopolitan personae present us with a politics according to which the articulation of Ubuntu is either overdetermined by globalising knowledge-production under Northern hegemony or by the idea that the quest for anything local and specific amounts to little more than an outdated intellectual nationalism. While the Archivist is an antipathetic persona, the Cosmopolitan is sympathetic, to the extent that it refuses to sacrifice African humanism on the altar of sovereignty politics, while retaining the belief that it can contribute to an emancipatory politics. Beyond this, the less said about the 'law of averages', the better. We are left with an Ubuntu that, because not unique, should never imagine itself as some kind of gift to the rest of the world. The tropes of uniqueness and the 'gift' really belong to what appear to be the two most stable, if least interesting, personae in Ubuntu discourse.

---

11. Further examples of texts manifesting the Cosmopolitan persona include Douglas (2010) and Cornell and Panfilio (2010).

The local: Conformist and Prophet

> Serious problems await the intellectual if she or he fails to perceive utopian and prophetic statements as such, and instead proceeds to an empirical critique as if such statements are meant not primarily to muse and to exhort, but to give a factual description.
> — Wim van Binsbergen, '*Ubuntu* and the Globalisation of Southern African Thought and Society'

There seem to be two main conceptual personae rooted in a political stance that maintains the possibility, if not always the desirability, of articulating Ubuntu as an endogenous tradition – an African philosophy, in the true sense of the word. These are the Conformist and the Prophet and, in what follows, I dedicate most of my attention to two subcategories of the prophetic, namely the Revolutionary and the Saviour. But first, some brief comments about the Conformist.

This persona presents a belief in the reality of Ubuntu as an original and endogenous or local philosophy, but sees in it no emancipatory praxis. Instead, it emphasises the ideological dangers of its conformism.[12] Ubuntu does exist and can be articulated, but it is not always clear that we should bother to do so because its inherent conformism is very much at odds with a liberal, democratic understanding of liberty and personhood. Some of the texts in the Conformist persona are more forgiving than others. Least forgiving are those who read Ubuntu as strong or restrictive communitarianism or, more dismissively, as a form of collectivism. This interpretation often exceptionalises Ubuntu and by glossing over the fact that all forms of communitarianism are routinely criticised for being coercive to some extent (because they prioritise collective good over individual rights), it must be recognised as at least, or very often, a quasi-racist refusal to engage with Ubuntu simply as part of this often-problematic communitarian tradition.

Less extreme are those texts that interpret Ubuntu as part of this general communitarian tradition, but nonetheless only foresee problems in deploying it as mode of critique of post-apartheid, neocolonial, Western modernity. The fact of its

---

12. Thomas Kochalumchuvattil states: 'This lack of individuation is at the root of the African crisis in identity and in the failure of the continent to sufficiently address its problems. The prevalence of communalism in African society is identified as the main barrier to the process of subjective becoming' (2010: 108).

being a racialised communitarianism (Western individualism versus African communitarianism) often means that Ubuntu gets sucked into Eurocentric developmentalist narratives. These then schizophrenically try to balance the acceptance of Ubuntu as a valid, local form of communitarianism with its dismissal as archaic, premodern communitarian praxis. In short, while Conformists still believe in the possibility of an endogenous or local articulation of Ubuntu, they have the inverse expectation to that of the Prophet – a negativity that presents as a doomsday prophecy regarding the realisation of Ubuntu as an ideology of conformism.[13] This persona is *antipathetic* and its image of thought shades off into what dominates the Prophetic persona in both its Revolutionary and Saviour articulations, namely thinking as *recollection*.

The conceptual persona of the Prophet includes the two related but distinct personae of the Revolutionary and, often but not always, building on it, that of the Saviour. The Revolutionary anticipates the end of oppression in the recovery of Ubuntu, clearly anticipated as a moment of self-recognition.[14] Here, liberation from physical oppression is no more important than liberation from intellectual colonialism – in fact, mental liberation is a condition for the possibility of meaningful material liberation. This movement of *recovery* is often inseparable from a second movement of *giving*, premised on the idea that a self so uncovered has something unique to offer the world. The thought behind it is that the recognised self contains a secret knowing, an insight into being that will either complete the range of human possibilities at the End of History – Senghor's Civilisation of the Universal – or play a more redemptive role in saving the world from the excesses of individualism. The latter is the nativism critiqued by Mbembe in its extreme form. The Revolutionary image of thought is that of *recollection*. It is possible, the image suggests, to recall the self, for thinking to re-member a dis-membered self, to recognise its former ways of thinking and being and to reinstitute these in the present, in order to give effect to Kwame Nkrumah's dream when he exhorted: 'We should write our history as the history of our society in all its fullness. Its history should be a reflection of its self, and contact with Europeans should only figure in it from the viewpoint of the African experience' (in Bayart 1993: 6).

---

13. Examples of texts predominantly in the Conformist mode include Marx (2002) and Mdluli (1987).
14. This persona manifests in some form in the vast majority of texts. Some interesting examples include Munyaka and Motlhabi (2009), Murithi (2009) and McDonald (2010).

In its most extreme manifestation, such an act of recollection promises to sweep away all Western ways of being and their institutionalised oppression, while in its less extreme versions, it aims to soften the blow of an inescapable alienation by 'Africanising' our postcolonial institutions so that, at the very least, we can recognise in them the contemporary residue of a historical self. If the mode of being presupposed by Descartes's *cogito* was that of the solipsistic Idiot, the mode of being implicit here is again, but for entirely different reasons, that of the *ghost* or *spectre* we have already encountered in the Archivist. A ghost is neither here nor there, trapped between this world and the next, neither of nor in this world, never wholly in/outside. Ghosts never simply inhabit the past or the present. We cannot commit them – or what happened to them in this life – to memory in order to 'move on' because they remain haunted by an incident that left them suspended between two worlds. The Revolutionary lives a ghostly life, premised on the belief that life, true life, is possible or must always remain a possibility: 'I will only truly exist,' the Revolutionary consoles him or herself, 'once I have recollected the self; until then, the self is a mere shadow of its former self; a shell, an oppressive invention of the Other.' Ghosts haunt us in the same way that we are haunted by the possibility of being ourselves. Driven by remembrance of things past and fervently hoping to bring about a future in which the self will no longer be different from that memory (being *différance*), the dream is not merely one of being present, but of existing as tautology ('I am my self'). In short, the Revolutionary mode of being is spectral because it inhabits neither the present, nor the past, or the future. Here, I am thinking of Nyerere who, addressing his fellow Tanzanians in this mode of Revolutionary, proclaimed: 'Our first step, therefore, must be to re-educate ourselves; to regain our former attitude of mind. In our traditional African society we were individuals within a community. We took care of the community, and the community took care of us' (1967b: 166) and furthermore, 'We must, as I have said, regain our former attitude of mind – our traditional African socialism – and apply it to the new societies we are building today' (167). At work in the Revolutionary discourse on Ubuntu is not only the belief and hope that Ubuntu can be recovered and articulated in all its locality, but also a problematic conception of *iteration*, in which Ubuntu is repeatable in the present as it was in the past, instead of recognising that the iteration of the past in the present renders the present a constitutive and defining moment of the past. Simply put, what the Revolutionary discourse on Ubuntu underestimates is that the meaning of Ubuntu will never be what we manage to recollect of it (so that we can bring the past into the present).

On the contrary, its meaning will always, in part, be informed by the reasons for its recollection (which places the present in the past).

Such a critique of the Revolutionary conceptual persona is not intended as a judgement or even as a criticism. On this point, there is tentative agreement between myself and Wim van Binsbergen that will further resonate with the statement by Deleuze and Guattari used as an epigraph to this chapter: 'We will not say of many books of philosophy that they are false, for that is to say nothing, but rather that they lack importance or interest, precisely because they do not create any concept or contribute an image of thought or beget a persona worth the effort' (1994: 182–3). For Van Binsbergen, and hypothetically Deleuze and Guattari, the least interesting question here would be to ask whether the Revolutionary is right or wrong, whether what he or she proposes is possible or impossible. For Van Binsbergen, Revolutionary Ubuntu claims are not locutionary (i.e., truth claims), but rather perlocutionary (i.e., they perform political work). In terms of the notion of hypermodernity to be discussed later, we can also say that Revolutionary calls to recollect Ubuntu – however contradictory and problematic – derive their urgency, legitimacy and relevance not in the first instance from their status as truth claims, but from the fact that they exhort and inspire, from *executing* political work that *may* (not will) otherwise remain inexecuted (and perhaps inexecutable) in the absence of a teleology of purpose. With the execution of political work in a context of nationalism, I have something very specific in mind. All nationalisms – political and cultural – require a transcendental sense of purpose to legitimise their performance or the execution of the work they imagine needs to be done. By teleology of purpose, I mean some *Blut und Boden* myth or a story about being God's Elect, predestination or, however metaphorically vague, of being a Promethean bearer of light to other peoples and nations. In the case of Africa, the nationalist myth is grounded in the grand-narrative myth of returning Africa to itself. Such myths need to be accepted as true in order for the political work committed in their name to be successful; that is, executable. In other words, the performance or execution of political work is a direct function of the extent to which its founding myth remains opaque (or sufficiently opaque) to a variety of actors in the relevant political domain, including those with executive powers and those who find themselves at the executed end, as Means to an End: the executors and executees, as it were.

Where a modernity such as postcoloniality is fundamentally constituted – due to larger theoretical frames such as postmodernism and world-historical developments such as the radical separation of political and economic sovereignty in a time of globalisation – as the impossibility of the politically opaque; that is, the impossibility of legitimating its execution with reference to what ostensibly exists outside the political domain, a whole range of questions have to be fundamentally rethought. What is the real possibility of constituting a 'we' in the absence of a legitimising myth or shared *nomos*? What is the nature of the relationship between locutionary and perlocutionary statements in such a political domain? Are the former necessarily superior (because true) to the latter that can, at best, claim some kind of family resemblance with the concept of truth? Or do performative claims perhaps gain increased legitimacy from the simple fact that, unlike locutionary statements *about* the world, perlocutionary statements are more directly instrumental in the creation *of* the world – in this case, the creation of a political collective subject or 'we'? The low-key drama that is the Ubuntu debate is shadowed, then, by bigger questions about how to legitimise and found the existence of the African cultural subject and its political projects – beyond the category confusion of claiming to have a 'right to a philosophy' – in a world that is increasingly becoming immanent, a world in which politics increasingly has to justify itself in the name of the political itself and not with reference to any extra-political legitimations, such as various forms of historicisms, the myth of the Promethean (traditional colonialist and contemporary United States alike) and so on. In short, the question becomes about how to create a foundation for the articulation of a self after a politics of the opaque. I think of such a context as the historical condition of the possibility for the dominance of one particular conceptual persona in the Ubuntu discourse, namely the Saviour.

The Saviour
The Saviour, not content with liberating the self through an act of self-recognition, sees in Ubuntu the additional potential to free the rest of the world from its misplaced infatuation with individualism.[15] Building on the Revolutionary commitment to emancipation, the Saviour finds in Ubuntu a communitarianism (now presented as paradoxical humanism) superior to other, particularly Western, equivalents. I say 'paradoxical' because in terms of this persona, Ubuntu's perceived superiority derives

---

15. Among the many texts that manifest the Saviour persona see, for example, Ngoenha (2006) and Nussbaum (2003).

from the fact that it combines what is most specific to humanism (a dedication to immanence, to the recognition that 'we are all we have') with what is most at odds with humanism, namely hints of the sacred that are no doubt traces of an ontological commitment to an onto-triadic understanding of community. As an interstitial humanism – poised in the difference between its sacred and profane commitments – it appears as an apophatic, even ecstatic humanism (reminiscent of Frantz Fanon) that holds out the promise of a politics beyond politics, a politics of grace, of grace as a way of doing politics (think Nelson Mandela). In other words, only against a backdrop of near global boredom with what it means to live in a disenchanted world, only in a world where the generative or creational dimension of violence has given way almost entirely to recreational violence, in order to reveal the apocalyptic horror of disenchantment as *nomos*, only in such a world can Ubuntu theorists repackage its historical proximity *to* the sacred as the new politics *of* the sacredly human.[16] And therein lies something very specific about Ubuntu, a specificity that derives not from *what* it is, but from the time *when* it becomes visible as alternative point of entry to the Abrahamic, as a source for the appreciation of what is sacred about human life. Ubuntu's specificity, then, lies not in *what* it is, but in *when* it is; more accurately perhaps, in *when* it gets to be *what* it gets to be, so that if we absolutely must insist on associating this specificity with *what* Ubuntu is, let the 'what' refer to u/Ubuntu as interstitial humanism.

With the persona of the Saviour, we enter the complex terrain in which the African theorist constructs a locally based, but globally influential *imaginaire* on the basis of the meaning of African ethics. This structure requires of the African subject to imagine how African ethics will fit into global ethical structures and demands. At a cultural-identity level, this often assumes the logic first articulated by Senghor in his notion of a Civilisation of the Universal. Essentially an argument for a vision of global pluralism, it suggests that if we want to understand what it means to be human, we need to consider the full range of contributions from all societies and civilisations on the subject. Here, the logic is one of *contribution*.

A slightly stronger and more optimistic *imaginaire* is one in which the African ethic circles out to redefine first, postcolonial African society, then the nation and

---

16. The theological overtones here are no mere accident. The discourse on South Africa's transition predominantly presents as a kind of political theology, of which Ubuntu-based talk of being a Saviour or World Redeemer would simply be an extension.

from there, proceeds to reconfigure the whole global system of interdependent societies and cultures. Again, Senghor's widening of the logic of the homeland is an example, as is Ali Mazrui's articulation of the expansionist dreams of Nyerere's Ujamaa project:

> Long before welfare socialism was established in Britain, Africa had developed a system of collective responsibility for orphans, the infirm, the aged and the needy. African communities had historically looked afer their most vulnerable members. From former German East Africa (Tanganyika), Nyerere expanded this African sense of family into the basis of the modern socialist ethic of sharing ... This chapter goes a step further to globalise *ujamaa* into an ethic for the human family as a whole (2009: 38).

Here, the logic is no longer one of *contribution*, but rather one of *re-creating* the world in its own image. This often amounts to visions of, as we can now articulate it, Ubuntu the interstitial humanism as salvific ethic. Claims range from the meek, who see Ubuntu as something that can 'supply something that our dominant scientific culture lacks' or that 'it has something unique that we can make use of for ourselves and also offer to the world' (Shutte 2009: 85, 99), to the stronger claim that 'African ethics can indeed be seen as a salvatory power in today's heartlessly globalising world, a potential moral saviour in a time of deep trouble' (Prozesky 2009: 12).

With this persona, then, I have in mind those knowledge-constructs that not only think it possible to recollect the meaning of Ubuntu, but also for whom the sense of purpose that motivates the recovery, far from being limited to the elusive promise of founding a national self, derives from the projection onto the world stage of one of the other familiar tenets associated with Ubuntu in the popular imagination, 'freedom is indivisible'. If the image of thought of the Revolutionary is *recollection*, the Saviour's is *redemptive*, perhaps even eschatological. Thinking may be about recollection or recovery as the Revolutionary maintains, but this, argues the Saviour, is only a preliminary to the real meaning of thinking, which is to act as a conduit to the global redemptive or eschatological. Implicitly at work in this mode of thinking is something vaguely Heideggerian, something of a 'world disclosure', in which an improbably post-sovereign subject merely discloses to the world the innermost nature of its interdependent being. In this instance, it is very difficult, if not impossible, to disentangle the appearance of grace and the politics of grace, a World-Disclosing Humility and the ultimate violence of sovereignty, power merely masquerading as humanism and grace. Ultimately I think there is indeed something of a world-disclosing possibility in this interstitial humanism, but in order to disclose it, the interrogation of its identitarian subtext needs further development, in order to reveal something of the violence involved in its flirtation with sovereign subjectivity and the seductions of soft power.

Anybody who speaks of how special or unique Ubuntu is inadvertently steps into a tradition that has prepared in advance a specific reception for that claim. I am thinking of Pliny the Elder (AD 23–79) who, in his *Historia Naturalis* (Natural History), memorably exclaimed: '*Semper aliquid novi Africam adferre*' (Africa always brings [us] something new) – a popular cliché about the continent in the sixteenth and seventeenth centuries. In fashionable contemporary academic discourse, this would refer to the exoticising eye, the eye that makes of a person or a place an exotic Other, always marvelled at, but *for that very reason*, never simply considered part of the community. In contemplating how Ubuntu theorists write and speak of themselves, we have to consider the extent to which this exoticising eye has penetrated consciousness and the reflection of the self on the self. Of course, this exoticism is not unrelated to the phenomenon of double consciousness that I touched on in the previous chapter. There, in the discussion of two global a prioris, I suggested that the whole nexus of issues we are dealing with here – blackness, being African, being communal, having Ubuntu – is a function of a very specific historical discourse or order of things, namely a racialised, Western modernity. It is only as a result of and through this discourse that Africans came to think of themselves in the binary terms of 'being black', of 'all having something in common', of 'being African', of having 'authentic ways of being and belonging' and of 'having u/Ubuntu'. The fundamental problem here is the dialectic of recognition through which a Revolutionary recovery of the self always proceeds as reappropriation of the self through the exoticising eyes of the Other – thereby, as Mudimbe was earlier quoted as saying, always returning in order to affirm and confirm the same epistemological and political order of things. In the introduction, I pointed out how Fanon justified his stance on violence as a response to exactly this problem: in order for a racist system to change, white people first have to recognise black people *as* people, *as* human beings. Where such recognition is unlikely ever to come about as the result of black people's commitment to the ethics of dialogue, they should stop waiting for it, suspend the ethical and instead resort to armed struggle, as the only way of bringing about a system premised on the humanist bottom line that *all humans are humans and therefore equal.*

South Africa's so-called miraculous transition to democracy has suggested an alternative: it is possible to negotiate a fundamental turnaround dialogically. However, there are at least two problems with this story: first, the transition was not a 'turn-about' (see Marais 2011: 69–96) as much as it was a carefully constructed agreement on how to change things without turning them about, so that the result has been little more than a changing of the guards that has left the racial fault lines of poverty more or less unchanged. Second, the transition was not peaceful – unless, that is, we exclude from the story the thousands of mostly black people killed, maimed and displaced in the struggle against apartheid (Praeg, forthcoming, in Redekop and Ryba's *Creative Reconciliation*). In recognising the extent to which South Africa did not go up in flames at the moment of transition, we like to give an occasional nod to the role Ubuntu played in the conceptualisation and proceedings of the Truth and Reconciliation Commission. There can be no doubting this role. But the mistake we make is to insert Ubuntu as shorthand for reconciliation, forgiveness and shared humanity into a violence/non-violence binary, in which Ubuntu is understood solely and simply as a gift that redeems, not one that conflicts and contests in a way that reproduces the violence of sovereignty. This violence needs to be surfaced as part of Ubuntu discourse, in fact, as a recognition of the condition of its possibility that follows directly from what it means to accept, as I argued in the introduction that we should, the political as First Philosophy.

In the remainder of this chapter, I trace the outlines of this relationship between African humanism and the violence of sovereignty inherent in its identity politics by considering a very timid, perhaps even soft version of that violence. It is a violence born of what I earlier called the paradox of differentiation that emerges when a philosophy of relationships is premised on the severance of relationships, a severance commited in the name of sovereignty politics, of wanting to use Ubuntu or the idea of 'shared humanity' as culural capital to purchase political ends that, while often committed in the name of our shared humanity, more often than not effect very little that is shared, exactly because, as Chapter 3 will demonstrate, the violence necessary to *conceive* of our shared humanity, as Ideology trickles down as the violence necessary to *sustain* our shared humanity as human*ism*, as Ideology. If we examine the logic of Ubuntu as a gift more closely, we will find that it too succumbs to the violence of soft power, to a certain self-mutilation or an autoviolation of the very subjectivity to which it seeks to restore dignity and a place in the world. To reinsert Ubuntu as humanist praxis in the world as a mode of critique also, and particularly *of* the violence associated with Western modernity and its sovereignty politics, we have to start at home and make visible Ubuntu's own complicity in this violence. I want to do this by starting at an individual level, by considering the logic of the gift in relation to the Other and how this violence plays itself out at the level of global politics.

The gift: Where Saviour meets Idiot

Let us pause, then, to consider another animal altogether, not one that was ever exported from Africa – in fact, not one that is particularly associated with Africa at all, but comes to us from a story Danish author Karen von Blixen-Finecke, writing as Isak Dinesen, recounts in the memoir she is most famous for, *Out of Africa* (first published in 1937), a story she was told, or perhaps read, as a child:

> A man, who lived by a pond, was awakened one night by a great noise. He went out into the night and headed for the pond, but in the darkness, running up and down, back and forth, guided only by the noise, he stumbled and fell repeatedly. At last, he found a leak in the dike, from which water and fish were escaping. He set to work plugging the leak and only when he had finished went back to bed. The next morning, looking out of the window, he saw with surprise that his footprints had traced a figure of a stork on the ground (in Du Toit 2008: 424).[17]

Now, what can we learn from this story of the stork? Blixen herself mused: 'When the design of my life is complete, will I see, or will others see a stork?' (in Cavarero 2000: 1). The idea of a pattern is comforting because it suggests the possibility of life as patterned meaning, a pattern that 'reveals the meaning of what would otherwise remain an intolerable sequence of events' (2). This is a comforting thought indeed, for it suggests that when all the ramblings and scramblings are over, if I were to sit back, a pattern would emerge to reveal that all the while, unbeknown to me, my life made sense; it unfolded a pattern that only appeared random to me at the time because I was too immersed in living my life to recognise it. Italian feminist Adriana Cavarero is more eloquent about this:

---

17. My gratitude to Louise du Toit for bringing this story to my attention (see Du Toit 2008). The story is also discussed and analysed in Cavarero (2000).

> The significance of the story lies precisely in the figural *unity* of the design, and in this simple *'resulting,'* which does not follow from any projected plan. In other words, the design – which does not consist simply of confused marks, but has the unity of a figure – is not one that guides the course of a life from the beginning. Rather, the design is what that life, without ever being able to predict or even imagine it, leaves behind (2000: 1).

For Cavarero, the recognition of life as meaningful is conditioned on recognising the importance of three things: *unity*, the *Other* and the *gift*. Let us consider these in the sequence of their unfolding. The meaning of a life results from or is a function of its unity, of everything somehow 'hanging together'. This unity, however, has an apophatic or negative quality about it because its very possibility is premised on its opposite, on not *going for unity*, of not planning in advance what that unity will be about, but on actively living one's life, being immersed in it, making patterns while going about the seemingly random and pointless business of living. In other words, the unity or meaning of life does not precede life as a pattern that we set out to make, but rather unintentionally results from it. When that pattern emerges, Cavarero writes, it is only from an external perspective of an *Other* who is looking on. Why can it not emerge from my own perspective? Why can I not stand back, like the man in the story, and look at the pattern of my life in order to narrate its unity? Why can I not gather the meaning of my life from looking at what living it has revealed about me? Is this not what all autobiography is about? Yes, and this is ultimately also the failure of autobiography: however self-reflective and self-critical I may be, given that my reflection is part of my life, it follows that my reflection will also replicate the very pattern that it reflects on. Try as I might, I cannot extricate myself from the life I live in order to reflect on it. Autobiography will always be only more tracks around the pond: because 'the one who walks on the ground cannot see the figure that his/her footsteps leave behind . . . he/she needs *another* perspective' (Cavarero 2000: 3) to reveal the figure to him/herself. It takes an *Other* person to look at my life, in order to narrate its patterned unity. This is why there is 'an ethic of the gift in the pleasure of the narrator. The one who narrates not only entertains and enchants . . . but gives to the protagonist of his/her story their own stork.' We all desire to be narrated by another – not so that we can get the facts right, but because we desire 'the unity . . . which this tale confers to identity' (xvii), the unity that can only come from another's mouth.

What does all of this have to do with Ubuntu? Let us start by noting an important difference between different forms of nativism, between *négritude* and Ubuntu, between Senghor's laconic vision of an anticipated future pattern called the Civilisation of the Universal and the banality of much local discourse on Ubuntu as a gift to the world. Mbembe touches on this difference between the softer version of Senghor's universalist nativism and the banality of the stronger nativism:

> In the most extreme version of nativism, difference is thus praised, not as the symptom of a greater universality, but rather as the inspiration for determining principles and norms governing Africans' lives in full autonomy and, if necessary, in opposition to the world. Softer versions leave open the possibility of 'working toward the universal' and enriching Western rationality by adding to it the 'values of black civilization,' the 'genius peculiar to the black race.' This is what Léopold Sédar Senghor calls *le rendez-vous du donner et du recevoir* (the meeting point of giving and receiving) (2002: 255).

Similarly, Nyerere comments:

> It was in the struggle to break the grip of colonialism that we learnt the need for unity. We came to recognize that the same socialist attitude of mind which, in the tribal days, gave to every individual the security that comes of belonging to a widely extended family, must be preserved within the still wider society of the nation. But we should not stop there. Our recognition of the family to which we all belong must be extended yet further – beyond the tribe, the community, the nation, or even the continent – to embrace the whole society of mankind. This is the only logical conclusion for true socialism (1967b: 171).

The issue at stake in both softer and more extreme versions of nativism is the reinvention of the self in a manner that presupposes as *archē*, or point of origin, a self-reflective appreciation of what this reinvented self is going to mean, prior to its engagement with the Other. To concretise: when Ubuntu is self-consciously reinvented as gift, we decide the unity in advance and therefore the meaning of being African prior to the dialogue that may (or may not) recognise Ubuntu as bringing a gift, as making a contribution. As the story of the stork illustrates, it is not for the bearer of the gift to decide this. It is for the *Other* to narrate that unity as constituting a gift by saying, 'I have received a gift.' In this manner, the meaning of Ubuntu will be left to temporality and time, to letting a difference emerge, instead of that difference being constituted as such in advance. To be sure, there are certain Western commentators who write in the gift mode about Ubuntu (as having received a gift) and one would have to investigate how or to what extent those writings reproduce the assumptions of exoticism that have always characterised writing on Africa. This is not my focus here. My concern is with writing from Africa, by Africans, in the mode of the Saviour, in which the meaning of Ubuntu is constructed through a definitional circularity that creates the space for the predetermination of Ubuntu as gift to the world. This predetermination amounts to little more than a narcissistic tautology, an act of self-definition or 'interior monologue' (Cavarero 2000: 35) masquerading as dialogue with the Other. It is a form of African autobiogaphical thought acting as biography, a self-definition that pretends to emerge from an imaginary encounter with the Other.

There is something deeply unsatisfactory about a self who narrates itself, as opposed to letting itself be narrated by another. As Cavarero notes:

> The life-story that memory recounts is not enough for the narratable self. Not so much because the memory proceeds like a voluble and discontinuous narration, or because the demon of self-interpretation produces mythical-biographical texts, but rather because memory claims to have seen that which was instead revealed only through the gaze of another (2000: 40).

The point I am making is that a discourse that self-nominates itself as gift to the world defines itself in a way that 'claims to have seen that which [should or can be] revealed only through the gaze of another'. Between this 'sort of interior monologue' and the dictum 'I am because we are', a radical tension arises that I earlier called the paradox of differentiation and which we can now also articulate as the paradox of postcolonial subjectivity, for that is what the excursion into the Dinesen story allows us to see: the mode of being or persona that engages in this interior monologue of a pre-emptive gift is not the persona or mode of being implicit in 'I am because we are', but one much closer to the Cartesian Idiot, one for whom the self self-affirms its own existence and identity and who inhabits a world in which 'I think therefore I am' effortlessly translates into 'I know my self is/as gift to the world therefore I am' – a tragic substitution of self-recognition for the eternally deferred recognition by the Other.

Augustine Shutte reminds us of the logic of the gift that would be consonant with the logic of Ubuntu when he writes that an important

> aspect of a person existing only in relation to others is that personhood is a gift. We have already seen that it is not something already there at the beginning of a person's life. But *nor is it something that one can acquire through one's own power*. Instead it comes to me from others as a gift. If it is not given it cannot be acquired (2009: 92).

In other words, 'personhood comes as a gift from other persons' (Shutte 2001:12; also Christians 2004: 241). This is not the logic we find at work in the persona of the self-nominating Saviour as bearer of redemptive gifts. Instead, here,

> the self is the protagonist of a game that celebrates the *self as other*, precisely because the self here presupposes the absence of another who truly is *an* other. In this sense, by bringing together the *auto*, the *bios*, and the *graphein*, the self conquers for itself an absolute unity and self-sufficiency (Cavarero 2000: 40).

This self-sufficiency (autonomy, sovereignty) is purchased both at the cost of what the self represents (I am because we are) and, by implication, any authentic relation with the Other, substituted by 'the fantasmatic product of a doubling, the supplement of an absence, the parody of a relation' (Cavarero 2000: xiv). At this point, it is difficult to avoid the conclusion that since so much local thinking about Ubuntu manifests the gift-bearing persona of the Saviour, Ubuntu thinking is deeply implicated in the violent logic of sovereignty, a logic constituted or arrived at through two forms of violence that we can denote as *Other*-violation and *auto*-violation.

The Other-violation is executed in the definitional circularity I discussed earlier. It is at work in any text that legitimises the *raison d'être* of Ubuntu with a violent differentiation that excludes any trace of a relational subjectivity from its image of the West (see Marx 2002: 59–62). Typical of this Other-violation are statements such as: 'The most important difference in the conception of human beings between Eurocentric and Africentric philosophical models is that the African viewpoint espouses harmony and collectivity, whilst the Eurocentric point of view emphasises a more individualistic orientation towards life' (Venter 2004: 152). Only through such an Other-violation can Ubuntu be posited as an alternative, a redemptive humanism that emphasises and reminds us of our interdependence, our communality. Only through this Other-violation is the enunciative space created for the emergence of a discourse on Ubuntu-as-gift.

This Other-violation is also a condition for the further, or secondary, auto-violation that follows. If the Other is violated through the construction of its identitiy in terms that purposefully and consciously omit central features of its intellectual and political history, the secondary auto- or self-violation consists in conceiving the resulting politics of the redemptive self or Saviour in terms of an individualism radically at odds with the communalism generated as a function of the Other-violation. The African subject becomes the very individualist subject it wants to redeem. Only on the basis of these two expressions of violence does a conception of the African self as world redeemer become possible. The Saviour steps onto the world stage of cultural politics through a movement that sees claims about our shared humanity deconstructed by the politics of sovereignty. Formulated differently, the Saviour emerges at the exact point where the politics of sovereignty is deconstructed by appeals to a shared humanity that remain deferred by the politics of sovereignty and a rhetoric, however implicit, that is not very far removed from certain oppressive historical tropes – of the black subject as Promethean bearer of light, the 'black man's burden' and so on. If the mode of being of the Cosmopolitan is that of *belonging*, the mode of being implicit in the Saviour is that of *solitary* redeemer who lives, at best, with a future anticipation of belonging.

None of this should be interpreted as a problem of blackness or Africanness. It is a problem of thinking identity and meaning in terms of the historical and conceptual a priori of Western modernity. The dilemma for the black subject here is that this a priori cannot but commit it to both an Other-violation and an auto-violation – two forms of violence that are a function of each other, as mutually constitutive of each other as the claim to interdependence in whose name they are committed.

The subject so invented is a teleologically conceived subject and much of African philosophy in general and the Ubuntu discourse in particular legitimised and continues to legitimise itself with reference to a teleological, even messianic End that lends it a certain performative urgency. Fundamental to concealing the secret at work in this teleological bootstrapping as belated politics of the opaque is what I earlier called the pretence of a certain World-Disclosing Humility, through which philosophical thinking is ostensibly alienated from the political subject, in order for (its) thought to present itself as the World contemplating its true interdependent nature. Both postulates – that of a Civilisation of the Universal and Ubuntu as

Redemptive Gift – erase, through sheer assumed necessity, a contingent, historical subject who posits the teleology only for the postulate itself to appear as but one anonymous moment in a seemingly inescapable, unfolding teleology (the historicism of nativism). Of course, there is a crucial difference between the postulate of the Civilisation of the Universal and Ubuntu as Redemptive Gift, between thinking as *contribution* and thinking as redemptive *re-configuration*. The former is predominantly (but not exclusively) teleological, in the sense that what it projects into the future is the realisation of pluralism as the minimum condition for the political. As Mudimbe comments about authors who project this view:

> They believe that there is an African tradition in itself and consider themselves as the interpreters of this particular experience . . . Yet in stating that Africans have their own distinct mode of being, they insist that this singularity is the condition of universality: if there were no particular individuals and traditions, there could be no real universals (1991b: 45).[18]

This is not the case for the Saviour persona. At work in its teleological projection is something of an Aristotelian understanding of teleology, of formal and final causes in which, as Walter Stace comments:

> The idea of the end, the final cause, is thus the real ultimate cause of the movement. Only, in the case of human production, the idea of the end is actually present in the sculptor's mind as a motive. In nature there is no mind in which the end is conscious of itself, but nevertheless nature moves towards the end, and the end is the cause of the movement (1962: 274).

There is a specific sense then in which, for the conceptual persona of the Saviour, the End is present at the Beginning or even anterior to it *as* Beginning.[19] In the

---

18. It seems to me that the contemporary version of the Civilisation of the Universal is the discourse on a global ethic, as argued by Mazrui (2009: 36).
19. Bearing in mind that Aristotle's notion of 'causality' includes whatever facts, principles or reasons necessary to explain the existence of something, the relationship between *négritude* and the Civilisation of the Universal would be one of matter to form, of history as a movement from matter *to* form – where matter, i.e., the characteristics of being African, derives meaning or reason from form; that is, from history as efficient cause, the Idea of *négritude* as formal cause and the Civilisation of the Universal as final cause.

interim – or postcoloniality conceived as interregnum – this difference manifests either, in terms of values, as a paradox of differentiation or, in terms of identity, as a hybrid subjectivity, whose putative self-understanding is temporarily contradicted by the politics conducted in its name. Of course, part of this bootstrapping teleology is the world-disclosing erasure of the paradox or hybridity itself, its anticipated overcoming at some distant point in the mythological future when Ubuntu's ontology of interdependence will have reconfigured the global political order in terms of this interconnectedness, an Ubuntu-based post-sovereignty. If there is a messianic structure in Ubuntu discourse, it reveals itself most clearly in this promise that a day, irreducible and heterogenous to the condition of postcoloniality, will arrive when Ubuntu's politics will once again be consistent with its ontology.

But it is not sufficient only to be critical of the image of thought and the mode of thinking associated with the Saviour and of how they conjoin to form a political stance riddled with overstretching contradictions and paradoxes. For this perceived failure of African humanism, the manner in which it can only position itself in the world through a paradox of differentiation, while articulating a subjectivity at odds with what it holds most dear, this 'failure' is not a failure of African humanism per se. On the contrary, it is a function of a historic a priori, of which the master trope in various contexts appears as 'individual', 'independence', 'autonomy', 'sovereignty' and so on. Second, in as much as it then still makes sense to talk about all these contradictions and paradoxes as 'failures', it is perhaps the *necessary failure* of any humanism, the failure that allows it to intervene in politics, only to withdraw again as a 'failure' in order to reappear again, later, as the renewed assertion of the imperative to humanise the world.

Everywhere humanism intervenes in the world, it cannot do so except on the basis of a fundamental denial or self-destructive contradiction of what it holds most dear, namely the belief that the human is sacred. Every time humanism is deployed to make a move in the world of politics, it can only do so by compromising *into* the world of politics, by adopting certain strategies, modes of thinking and by acting politically, strategically and with some end in mind. This is, after all, the problem with thinking of humanism as human*ism*. The moment we conceive of it as an '-ism', we have already sacrificed what is most particular about it, namely that it is not an ideology or a thing, but a mode of critique, a mode of advancing the ideal – the quasi-transcendental ideal – of human plenitude. But this sacrifice is as necessary as the political engagements made possible by it. The persona of the

Prophet, in its twin manifestations as Revolutionary and Saviour, exactly *because* they advance the emancipatory project and not *despite* their failure to do so without contradicting themselves, can therefore be considered truly sympathetic personae – or, perhaps simply *pathetic*, in the original sense of the word that originated in the sixteenth century, via late Latin from the Greek *pathêtikos*, based on *pathos*, 'suffering'.

The dirty work of grace
A week after Tanganyika achieved formal independence from the British, Nyerere made the following statement to the United Nations General Assembly:

> It *goes against my grain as a nationalist* to say thank you to anybody for the achievement of our independence except to the people of Tanganyika. But . . . I want to express our most sincere appreciation both to this Organization for the keen interest it took in our affairs and to our former governors, and now our friends, the British. I might say that *I do congratulate the British for taking yet a further step towards their own achievement of complete independence and freedom because I believe that no country is completely free if it keeps other people in a state of unfreedom* (1967b: 144–5, emphasis added).

In what reads in many ways as a ceremonial acceptance speech, the representative of the formerly oppressed, instead of indulging in realist politics, celebrates freedom – not their own freedom, autonomy and sovereignty, but that of the former oppressor who now, *only now*, is decolonising itself, realising its own freedom from oppressing itself via and through the oppression of the colonised. This is treacherously close to grace as hubris or the hubris of grace. But we need not be that negative. In fact, such negativity is possibly a racist form of hubris itself. For we know this gesture, we have been witness to it many times since. It is what happens when humanism in general, but postcolonial interstitial humanism specifically, enters the world of politics in order to do *what it cannot but fail to do*. We know this gesture as the claim that freedom is indivisible as argued, replayed, reiterated again many years later by Mandela: 'I knew as well as I knew anything that the oppressor must be liberated just as surely as the oppressed' (in Nussbaum 2009b: 105). More heart-rending is Cynthia Ngewu's statement quoted in the previous chapter:

This thing called reconciliation ... if I am understanding it correctly ... if it means this perpetrator, this man who has killed Christopher Piet, if it means he becomes human again, this man, so that I, so that all of us, get our humanity back ... then I agree, then I support it all (in Praeg 2000: 275).

What is so profound about these statements? Perhaps it is simply that as acts of ubuntu or ubuntu praxis, they somehow speak to us from beyond the limitations of the episteme or historic a priori that ensnares the discourse on Ubuntu in so many paradoxes and contradictions. The statements by Ngewu and Mandela (and, of course, I am taking them out of context here in order to make a point) are truly sublime because they speak the language of a certain post-subjectivity that reveals the possibility of a World-Disclosing Humility. What we do not see in these two statements, though, and what we must remain sensitive to, is the sacrificial logic of this Disclosure that both Ngewu and Mandela would have to confront outside of the idealised context into which I have abstracted them here, namely the manner in which this humanism always must compromise into the dirty work of politics in a way that reveals a fascinating oscillation between accomplishment and failure – the accomplishment of politics as the failure of humanism and the accomplishment of humanism in revealing the failure of politics. This we see clearly in Nyerere's speech, delivered at a place that can in many ways be considered the heart of the political, namely the United Nations General Assembly, where states battle to defend and promote their real interests.

The sacrifice presents as the conflict between the two hearts in Nyerere's breast, in the manner in which his soul is presented as a battleground, where the Revolutionary nationalist and the World-Redeeming Saviour have to battle it out. Who will he be in this moment? Will he be the self-congratulatory Revolutionary, proud politician, master of the agonistics of the political? Or will he be the humble Saviour, mere conduit of the freedom of us all? And if he were to act as mere conduit of our collective freedom, would he avoid turning this status into soft power, in order to advance the self-interest of the Tanganyikan state?

He wavers. He recognises that it 'goes against my grain as a nationalist to say thank you to anybody for the achievement of our independence except to the people of Tanganyika'. And yet, and yet ... he goes on to to thank not only the United Nations, but also his country's former governor for this freedom. Why does he hesitate so? One might ask: What is so terrible about thanking the coloniser for granting freedom? And one might answer: power. If Fanon understood one thing clearly, it is that a slave who is set free by the master is not yet free, precisely because he or she was set free *by the master*. Only a freedom willed and seized by the slave amounts to true freedom. A freedom granted is not real; freedom asserted is. But this is Nyerere's problem. The independence of Tanganyka did not come at the end of a violent historical revolution, through which the formerly oppressed asserted their freedom. To be sure, there was significant anti-colonial resistance, but the independence that arrived could never simply be construed as freedom seized. Enter the sacrificial movement of a World-Disclosing Humanism. There is only one way out of this dead end and that consists in turning the tables on the former governor, to assert that in perhaps *the most important sense possible* and therefore the only sense that, being irreducible to mere politics, truly matters, it was never (only or primarily) about the Tanganyikans achieving independence but (at the same time, or rather) about the British governors 'taking yet a further step towards their own achievement of complete independence and freedom'. After all, 'no country is completely free if it keeps other people in a state of unfreedom'. Freedom is indivisible. The inversion is complete: a graceful move has allowed Nyerere to slip out the back door of the dialectic of freedom posited by Fanon. Between an emasculating freedom granted and a virile independence asserted, a third option suddenly appears: a graceful exit that asserts the indivisibility of freedom, an insistence that refuses the reduction of freedom to the agonistic of individualism, a true and sublime communitarian praxis that seems to trivialise realist politics with its humanist splendour.

But things are invariably more complex than they seem. As the first president of a newly independent country, Nyerere only had a couple of minutes to make a good first impression on the other world leaders present at the General Assembly. He had already started with an apology for the fact that his speech was going to be 'slightly longer' than convention allows. He was motivated by the fact that he had to establish the imprint of his nation on the minds of the wary, tired realists of state politics, to show them that he and his people would be of value to this austere collection of states and that they did not come empty-handed to the table – much in the same way that Senghor invented *négritude*, in order not to arrive empty-handed at the cultural version of the United Nations, the Civilisation of the Universal. In short, the truth of his World-Disclosing Humility has to be actualised as politics and therein lie the sacrifice and the necessary failure of humanism.

For some states (but also individuals), there is only one way to redeem their insignificance and that is to augment it, emphasise it and then to demonstrate the inherent usefulness, even superiority of this radical insignificance. It is a paradox Nyerere had negotiated before in an article published in the *Royal Commonwealth Society Journal* of December 1961:

> It is in the latter respect that we may have something to contribute to the Commonwealth. Our present *unimportance* in world power terms, and our comparative freedom from past involvements in world politics can be *of signal assistance* in bringing a new view to the councils of the Commonwealth ... And *the only way we can hope to gain any prestige in the world is by a record of honest and serious consideration* of any issues which might arise, and by the taking of attitudes based on what we believe to be right. In other words, *our unimportance gives us an opportunity to be somewhat objective – which can only be of value to the Commonwealth* (1967b: 135–6, emphasis added).

Effectively it is Tanganyika's supreme unimportance that could make it supremely important. It is our unimportance, Nyerere says, which enables us to be objective – which could be of great importance to the Commonwealth and, by deduction, the rest of the world. What may appear as one of the most marginalised spaces in the topography of geopolitics may in fact be the Archimedean point from where we can *collectively* obtain leverage on the petty logic of political realism. The pathos aside, it is the tension between the transcendent and the immanent world of the political that is intriguing. Nyerere argues that we have no power, no history of involvement in conflicts, we 'do not have to think of political prestige' (1967b: 135–6); we are honest, humble, objective, the humanist force of reconciliation and mediation – in short, *beyond mere politics*. All this is the transcendent claim of humanism, but it is a humanism that can only enter the political on the back of a compromise that turns humanism as mode of critique into human*ism*. In other words, what is most transcendental about humanism – the fact that it beckons to a world 'beyond' mere politics – only becomes visible once it is actualised as its opposite: an immanent move wholly within the domain of the political. If, unlike powerful states, 'we do not have to think of political prestige', we can nonetheless leverage our humble objectivity, 'as the only way we can hope to gain any prestige'. Transcendental humanism is converted into political capital in order to do the dirty work of immanent politics, the kind that will earn it, too, some privilege and prestige.[20] What is revealed through this sacrificial incarnation (and incarceration) of the transcendental as immanence is the fact that Nyerere does not manage to sneak out the back door of the Fanonian dialectic of freedom. Rather, he doubles up on the idea of a freedom asserted, through the messianic anticipation that Africa in general, perhaps, but certainly Tanganyika in particular, can set the world free. This is Nyerere the realist who truly understood the politics of the gift: one *is dependent* as long as one relies on gifts; one *becomes independent* when one no longer needs them, but one can only *assert independence* when, in turn, one becomes the dispenser of gifts, the giver or gifter, the one who is relied upon and imitated in being.[21]

Conclusion

In some misguided way, the meta-critique of Ubuntu offered in Part I of this report, specifically the analysis of the conceptual personae through which the meaning and place of Ubuntu in the world is articulated, invites the question, 'Then who is right – the Prophet, the Conformist, the Cosmopolitan, the Archivist?' But this is the wrong question for two reasons: First, there is no adjudication possible that will not present itself in the mode of one of these personae (or, admittedly, another one that yet awaits articulation). In the metaphoric language of Dinesen's story,

---

20. This logic is also evident in in Ubuntu-based management discourses, where 'the human' is invoked 'to effect spiritual reconciliation between the workplace and African beliefs' (Dandala 2009: 260), or where '*Ubuntu* might be harnessed to soften the hard face of the economy' (263). This reconciliation aims, not primarily at the spiritual growth of the individual; that is, the realisation of the transcendent potentialities, but at actualising the potential of the immanent, the workplace – the human, not as an end in itself, but as a means to increased productivity for the company and increased power of and profits for corporations: 'To be seen as vulnerable can be an enhancing factor allowing managers to be seen as people behind the façade of power' (260). Behind the first façade of power lies the second façade of fake vulnerability as both cultural and economic capital.
21. For Thomas Hobbes, pride is such a social construct and the most dangerous of the three causes of war because 'the criterion of success is universal envy; vainglory cannot be slaked by prosperity, and it creates a competition that security cannot defuse. There logically cannot be more than one top position; if that is what we seek, the conflict between ourselves and others is absolute' (Ryan 1996: 221).

they are (some of the) tracks made by the searching Ubuntu theorist. This theorist cannot, through an ostensibly detached act of autobiographical reflection as writing, remove him- or herself from the modes of being revealed here in order to decide, once and for all, on the meaning of track-making in a way that will not amount to more track-making, the generation of more and more conceptual personae. Second, if we take as a point of departure the principle or the logic of interdependence – what we generally refer to as African humanism or specifically as Ubuntu – the question of its relative out-of-placeness in an episteme biased in favour of a politics radically at odds with it, these personae present no more than various ways in which to conceive the sacrifice that humanism makes in order to become political, to engage the political. The conceptual personae presented here are nothing more than various political actualisations of the necessary failure of humanism.

Part II

> I would turn on the TV, but it's so embarrassing
> to see all the other people, I don't know what they mean.
> It was magic at first, when they spoke without sound
> but now this world is gonna hurt, you better turn that thing down,
> turn it around.
>
> — Jack Johnson, 'Cookie Jar'

Part III

CHAPTER 3

African Socialism

> If he were to define what African Socialism means, and what it does not mean, he would render yet another great service to Kenya.
> — *Kenya Weekly News*, 12 February 1965

The analysis in Part I of this book is concerned with understanding the conditions under which we have come to think and write about Ubuntu in certain ways, as well as the different political stances we assume in the process of imagining its place in contemporary, post-apartheid South Africa. In Part II, I am broadly concerned with the third dimension of Lewis Gordon's threefold distinction, namely the emancipatory promise and limitations of a reappropriated Ubuntu, framed by a greater, universal concern with the emancipatory potential of critical humanism.

In this chapter, I explore one specific historical attempt to rearticulate the precolonial logic of interdependence in the abstract form of an emancipatory ideology, namely Julius Nyerere's Ujamaa project. This is followed in the last two chapters by a discussion of the South African debate on the emancipatory potential of Ubuntu in constitutional jurisprudence. In order to develop Ubuntu in the direction of an emancipatory praxis, two important questions need to be addressed: the question of violence and the question of definition. This chapter addresses the question of violence and I use the Ujamaa project to demonstrate the danger of not making visible the constitutive violence of ujamaa/ubuntu when we translate or codify the praxis into an ideology or philosophy.

Let me reiterate what I have already stated in the introduction: my critique of the Ujamaa project should not be taken to exceptionalise the violence it invoked. Rather, the aim is to demonstrate the importance of making violence or coercion visible as a political choice. Having considered the question of violence, the last two chapters will address the issue of definition. If there is one common concern in Ubuntu-engaged jurisprudence, it is the problem of definition. Can or should judges be allowed or encouraged to invoke in their adjudication something they cannot define to a plausible degree of consensus or certainty? At this point, it should be clear that I consider the question of definitional consensus moot. The difficulty we have in defining Ubuntu lies not with Ubuntu itself, but with the fact that Ubuntu is the product of subtle interfaces between endogenous memory and exogenous, global discourses. Simply put, Ubuntu is not to be defined to the satisfaction of legal scholars who expect of this concept a clarity of articulation that they, by and large, do not expect from concepts that are just as difficult to define, such as dignity. Of course, dignity scholarship has a history that Ubuntu scholarship does not. But this is not a criticism. Rather, it is an invitation to deepen Ubuntu scholarship. When it comes to the law, I argue, we need to ask a different question altogether. Not what does Ubuntu mean, but rather, how do we position this glocal articulation of our shared humanity in relation to a constitutional regime of individual rights, in order to maximise its emancipatory potential?

The ujamaa/ubuntu analogy: Some preliminaries

When colonial powers left Africa, they did not leave behind viable independent economies and coherent political forms, for the simple reason that neither of these things were ever colonialist intentions. Instead, administrative frameworks were put in place that aimed at economic exploitation and political domination and, later, to ensure that the future postcolonial African state would remain economically and politically dependent on metropolitan states. When African states started to gain their independence from the late 1950s and 1960s onwards, these emerging economies were so thoroughly intertwined with the political fate and market economies of metropolitan countries that it can rightly be said that they had gained 'the ability to make laws within the country but not the power to change the structure of the economy or the pattern of trade with the outside world' (Mohiddin 1981: 12).

Every new African state has had to create exactly what the colonial powers failed to establish, namely viable economies and coherent political identities. The duality of these concerns reflects the twin conditions of human existence in general and that of the postcolony in particular: on the one hand, a materialist concern with the best economic policy for the generation and distribution of wealth (development) and, on the other hand, an idealist or political concern with conceiving an authentic postcolonial identity and the political form most suitable for its articulation. The materialist concern had to be negotiated within the context of a Cold War ideological binary opposition between capitalism and socialism, while the idealist question of identity had to steer a course between those who advocated African unity or pan-Africanism and those who argued for the Western-style autonomy and sovereignty of individual postcolonial African states – a debate that came to a head at the first meeting of the Organisation of African Unity (OAU) in 1966, where the principles of the inviolability of colonial borders and the sovereignty of African states were accepted. Within the parameters of these two sets of choices, most African societies were determined, 'at least at rhetorical level, to restructure their societies in a manner consistent with their own traditions, needs and desires' (Mohiddin 1981: 12). In order to unify their materialist and idealist concerns, nothing less than a grasp on the totality of things, both materialist and idealist, was needed; in other words, an ideology that would enable Africa leaders to exercise what was effectively a very limited set of choices, in a manner that would make future development seem natural or somehow in line with traditional African values and traditions.

In the 1960s, African Socialism emerged as the most promising ideology for such a unity of expression. Senegalese poet and politician Léopold Sédar Senghor coined the term in the late 1940s (Onuoha 1965: 28–9) and it gained particular prominence after he convened the Colloquium on Policies of Development and African Approaches to Socialism in Dakar in 1962, which was attended by a large number of African leaders and intellectuals. So well suited did African Socialism appear to the task at hand that Bede Onuoha could comment that African leaders 'from Algeria to the Congo and from Senegal to Malagasy, as if by some common intuition... have unequivocally declared themselves in favour of what they call African Socialism' (in Mohiddin 1981: 13).

That the debate on African Socialism would fade into obscurity twenty years later does not mean that it is no longer relevant to us. In fact, the basic premise of this chapter is that the attempt to rearticulate the precolonial logic of interdependence in the more or less coherent form of an ideology remains pertinent to our contemporary attempt to rearticulate this logic in the more or less coherent form of an abstract philosophy, with possible emancipatory or developmental potential. Philosophers interested in the re-presentation of ubuntu as Ubuntu can learn much from the way in which first-generation, post-independence African leaders went about reinventing the precolonial logic of interdependence in terms of a contemporary ideology – in the case of Nyerere's Tanzania, how he translated and codified a precolonial political economy of obligation (ujamaa) into full-blown postcolonial ideology (Ujamaa). Those who find the analogy between ideology and philosophy, between ujamaa/Ujamaa and ubuntu/Ubuntu perplexing would do well to bear in mind Christopher G. Thomas's reminder:

> South Africa's efforts to promote an indigenous knowledge system linked to collectivist solidarity values for nation-building and development projects are not unique. Although embedded within a development model framework, Julius Nyerere's philosophy of familyhood, or communitarianism, *ujamaa*, and the policies implemented in independent Tanzania between the 1960s and 1970s... bear a similar ethos to the isiZulu *ubuntu* expression of the individual's interdependence with the community: '*Umuntu, ngumuntu, ngabantu*' (a person is a person through other persons), and similar renditions in Bantu languages in eastern and southern Africa (2008: 44–5).

Further evidence of the similarity between Ujamaa ideology and Ubuntu philosophy is to be found in the fact that post-apartheid discourse has already mobilised Ubuntu in the production of at least two such hybrid ideologies of postcolonial modernity: an Ubuntufied Christian theology of reconciliation and forgiveness and a sentimental Ubuntu nationalism, briefly embraced around the moment of transition to democracy.[1] My argument here is simple: with both Ujamaa and Ubuntu, the point of departure is a precolonial political economy of obligation that, never before systematically articulated in the abstract, was or is being codified in the abstract terms of either glocal ideology or glocal philosophy. There is one important difference, though: African Socialism tried to unify both the materialist and idealist demands of postcoloniality into a coherent vision, while Ubuntu, as argued in Chapter 1, is primarily quarantined at the idealist level, as a philosophy tasked with the articulation of the imaginary 'we' in a postcolonial nationalist version of 'I am because we are'. Only in a secondary sense is it sometimes assumed or conceded that Ubuntu may have some relevance as a political philosophy with emancipatory potential. That Ubuntu is more or less quarantined within the constellations of culture and (occasionally) the political (and is conspicuously absent in most discourses concerned with our material as opposed to political equality)

---

1. Those interested in the possibility of converting Ubuntu into full-blown ideology reminiscent of the Ujamaa project need look no further than the educational intervention introduced by Inkatha in KwaZulu in 1979 (see Mdluli 1987).

can perhaps be explained as the combined outcome of the failed African Socialist experiment and the so-called post-ideological times we live in. The fact that Ubuntu has played an extremely limited role in emancipatory politics so far does not mean that it is not suitable to the task. In a liberal democracy – particularly one marked by a radical asymmetry between institutional mechanisms devised for the protection of individual rights and those that could give substance to social obligations – there will always be an urgent need and place for communitarian philosophies and praxes.

Just like Ubuntu, African Socialism can only really be understood through V-Y Mudimbe's notion of a retrodiction, according to which a historical, local praxis came to speak the language of contemporary, global ideology. And as with the majority of contemporary texts on Ubuntu, this was not generally acknowledged at the time. In the same way that most texts on Ubuntu assume a seamless continuation of ubuntu as Ubuntu, there was a real sense in which intellectuals such as Senghor and Nyerere did not think of African Socialism as an ideology or theory about existence and labour, but rather as the continuation of the traditional economy of obligation in the abstract form of an ideology. This idea of a naturalised modernity is evident in Tom Mboya's definition of the term: 'In brief, [African Socialism] reflects and implies the development of a society based on our own ideas and concepts, with our own relations between man and man, between labour and profit and the attitude to work, or production and its results' (in Mohiddin 1981: 15).

The idea that African Socialism merely reflected Africans' 'own ideas and concepts', their 'own relations between man and man' and 'between labour and profit' was succinctly captured by Senghor, for whom Africans did not need to be taught socialism because their communal ways amounted to a form of socialism *avant la lettre*. To be sure, it was accepted that African Socialism was the abstract articulation of a historical praxis, but it was nonetheless held that African Socialism represented the essence of that praxis, the essence of a certain relationship between being and belonging and the essence of a specific understanding of personhood, which was to be preserved by retrodicting it in the jargon of socialism as the absence of class relations and by celebrating the logic of subsistence production as a sign of the absence of a concern with the generation of surplus. Abdulrahman Babu notes:

> *Ujamaa*'s declared target is to improve the material conditions of the peasant, 'at his own risk and responsibility for the market,' by methods firmly rooted

in the old system, at the same time resuscitating social values corresponding to a pre-feudal mode of production. The policy does not in the least envisage the need to *transform* him into a new person belonging to a new class – a need created by the development of the productive forces and new relations – with corresponding new social values (1981: xv).

What I am interested in tracing in this chapter are the conceptual moves through which Nyerere's Ujamaa was first constructed (the process through which a traditional praxis of familyhood [ujamaa] was transformed into an ideology of national familyhood or Ujamaa) and, second, how this construction was legitimated or naturalised. By the latter, I mean what conceptual moves or strategies accompanied the translation of ujamaa as Ujamaa, in the form of legitimations for positing Ujamaa as naturalised postcolonial modernity?

In considering African Socialism, I limit my analysis to one theorist and one example only, Nyerere's Tanzania, more specifically the decade of 1967 to 1977. I chose Nyerere because after the publication of the *Arusha Declaration* on 5 February 1967, there was a general sense in which, as the British *Guardian* put it, 'President Nyerere's move has now confirmed him as perhaps the most serious exponent of African Socialism – a socialism inherent in native institutions that was corrupted by the colonials' (in Mohiddin 1981: 205). The year 1977 is important because it marks the year when the East African Community eventually collapsed and Nyerere's Tanganyika African National Union (TANU), which had introduced African Socialism under the name of Ujamaa, amalgamated with the ASP (Afro-Shirazi Party), after which the minimal private enterprise allowed by the *Arusha Declaration* was again permitted, even encouraged, to play its designated role in the economy. In a sense, then, 1977 marks the end of the socialist dream and a recognition of the reality of capitalist modes and relations of production that not only pre-dated colonialism, but also continued alongside Ujamaa as the driving force of Nyerere's socialist project.

Nyerere declared his own intention to reappropriate ujamaa as African Socialism through a process of translation or formal codification usefully described by Onuoha:

The marvellous integration of ancient African life was thanks to the operation of certain principles of economic, social, cultural and political life based on human nature *but not articulated*. It is the objective of African neo-Socialism to set out these values and principles, assimilate and inculcate them and devise the best techniques, the best institutions and processes for incorporating and perpetuating them under modern conditions (1965: 123, emphasis added).

The idea that, as Jomo Kenyatta stated in 1963, Ujamaa can be 'roughly translated as Socialism' (in Mohiddin 1981: 17) suggests that it is perhaps with the politics of translation broadly conceived that we should start – more precisely, by separating out the two-way interaction between past and present (the past *as* present and the present *in* the past) that accounts for the logic of retrodiction. How did the lived memory of a past ujamaa praxis inform the interpretation, in the present, of socialism? Inversely, how did the intellectual knowledge of socialism determine or influence the recollection and interpretation of ujamaa? We can transpose these into more abstract questions about translation in general: when we translate a historical praxis into a contemporary ideology or philosophy, which elements of the praxis are included in that translation and which are not? Which elements are explicitly transferred into the ideology or philosophy and which elements can, at best, be said to shadow the ideology or philosophy, exactly because they remain problematic or at odds with the context that called forth the translation in the first instance? Further, is it possible that certain aspects of this precolonial praxis have functioned and continue to function in between the cracks of what is explicitly included and excluded, in order to function as indispensable supplement to, or sine qua non of, the abstract ideology of philosophy?

In what follows, I argue that what I have so far referred to as the constitutive violence of African humanism has exactly this status of indispensable supplement or sine qua non of the translations of ujamaa as Ujamaa and ubuntu as Ubuntu. There is nothing radical or outrageous in this idea of the constitutive violence of Ubuntu. What may be new in my overall argument is that the relative obscurity, even invisibility, of constitutive violence in this discourse is largely the result of identity politics, of the Revolutionary assumption that in Ubuntu we have something 'authentic' and 'new' that, through the conceptual persona of the Saviour, can be said to account for its salvific, even messianic, potential. It seems to me that these essentially identitarian claims can only be legitimated and substantiated through a constant repression of the constitutive violence that makes of Ubuntu a philosophy and a praxis comparable to other communitarian philosophies and praxes, which are routinely criticised on exactly this issue of a minimum violence implied in any prioritising of the common good over individual rights. In order to make visible this violence and its role in the translation of ujamaa praxis as Ujamaa ideology, I think it is necessary to start with a brief discussion of a major fault line in socialist discourse in postcolonial Africa.

Socialism: Uncanny memory or utopian possibility?

Ahmed Mohiddin describes the fault line I have in mind as follows:

> At one end of the ideological spectrum were those who argued that 'African Socialism' was a unique ideology, basically socialist in its origin, content and orientation, but appropriately modified to meet the peculiar condition of erstwhile colonised Africa. At the other end of the spectrum were those who asserted that there was only one socialism and that was 'Scientific Socialism,' propounded by Karl Marx and his followers. Those who belonged to this latter school of thought maintained 'African Socialism' was nothing more than a bourgeois attempt to Africanise the colonially established capitalism (1981: 14–15).

This polarity between African Socialists and scientific socialists presents us with two perspectives from which to interpret or account for the eventual failure of African Socialism as an ideology in general and Nyerere's Ujamaa project in particular. External to the African Socialist project; that is, from the vantage point of scientific socialism, Nyerere's project was essentially a 'bourgeois attempt to Africanise capitalism', legitimised by a misguided historiography, by a mistaken, *because merely identitarian*, interpretation of the social-developmentalist status of African communalism. Authors such as Michaela von Freyhold and Issa G. Shivji have argued that since the Tanzanian working class did not seize state power, the expansion of the state economy was never going to be the articulation of working-class interests. In fact, writes Von Freyhold, 'the state economy was not the creation of the working class but the creation of a petit bourgeoisie which tried to gain an economic base by integrating metropolitan capital into peripheral state capitalism' (1979: 119). The state so conceived gained its legitimacy from presenting itself in terms of its ideological inverse, as African Socialism and the claims through which this inversion articulated itself were, on the face of it, intuitively respectable. It is the nature of these claims and their deconstruction that I want to pay attention to, as a second way of accounting for the eventual failure of the African Socialist project.

The intuitively attractive train of thought that African Socialists advanced can be presented as follows. Colonialism amounted to the introduction of a political economy of commodity capitalism, premised on the pursuit of individual self-interest on a continent predominantly characterised by a very different political economy of social obligation and reciprocity. The dominance of the former over the latter was sustained until the wave of independence that swept across Africa, beginning in the late 1950s. Independence meant that African states subsequently had to choose between two ideologies of development that defined the post-Second World War era: capitalism and socialism. While capitalism seemed more entrenched globally, at least two factors made socialism more attractive: first, as in traditional African societies, socialism was premised on an ontology of the human as social; second, socialism legitimised this ontology through a Marxist historical grand narrative that presented socialism as the way of the future, as what comes *after* a capitalist emphasis on individual self-interest. These two theses – a *social ontology* and the grand-narrative historicism that placed socialism *after capitalist individualism* – generated a profound tension between African Socialists and scientific socialists: like socialism, precolonial African societies prioritised the social over the individualist, but unlike the grand narrative that tells of the manner in which socialism comes about after a capitalist mode of production, as a solution to the tensions generated between capitalist forces and relations of production, African societies had never gone through a capitalist phase of development. The question then arises: in what way can precolonial African societies be said to have been socialist? Logically, the tension could only be resolved in one of two ways: either capitalism was not a necessary stage of development *or* precolonial African societies cannot be said to have been socialist – perhaps they were simply communalist, in the precapitalist sense described by the Marxist grand narrative. The particularities of the debate between social and scientific socialists and the question of whether scientific socialists such as Babu had a thorough understanding of Marxism in general are not important here. What does matter is the very different status attributed the precolonial political economy of obligation in their two very different understandings of emancipation.

By insisting on using the word 'socialism', African Socialists essentially tried to subvert the patronising, linear developmentalism of Western modernity. By arguing that socialism had existed in precolonial Africa and that as a way of being and a mode of production it was something to be *recollected* after the forceful introduction of commodity capitalism, African Socialists attempted to de-historicise development or to insist on its atemporality. Scientific socialists, on the other hand, were quite content to argue that what African Socialists interpreted as 'traditional socialism' was really only a 'precapitalist social formation', the communalism posited by Marx as an early stage of socio-economic development. In this view, colonial-induced modernity 'transformed the people, both in their outlook and in their mastery of technological skill. The peasants were liberated from backwardness and superstition; they broke loose from the constrictive "traditional" practices inherited from the medieval and feudal past, which had their basis in peasant agriculture' (Babu 1981: x). Accordingly, socialism proper should be thought of, not as something to be recollected, but as something to be *anticipated*, not as past idyll, but as future possibility. The difference between a socialism recollected by the Revolutionary nationalist and a socialism anticipated by the Cosmopolitan Marxist allowed for a further difference to emerge between, on the one hand, what some argued was a necessary, but always problematic bourgeois politics of identity and, on the other hand, an Afro-radical politics centred on the role of the working class as the only historic agent for the realisation of true socialism.

In retrospect, it is easy to understand the profoundly aporetic nature of the tension between these two positions. One the one hand, the scientific socialists' adherence to the grand-narrative anticipation of socialism and their implicit (and sometimes explicit) historicist dismissal of African communalism could not but resonate with the kind of social evolutionism that legitimated colonialism in the first instance. Was an essential part of Europe's civilising mission not a condescending view of African communalism, in which the European civilising mission depended on what Sir Philip Mitchell, governor of Kenya (1944–52), referred to as a 'radical transformation of the subsistence society enmeshed in atavistic superstitions' (in Mohiddin 1981: 25)? As Mohiddin notes:

> The African and his way of life at that time were considered by the Europeans to be the lowest in the historically established stages of human development. At best the African was regarded by the European as a moral responsibility, to be gradually and carefully raised to the levels of those already civilised (1981: 24).

In order to rescue African communalism from this historicist dismissal, African Socialists attempted a move that was conceptually as complex as it was ideologically incoherent, a move that amounted to accepting temporality, while denying historicity. Temporality is a co-ordinate of existence; it signals awareness of the passing of time, the movement from, say, the time of precoloniality to the time of colonialist intervention to a present that is postcolonial. But we never understand temporality simply in the abstract categories of before, during and after. These categories become meaningful only as historical categories or when they are allowed to signal something of the meaning of the historicity of existence. And with that recognition, we find ourselves back at the starting premise of this book, namely that the political is First Philosophy or, simply put, that everything is fundamentally, first and foremost, political. After all, what can be more political than the act and the contestation of the act of making meaningful the historicising or temporality of existence?

In the intellectual climate of the 1950s and 1960s, African Socialists took on an almost impossible task: to insert their societies into the grand narrative of human evolution as *equal participants* in the making of human history while, at the time, the very thinking of what it meant to understand temporality in historical terms departed from a historicist assumption that equated 'change' with 'evolution', evolution with 'progress' and progress with re-enacting a linear and teleological path of development, at the beginning of which we find communalism and at the end socialism – an a priori that predetermined difference in terms of absolute time and space. As I argued in Chapter 1, at the time of independence, this *historicist* a priori was only gradually giving away to a postcolonial, *relativist* a priori that would eventually enable theorists to conceive of evolutionary differences in terms that are non-linear or non-teleological; that is, non-ideological.[2]

The manner in which African Socialism tried to negotiate this epistemic impasse made visible the full extent to which the ideology was born *of* Western modernity as a form of resistance *to* Western modernity, a contradictory status that manifested a number of profound paradoxes that troubled its conceptual coherence as ideology: in accepting temporality, but denying historicity; in simultaneously legitimising the dominant grand narrative of historicised temporality – by 'recognising' itself as 'socialist', supporting the argument that socialism is superior, the 'way of the future' – while delegitimising that grand narrative by contesting the manner in which it historicises temporality; by claiming that Africans always had socialism, that they did not need to be taught socialism, that theirs is a socialism *avant la lettre* and so on. In a nutshell, within the racist historic a priori of Western modernity, African Socialists attempted a complicated de/legitimation of historicity that, on

---

2. For a genealogy of the changing perceptions of Africa over time, see Praeg (2010a).

the face of it, made the End (socialism) *also* the beginning, or the Beginning (communalism) also the End, but which really amounted to inserting African communalism into the grand narrative as both Beginning *and* End. This was perhaps the deeper meaning of claiming, as Nyerere did: 'We, in Africa, have no more need of being "converted" to socialism than we have of being "taught" democracy. Both are rooted in our own past – in the traditional society which produced us' (1967b: 170).

Of course, these are primarily identitarian moves and the very reason why scientific socialists, who were more concerned with changing material living conditions than with restoring dignity through a politics of recognition, could dismiss African Socialism as a bourgeois pastime, as a simple question of trivial 'national self-confidence' (Babu 1981: 53). It is also the reason why Babu could provocatively title his tirade against Nyerere *African Socialism or Socialist Africa?* and why some scientific socialists warned that 'if we are not careful the word "socialism" will be emptied of its meaning and bourgeois systems of the most reactionary kind will be able to camouflage themselves under the sign of socialism' (Keita in Mohiddin 1981: 15).

However, to dismiss as identitarian a certain political gesture does not exhaust what there is to be said about it. Considered in terms of the Revolutionary conceptual persona, African Socialists embodied what was most empathetic about a certain way of connecting thinking and being Africa(n) at the time; *empathetic* because it attempted to do what was epistemically impossible, namely to articulate the African self as equal within an historic a priori that could only interpret who that self was and what it had to offer in terms of its own linear developmentalism; that is, as a sign of Africa's radical inequality.[3] This urgency to do what was impossible was the pivot around which the debate between African and scientific socialists turned, in which yet again, we recognise the *aporia of the untimely* that we have already encountered twice before in the preceding chapters. I want to spend some time on this aporia, in order to lay the foundation for the analysis of the question of violence that follows.

---

3. There are suggestions of an equivalence according to which Africa, like the West, has indeed gone through feudalism and capitalism and, like the West, is trying to find its way to socialism. For instance, Nyerere's *Arusha Declaration* states: 'Tanzania is a nation of peasants but is not yet a socialist society. *It still contains* elements of feudalism and capitalism – with their temptations' (1967a: 5, emphasis added).

The untimely: Between memory and possibility

Our first encounter with the untimely was with reference to Frantz Fanon's claim that the recognition of the ethical will be untimely in those instances when a revolutionary suspense of both ethics and the political order is called for, so as to bring about the truly ethical as foundation for a new, politically just order. The second instance was when, following Arif Dirlik, I argued that what Achille Mbembe glosses over in his critique of historicism in postcolonial African studies is that *at the time* of adopting certain nationalist (teleological) and/or nativist positions, the criticism that in doing so, liberation fighters were simply replicating colonial categories of nation, class and race 'would have been impossible to entertain . . . [because] a unified national entity [premised on the "myth" of race and Africanness] was the only conceivable agent capable of overthrowing colonialism and withstanding its ravages' (Dirlik 2002: 613).

At the heart of the project of emancipation is the need to address both material conditions and psychological recognition, of having to realise recognition through political freedom, *while* bringing about the socio-economic conditions that will make that political freedom meaningful. It is a trite comment on the Marxist distinction between a first and second transition that political freedom without an accompanying improvement in material conditions is empty, but it is equally true that an improvement in living conditions without the accompanying recognition of one's humanity would also be meaningless. In retrospect, the debate between African and scientific socialists appears to be less a debate and is rather two arguments working different sides of an aporetic impasse: *at the time*, nothing seemed more urgent than an Marxist-motivated improvement in material conditions but, *at the same time*, the grand narrative of social evolution invoked to militate for that improvement did so on the back of a historicism that did nothing to gain recognition for Africa in the eyes of the former colonial powers. If an African Socialist such as Nyerere overestimated the importance or the priority of recognition, it could be argued that scientific socialists underestimated it, by simply dismissing it as a matter of national self-confidence, as 'an idealistic view of the world [that] has little relevance to the real world . . . as it exists outside our consciousness' (Babu 1981: 57). In the context of a Western, modernist understanding of change as linear progress, African intellectuals would have had a very hard time forcing the European hand of recognition, by acknowledging that their communalism was merely a primitive stage of development in the grand-narrative realisation of socialism. In a very real sense then, the truth of the scientific socialists' claim was superseded by the fact that their claim was untimely.

In terms of the political work of recognition that African Socialists were trying to *perform*, to dismiss African communalism as a primitive stage of development and to argue for the insertion of the newly independent states into the grand-narrative march of the universal proletariat was untimely, in the precise sense that it threatened with *inexecution* the founding moment of postcolonial modernity, when newly born states had to perform themselves into a Western-dominated modernist discourse of equality, understood in terms of self-determination, autonomy and sovereignty.[4] That they could only execute this modernity on the basis of a range of contradictions and paradoxes, of which the undecidable status of African Socialism as both (r)evolutionary Beginning and End is a prime example, was symptomatic of a condition perhaps best described as *hypermodernity*. I say more about this in the last chapter, but a short digression here is indispensable for framing the question of violence that concerns this chapter.

Hypermodernity and the (im)possibility of the founding

For the purposes of this chapter, we can identify as an instance of hypermodernity the peculiar paradox that shadowed the embrace of African Socialism as ideology. This paradox consisted in the self-conscious recognition of the *need* to embrace African Socialism and of the fact that doing so would amount to a declaration of independence of sorts, accompanied by an equally self-conscious recognition of the complete lack of consensus on what African Socialism actually *meant*. We can only understand this willingness to embrace an ideology that has as yet no meaning in terms of a difference between constative and performative claims. Constative claims *say* something about the world, while performative claims *do* something in the world. At the time when African leaders embraced African Socialism, the claim that 'we have African Socialism' was not a constative claim, for the simple reason that it did not refer to an existing theory or tradition. Nobody could say what it meant. Rather, the claim was a performative one, a claim designed to effect something in the world, namely to state or assert and thereby to *perform* an African identity, at once different from both the capitalist West and socialist East.

---

4. The picture is, of course, more complex than this because the post-Second World War state system was not simply dominated by the West. What the West did manage to do successfully, though, was to persuade post-independence African leaders that they somehow had to 'choose between independence and Marxism' (Babu 1981: 36–7) – as if joining the evil Russian empire amounted to a renunciation of sovereignty in a way that submitting to the Bretton Woods monetary system would not.

At the moment when a political order is founded, the relationship between the constative and performative is quite complex and can perhaps best be described in terms of a 'performative tautology', which tries to conceal the emptiness of its constative founding claim ('We the people . . .') with performances to the contrary. We know, at least since Ernst Renan's 'What is a Nation?' (1990), that somewhere in the history of any political collective, we can identify the precise moment when a collection of individual persons or states first came to think of themselves in terms of a collective – typically, when a first history of the people was written and published or, in the case of revolutionary overthrow, when the people adopt a Constitution prefaced by the statement, 'We the people . . .' or, as in this case, when it is claimed that 'we are African Socialists'. However, as pointed out by Emmanuel Joseph Sieyès in *What is the Third Estate?* (1963 [1789]), Hannah Arendt in *On Revolution* (1963) and Jacques Derrida in *Force of Law* (1992a), at the precise moment of founding, when the collective first speaks on behalf of a We, the We does not yet exist. On the contrary, it is only through the iteration of this claim over time – through the continued singing of the national anthem and the celebration of national events and so on – that the We will eventually come into being, so that the collective can start acting, not *as if* they were a We, but simply *as* a collective We. Formulated differently, at the time of its articulation, the original statement, 'We the people', has no constative truth because the We it refers to does not yet exist. The statement does not say something about the world. Instead, it *does* something. It is a performance in time and as such should be interpreted as a performative statement that, while making us believe that there is a We, will actually only perform the We into existence *over time*. People and peoples alike become the collective identity they embrace through the perpetual performance of that identity – which means that somewhere near the origin of nations where that identity is adopted, somewhere near the first performance of that claim, we invariably find a double-thinking at work: *We assume to already be what We will only become over time.*[5]

What makes this relationship between the constative and performative and their combination as performative tautology truly complex is the fact that the double-thinking logic of the performative tautology has to remain invisible to those

---

5. Think, for instance, of the 1994, SABC 1 jingle, 'Simunye: we are one'. For a discussion, see Praeg (2010b).

participating in the moment of the founding, for the simple reason that any self-conscious awareness of the double-thinking at work would threaten the eventual formation of the We with *inexecution*. To put it crudely: the success of the performative claim wholly depends on its not being recognised as such. Any recognition of the vacuity of the constative claim and the superficiality of the performative iteration will threaten with *inexecution* the founding moment. Where the origin is transparent to itself, where we cannot but recognise the performative for what it is, different strategies have to be deployed to effect or execute the founding – one of which, I contend, is the violence of pure force or enforcement. And that is the violence of the Ujamaa project that I am concerned with here.

In the case of African Socialism, the performative tautology or double-thinking that accompanied the founding of the postcolonial state manifested in the adoption of an ideology by a range of African intellectuals who, while they publicly agreed on the necessity of adopting African Socialism (because doing so would perform independence), nonetheless admitted that there was no *doctrinal clarity on what African Socialism meant*. In other words, the doctrine of African Socialism was accepted or posited *as fact*, in order to make a politico-identitarian statement that would *perform* independence, self-reliance, authenticity and separation from the West, in a way that quite self-consciously recognised the pure performativity of doing so. In effect, we accept this ideology, not because we agree on what it means, but because doing so *makes a difference*. This priority of the identitarian performance over constative truth is clearly articulated by Onuoha: 'African Socialism is an expression of the desire of all Africans to *find* themselves, *be* themselves, and *assert* themselves. It is a crystallization of the African genius and a declaration of ideological independence in a world flooded with learned masters' (1965: 30). Should we be at all surprised that many commentators and writers preferred then, as they still do, to think of African Socialism as a form of nationalism?

The lack of agreement on what African Socialism meant at the precise moment when it was adopted as an identity marker produced a range of curious statements that were at worst, paradoxical and at best, self-contradictory – such as the claim by the chair of Democratic African Socialism and its Challenges, organised by the East African Institute of Social and Cultural Affairs in Nairobi, 1–6 February 1964: 'Is there such a thing as "African Socialism"? There is agreement that there are no socialist societies in existence yet in East Africa . . . In so far as this form of socialism differs from other forms of socialism it is legitimate to speak of African Socialism' (in Onuoha 1965: 89) – and open to future determination, such as the formal, identitarian definition of African Socialism adopted at the same event: 'African Democratic Socialism means democratic socialism as conceived by Africans in Africa, evolving from the African way of life and formulated in particular terms as *the result of a continuing examination* of African society' (108, emphasis added).

What I am emphasising here is that fundamentally at work in this embrace of African Socialism was *the performativity of the founding* as political statement, an identitarian performance that explains why 'some African political leaders could describe themselves as socialists, or publicly commit their countries to the socialist pattern of development, without really and seriously meaning either, alternatively [to] ... go ahead with a socialist pattern of development for his country without having to label it as such' (Mohiddin 1981: 14).

But it is one thing to make a performative gesture in order to make a difference. It is quite another to self-consciously *know* that one is making a performative gesture in order to make a difference, for that self-consciousness will threaten with inexecution the very difference that needs to be made. The problem here is the transparency to itself of a founding that needs to remain opaque and invisible for, as Blaise Pascal, citing Michel de Montaigne, warns us: 'Whoever traces [custom] to its source annihilates it' (in Derrida 1992a: 12). In the case of the postcolonial state, this self-conscious awareness of what needed to remain invisible, in order to be executed, amounts to a form of *hyper*modernity that leaves only two options for a successful execution of the founding. The first consists in exaggerating the performativity of the founding gesture, to *will* the performance of the origin, despite its transparency to itself, and to *act as if* the origin is not threatened with inexecution by self-conscious identity politics – as Harold Bloom comments in his introduction to Miguel de Cervantes's *Don Quixote*: 'A fiction, believed in even though you know it is a fiction, can be validated only by sheer will' (Bloom 2003: xxvii). The second option consists in the violent enforcement of the founding.

The power of the as-if

Nyerere understood both the dilemma of hypermodernity and the first solution very well – as we can see from the manner in which he tried to effect the founding of a United States of Africa at a time when, from his perspective, that possibility had become mired in too much talking and not enough doing. The power of the *as-if*, he effectively argued, could put a stop to all the procrastination and obliterate the untimely self-consciousness that threatened this potential founding with inexecution. In a 1963 article, 'How to Overcome the Transition That Will One Day Lead to the Formation of a United States of Africa', Nyerere writes: 'But there is only one way for us really to deal with this transitional problem. That is for us all to act now *as if we already have unity*' (1967b: 192, emphasis added). If ever there were an articulation of the challenges of hypermodernity, it is this desire to 'overcome the transition'. What does it mean to 'overcome' a transition? Obviously there were a lot of real political concerns and policy questions that complicated the adoption of a political framework for a United States of Africa, not to mention the obvious tension between pan-Africanists and those who supported Western-style sovereign states. But I think Nyerere was already grappling with a different, additional issue relating to the condition of hypermodernity, an issue that haunted both African Socialism and the notion of a United States of Africa as forms of cultural, even racial, nationalism.

In political discourse, this gap between the founding-as-promise and the eventual founding that is realised through repetition of the original promise, is referred to as an *interregnum*. Over and above all the real political complications and the lack of consensus in this debate on a future United States of Africa, the interregnum is the problem that Nyerere is acutely aware of, the 'problem of the transition' he is trying to find a solution to: how to escape the self-conscious recognition of a moment as a moment of transition when no founding myth can be appealed to in order to drive the transition by making it seem inevitable? How to find, amidst all this self-conscious identity politics, the necessary blindness that will allow for an unreflective or unself-conscious passage through the interregnum? In short, how does one find a transition through the transition? Or, how does one execute a founding that is recognised, in advance, as a founding? For Nyerere, there is only one solution to this aporia of the self-conscious interregnum, which is 'for us all to act now *as if we already have unity*' (1967b: 192, emphasis added).

Hypermodernity, then, is constantly threatened by the *inexecution* resulting from an untimely self-consciousness. Where would European modernity be if it too were shadowed *from its inception* – and not as a result of it – by a human rights discourse? Where would European modernity be without colonialism and the transatlantic slave trade – the inhumanity of which returned to haunt the imperial project *after* its execution, after having been instrumental in the founding of that modernity? What is distinct about postcolonial modernity, then, is the fact that the performative tautology, which would otherwise allow for the creation and execution of its collective will, remains visible to the collective *as* tautology. The self-consciously recognised lack of agreement among African Socialists on what the doctrine meant was always already understood as sign of something else, namely the abysmal superficiality of identity politics and the need to embrace an ideology, in order to perform a difference that could not be substantiated with any degree of satisfaction. In this instance, to continue to act *as if* African Socialism meant something, to keep iterating the same set of claims over and over, in the hope that doing so would, in the long run, perform consensus on their meaning, to attempt a negotiation of the founding of African Socialism in the way Nyerere suggested the founding of the United States of Africa be negotiated, *that* solution to the problem of hypermodernity was not going to work. Nyerere would discover that it could only work if, and for so long as, the performative *as if* of its invention were accompanied, bolstered and given effect by the second solution to the challenge of hypermodernity, namely to plug the hole created by self-conscious identity politics with the violence of enforcement. This violence, in order to find its own internal or immanent legitimation, had to derive internally from the ideology itself, for the simple reason that an ideology such as African Socialism that desperately tried to naturalise itself could not appeal for its legitimation to anything beyond itself.

My aim in the remainder of this chapter is not to offer a critique of the Ujamaa project from a scientific socialist perspective. Readers who are interested in such critiques are referred to the work of, among others, Babu and Shivji.[6] My aim is somewhat different, namely to offer an internal critique of the manner in which Nyerere constructed the Ujamaa ideology through a process of violent enforcement that depended on the twin strategies of the *ban* and *supplement* for its execution, a process that implicitly relied on the constitutive violence of the precolonial political economy of obligation, transposed to the level of ideology.

The ban
For Igor Kopytoff (1964), it is pertinently not the case that we can simply equate traditional African communalism with socialism because the central claim of African Socialism simply does 'not square with the empirically discovered reality' (in Sprinzak 1973: 629). Once we delve beneath the image of Africa offered by Revolutionary myth-makers such as Nyerere, we discover that precolonial African

---

6. See Babu (1981) and Shivji (1973, 1976, 2006a, 2006b, 2008, 2009); see also Von Freyhold (1979).

societies were indeed stratified and had developed different degrees of co-operation, alongside various forms of individual ownership. In other words, we discover that they were not simply communal. The subtle stratifications of precolonial African societies are obscured when philosophies such as Ubuntu or ideologies such as African Socialism are used reductively; when, through a form of auto-violation, we exclude from our image of precolonial Africa those forms of individualism and stratification, notably class, that complicate the picture. Nonetheless, this often happens and when it does, it is through a 'ban' of stratification and individualism from the image of precolonial Africa that the idea of a communalism as synecdoche of precolonial African societies emerges. The logic of the ban is of course closely related to the conceptual violence of the definitional circularity regularly deployed to reinvent Ubuntu as redemptive communalism.

Here is an example of the ban at work. In his 1961 article, 'The African and Democracy', Nyerere challenges the idea that precolonial Africa was not egalitarian. He does so through an essentially nativist distinction between true or original and untrue and foreign Africans, in which class differences are associated with the latter, in order to construct the egalitarian nature of all truly African precolonial societies: 'In my own country, the only two tribes which have a distinct aristocracy are the Bahaya in Bukoba, and the Baha in the Buha districts. In both cases the "aristocrats" are historically foreigners, and they belong to the same stock' (1967b: 103).

What the logic of nativism invariably reproduces is the cultural equivalent of what Paulin Hountondji calls the 'myth of primitive unanimity' (1996: 60): the collapse of the subtle differentiations between individual and society and between various societies, a process, Kopytoff argues, which ironically borrows its categories 'from an old European social mythology whose origins could well be traced back to the "noble savage" and other idyllic images of the spontaneous tribal society' (in Sprinzak 1973: 629–30). We can avoid this danger by using the phrases 'traditional African society' or 'precolonial communalism' self-reflexively in a manner that retains a meta-critical awareness of the pitfalls of reasoning. Here, a distinction suggested by Ehud Sprinzak is useful. At the level of *institutional comparison*; that is, as far as their social and political institutions were concerned, we can say that, despite subtle differentiations, an image of precolonial societies emerges as *predominantly* communal or communalist. Here communalism functions as what Max Weber called a pure type or abstract generalisation that, although not absolutely or consistently true, remains a useful concept to work with, on the proviso that we remain attentive to instances where the theory we construct on this basis is troubled by the facts. A pure or ideal type 'is an intellectual tool, a mental model designed to make historical reality more comprehensible – without it being necessary for there to have been any complete or perfect implementation of the construct in the real world' (Todorov 2003: 6).

At the level of pure type, there can be said to have been predominantly communal ownership of land, a low degree of stratification and an extensive network of obligations, suggestive of a society that prioritises social relations over the pursuit of individual interests (Friedland and Rosberg 1964: 5), while in empirical reality there may not have been complete equality, since 'some societies developed "castes" and others "aristocracies"; many had private property of cattle and other goods, and certainly there were both poor and well-to-do members of the same community' (Sprinzak 1973: 636). Such attentiveness to the subtle interplay between communalism and individualism, between equality and stratification, encourages us to ask much more sophisticated questions about African humanism that will eschew the Saviour rhetoric of damning individualism and salvific communalism. In addition, it will also liberate Ubuntu *qua* critical humanism for application in/to contemporary postcolonial African societies, where we find some of the most inhumane and pernicious forms of frenetic individualism devised to protect the interests of the few from the needs of the many.

Nyerere, however, appropriated ujamaa with anything but such a self-critical awareness or provisionality. Quite the contrary, the twin logic of the ban and supplement were deployed to naturalise Ujamaa as ujamaa writ large. As a first step in retracing the process through which this translation unfolded, we may note that one of the first things many African intellectuals did in their attempt to give substance to the 'African' in African Socialism involved an abstraction away 'from the [comparison of] formal institutions to the psychological or attitudinal aspects of the theory' (Sprinzak 1973: 637). For example, in his 'Ujamaa: The Basis of African Socialism', Nyerere explicitly focuses not on an institutional comparison, but on socialism as an attitude of mind. As he explains: 'Socialism – like democracy – is an attitude of mind. In a socialist society it is the socialist attitude of mind, and not the rigid adherence to a standard political pattern, which is needed to ensure that the people care for each other's welfare' (1967b: 162). Typical of such a state of mind is a trust or vote of confidence in the social that, so it is argued, is completely absent in the mind of the acquisitive capitalist. Nyerere's elaboration on what this trust means for those who have acquired the right state of mind not only illustrates the point, but also confirms why we should take this thinking about African Socialism as an important point of reference in our thinking about Ubuntu:

> Apart from the anti-social effects of the accumulation of personal wealth, the very desire to accumulate it must be interpreted as a vote of 'no confidence' in the social system. For when a society is so organized that it cares about its individuals, then, provided he is willing to work, no individual, then within that society should worry about what will happen to him tomorrow if he does not hoard wealth today. Society itself should look after him, or his widow, or his orphans. This is exactly what traditional African society succeeded in doing. Both the 'rich' and the 'poor' individual were completely secure in African society. Natural catastrophe brought famine, but it brought famine to everybody – 'poor' or 'rich.' Nobody starved, either of food or of human dignity, because he lacked personal wealth; he could depend on the wealth possessed by the community of which he was a member. That was socialism. That is socialism (1967b: 164).

And that, we may also add, was ubuntu; that is ubuntu. Here I want to follow Sprinzak (and Robert Horton) in their analysis of the meaning and implication of this kind of soft talk about *socialism as a state of mind* because understanding it will, I think, reveal something important about the role, perhaps even the *inescapable* role, of violence in the translation of praxis into ideology.

Elaborations on socialism as a state of mind often start with a 'hard' or quasi-theoretical statement to the effect that what is specific about African Socialism is social fraternity and the pre-eminence of group interests over personal interests. Over this is layered additional 'soft talk' about how we should think about this pre-eminence of the social over the individual. Illustrative of the latter is Senghor's statement that precolonial African societies were 'collectivist or, more exactly, communal because it is rather a *communion* of souls than an aggregate of individuals' (in Sprinzak 1973: 631). Sprinzak takes this to imply that 'the emphasis here is on a type of fraternity that is expressed by the hegemony of the group over the individual . . . by the psychological deference of the individual to the collective norms of the social unity' (637). For Sprinzak, Sékou Touré's 'social fraternity, the pre-eminence of group interests over the personal interest' or Senghor's 'communion of souls' suggests, not the absence of conflict in precolonial African societies as much as the fact that conflicting opinions were 'not expressed ... in a counter-ideological form that might threaten accepted beliefs and social norms' (638).

Characteristic of an open society is the existence of a meta- or self-reflective discourse on the general rules that are followed, in order to distinguish between good and bad arguments, as well as in free speculation about what we can ever claim to know about the world. Horton's articulation of this difference is somewhat crude, but not without merit:

> The feasibility of raising these critical questions is what makes modern thinking, led by science, an 'open' system, ready to renounce old beliefs for new and better ones. The traditional system is 'closed,' both in the sense that it does not go beyond accepted beliefs and traditions, and that at the same time it knows the answers to everything (in Sprinzak 1973: 640).

Religion-based societies indeed have the answer to everything; science-based societies do not and that is the difference between a closed and an open society. This is complex and contested terrain. Among other things, we have to bear in mind that there is not one open society that was not at some stage a closed society. But I want to sidestep this volatile terrain by invoking the same right to generalisation that allows us to talk about African communalism as pure type. Open and closed, here, are no more than ahistorical, Weberian general types, according to which 'open' refers to societies that allow for, even encourage, meta- or self-reflexive, critical reflection on the ontological assumptions, on the basis of which the social is imagined and which is a condition for its reimagining. Such openness does not typify precolonial African societies, for 'the single most important claim of the "socialist" thesis is that the structure of social thinking of the traditional society in Africa was communal. The sense of this communality was the fact that no individual or group within that society developed a counter-ideology that might question traditional cultural norms' (Sprinzak 1973: 642).

While some may find such a description of precolonial societies problematic, the very idea that they were characterised by the absence of counter-ideological positions was, nonetheless, the sine qua non of the description of precolonial societies as socialist. We can take our cue here from Nyerere himself, for whom socialism in Africa was not the result of a long class struggle, but rather derived from the extended family structure, the socialist 'state of mind' of precolonial African societies. He writes:

> European socialism was born of the Agrarian Revolution and the Industrial Revolution which followed it. The former created the 'landed' and the 'landless' classes in society; the latter produced the modern capitalist and the industrial proletariat. These two revolutions planted the seeds of conflict within society, and not only was European socialism born of that conflict, but its apostles sanctified the conflict itself into a philosophy (1967b: 169).

In other words, a description of precolonial African societies in terms of the absence of conflict expressed in ideological terms is essential because therein lies the possibility of the analogy with socialism in the first instance. Recall that for Karl Marx in *The German Ideology* (published in 1846), the end of ideology will only come about when all antagonistic class relationships have finally been eliminated. All ideologies are class phenomena because they represent the interests of certain classes; ideologies rationalise, legitimise and defend the norms, values and interests of certain classes. Because ideologies express particular class interests, it follows that the classless society will also imply the end of ideology. In other words, socialism is not only characterised by the withering away of the state, but also by the end of all ideologies that, at the level of superstructure, justify and contest the necessity of the state. When the state withers away, so will all ideologies that historically supported or contested its existence. As a result, humanity will be redeemed of its alienated existence to find its true nature in an original, restored communality. In this projected or anticipated world after ideology lies the key to reading traditional African societies as essentially socialist.

Such societies were also characterised by an absence of conflict expressed in terms of ideological conflict and thus the similarity with socialism seems obvious. If the one-party state is the form of government par excellence, in which differences and conflicts are not allowed to assume ideological expression, this would explain why subsequent to independence this idea of government would have been at once so obviously alluring and problematic: *alluring* because it seemed to offer the possibility of seamless continuity, of carrying forth into the postcolonial political domain that which was most specific about precolonial societies, namely a unity conceived in terms of the absence of ideological conflict – society, in fact, as 'a direct extension of the family' (Nyerere 1967b: 105) – *problematic* because, in so doing, the one-party state effectively attempted to ontologise politics in communal terms at the very moment when modernity was continuing the individualising of the social and political domains – a process which, in Tanzania, had started even before colonialism and which could only be sustained *by violently enforcing an out-of-step conception of democracy as familial praxis*. By the phrase 'ontologise politics in communal terms', I mean to suggest that where the possibility of critically interrogating the moral and ontological basis of society is foreclosed, an individualised notion of personal independence and its expression, in terms of or *as* a healthy ideological difference, cannot be imagined. In a world where, to quote from one of the more problematic sources in African philosophy, Placide Tempels's *Bantu Philosophy*, 'moral standards depend essentially on things ontologically understood' (1969: 121), it follows that the 'compliance of the individual member with the social and religious norms of the group is not, therefore, a matter of choice but one of necessity or inevitability' (Sprinzak 1973: 640).

When African theorists equated precolonial African communalism with socialism to signify a continuation with the past, their reappropriation of communalism as socialism was never simply the continuation of that praxis of interdependence, but rather a translation of that praxis into a contemporary ideology that had to be defined, constructed and propped up by political and juridical measures that excluded ideological contestation, because that would have meant a violation of what was taken to be essential about African societies as socialist *avant la lettre*; in short, ujamaa praxis had necessarily to be *enforced* as Ujamaa ideology because the lack of ideological conflict that constituted ujamaa could no longer be assumed to exist in the latter. Here is a simple example of how the technologies of discipline that were constitutive of a political economy of obligation were transmuted into a conscious ban of difference, expressed in ideological terms. Nyerere effectively romanticises ujamaa as a political economy of obligation:

> Those of us who talk about the African way of life and, quite rightly, take a pride in maintaining the tradition of hospitality which is so great a part of it, might do well to remember the Swahili saying: '*Mgeni siku mbili; siku ya tatu mpe jembe*' – or in English, 'Treat your guest as a guest for two days; on the third day give him a hoe!' In actual fact, the guest was likely to ask for the hoe even before his host had to give him one – *for he knew* what was expected of him, and would have been ashamed to remain idle any longer (1967b: 165, emphasis added).

But by 1967, when it was already clear that socialism however conceived was not a natural developmental option and that the capitalist tendencies that had started even in precolonial Africa would grow exponentially if left unchecked, the *Arusha Declaration* turned this implicit, unreflective and unarticulated participation in a political economy of obligation and reciprocity ('for he knew . . .') into a policy-based admonishment, in which loitering and the exploitation of selflessness were equated with an exploitative and selfish capitalist frame of mind: 'Nobody *should* go and stay for a long time with his relative, doing no work, because in doing so he will be exploiting his relative' (1967a: 28, emphasis added). This 'should' amounts to nothing less than the acknowledgement that, in the 1960s, people no longer knew what they needed to know in order for memories of communalism to be naturalised as socialism.[7] People no longer acted spontaneously on the basis of communitarian principles. Instead, like a virus, the capitalist frame of mind had taken root in large sections of the popular imagination and something more than Revolutionary memory was necessary to reinvent communitarian praxis as nationalist ideology, to project ujamaa as Ujamaa. Understanding what that something was will reveal the relationship between the logic of the ban and the role of violence as a necessary supplement in the translation of praxis into ideology. To set the stage for such an analysis, we need to briefly retrace the history of Tanzania.

The supplement
In 1885 Germany colonised Tanganyika and ruled until 1918 when, following the country's defeat in the First World War, the territory came under British administration as a League of Nations mandate. The Germans never intended to settle Tanganyika, but rather to use it for exploitation-plantation. Peasant farmers were actively encouraged to grow cash crops – if only because the governor of the time, Albrecht Freiherr von Rechenberg, saw economic grievances as the greatest threat to German supremacy and thought it better if the peasants were able to sustain themselves economically. The British administration continued this emphasis on farming, but for different, more liberal reasons. For Sir Horace Byatt, the first British administrator, the 'future of the country lay in developing native cultivation only' (in Mohiddin 1981: 42). In this way, cash-crop farming became an export-size business that assured the African peasant farmer a place in the national economy. The second governor, Sir Donald Cameron, similarly insisted that 'the

---

7. Wiredu (2002: 293–4) describes a similar trajectory.

African [be] developed politically on lines suitable to the state of society and natural environment in which he lives and must continue to live' (43). As a result, when in 1930, the British officially adopted a policy of indirect rule with regard to Tanganyika, 'it was insisted that African social and political institutions should... constitute the basis for Africans' development' (44). This paternalism was balanced by a continued appreciation of the need for and benefit of Western-style education as part of the logic of tutelage. Through education, Africans were exposed to British values and by the time of independence in 1961, Tanganyika had been firmly integrated into the international capitalist system as an export economy, dependent on the importation of European commodities. This induction of the country into the global capitalist system was complemented by some interesting internal developments:

> The unhindered development of the peasant cash economy did, in its own way and speed, bring about social differentiation within the rural population. The efficient or enterprising peasant farmer, employing family or clan labour, progressively became richer than his less enterprising neighbours. With capital (money) accumulated from the sale of his crops, the enterprising peasant gradually acquired more land to put under cultivation and hired more labour to work on it. This kind of capital accumulation, which was responsible for the rise of the 'kulaks' (rich peasant farmers), *had its beginnings much earlier than the Western colonial impact*. It was these enterprising peasant farmers who sustained the Arab-Swahili slave caravans, and also supplied Zanzibar with virtually all her food supplies (Mohiddin 1981: 46, emphasis added).

This development of a capitalist economy before colonialism had two important implications: first, many farmers 'increased the acreage under their cultivation and employed more and more labour, thus initiating the evolution of a land-owning class and the beginning of employed rural labour' (Mohiddin 1981: 46); second, a class of African traders emerged to locate and market crops. As a result, while the British did not directly interfere with the traditional land-tenure system, these developments placed a lot of pressure on that system so that, by the 1940s, it was slowly losing its meaning and prevalence. In short, 'by the time the British attempted to bring about radical changes in the method of agriculture and in the traditional system of land tenure, these internal differentiations were already in evidence'

(48), so that the introduction of a capitalist economy by the British became a matter of converting already existing trends into the kind of policies that had

> the inevitable effect of producing precisely that type of farmer who valued his land and who wished to improve it. Thus, as a by-product if not by a design, a landed African class was being created and it was the members of this class who eventually joined TANU in a bid to achieve the political independence of Tanganyika (Mohiddin 1981: 48–9).

By the 1950s, no doubt influenced by the Swynnerton Plan adopted in neighbouring Kenya as well as the Report of the Royal Commission, which both advocated developing individual land ownership, the British embraced a more aggressive policy, aimed at destroying the communal system of land tenure. Evolution in that direction was no longer sufficient; it had to be actively encouraged. But when, as an initial step, the government proposed a fundamental overhaul of the land ownership system that existed on the back of the Land Ordinance of 1923, in order to encourage and facilitate land-transfers, it encountered two fundamental oppositions: first, from the wealthy cash-crop farmers in Tanganyika, who feared competition from Kenya where white settlers had already acquired most of the land; second, 1954 saw the founding of TANU, headed by the 'most articulate, consistent and effective socialist ideologue of the party' – Nyerere (Mohiddin 1981: 50).

At its annual conference in 1958, TANU formally condemned the government's attempts to introduce private ownership of land. As a result of this development, much of Tanganyika's land-tenure system was still intact at independence. In fact, 'apart from the internal changes brought about by the development of cash-crop farming, *the principles governing the ownership of land*, as well as its utilisation, were still based on African traditions' (Mohiddin 1981: 51, emphasis added). Given Nyerere's determination to stifle any further class differentiation, Tanganyika became independent with a very weak African middle class. Importantly, Nyerere assumed that 'in spite of the colonial impact the extended family was still basically intact, although he admitted that the institution would collapse if no measures were taken to counteract the pressures against it' (52). In other words, the principles that governed communal land ownership or familyhood (ujamaa) could still be saved and used as cultural capital for development, but only if familyhood were not left to its own devices, only if it could somehow be transposed into an ideology of Familyhood, or Ujamaa.

The process through which this was to be achieved in a way that would insert Africa into the global economy, while fulfilling a local identitarian demand for authenticity, can be broken down into three steps: (1) the precapitalist (not simply precolonial) was identified as locus or source of an original or natural socialism, which Nyerere argued could be mined for principles that could function as the cultural capital needed to fuel the quest for development and the need for an authentic African identity; (2) from this precapitalist, ujamaa praxis, three principles of human communality were abstracted that were then (3) recast as the cornerstone for a postcolonial ideology of Ujamaa. In *Freedom and Unity*, Nyerere is clear about what these three principles were. Prior to capitalism,

> there was an attitude of mutual respect and obligation which bound the members together – an attitude which might be described as *love*, provided it is understood that this word does not imply romance, or even necessarily close personal affection. The property which is important to the family, and thus to the individual members of it, is held *in common*. And every member of the family accepts the obligation to *work* (1967b: 8–9, emphasis added).

Love, sharing and work (Nyerere 1967b: 13; see also Babu 1981: 55) – these were the three principles that informed precapitalist African societies and which had to be reconstituted as African Socialism in postcolonial Tanzania.[8] For Nyerere, what made such a translation of praxis into ideology desirable was the fact that 'the principles which worked in this one case are equally valid for larger societies because, however large it is, men are always the purpose and justification of society' (1967b:

---

8. In 1963 the TANU national executive decided that Tanganyika would become a one-party state. The Presidential Commission tasked with investigating the implications of this decision was provided with documentation submitted by the president, in which the three principles of love, sharing and labour do not appear explicitly, but are combined under the rubric of a 'national ethic'. In 1962 Nyerere had already advanced the idea of a national ethic when he spoke on the proposal for a republican Constitution for Tanganyika. He argued that Constitutions are not foolproof and that only a national ethic can protect the people against tyranny (1967b: 174–5). Whether such an ethic amounts to a nationalism without the state, one that would enable a perpetual revolution against statism, corruption and elitism (the seemingly inevitable consequences of any revolution that culminates in state-making) cannot be explored here. The last two chapters of this book explore Ubuntu similarly as a national ethic, supplementary to the Constitution.

12). In other words, all human collectivities have the same purpose, namely to increase human welfare and flourishing. We enter into society because it is only through collective effort that we can satisfy the basic needs of security and well-being. In order to enable that association, we have to forfeit incompatible needs driven by self-interest. To this, end the principles of love, sharing and work form 'the only basis on which society can hope to operate harmoniously and in accordance with its purpose'. Because precapitalist African society practised these three principles to achieve this end, they can be reappropriated as abstract principles to do the same in a postcolonial context.

More ambitiously, Nyerere generalised these principles as the only ones upon which *any* human society can be founded. As he put it: 'The question to ask is not whether [these principles] are capable of achievement, which is absurd, but whether a society of free men can do without them' (1967b: 13). This universalist claim only apparently contradicts the identitarian claim to have uncovered a precolonial self that is uniquely African because Nyerere's idea of what it means for Africa to be unique is more ambitious than one expects. By making the principles of love, sharing and work fundamental to the very idea of human society, the Africa of Nyerere's imagination becomes foundational to the very possibility of human society as such, affording us a glimpse of the messianic teleology that always shadows African modes of self-writing in the conceptual personae of Revolutionary and Saviour. However, Nyerere admits:

> There are very great problems involved in adapting the principles to really large units where individual brotherhood and interdependence is not as immediately obvious as in the family unit. But they are still the only basis on which society can hope to operate harmoniously and in accordance with its purpose. Unless they are adopted there will always be an inherent, although sometimes concealed, danger of a breakdown in society – that is, *a split in the family unit, a civil war within a nation, or a war between nations* (1967b: 12, emphasis added).

In a postcolonial world where people no longer remember what they need to know in order for communalism to simply reappear as socialism, the threats of fratricide and civil strife are very real and need to be legislated against. For Nyerere, the best way to do this consisted in taking from precapitalist society not only the three *principles* of love, sharing and labour, but also the *idea* of a communal or socialist society, in which difference is never expressed in ideological terms. This meant banning from the Kingdom of Fraternal Unity the very logic of ascending individualism and its ideological representation. How we theorise this ban is a complex question. My suggestion is that in a postcolonial setting, unity conceived as fraternity (the nation as extended family writ large), this Familial Ideology or Fraternal Socialism needs a fourth principle to account for and sustain the holy trinity of love, sharing and work as a coherent ideology, a fourth principle that would make the construction of a Socialist Ideology possible, but without necessarily being recognised as one of its principles – in short, a necessary supplement. What this fourth, shadowy principle is becomes clear when we note the manner in which, according to Nyerere, the coherence of love, sharing and work was always sustained as familial praxis (ujamaa):

> The child is *indoctrinated* with [the three principles] in practical terms . . . And he is *criticised and punished* if he disregards the courtesies due to other members of the social group [read: when s/he fails to love], or fails to share the remaining food with a late-comer [fails to share], or ignores the small duties entrusted to him [fails to work] (1967b: 14, emphasis added).

If love, sharing and work are positive principles, they nonetheless only function coherently because of a fourth principle, which can be described as indoctrination, technologies of discipline or benevolent cultural practices of coercion.[9] More so, this fourth principle of coercion is in a sense more fundamental that the first three because it is the condition for their possibility. The fourth is a negative principle, in the sense that it is an unarticulated absence that defines what is present; it is the negativity through which the positive news of love, sharing and work is made possible, created, ingrained in the individual and sustained as cultural praxis (habitus). Where indoctrination, criticism and punishment are embodied in cultural practices, ritualised admonishments and the like function to *ban* certain forms of behaviour, while *filtering* into the social domain other, more desirable forms of behaviour. It embodies the kind of *coercion* that we associate with the reproduction of culture and tradition. My argument is simple: this fourth, implicit principle was

---

9. Similarly, in a Heritage Day opinion piece in the *Cape Times* on 28 September 2009, Simphiwe Sesanti wrote of the need to educate children to be 'true Africans' so that they 'will know from an early age that it is culturally offensive when one child eats bread . . . without offering it to the one who is without' (in Douglas 2010: 22).

constitutive of ujamaa/ubuntu praxis and is as essential for the reconstitution of that praxis as ideology or philosophy as the three explicitly articulated principles.

This fourth principle can best be described in terms of its function, which is to *filter, ban, coerce*. These are not separate functions, but various manifestations of the same principle, depending on whether one is considering the way it works in articulating and constructing an ideology, formulating policy or implementing a development programme. By *filtering*, I mean that socialism as a Western ideology is used here as a lens or filter through which to decipher and retrodict the past. If one approaches precolonial (here, precapitalist) communalism as essentially socialist, one will only see what is socialist about it and filter out what is not (for example, pre-existing and evolving class differentiations). Onuoha is quite explicit about this. Having offered a short, general description of traditional African societies, he continues:

> The fore-going general statements about African life are obviously selective. Among African traditions and values, some of which are positive and others negative, we have mentioned only those that are positively socialist in order that, later on, these may be called upon to serve as the basis of a new, twentieth century *African* Socialism (1965: 35–6).

The circularity is astounding: Africa will be decoded *as* socialist so that we can show that it always *was* socialist. We can refer to this particular dimension of retrodiction as *theoretical filtering*. African Socialism filtered out numerous features of precolonial African society incompatible with socialism, in order to filter in the three principles of love, sharing and labour.

As Nyerere admitted, however, an ideological construct is not sufficient for postcolonial Africa, where people no longer live in a world of interdependence as praxis. People have forgotten that *one simply does not* live off friends for days without taking up the hoe; they now need to be reminded that *one should not*. This is symptomatic of the virus of capitalist individualism and self-interest that has taken root in a part of the Tanzanian imagination. As a result, the ever-present threats of fratricide and civil war, in short, *difference expressed as ideology*, loom. This is where the fourth principle manifests its second function, namely the *ban*. Babu critically articulated this logic of the ban in Nyerere's thinking. After listing the three principles of love, sharing and work (1981: 55), he goes on to state what would be required to make them function coherently as ideology:

Since these traditional principles (the argument goes), which kept the family and the community together, are thus demonstrably desirable for the maintenance of social order and the well-being of the community, they must be made part of the educational system of the present just as they were part of the educational system of the past. In consequence, as these values have thus become desirable in themselves, they must be presented as general aspirations as a matter of policy, and *any expression of opposite views to these principles must be suppressed* (Babu 1981: 56).

In 1967 Nyerere released the *Arusha Declaration* – both a politico-ideological declaration of independence, as well as an identitarian promise to reconstitute the principles of love, sharing and labour as cornerstones of a truly African state. As such, it is the founding document for an officially socialist Tanzania and contains the rough outlines of what a utopian state premised on African Socialism would look like: there will be neither feudalism nor capitalism; no class differentiation; nationalised means of production; democratically elected representation; work for every able-bodied person, with salaries not grossly divergent; no exploitation of the undeveloped rural by the urbanised elite; no exploitation of women by men and so on. But at this point in Tanzania's history, this is no more than what Walter Benjamin called a 'wish image' (of the state that is yet to come), for there is a virus present at the founding that must be recognised, banned and instituted against. The *Declaration* admits the existence of classes in Tanzania, which, though considered weak, nonetheless have considerable potential for growth if left unchecked. Indeed, one primary objective of the *Declaration* is precisely that of 'preventing the property-owning and commercial classes from taking over political power in the country' (Mohiddin 1981: 83). And so, shortly after independence when Nyerere for the first time articulated his ideas on socialism in 'Ujamaa: The Basis of African Socialism', he made clear what this meant: 'The TANU Government must go back to the traditional African custom of landholding. That is to say, a member of society will be entitled to a piece of land on condition that he uses it. Unconditional, or "freehold" ownership of land ... *must be abolished*' (1967b: 167, emphasis added; see also the pamphlet, 'Mali ya Taifa', published in 1958).

The story of the ban on capitalist individualism is complex. According to Onuoha, 'no spokesman of African Socialism that we know of is opposed to free enterprise in principle' (1965: 77). Some embraced this on principle while others, such as Senghor and later Nyerere, embraced it simply as a way of not scaring off investors. Mohiddin, too, writes: 'Although at that time Tanzania's economy was not decidedly socialist, the official indications were clear that the preferred mode of future development would be socialist' (1981: 53). These socialist leaders, by contrast, would 'seek to work out a set of empirical principles that will indicate in a *particular* instance whether a specific *industry or service* is to be transferred to public ownership and control' (Ebenstein in Onuoha 1965: 119). In other words, there would be room for private enterprise, but not for excessive profiteering. The reason for this was that Senghor and Nyerere thought of the present in terms of the logic of the transition or interregnum discussed earlier, of 'living in a period of transition between monopolistic capitalism . . . and democratic socialism' (91).

As a result, it is fair to say that capitalism was banned as an ideology and general economic alternative, but at the same time very much relied upon by government itself to generate the profits necessary to finance the socialist development programme. Exactly this ambivalence is what made the exclusion of capitalism not an *exclusion* (which was never the intention), but a *ban*, in the precise sense theorised by Giorgio Agamben in *Homo Sacer* (1998): the person banned from a community remains a necessary supplement and, as such, central to its survival. Social cohesion is in part a function of the ban or exclusion of those who can be said to threaten or undermine it, but it is always a necessary ban because without it, the community can have no sense of itself. In this sense, the banished are always at once outside *and* central to the community they are banned from. The working of the fourth principle of constitutive violence demonstrates this logic. Banned from the official list of principles that Nyerere adopted from ujamaa in order to reconstruct Ujamaa, it was nonetheless the one principle indispensable to the realisation of love, sharing and work. It shadowed Ujamaa as ideology in much the same way that the banned individual shadows the community he or she is banned from, a community that only has a sense of purpose because of its relationship with the banned, the negative *we are not*. The banned principle of violence promised to actualise the founding of the state, to get Tanzania from here to there; that is, past the moment of the founding that threatened to remain inexecuted by the debilitating superficiality of a self-conscious identity politics.

In 1962 and in line with this complex ambition, the independent, TANU-led government of the one-party Tanzanian state declared freehold a foreign, unAfrican concept, incompatible with African tradition – despite the precolonial developments cited earlier. For the next three years, confusion reigned. Accepted was Tanzania's place in the capitalist world economy and the existence of limited private enterprise and foreign investment in the country, but this was not encouraged. While a limited form of capitalist practice was accepted – even practised by the government itself – capitalism as ideology was banned and, as a 'state of mind', effectively criminalised. In a speech delivered in China in February 1965, Nyerere commented: 'We inherited an economy linked and geared to the capitalist world, we are shaking off the restriction which that implied' (1967b: 323). Because of the complex mixture of capitalism in a devout socialist development plan and because capitalism was simultaneously banned and practised, we see the logic of the ban more clearly reflected in its inverse function, the logic of *coercion*.

Where the possibility of expressing difference in ideological terms does not exist, the *actions* of an individual no longer suffice to judge his/her commitment, morality or thinking. Where ideological differences are encouraged or at least allowed, one can judge somebody by the ideology they explicitly support, by what they do and say. Where it is not allowed, scrutiny of intention becomes the only way to ensure compliance with the sole remaining ideology; *intention* becomes the real criteria. Instead of judging somebody's lack of commitment by their overt actions, we perpetually interpret the covert intention of the individual: secure it, know it, have them confess it, illustrate it or interpret it as we wish – as Arendt so powerfully demonstrated in 'On the Nature of Totalitarianism' (1994). And this is what is deeply worrying about the 'soft' or psychological turn that accompanies all descriptions of African socialism as a 'way of life' or a 'state of mind', the suggestion that 'African Socialism must, therefore, be defined in psychological and sociological terms – in terms of a will, an attitude, a people, a conception of life' (Onuoha 1965: 123–4). The only way to ascertain whether or not somebody has reconciled themselves to socialism, whether they have become good, committed socialists and embraced it as a way of life, consists in introducing a series of malleable binaries that, as every totalitarian leader knows, remain infinitely open to interpretation: between committed and non-committed socialists, between those who have and those who have not *fully* embraced it as a way of life and promise never to 'live off the sweat of another man, nor *commit* any feudalistic or capitalistic actions' (in Mohiddin 1981: 85, emphasis added). As Nyerere stated in his public broadcast on becoming prime minister in March 1961:

> If you have cotton unpicked in your shamba, if you have cultivated half an acre less than you could cultivate, if you are letting the soil run needlessly off your land, or if your shamba is full of weeds, if you deliberately ignore

the advice given to you by the agricultural experts, then you are a traitor in the battle (1967b: 115).

This is socialism as psycho-juridical regime, in which to engage in or neglect duties, to show a lack of fervour, or be actively capitalist are all tantamount to *committing a crime* – in the words of Onuoha: 'African Socialism will deal firmly with saboteurs. African nationals who refuse to harmonize their freedom with national well-being will be given opportunity in prison to meditate on the reality of society and the absurdity of individualism' (1965: 131). This is individualism as a crime that can become visible as such only in a context of the coercive ideology of Familyhood/ Ujamaa. The signifiers of criminal individualism are all those activities – lack of love, sharing and work – that would amount to acts of betrayal in this war on poverty and underdevelopment. As Nyerere noted in his presidential inaugural address on 10 December 1962, with regard to the combined threat of poverty, famine and careless hygiene:

> These, then, are no mock-enemies; they are the true enemies of our people. And anybody who refuses to take part in this war, or who hinders the efforts of his neighbours, is guilty of helping a far more deadly foe than is he who helps an armed invader. So, I repeat, this war is a very real war; it is no sham battle in which we are engaged. I look to every citizen of our country to join in the fight. And anyone who interferes with our war-effort, I, for my part, shall look upon as a traitor and an enemy of our country (1967b: 177).

Nyerere was quick to defend himself against those who effectively, and in terms of the languages of their own discourses and analyses, pointed out what I am referring to here as a constitutive violence at work in the abstract level of ideology, by claiming that 'this is not a negation of the freedom which the principles claim to uphold' (1967b: 14). In saying this, he was both right and wrong. Right, because the principle of coercion does not simply negate the freedom made possible by love, sharing and work, but rather, in a limited sense, enables that freedom, makes it possible. But he was wrong to insist that 'freedom and well-being ... depend upon there being a generally accepted social ethic' (20). Freedom and well-being can indeed exist without a generally accepted social ethic. In fact, many would argue that it is exactly the absence of consensus on a social ethic that is sine qua non of freedom and well-being. Of course, if such consensus were to arise from the bottom up, it could be a form of social well-being. But this was top-down consensus, the reinvention of a logic of interdependence as ideology, which could only be constructed on the basis of a ban and its supplement. The consequence of all this was the institutionalisation of Ujamaa and its constitutive violence.

Violence writ large

In 1969 Tanzania published its second five-year development plan, one of the central components of which was the establishment of Ujamaa villages on the basis of extended family principles. Because it anticipated a lack of buy-in,

> the *Plan* ... admitted that although the development of the *Ujamaa* villages would be based on democratic principles and voluntary participation, TANU and the Government must endeavour strenuously to promote the acceptance of the ideal and the reality of *Ujamaa* villages. This must be done because 'the tendency towards capitalist development in the rural areas is unlikely to be checked without a vigorous initiative being mounted' (Mohiddin 1981: 148).

Because of these capitalist tendencies, the government opted for a 'frontal', rather than a gradual or 'selective' implementation of the Ujamaa scheme, a full-scale mobilisation of rural communities all at once. The government envisaged the establishment of these villages in three stages: (1) formative: when a group of farmers, after 'some persuasion' (Mohiddin 1981: 149), would agree to join and form an Ujamaa village; (2) when the farmers would have acquired a thorough understanding of the advantages of living and working together, in other words when they have *re*appropriated the tradition of loving, sharing and labour in the ideological terms of socialism; (3) when the Ujamaa village would have proven itself economically viable and 'self-reliant'. In retrospect and through the lens of postmodern irony, the creation of these villages resembles nothing more than the self-conscious construction of a precolonial theme park; large-scale Ujamaa/Ubuntu villages inhabited by people who have increasingly become out of practice with what it means to live communally:

> In fact, partly in order to avoid the inevitable variations in the structure and organisation of *Ujamaa* villages, and partly to ensure that the village

does conform to the officially accepted pattern, TANU and the Government provided a model *Ujamaa* village. Included in the model *Ujamaa* village are such things as the optimum size of the village, a constitution and a manual showing how meetings are to be organised, elections to be conducted; how work in the village is to be divided and organised; the kind of activities – economic and social – the village ought to undertake and so on (Mohiddin 1981: 150).

But the comparison with the theme park should not conceal that this was essentially an exercise in social engineering, planned and executed as part of a war on poverty. Quintessential about this postcolonial creation of a precolonial theme park was that it replaced the familial mechanisms of social cohesion – witch-hunts and the like – with the familiar coercion of nationalist social engineering. After all, as Nyerere commented, these were 'proper villages', not the old-fashioned ones in which people lived 'scattered over a wide area, far apart from each other, and still haunted by the old superstitious fear of witchcraft' (1967b: 183).

Planning assumed the form of military strategy and rhetoric as Nyerere's comment on nationalisation in 'Freedom and Socialism' makes clear: 'In the division the key positions of the economy have been secured for the nation in the same way as, during a war, an army occupies the sites which dominate the countryside. Our war is a war against poverty, and for the freedom and self-government of our people' (in Mohiddin 1981: 131). If nationalisation occupied the 'sites' for the freedom, the Plan mapped out how the civilians would be mobilised to occupy those sites. Operation Dodoma (of 1971) encouraged thousands of Wagogo people to abandon their homes and move to Ujamaa villages, while later the same year, at the end of the Kigoma Operation, 12 000 families lived in 44 Ujamaa villages (150). A year later, 15 per cent of the population lived in such villages. By the end of 1972, 342 villages reached the second and third stages of development. By 1977, there were a total of 7 684 villages, accommodating 13 million people of Tanzania's then approximate total population of 14 million.

Key to understanding this 'success' is to keep in mind that the formation of these villages was only nominally voluntary. In fact, through a combination of legal and political measures – tax rebates and famine relief for those who had agreed to live in Ujamaa villages and none for those who had opted not to, directives and laws in combination with various 'mopping up' operations – it became very difficult to survive outside one. Central to these coercive measures was the Villages and Ujamaa Villages Act of 1975, which provided the legal basis for the constitution of village assemblies and election to them, as well as the legal framework for villages to become co-operative units that would enable them to act on behalf of national authorities, which in turn would allow them to borrow money for development purposes. In short, 'first, it provided the legal and compulsory basis for a new form of rural local government; secondly, it made it mandatory for a village which has attained a given minimum population to come under the provisions of the Village Act itself' (Mohiddin 1981: 161). Of course, this was not totalitarian or social engineering as seen elsewhere in the world: 'The Villages Act does not compel the formation of Ujamaa villages; that has to be decided by the villagers themselves. But the Villages Act does provide the legal – compulsory – basis and the persuasive administrative machinery for the foundation of *Ujamaa* villages' (161–2).

Through its subtle combination of financial and juridical measures, the 'ultimate objective of the Villages Act [was] the establishment of *Ujamaa* villages as viable economic units and effective bases for local government' (Mohiddin 1981: 162). To the extent that we can talk of coercion – and there were explicit instances, but this was the exception rather than the rule – 'the first priority was to bring people together in villages and then, through persuasion, and the gradual application of the Villages Act, these villages would eventually become Ujamaa villages' (163).

Conclusion

Underlying the Ujamaa project was, as Shivji (1976) points out, an astounding naivety regarding the nature of the class struggle in postcolonial Tanzania.[10] Nyerere premised his whole project on the persuasive nature of a highly developed nationalism and the altruistic dedication of the Tanzanian bourgeoisie – the bureaucrats and politicians who had to drive and implement the Ujamaa project. But as Shivji argues, the combination of nationalisation and the retention of existing

---

10. The spectre of a certain naivety seems to shadow Ubuntu discourse. The ANC's proposed Media Appeals Tribunal 'assumes that officials are, by default, benevolent people and always have the best interests of citizens at heart' (Van Vuuren 2010). The ANC's working document justifies the tribunal with reference to the state's expectation of 'the media to instil a "caring society" instead of being a watchdog' (Tshwaku 2010). In light of the analysis offered in this chapter, we have to be concerned about the logic of the ban at work in this suggestion. Care is a function of democratic praxis, not a substitute for it.

bureaucratic and political leadership left the ownership of the means of production in the hands of these elites and not in the hands of the people, effectively creating a common class interest between bureaucrats and politicians. The only way Nyerere could have avoided this continuation of the class struggle at the heart of his socialist project was to have recognised it in the first instance and to have avoided the formation of a politico-bureaucratic class, while at the same time encouraging the building of socialism from the bottom up, by the people themselves. But African Socialism was too much of a self-conscious identitarian ideology to have fostered this kind of growth. As Onuoha puts it, that was exactly its 'strength' – for African Socialism was 'being advocated by the powers that be, not upstarts within some underground movement' (1965: 132).

This said, it is the fact that African Socialism grappled with the profoundly aporetic structure of postcolonial hypermodernity that reveals as deeply empathetic the Revolutionary conceptual persona it presents. While Cosmopolitan scientific socialists were content to dismiss as bourgeois Nyerere's attempt at unifying the idealist and materialist conditions of liberty in a more or less coherent ideology, they had little more to offer than the oppressive universalism of another master narrative of Western modernity that reduced every particular struggle to 'the continuation of . . . class contradictions in a different setting' (Babu 1981: 52), one that posited the universal class struggle as the means for the realisation of humankind's 'historically ordained destination' (xii).

What the conflicting status of African communalism in the different emancipatory visions of African Socialists and scientific socialists demonstrates is that not all manifestations of the Revolutionary conceptual persona are equally empathetic. In fact, some can be quite antipathetic for valorizing particularity over the very possibility of the universality of experience; others, for doing the inverse, by subsuming the particularity of experience under the aegis of participation in an oppressively universal historicism. Only those manifestations of the Revolutionary conceptual persona that somehow try to articulate the universal in the particular, or who see a universality at work in their particularity, will be empathetic. In as much as the African Socialist project in general and Nyerere's Ujamaa project in particular can be said to have failed, it is not simply because it prioritised the importance of recognition, but because, as an ideological construct, African Socialism simply could not contain anything resembling a coherent doctrine or, without a significant measure of violence, live up to all that was expected of it: to position Africa globally by aligning it not with capitalism, but with socialism; to balance this nod in the direction of universalism with a nationalist project of development and authenticity, premised on a robust identity politics riddled with paradoxes, of which the most salient was an undecidable historicism that found in socialism an articulation of the precolonial past, only to advance the past so conceived as the foundation of socialism. If ever there were a single explanation for the 'orgy of definitions and interpretations of "African Socialism"' (Mohiddin 1981: 14) that proliferated throughout the sixties and seventies, it must surely be the simple fact that no single theory could possibly satisfy this combination of global, nationalist-developmental and identitarian demands.

The aim of this excursion into Nyerere's African Socialist project is to make a very general point about any translation of the precolonial logic of interdependence into a postcolonial ideology or philosophy. Whenever an ideology of unity and interdependence is conceived, literally, in fraternal or familial terms, that ideology will necessarily retain an element of the ritualised coercion and conformity that marked the originary praxis of familial interdependence. Is it surprising that the South African liberation struggle, which drew so deeply from this well of interdependence with its rhetoric of solidarity ('an injury to one is an injury to all'), should have given the world one of the most atrocious and archetypal forms of the ban, the sacrificial witch-hunt known as the necklace murder, reserved for those who betrayed that solidarity (see Praeg 2007: 61–98)? This fourth principle of *coercion*, of which the praxis of love, sharing and work – in short, solidarity – is a function, makes its way into all postcolonial understandings of the 'common cause', which so often decodes *differences* of opinion in ontological terms as a *betrayal* of belonging. Again, none of this should come as a surprise to anyone familiar with the literature on Ubuntu. Whoever surveys this literature will find an equal number of authors praising its transcendent humanism and those who caution against its coercive conformism. At stake here is not violence as such, not the existence or even the praxis of Ubuntu's constitutive violence. Any communitarian philosophy or praxis will be shadowed by this principle and identifying it at work is not reason enough to dismiss either philosophy or praxis. The problem, as I stated at the beginning of this chapter, is not violence, but its invisibility, the desire to naturalise communitarian praxis as if it were not a function of violence – which means that, for us, the challenge consists in making the violence of coercion visible as political choice.

In many ways, the first widely visible translation of ubuntu praxis into Ubuntu philosophy in South Africa came with the proceedings of the Truth and

Reconciliation Commission. It is perhaps no exaggeration to say that in some sense democratic South Africa was founded upon the value of ubuntu, appropriated more as lived experience than theorised philosophy, but nonetheless appropriated in a way that allowed us to make sense of how to forgive and reconcile in a manner consonant with the lived experiences of the majority of South Africans. In retrospect, we can now see that, admirable and moving as this implicit trust in the lived reality of ubuntu praxis at the time of the transition may have been, it also afforded us our first glimpse of the coercive shadow that haunts the translation of this praxis into philosophy or ideology. I am thinking of the complex legacy of Steve Biko, champion of human rights and advocate of Black Consciousness. What accounts for the complexity of his legacy is the fact that as a champion of equality and individual rights, his legacy is situated in the tradition of political Revolutionary that stretches back at least as far as Robespierre and the French revolutionary pursuit of freedom, equality and fraternity. This tradition has become mostly associated with the calls to freedom and equality, while it is widely acknowledged that the institutionalisation of fraternity or human solidarity has had a much more ambivalent relationship with democracy.[11]

In Biko's case, the legacy of fraternity is represented by his call to Black Consciousness and the pride he took in his African identity, the African values of communality and solidarity – in short, in his role, not only as political Revolutionary, but also as intellectual Revolutionary, in the sense used so far in this book: the desire to uncover and live what it means to be African. What complicates his legacy is his dual demand for equality and individual rights *and* his celebration of African values of communality and solidarity. This need not have been and probably was not a tension for Biko the person, but it became a profound tension in the memory of Biko the struggle icon when his family insisted that reconciliation was not enough; what they wanted was justice for his callous death at the hands of the apartheid police force. Along with others, they challenged Act 34 of 1995 that established the Truth and Reconciliation Commission, specifically the constitutionality of the clause that provided for conditional amnesty for those who would disclose their part in apartheid violence (*S. v. AZAPO*, 1996). The problem

---

11. For instance, John Rawls's *A Theory of Justice* (first published in 1971) specifically provides an analysis of liberty and equality, but fails to meaningfully engage with fraternity or community (see Kymlicka 2002).

was that the architects of the transition, or formulated more generously, *the logic of the founding*, required that what South Africa needed *at that time* was not justice, but reconciliation. I look at this judgment in more detail at the end of the last chapter. Suffice it here to say that by prioritising in that moment and in that particular judgment, as the postamble of the Interim Constitution of 1993 puts it, the 'need for understanding but not for vengeance, a need for reparation but not for retaliation, a need for *ubuntu* but not for victimisation', we are left with a very complicated memory of Biko indeed.

It would be the easiest thing in the world to interpret this judgment as a denial of Biko's legacy as a human rights activist – as indeed it was seen in some quarters. But the same judgment was also a celebration of Biko the African. The fact is, whichever way the judgment went, it would have violated one dimension of what Biko stood for. While Biko the activist demanded commemoration, in terms of the acknowledgement of an individual right to freedom and justice, Biko the Black Consciousness advocate demanded a recollection and remembrance of what colonialism had dis-membered of the African subjectivity. Ironically, then, we are left with two incomplete lamentations: on the one hand, recognising that his right to justice in that moment would have meant violating, and relegating to the margins yet again, the possibility and reality of ubuntu as political praxis; on the other hand, the celebration of ubuntu in that moment could only occur through the violation of the fundamental rights he had fought for. In this complex sense, we may well draw some consolation from the question: What could have been a more fitting commemoration of his legacy than the brief transformation of the public sphere into one where the legacy of Biko the human rights activist contested the legacy of Biko the Africanist?

The reasons why I am concluding this chapter with the ambivalent status of Biko in this precarious interregnum is because the only thing that made this violation of Biko's legacy as human rights activist bearable was the *visibility of the violence* that briefly prioritised ubuntu over individual rights.[12] In the clear articulation in Mohamed D.P.'s judgment of the need to violate, through a temporary suspension, individual rights in the name of the common good, we find the violence of communitarianism made visible as political choice. And this is the point with which I want to conclude this chapter. As one of the theorists that I will be appealing to

---

12. See Praeg (2008b: 218, especially footnote 33).

in the last chapter, Duncan Kennedy, puts it in 'Form and Substance in Private Law Adjudication':

> True, collective self-determination, short of utopia implies the use of force against the individual. But we experience and accept the use of physical and psychic coercion every day, in family life, education and culture. We experience it indirectly, often unconsciously in political and economic life. The problem is the conversion of force into moral force, in the fact of the experience of moral indeterminacy. A definition of freedom that ignores this problem is no more than a rationalization of indifference, or the velvet glove for the hand of domination through rules (1976: 1774).

Surely the most overdetermined 'difference' between liberals and communitarians is the suggestion that only the latter implies violence or coercion. On the contrary, the choice is never between a world in which we accept the violence of coercion and a world in which it is absent. The choice is only ever between a world in which violence remains invisible and a world in which we insist on making it visible – and by visible, I mean converting violence into a moral force and thereby rendering it a political choice. That, in *S. v. AZAPO*, the violence of ubuntu (however indirect the reference) was made visible, seems clear. Less clear is how we are expected to proceed, beyond the relative ease with which we could discern what this founding moment required of us, today and in future, in relation to this founding *aporia-archē* of the South African politico-juridical order: how do we continue reconciling individual rights with the memory, for many still rooted in daily praxis, of our human interdependence? This is the question I explore in the next two chapters. I do so very much in recognition of the fact that in this our thinking will forever be haunted by the ambivalent spectre of Steve Biko.

CHAPTER 4

The Law
First *Epoché*

> Bifurcation is the source of the need for philosophy.
> — G.W.F. Hegel, *The Difference Between Fichte's and Schelling's System of Philosophy*

Introduction

In Chapter 2, I discussed Achille Mbembe's critique of the dominant forms of postcolonial historicism that, he argues, uncritically replicated the basic assumptions of Western modernity. In response to his analysis, I quoted Arif Dirlik, who argues that *at the time* a racialised knowledge-construction was the only viable way through which the unity of a historic agent capable of resisting white colonialism could be conceived. In Chapter 3, I argued that this *problematique* of an untimely criticism manifests as a tension between constative claims that may be true (race does not exist) and performative claims that, although they 'buy into' an oppressive logic (race exists), nonetheless allow important political work to be done (effect independence, sovereignty, equality and so on). I also teased out some of the implications of this tension for the condition I describe as hypermodernity. Typical of this condition is that the political work that needs to be done through performative claims is perpetually threatened with inexecution by claims concerned with constative truth. I used the logic of nationalism to demonstrate the point, but the example referenced in the introduction would have served just as well. When Nelson Mandela was released from prison and started to live the role of reconciliator, largely scripted for him by the African National Congress (ANC), by reconciling and forgiving the left, right and centre, many legitimised his actions both *epistemologically* (he was living an African truth) and *morally* (his actions seen as superior to Western juridical retribution). But it took the ANC Youth League to point out that although his actions may have been epistemologically true and morally austere, they were politically naive because they undermined an important *political truth*: forgiveness comes at the end of a political process of confession and contrition. To honour the epistemological and moral truths at the cost of the political truth, to short-circuit a process that should have unfolded over time – white people apologising and making amends in a way that would have restored African dignity (because it would have treated them as worthy of an apology and left them with sufficient agency to decide whether or not to forgive white people) – amounted to reinforcing and perpetuating the asymmetrical power relations that marked the conflict of domination in the first instance. An ethical truth, *when untimely*, may become instrumental in self-oppression because it may render political truth inexecutable.

The twin political categories of the *performativity* of the origin and the dilemma of the *untimely* haunt the condition of hypermodernity, irrespective of whether we are considering the timing of forgiveness, the double-thinking involved in claiming that a national We exists or whether we are imagining a unified 'racial subject', capable of overthrowing white domination. That African ethnophilosophers ontologised their essence racially in their attempt to liberate themselves from colonial domination is true. That they, by and large, did so without fundamentally questioning the very axioms of the game they were inducted into – a game that predetermined the meaning of being human in terms of the categories of race, cultural authenticity, political sovereignty and personal autonomy – is perhaps also true. The fact remains that what made it plausible for them to do so (and what enabled them to overlook the limitations of replicating the rules of the game in their attempts to liberate themselves from it) was the political necessity and therefore the *political truth* of having to do so. V-Y Mudimbe and Bogumil Jewsiewicki articulate this dilemma with characteristic clarity:

> Those with less power are always in some sense in a double-bind: there is no good answer to the prevailing universalisms. If they accept the wisdom of those universalisms, they find themselves excluded or demeaned by the very premise of the theorizing. But if they hesitate to act with regard to the prevailing universalism, they find themselves unable to function adequately within the system, either politically or intellectually, and therefore impede ameliorating the situation. The consequence is that, initially, those who are excluded move back and forth, both politically and culturally, between integration and separation (1996: 59).

This notion of a double-bind or aporia, the description of a moment weak on epistemological and moral truth, but strong on political truth, a moment that Jean-Paul Sartre immortalised as the weak moment in a dialectic of recognition, renders the moment of political transition and the ambivalent status of *political truth* profoundly complex, beyond what now appears as Mbembe's rather simplistic critique of these forms of historicism.

At work in this tension between the epistemological, moral and political is not simply a contradiction, but an aporia: 'Every new order announces itself through the violation of what it stands for' (Praeg 2008b: 218). It does not seem to matter whether the founding is violent or non-violent, the logic of the transition seems to require that what is *new* can never simply arrive in all its newness; that in order for the new to arrive, the new (or the We who stand for the new) needs to engage the old, even repeat the old, in a manner that cannot but violate, by contradicting, the new that is being announced. This is how the 'people' reconcile a violent decapitation of the *ancien régime* with a new vision of equality, fraternity and liberty, how the We brings about a new order of individual rights and due process by necklacing those whose actions threaten to prevent the realisation of this vision. This is how the We in South Africa reconciled actualising a constitutional regime of individual rights by suspending the Biko family's right to due process, in the name of a constitutionally declared exception, legitimised by the anticipation of a new *nomos*. Lastly, this is how the We has reconciled the need to theorise a philosophy of shared humanity with the claim that this philosophy is a marker of cultural sovereignty, of that which is *not* shared by all humanity.

As complex as this aporetic moment of the founding may be, there is also something deceptively simple about it when it marks a clear transition from the old to the new. For, where a successful founding is anticipated, we also anticipate the immanent criminalisation of such repetitions of the old: once the democratic order is established, we know that in future no individual will retain the sovereign right to declare him or herself an exception to the law and no community will be free to curtail individual liberty through the logic of benevolent communitarian coercion, however legitimised in terms of a 'right to culture'. These claims, we know, will soon be illegitimate and criminal – a comfort that derives from the fact that we are dealing with a relatively simple or clear transition from the old to the new. In Ubuntu discourse, this anticipation assumes the form of a temporary tension between its claim to articulate our shared humanity and its sovereign, identity politics (Ubuntu is not shared by all humanity) – a tension, we are told, that will be suspended or overcome one day when the global order is reconfigured as post-sovereign on the basis of Ubuntu.

All of this becomes even more complex when the new is not simply understood as what comes *after* the old, but is envisaged as that which will *enable*, in the sense of giving effect to, the old. Here, what seems obvious at political level – the transition from apartheid to democracy in South Africa was about leaving behind an 'old' authoritarian South Africa, in order to embrace a 'new' democratic South Africa – becomes problematic at a cultural level. For, what does it mean to say that the struggle for liberation was about an *imayibuye* or return of Africa to Africa(ns), if that very return marks a transition from a traditional political economy of obligation to a modern, democratic regime of individual rights? What does it mean to embrace constitutional sovereignty as the mark of a return of Africa to Africa(ns)?

However we answer these questions, we cannot deny that this moment marks a simultaneous loss and gain. What Africans gained through the liberation struggle they/we did so by mobilising the best from the interaction with Western modernity (the co-creation of a global culture of human rights), in order to transcend both the phallo-logocentric violence of the West and the phallo-primocentric violence of precolonial African societies. But this double negation of what the return to/of Africa could possibly mean – *double* because Africa simultaneously articulated its liberation from the West through the adoption of Western political forms, such as the democratic nation-state, in addition to embarking on the inescapable process of reinventing traditional values, in line with a regime of individual rights – this double negation cannot but create among people a sense of postcolonial disillusionment, often articulated as an estrangement from the law itself – as if the very juridical that promised to restore the dignity of Africans ended up having nothing to do with the real lives of Africans, as if the promise of a new *nomos* was never more than a dream, which will remain in future, as it was in the past, eternally deferred.

The vacuum left by this double negation is the enunciative space of the call to 'Africanise the law'. Of course, the standard knee-jerk reaction to this call often trivialises it by pointing out that the Bill of Rights contains universal rights that are per definition not African. This is an easy way out. I think once we recognise the irreversibility of the double negation (a function of what I shall below refer to as the 'arrow of time'); that is, once we recognise that 'Africanising' is necessarily eternally deferred, the difference between two options emerges: on the one hand, 'Africanise' understood as a noun, a state of being which, because it is in principle recognisable, can also be instituted, so that we can have a fully Africanised or transformed law. This is not going to happen: juridically, because universal rights are *universal* and politically, because of the double negation or movement *away* from Africa. But there is a second, more interesting way to think through this call to Africanise the law, which consists in recognising the word 'Africanise' not as noun or state of being, but as a verb or process of becoming, a process that, given the irreversibility of the double movement away from Africa, will always remain endlessly incomplete or necessarily deferred.

These two models of what 'Africanise' should be taken to mean roughly correspond to two models of understanding law in relation to politics. First, when it is understood as a noun, the call to Africanise the law is premised on a legal positivist understanding of that relation: the law may open to Africa *once and for all*, in order to be transformed into something African; once that has happened, it will be sealed off again and continue to exist as a complete set of African(ised) rules that will in future remain impervious to the political in general and the changing demands of postcoloniality in particular (because we will have Africanised). Second, understood as a verb, the call to Africanise the law can be interpreted as a rearticulation of transformative constitutionalism; that is, of the recognition that exactly because the border between law and politics is permeable, the law has a fundamental role to play in transforming society. When I say that we have to take the call to Africanise the law seriously, it is in this second sense that I mean it; when I insist on its urgency, it is because the call emerges from the enunciative space of a vacuum, left behind by an inescapable double movement away from the very *nomos* that historically has animated and in future will continue to animate the struggle for justice.

In these last two chapters, I want to consider the meaning of Ubuntu in relation to this double movement away from Africa. Ultimately, I shall relate this movement back to a double structure of justice in South African Constitutional Court jurisprudence. But before this, some preliminaries need to be addressed.

Preliminaries
On the relationship between Africa and the law
There are at least three ways of understanding the relationship between Africa and the law implicit in this call to Africanise the law, three ways in which to think about filling the vacuum left first by colonialism and, since 1994, by the liberal-democratic retrodiction of tradition. I think of them as the *sovereign*, the *pluralist*

and the *cosmopolitan* options. I will say just enough about each one to demarcate in the broadest of terms the kind of questions I am concerned with in these last two chapters.

The first, the *sovereign* stance is best represented by Mogobe B. Ramose who, in several publications on conquest and sovereignty (2002a, 2002b; see also 1999, Chapter 6), has argued for a particular conception of decolonisation, according to which we can speak of neither decolonisation nor postcolonial justice until the sovereignty of the African claim to land and the parity of African law with Western constitutionalism have both been recognised. In the case of Zimbabwe, he argues, this has not happened and the result is a 'memory of *the original injustice* which prompts . . . [Zimbabweans] to seek justice beyond the Lancaster Agreement' (2002b: 470, emphasis added). In South Africa, constitutional arrangements merely make provision for a willing buyer-willing seller arrangement that remains fundamentally unjust for converting questions of collective rights and sovereignty – that is, the *'original injustice'* – into matters of individual rights and private property (473). Ramose is, of course, right. It is the fact and the memory of an *'original injustice'* that drives the popular imagination and its discontents.[1] I call this the *sovereign* option because, depending on how it is construed, it will argue for greater sovereignty of Africa law, either as wholly sovereign (difficult to imagine in tandem with a unitary state) or as relatively sovereign – various federalist agreements that would amount to 'the reversion of title to territory to its rightful holders – the indigenous conquered peoples – the restoration of absolute sovereignty over the same territory and restitution' (471) – a call for federalism that did not materialise during the transition to a democratic South Africa for a number of reasons, not least of which was that it may have ended up re-entrenching apartheid in the form of a postcolonial, ethnic neo-medievalism.

---

1. For example, Article 3 of the Preamble of the Manifesto of the Economic Freedom Fighters (EFF): 'Those who fought the gallant wars of resistance did so to resist forced dispossession of land, wealth, livestock and heritage, which they had cherished and inherited from their forebears. More than 350 years later, the war of resistance has not been won, and the battles that were fought almost represent nothing, because 20 years after the attainment of formal political freedom, the black people of South Africa still live in absolute mass poverty, are landless, their children have no productive future, they are mistreated and they are looked down upon in a sea of wealth.' The full manifesto is available at http://allafrica.com/stories/201307261484.html.

The second, *pluralist* alternative refers to a variety of arguments that, while accepting the sovereignty of the constitutional framework, nonetheless insists on giving more substance to the idea of legal pluralism, first introduced when Britain officially recognised indigenous African law alongside Roman-Dutch law.[2] The most acute articulation of this position in recent times has been the debate on the Traditional Courts Bill, a debate that historically revolved around the two master tropes of *sovereignty* and *identity*. The first moment of sovereignty was really concerned with power: how to reconstitute the power of traditional leaders in a way that would not threaten the state's claim to authority, premised on the monopoly on the means of violence (the right to make and enforce the difference between life and death most vividly asserted in the state's compulsory health provisions for circumcision rituals). This was negotiated in Chapter 11 of the 1993 Interim Constitution, which recognised traditional authorities and established the National Houses of Traditional Leadership (carried forward as Chapter 12 of the 1996 Constitution), but subjected the power of traditional leaders to the Constitution in general and the Bill of Rights in particular. Of course, even then, the struggle for power was always influenced by a background concern with identity and justice:

> It was accepted implicitly that traditional leadership contributed immensely to the development of systems and a body of knowledge for dispute resolution, thereby contributing to communal harmony. It was accepted that the processes by which lineage disputes were resolved and how genealogies were preserved and used constituted a body of knowledge to be preserved (Nkasawe 2012).

What 'communal harmony' and 'dispute resolution' refer to here, of course, as Chief Phathekile Holomisa stated, is the idea that 'traditional courts operate on the basis of ubuntu' (in Nkasawe 2012). But ubuntu, as we saw in Chapter 1, was historically a function of a praxis constituted in terms of a phallo-primocentric constellation of values. The process of abstracting Ubuntu from this political economy, in order to retain its relevance in and for a post-apartheid constitutional

---

2. Of course, there has never been equality between Roman-Dutch law and indigenous African law and, in this sense, no real pluralism. For an approach that goes into the legal aspects in more detail than the pluralist option advanced here, see Van Niekerk (2000).

democracy, has marked a second phase in the debate, in which the struggle for power implicit in the question of sovereignty, far from disappearing, has been complemented by a number of concerns revolving around the nexus of *identity* and *justice*.

Identity and justice are not separate driving forces of the political, the one particular and the other universal. They feed off each other, in the sense that a certain identity claim is often reinforced by the assertion that the bearer of that identity can make an important contribution to, say, the question of justice – in this case, the 'spirit of give and take embodied in our tradition of ubuntu' has 'bequeathed to us the legacy of consensual decision-making, a critical element in our endeavour to enhance the discourse of democracy' (Nkasawe 2012). But this claim can only purchase credibility on the back of the sacrifice of those very constituent elements of ubuntu praxis that seem most *un*modern; that is, the phallo-primocentric structure of onto-triadic communality that gave it ontological substance in a political economy of obligation.[3] 'Accordingly, the transformation of traditional leadership, especially between 1997 and 2003, sought to bridge the gap between hereditary and democratic leadership . . . This was done by bringing a gender balance to an institution based on male lineage', through the Traditional Leadership and Governance Framework Act of 2003. The continued debate on traditional leadership in relation to the Constitution is complex and cannot be discussed futher here. It is possible that, within a pluralist framework, the question of Ubuntu and the law will play itself out in traditional courts, gaining some institutional autonomy from the state on the back of 'service delivery' arguments (making justice more accessible), in addition to which, considered as a political strategy unconcerned with justice, it will allow the political elite to consolidate political power, by articulating their ethnic identity in terms of locality. Countering the former argument, Nomboniso Gasa (2012) has argued that the differentiation between rural traditional courts and urban constitutionalism will graft a *double structure of justice* on the South African political geography that is unacceptable.

---

3. 'The basic bond of this kind found in traditional African societies is the one existing between members of the patrilineal, extended family, the majority of whom also share co-residence. The senior members of this *rixaka* in Tsonga, *umndeni* in Zulu, *lesika* in Tswana or *moloko* in North-Sotho have already departed to the spirit world in the hereafter but retain their interest in the good relations maintained with them and those existing between their kinfolk on earth' (Coertze 2001: 113).

Where a dual system of law 'is forced on sections of the population and is framed geographically, it not only reminds us of the apartheid system of separate development, it also exposes the complex ways in which the past lives in the present'.

Authors such as Gasa will perhaps be more inclined to the third position, what I think of as the *cosmopolitan*, on the question regarding Ubuntu and the law, one that seeks to incorporate an abstraction derived from African law (Ubuntu) into the constitutional regime. What is most appealing about this option is that instead of a quasi-, if not explicit, nativist legal thinking pivoting on the right (sovereignty) or need (pluralism) to limit African law to the African subject, it effectively argues for the expansion of an abstraction derived from African law, applicable to all postcolonial citizens. And is this not what intrigues about the debate on Ubuntu and the law – the fact that Ubuntu can be and has been deployed (as far as the status of Constitutional Court judgments are concerned) in reference to an imagined, postcolonial We? The questions I am interested in pursuing in these last two chapters are effectively: What are the conditions of possibility for such an understanding of Ubuntu in relation to the law? What are the implicit understandings of Ubuntu, modernity and legality presupposed by the idea that Ubuntu can and should be invoked in reference to this imagined We?

Let us proceed with the first of these questions and ask: What conception of Ubuntu is suitable to this task? In what follows, I briefly consider two options. In the first, the idea of Ubuntu as quasi-transcendental derives from the general framework of critical humanism, while in the second, Ubuntu as Law of law derives from the jurisprudence of Drucilla Cornell and Yvonne Mokgoro. Finding both wanting, I develop in the next chapter a third conception of Ubuntu as un/familiar or uncanny.

Ubuntu as quasi-transcendental, Ubuntu as Law of law
With regard to the idea of Ubuntu as quasi-transcendental, the claim to be human is the most fundamental claim we can make about ourselves because it is the most fundamental category of our existence. All other categories – that we love, pursue justice, that we sometimes act rationally, that we are emotional and so on – presuppose recognition of the deceptively simple fact that we are human. I say 'deceptively simple' because there is no single definition of human subjectivity that all people can agree on. The reason for this, I think, has a lot to do with the fact that there is no human society that did not at one point have a concept of the sacred. Having had a concept of the sacred historically did (and in future will

continue to) influence and determine any society's secularised understanding of what it means to be human. The Christian West, for instance, has a concept of the human that, even in the ostensibly secular understanding of itself as premised on nothing more ontological or profound than human rights, continues to derive much of its appreciation of the sacredness of human life from the Abrahamic tradition (Derrida 2001).[4]

However, all is not relative. Exactly because 'human subjectivity' refers to the condition of being human, its culturally and historically specific meanings also shade off and overlap with those of other traditions and cultures. Regardless of the differences in beliefs and traditions, human beings recognise each other as *human beings* and appreciate shared commonalities in what that means. This universality is a bottom line we recognise, although we may find it very difficult to describe or give content to it exactly because every attempt to do so will necessarily draw on our own beliefs and traditions, rooted in the heritage of our understanding of the sacred.

The introduction made a couple of comments in this regard: (1) there is no coherent and universally agreed upon understanding of human subjectivity upon which any emancipatory project can be based; (2) those who take the project of emancipation seriously should therefore never be expected to have such a definition at hand as a condition for the possibility of advancing a humanist critique of political arrangements; (3) this lack of definitional clarity is not a problem that we need to solve, in order to 'get on with politics', as much as it is a condition for the possibility or sine qua non of any meaningful engagement with the political. In short, there is no such thing as human*ism*, but only a sustained praxis aimed at humanis*ing* the world, guided by a quasi-transcendental idea of what being human means. In the spirit of this quasi-transcendental understanding of humanism, Chapter 2 recognises in a range of conceptual personae the different compromises that the abstract ideal of the human makes in order to do the dirty work of politics. The incarnation of the 'human' in politics – an incarnation that always conjoins an image of thought with suppositions about possible modes of being – can never exhaust what it means to be human. The world can never be humane enough and humanism is nothing if not the perpetual deconstructive recognition of the residual inhumanness of all political arrangements.

---

4. For an interesting argument that Hannah Arendt provides us with an ontological foundation for human rights, see Birmingham (2006).

For a humanist, the 'human' is a question that must be raised again and again, not in the hope of settling it, but in order for it to remain open as a horizon for the critique of unrealised potentialities. Humanism is by definition at once the most abstract and the most concrete of terms: the most *abstract*, for all the reasons described here and the most *concrete* because it is a fundamental fact of my existence that I can and must engage in critique as emancipatory praxis. As such, it seems to be a transcendental category – like *justice* it will never arrive in the world in all its perfect splendour. Yet, at the same time, we do not hesitate to use the word to criticise concrete examples of behaviour or policy that we find inhuman (in the same way that we can call a law unjust without being able to offer a definitive definition of justice). Humanism, then – and by implication Ubuntu as signifier of our shared humanity – can be understood in such quasi-transcendental terms: as an abstract, regulative concept or idea we cannot define, but which we nonetheless invoke in order to create a world that should manifest that idea, all the while knowing that a final manifestation of the idea is not possible.

An analysis of Ubuntu *qua* sign of our intersubjective humanity, premised on the quasi-transcendental status of Ubuntu, would be interesting were it not for two limitations: it would threaten to subsume Ubuntu under a general discourse on critical humanisms; that is, the particular (Ubuntu) would be subsumed as mere instance or at best an example of the universal (critical humanism) and, second, nothing better captures what is most characteristic about Western philosophy than the secularised messianic or quasi-teleological structure of the quasi-transcendental (see Hurst 2004). As a consequence, nothing could be more foreign to the context in which we are trying to think through the question of Ubuntu in relation to the law. However, there is another way of thinking through this relationship: Ubuntu as Law of laws.

Any political declaration, such as a country's Constitution, which starts with the phrase, 'We the people . . .' and then proceeds to elaborate a set of meta-rules that citizens agree to live by and be ruled by, at the risk of returning to an earlier state of civil war or chaos, effectively reiterates the master conception of the political inherited from the Anglo-European tradition of political thought, which posits the theoretical fiction of a 'social contract' among fully individualised citizens as the only viable way to conceive the legitimate constitutive power of a constituted government.

As Cornell (2004: 668) has argued, this postulate of the 'contract' provides us with a very culturally specific understanding of the founding principles of the constitutional state. The founding principle of the legality of the constitutional state, the 'Law of law' that animates it or the axiom that grounds it, represents the 'internal limiting principles of the social contract, based on maximising the negative freedom of all' (669). Three comments need to be made about this basic axiomatic or Law of laws: first, it is a culturally specific vision of both the political and the law that is thoroughly Anglo-European; second, its most fundamental constituent element is the idealised notion of an always already individuated individual; that is, an individual who enters into social arrangements and political agreements, not in order to become fully human, but as a fully actualised human who wants to maximise his or her interests; and third, for a variety of systemic reasons related to what is generally referred to as globalisation, the adoption of such a vision of the political marked the culmination of the struggle against apartheid and colonisation in South Africa, eroding in the process the basis for any easy juxtaposing of the law of the colonisers with the law of the colonised. Questions about what it means to Africanise and decolonise the founding contract of an inclusive, post-apartheid South African imagined community have become complex far beyond simplistically identitarian appeals to African law, indigenous or customary law. Decolonising will not come from a return *to/of* precolonial traditional forms of the political *and/or* law, but rather from an elimination of the postcolonial, racialised fault lines of rich and poor, through the realisation of socio-economic rights. I take this to be Cornell's point: an understanding of law solely premised on the social contract between already individuated individuals – although useful and valuable in itself – is inadequate to this task because the playing field was not level when 'We' entered the contract. In order to level the playing field, we need something more than a juridical axiomatic that departs from the assumption that it was level in the first place.[5]

Cornell (2004) and Mokgoro (1998) have both argued that in order to better respond to this challenge, 'African ideals of solidarity and mutual sustenance could potentially provide a new and important way to think about the "Law of law", or

---

5. '... contemporary human rights discourse ... is incapable of true transformative force. The central philosophical and jurisprudential features of liberalism are calculated to uphold the status quo. Prominent among these features is the metaphorical veil of ignorance through which legal norms and relationships are created, viewed, and judged. The veil imparts an aura of neutrality, formal equality, and moral relativism, legitimizing the prevailing relationships of power in society and shielding them from scrutiny' (Woods 2003: 53).

the grounding principle of legality itself' (Cornell 2004: 670). This alternative understanding of the founding principle and purpose of the law perceives the law,

> not as a tool for personal defense, but as an opportunity given to all to survive under the protection of the order of the communal entity; communalism which emphasises group solidarity and interests generally, and all rules which sustain it, as opposed to individual interests, with its likely utility in building a sense of national unity among South Africans; the conciliatory character of the adjudication process which aims to restore peace and harmony between members rather than the adversarial approach which emphasises retribution and seems repressive (Mokgoro 1998: 20).

As appealing as this may sound, what we are presented with here are not only very different kinds of claims made respectively by the social contract and Ubuntu as competing visions of the Law of law, but also a very big difference in the way each axiomatic *qua* Law, relates to the law. In the case of contract theory, what the Law represents is implicit or constitutive of the law. After all, the Law of law refers to the 'internal limiting principles of the social contract' itself (Cornell 2004: 669). In the case of Ubuntu, things are very different. The logic of Ubuntu *qua* Law is not constitutive of the law, nor does it derive from the contractual logic of the law itself, but rather it is invoked, normatively, to argue what the Law of law *should* be. To achieve this, it is argued, the Constitution can be used to reinvent Ubuntu so that Ubuntu can be deployed, either as a critique of the limitations of a contractual understanding of the Law or in order to 'actualise the democratic values of human dignity, equality, and freedom' (671). Here, the law plays a fundamental role in generating the Law, not as that which is constitutive of it, but rather as that which, because fundamentally Other to it, can modify and/or enhance it. In a perfect example of retrodiction, Cornell describes how Mokgoro reinvents Ubuntu as Law of law by way of what Cornell calls a 'conversion principle':

> A conversion principle generally both converts the way we understand the past, and converts or translates any current practice of interpretation as we attempt to realise it in the reconstruction of law and legal principle. Given Mokgoro's profound concern with discrimination against women, she is, on my reading of her, converting the world-view and ideal of ubuntu into law by both recollecting it and then also reimagining it in accordance

with a constitution that is explicitly teleological and thus performative in that it attempts to actualise the democratic values of human dignity, equality, and freedom (2004: 671).

What we are left with in the end are not only two claims to the position of fundamental Law of law, but two very different kinds of claims altogether. As Cornell acknowledges: 'Ubuntu and social contract theory are in tension with one another, but if postcolonial theory has anything to teach us, it is that that tension can be productive, even as we attempt reconfigurations of possibly divergent notions of the "Law of law" and the axiomatic principles they generate' (2004: 670). But I think there is more than a tension at work here. There is a fundamental difference between *recognising* the Law of law as contractarian and the invitation to *posit* Ubuntu as Law of law. In the case of the former, Law is constitutive and constituted by law *qua* contract, in the sense that it refers to the logic of the contract and its constituent assumptions (the individuated individual and so on). In case of the latter, the Law does not inhere in the law in the constitutive sense at all, but relates to the Law in the normative sense of what the purpose of the law *should* be. More succinctly, the contractarian Law does little more than reflect, at a meta-level, the essential constituents of the constitutional law regime as a social contract. The postulate of Ubuntu *qua* Law of laws does no such thing. It does not reflect the essence of the law but, normatively, what the purpose of the law *should* be. It reflects, not the abstract constituent *elements* of the law, but a normative vision of the teleological *purpose* of the law. Ubuntu can only play this normative role to the extent that it is created *by* the law as normative critique *of* the law: effectively, through the law retrodicting its own deconstruction.[6]

---

6. Perhaps a more convincing way of advancing the 'Ubuntu as Law of laws' argument would embrace Ubuntu as animating the harmonisation of different legal traditions in a context of legal pluralism. We can accept the Constitution as a meta-standard, while allowing the tensions that arise between the Constitution and customary law to be harmonised, by conceiving the former as a critique of the latter and the latter as an expansion of the former. 'What is uniquely African of *ubuntu*, are methods, approaches, emphases and attitudes. If, as [Mokgoro] pointed out, "at least key values of *ubuntu* (-*ism*)" converge with the values entrenched in the Constitution, the Constitution as meta standard could eventually be a means of harmonising the laws of South Africa. But a state of accord or consonance will only be realised if the key values of *ubuntu* are not disregarded' (Van Niekerk 2005: 487).

But this raises a number of related questions: if the above is an accurate description of the difference between a constitutive and a normative view of the Law of law and if Ubuntu is an example of the latter, does casting Ubuntu as the 'Law of law' add anything to our understanding of the relationship between Ubuntu and the law that we do not already get from the distinction between legal rules and social standards? According to this distinction, there are legal rules to guide adjudication in instances of conflicting rights and enable us to prioritise rights. But when, for a variety of reasons, we cannot make a decision solely on the basis of legal rules of interpretation, we may invoke social standards or values to justify a certain decision. We may, for instance, invoke Ubuntu to say, 'It is not in the spirit of Ubuntu to dispossess shack-dwellers of their land until the property owner has made alternative arrangements for them, because we value ubuntu and so I rule that they cannot be evicted.'

But there is a second reason why I am suspicious of the 'Ubuntu as Law of law' argument and this is its implicit tendency to exceptionalise postcoloniality as the only locus in law of a profound tension between the contractarian and the communitarian, between using the law to protect self-interest and the obligation to use it to enhance communal well-being. I have more to say about the racialised politics of this exceptionalism in Ubuntu discourse towards the end of this chapter. Suffice it here to say that this tendency is a function of a third, equally problematic and related tendency to ontologise the difference between individualism and communitarianism in terms of the tired Western individualism versus African communalism opposition: as if, by the end of colonialism, Africans had not found in the contract *qua* Law of law a guarantee of the individual rights they fought for and as if, conversely, only Africans ever appeal to the Law to prioritise altruism over individualism. I address this nexus of closely related tendencies in the last chapter.

To posit a meaning of Ubuntu that will allow us to sidestep such problematic Idols of the Mind is the challenge of these last two chapters. They essentially offer a version of a universalist argument that temporarily suspends (through a double bracketing or *epoché*) the particularity of the Ubuntu debate, only to return to this particularity in light of what is revealed by each *epoché*. The overall argument of these two chapters is that the tension between the two conceptions of the Law of law articulated here is peculiar, not to postcoloniality, but to modern legal cultures as such. Consequently, the place and meaning of Ubuntu in South African jurisprudence is not that of an ontological Other, which somehow needs to be squared with a Western law that is not of Africa's making, but rather of a contextually relevant uncanny (un/familiar) reminder of a profound tension between self-interest and Other-care that is familiar to all modern subjects for whom *belonging has become a problem for thought* and who in many ways have come to think of the law as one mechanism through which to negotiate this problem.

The first *epoché* of this chapter reveals, in very general terms, the question of Ubuntu as a question of modernity, while the second *epoché* of the following chapter builds on that generality by interpreting the question of Ubuntu in relation to the law, first and foremost, as the kind of question raised by modern legal cultures. The first *epoché* is particularly risky in the sense that, if interpreted as more than an attempt to model a certain analogy, it may come across as the kind of grand-narrative theorising – Thabo Mbeki's African Renaissance comes to mind – that has always rendered Africa 'epistemologically anachronistic' (Farred 2003: 69) by taking the European experience as timeless and eternal. This is the risk. What we stand to gain from taking this risk is the possibility of substantiating the intuition that there is something familiar about the transition from ubuntu to Ubuntu, something not dissimilar to a transition from *sinnliche* to *moralische Harmonie* (see Cornell 2004: 670). My overall argument is that this intuition contains an important half of the truth. The transition from ubuntu to Ubuntu is un/familiar. What is *familiar* about it can only be revealed by taking the risk of a general *epoché*; likewise, what is as yet unfamiliar about it can only become visible after the *epoché* and as a result of it, when we return to the particularity of South Africa's post-apartheid modernity.[7]

First epoché

> εποχη [*epoché*]: Greek term for cessation or stoppage; hence, in the philosophy of the sceptics, the suspension of judgement.

On 7 August 1788, a schoolboy at Stuttgart's Gymnasium Illustre in the Duchy of Württemberg handed in a homework essay titled '*Über einige charakteristische Unterschiede der alten Dichter [von den neueren]*' (Some characteristic differences

---

7. The category of the uncanny or un/familiar is posited here as a way of escaping the problem Claude Lévi-Strauss, Michel Foucault and V-Y Mudimbe grappled with in their various archaeologies, namely the reduction of the Other to the Same (see Mudimbe 1988: 33–4). In what follows, there is no tyranny of Western history, only the recognition that the transition from ubuntu to Ubuntu is at once old or familiar and, because of the time and context of the iteration of that transition, unfamiliar and new.

between ancient and contemporary poets). It was two weeks before his eighteenth birthday and the young man was very concerned with understanding why, compared to the ancient Greeks, German poets of his time were having such difficulty being understood by a general German audience. His diagnosis was as simple as it was profound: German poets were misunderstood because there was no general German audience. Greek poets could assume a cultural homogeneity in their audience that German poets could not. As a people, Germans lacked a shared conception of their own history that would unite them as a living people and a homogenous reading audience. Instead, the young G.W.F. Hegel argued, the difference between educated and uneducated Germans was vast. The educated classes had an alienated ('external') relationship with their own history that derived from the fact that German history was mostly written by foreigners, while for the uneducated classes, history seemed to be a mere matter of hearsay or superstition, regarding matters that were of little relevance to their daily lives. In such an atomised society, history can be nothing but a divisive force.

The essay was not prescriptive; the young Hegel did not try to offer solutions to the problem. Instead, his concern was diagnostic. He wanted, first, to understand the causes for the lack of homogeneity among Germans and, second, to advance an understanding of human beings, society and history that would allow the German people to overcome the sense of alienation he described as being both personal and collective. As one of his intellectual biographers, Raymond Plant, comments: 'It is in this essay that the twin themes of personal fragmentation and social division, the two keys to the identity of Hegel's thought, make their appearance for the first time' (1983: 28).

Hegel was not original either in defining the problem of personal fragmentation and social division or in juxtaposing contemporary German society with ancient Greece (as an ideal state of personal and social unity). A preceding generation of German thinkers, the so-called *Stürmer und Dränger*, including Johann Wolfgang von Goethe, Friedrich Schiller and Friedrich Hölderlin, had already articulated the need to 'restore the harmony of personal experience and to recreate a closely-knit community in contrast to the fragmentation of the person and the growing social divisions' of the time (Plant 1983: 16). The writings of this generation basically divided into two thematics that represented, not so much a divide between the authors, but rather a different emphasis at different times by various thinkers and texts. On the one hand, there were those texts we can refer to in the language of Africana thought as *poeticist* because they focused mainly, although not exclusively, on the manner in which the modern individual's consciousness had become 'deeply divided within himself' (20), a divided state of affairs epitomised by the philosophical anthropology of the Kantian individual, who was forever divided between reason and passion, duty and inclination, and the autonomous and heteronomous self. On the other hand, there were those texts and authors who were *historicists* – 'the more socially aware members of the generation [who] realized that the ideal of personal harmony, the achievement of the full potential of all the human powers could only be achieved satisfactorily if there was a corresponding renewal in *community*' (21). In their combined resistance to the fragmentation brought about by modernity, three things emerged quite clearly (16): first, a discontent with modernity that often took the form of a revolt against the depressed social, political and religious state of affairs in the territories of the Holy Roman Empire; second, an idealisation of Greek, particularly Athenian, society as one in which 'no distinction could be drawn between man as a citizen and man as a private individual'; a vision of the Greek polis as a 'work of art' because, as Hegel argued, 'no one part could be separated from the others, it was an ideal and harmonious entity' and in which, Schiller stressed, 'political, social, family and religious obligations were [closely] interwoven' (in Plant 1983: 24). What emerged in the third instance was an appreciation of the work of Scottish Enlightenment thinkers Sir James Steuart and Adam Ferguson who, in *An Essay on the History of Civil Society* (published in 1767), traced the inescapable forms of alienation that seemed to accompany humankind's evolution from 'primitive simplicity to complicated refinement' (21). Echoing what at this point should be a familiar opposition between modern individualism and premodern communalism, Ferguson wrote: 'To the ancient Greek . . . the individual was nothing, the public everything. To the modern in too many nations of Europe the individual is everything and the public nothing' (in Plant 1983: 24).

Such was the world the young Hegel grew up in and the context in which he wrote the school essay of August 1788. The concern first addressed in this essay would drive his lifelong intellectual project – so much so, that many years later in a letter of 11 November 1800 to Friedrich Schelling, he would comment: 'In my scientific development which began with the more subordinate needs of men, I was compelled towards philosophy and the ideal of my youth had been transformed into a system' (in Plant 1983: 15). It is this question of what it means to be 'compelled towards philosophy' as a response to modernity that I want to focus on in the remainder of this chapter. To do so, I want to suggest that from this story about the unity of his life (narrated by Hegel himself), we can extract four principal moments that mark the process through which philosophy in a general sense becomes a response to modernity.

The first two are *diagnostic* moments and here there is a clear distinction between a *poeticist* and a *historicist* response to personal and social fragmentation: poeticists, in the language of the European experience, articulate the fragmentation of personal experience by pointing out how premodern religion was 'not rationalistic or cerebral like the Deism of contemporary Enlightened Europe but was thought to have appealed to the heart and to the imagination more than to the intellect' (Plant 1983: 20), while historicists understand this division of the modern self as no more than a function of deeper, historical, social divisions – that is, as symptomatic of socio-economic changes.

Accompanying these two diagnostic moments are two *prescriptive* moments, aimed at offering solutions to both forms of fragmentation. The first prescriptive response centres on the reinvention of tradition – specifically religion or spirituality – as a marker for the sacred sense of belonging associated with premodern forms of communality.[8] The second prescriptive response marks a turning away from (often driven by a disappointment with) the reinvented spiritual towards historiography; that is, towards a *philosophy of history* that promises to overcome individual and social fragmentation, by historicising the temporality of the experience of fragmentation. In Hegel's narration of the unity of his life, he is referring to his early or initial attempt to 're-enchant' the world through a reinvention of the traditional sacred, namely German folk religion. He would later reserve the description of 'a philosophical response proper' for the second prescriptive moment, which, by historicising *as* temporal the experience of fragmentation, would mark a turn to the philosophy of history.

There is something important to be gained from retracing the young Hegel's first non-philosophical response to the problem of European modernity. It resides in the suggestion implicit in doing so, namely that the problem of Ubuntu is, in a complex but very important sense, irreducible to the problem of colonialism as such. By this I mean that, at a very general level, Ubuntu discourse is first and

---

8. Here I explore only the thought of the young Hegel in relation to this question. Others have made a link between Ubuntu as a civic religion response to modernity; see, for instance, Barrett (2008).

foremost, in its most fundamental form (*archē*), a confrontation with modernity and the dual fragmentation of individual and social that marks the modern moment.[9] To make the commonality visible, thereby allowing for an *archē* humanism to emerge, nothing less than a temporary suspension or bracketing (*epoché*) of that which predisposes us to a judgement that obscures this commonality, namely 'colonialism', is necessary. This *epoché* and its resulting distinction – which, I must insist, is purely conceptual – will enable us to appropriate a meaning of Ubuntu appropriate for today, if only because it will remain irreducible to the two forms of historicism critiqued by Mbembe (2002).

The notion that a suspension or *epoché* of the narrative of colonialism will remind us that there is something general or universal going on depends, of course, on how we understand 'modernity'. If anything has emerged from the brief introduction to the story of Hegel so far, it is that the encounter with modernity is a deeply ambivalent moment. We associate it with the increased recognition and protection of individual rights and with the demise of traditional, communal bonds or moral praxes of custom and tradition, in which individuals used to live with a certain givenness of their belonging. We gain the recognition of our individuality by losing the givenness of belonging; inversely, we gain the givenness of individualism by denaturalising the assumption that we belong. Only once it is lost and has to be reimagined all the way from its ontological bottom up (by contrasting competing axiomatics of the juridical, for instance), only then can we say that *belonging has become, first and foremost, a problem for thought*. Beyond all its complexity, this is fundamentally what we recognise as the modern moment.

In Chapter 1, I suggested that we can also articulate the idea that homelessness (*Unheimlichkeit*) is a condition for theorising the possibility and meaning of being at home in the world (*Heimlichkeit*) in terms of my own concern in this report as follows: only when belonging becomes a problem for thought does ubuntu become possible as Ubuntu; only then does a philosophy emerge that seeks to re-present in a contemporary idiom the givenness of belonging that historically existed as a function of a political economy of obligation. Ubuntu or the reinvention of the sacred *as* philosophy, then, becomes possible *because of* modernity, as a *reaction against* modernity.

---

9. *Archē*: the Greek word for 'beginning', in the dual sense of 'beginning' and 'principle' or 'origin' and 'rule'. See Birmingham (2006: 9).

But to the young Hegel, such a reinvention of the sacred as civic religion amounted to little more than a first unphilosophical and prescriptive response to modernity that must pass into a proper philosophical or historiography-driven response to modernity. I want to focus on what this transition meant to Hegel and its implications for our own attempts at historicising the loss of ubuntu and its reinvention as Ubuntu. But before I can do this, there are a couple of important moments in Hegel's own initial unphilosophical response to modernity that remain relevant – not only because they reveal powerful commonalities, but also because in those very commonalities lie important clues to what I think of as the *archē*, the *origin and rule* of critical humanism.

In a series of essays published between 1788 and 1793, Hegel pursued the possibility of 'social theology' or 'civil theology' (as per Augustine) through a constant comparison of the Greek religious *experience* with the nature of Christian *faith*. The former was 'integrated into the life of the community', while the latter created 'deep social divisions' (Plant 1983: 32); the former was concerned not 'with viable religious truths but with social peace' and as such was an example of *subjective religion*, 'which appeals to the whole man so that religion becomes an affair of the heart, a matter of emotion and imagination as well as reason and intellect' (33). Hegel deemed Christianity an example of *objective religion*, 'based upon truths about man and God discerned by the light of reason alone . . . which pays no attention to the conative and affective sides of man's nature'.

The reason why objective religion is divisive or fragmenting follows not only from the fact that it enervates the conative and affective side of human nature. Its 'anticommunitarian spirit' (Plant 1983: 35) also leads to social fragmentation because 'it leaves a gap between religious belief and social morality' (33): 'The task of any religion in the young Hegel's view is that of fostering social morality, but an objective religion cannot fulfil this role because the impulse to morality is not, *pace* Kant, primarily intellectual. Reason by itself cannot move a man to action.' Summarising Hegel's view on premodern folk religion with a statement that resonates strongly with Placide Tempels's succinct summary of premodern African thought as one in which 'moral standards depend essentially on things ontologically understood' (1969: 121), Plant notes that for the young Hegel, 'to act morally a man must act as a total being, with all his powers engaged'. Again the Greeks are held up as an ideal of this premodern idyll of a social sacred and a sacred social, one in which, Schiller argued, the Greeks were 'aware of the divine in every aspect of their existence, both in the social and the natural worlds' (in

Plant 1983: 37). At this stage, then, the solution the young Hegel proposes for modernity as a condition of personal and social fragmentation is clear:

> It is Hegel's strongly urged view in the fragments on folk religion that only something akin to Greek folk religion could recapture social and political homogeneity. He argues that a folk religion is necessary to replace Christianity in the hope that it would permeate society and so remove the dissonance and fragmentation which he regards as characteristic of his age. Such an effect could only be achieved by the creation of a folk religion which would find its gods, its symbolism and its ritual in the history and the traditions of the people and thus provide a core of common culture (Plant 1983: 36).

In Hegel's early development, the period 1788–93 marks the first moment of a deep engagement with the fragmentation that is modernity; he called it a diagnostic moment, but I prefer to think of it as the first moment in the process of reinventing tradition when we remember the (always romanticised) integration that seemed to have typified premodernity; when we lived integrated lives as human beings, prior to the division of labour and the fragmentation of the personal and the social. The second moment of reinvention is *critique*, when we address the question of how to mobilise this memory to overcome the fragmentation of the present.

In exactly such a second phase, starting in 1795, Hegel responded to this challenge by moving away from a purely religious diagnosis to a politico-religious analysis. The question became how to develop or reinterpret Christianity so that it may evolve into a viable, contemporary folk religion. What followed was a reinterpretation of the historical figure of Jesus in wholly immanent terms as (no more than) a prophet. In this period – inaugurated with the essay *Das Leben Jesu* – the aim became 'changing people's perception of their actual religious practices so that these practices, once reinterpreted, could develop into a folk religion' (Plant 1983: 43). Just as ubuntu is being reinvented as an Ubuntu suitable to a modern, nationalism project through a local, a priori circumcision of its problematic transcendental (living-dead) and gender (phallo-primocentric) dimensions, *Das Leben Jesu* responded to the demand for a modern reinvention of the Christian sacred, 'in such a way that all transcendental, authoritarian elements in it would disappear in the hope that out of this demythologized, humanized teaching a folk or civic religion might grow'. In both cases, the result represents a concern 'not so much to make claims about the relation of man to God [or the living-dead] but rather with fostering human relations and morality'.

If the reinterpretation of the premodern sacred in wholly immanent and post-patriarchal terms formed the first moment in the critique of the reinvention, the second moment for Hegel consisted of the realisation 'that schemes for reform in contemporary society based solely upon some intellectually-founded attempt to change contemporary religious experience would come to nothing without correlative changes in general social and political conditions' (Plant 1983: 47). In other words, to counteract individual and social fragmentation, a reinvented sacred had to be considered as merely one aspect among a complex set of other social factors. What followed for Hegel was an exploration of the interaction between the general social and political conditions that could explain the decline of Greek folk religion and the rise of Christianity as a subjective religion, from a communitarian experience of the religious, 'predicated upon a feeling of close identification with and integration into the community' (48), to an objective experience of rationalised faith, symptomatic of both the fragmented individual and society.

The seismic shifts in the socio-political landscape of Rome that accounted for the rise of Christianity as a subjective religion, the fact that this religion 'arose out of the unhappy consciousness generated by the lack of political *community* in Rome' (Plant 1983: 49) is not important here. What does matter is that Hegel recognised the seemingly simple fact that the reinvention of the modern sacred as a solution to the fragmented social must be predicated upon a profound understanding of the socio-economic and political shifts that caused the decline of communitarian spirituality in the first place.

The publication of *Die Positivität der christlichen Religion* in 1796 marks a crucial moment in the development of Hegel's thinking about the problem of modernity. Plant comments:

> His work during this period is vital for understanding the remarkable change which his thought underwent during the final years of the century – the change from socio-religious reformism with an emphasis upon the desirability of the foundation of a political community of free, self-directing, active participating individuals held together by common values predicated upon a non-transcendental interpretation of Christianity, to a philosophically-based understanding of the contemporary world (1983: 56).

Pivotal to this change is the move away from socio-religious reform to philosophical comprehension – a change that Hegel would later square with his understanding of philosophy: 'The task of philosophy . . . [is] to make thought adequate to reality, to develop a conceptual framework which would be capable of encapsulating the life of society, a framework which once shared would enable men to live at home in the world and with one another' (in Plant 1983: 31). Central to this movement towards philosophical comprehension was the work of Steuart, particularly *An Inquiry into the Principles of Political Economy* (published in 1767). From this work, Hegel derived a concept that would remain fundamental to the rest of his life's work, namely a 'rationally discernible development in history, a development which, once comprehended, would change the attitude of people towards their social environment' (57).

Until this moment, Hegel had at best an implicit philosophy of history. It was regressive and viewed social evolution in terms of a gradual decline of humankind, from integrated spiritual communality to fragmented modernity. But all of this was to change through his encounter with Steuart's theory of socio-economic evolution. The resulting impact on Hegel (according to Plant) is worth quoting at length:

> The modern world was no longer seen in such a jaundiced light but was regarded by Hegel as embodying certain values and principles and actualizing certain human powers and capacities which could not find realization in the Ancient world. The present began to be looked upon as part of man's *fate*: there could be no sense in trying to go back to more ancient types of social, political and religious organization – these were predicated upon quite different circumstances. What was required was some comprehensive grasp of the values, principles and human powers actualized in the modern world, how these were worked out in the modes of experience to hand in society and how they were related to other, earlier, different and less developed societies. The modern world was no longer to be condemned as irrational because it failed to correspond to a paradigm taken from the ancient world; rather, the rationality which the contemporary world had needed to be grasped. Only then could men find a home in it and be satisfied with the forms of community which it offered (1983: 65).

What Steuart's work allowed Hegel to grasp was that modernity was not somehow a mistake that had to be rectified through a reinvention of Christianity as folk religion, but rather that the present came about as the natural result of a *necessary* process of *progressive* social evolution that, through a combination of exogenous pressure and endogenous potential, saw European societies drift from pre-agrarian, pastoral societies to agrarian societies and then to the exchange economy of commercial societies. Only when we have understood the necessity and inherently progressive nature of this process, Hegel now argued, will we have understood and reconciled ourselves to our 'fate'.

'Fate' for Hegel is nothing but the recognition that history has a mind of its own and for 'mind', we can also read in the vocabulary of the time, 'Spirit' or the 'Absolute'. The proper attitude we should adopt vis-à-vis the manner in which Mind works itself out in and through history – in fact, *as* history – is not struggle and resistance, but reconciliation and acceptance. This was no simple *'c'est la vie'*, but rather a 'profound grasp of the principles, the values and the patterns of human experience realized in the modern world' (Plant 1983: 71). One of these principles was the recognition that modernity marks the attainment of self-consciousness that fundamentally ruptures our being in the world. This rupture or quantum leap in self-consciousness is the modern moment when the historical praxis, of which belonging had been a function, fragments in order to re-present belonging as a problem for thought, a problem that henceforth will only find a solution *through* thinking and *as* thought, in rational agreement.

This is not to suggest that a historical praxis such as ubuntu never contained as part of its praxis a critical engagement with what belonging was understood to mean, or with the conditions for its possibility, or that there did not exist (ritualised) ways of safeguarding the coherence and continuity of belonging. By suggesting that modernity is the moment when belonging becomes a problem for thought, I mean two things: one, that it marks a moment when the sacred (ontological) bottom of belonging, the religious or transcendental grounding of our belonging, falls out or gets questioned to the extent that it can no longer contain or function as a referent for a discourse on the limits and possibility of belonging. Historically, to say of somebody that he or she lacked ubuntu was to recognise oneself and the community as approaching, or having approached, the limits of belonging. A threat had been posed to belonging and a potential crisis loomed. Historically both the diagnosis and the solution to the crisis of belonging were articulated with recourse to a transcendental reference, the living-dead, who functioned as a transcendental legitimation for the rituals through which individuals were expected constantly to re-enact the meaning of belonging as love, sharing and work. When such references to the transcendental lose their givenness or when the master trope of belonging that characterised this notion of belonging, namely ubuntu, is extended to include those for whom any such reference would be meaningless or irrelevant, belonging becomes a problem for thought.

This is the second thing I have in mind with the phrase 'belonging becomes a problem for thought'. In the absence of any transcendental legitimation, belonging becomes not simply a problem for thought, but *first and foremost* a problem for thought. This is how we should understand what Hegel meant by viewing modernity as a moment of self-consciousness that marks a transition from *sinnliche Harmonie* – a communitarianism based on unmediated imagination and feeling, epitomised by the hometown structures of Württemberg life, layered over by the guild as 'second family', which protected individuals, buffered them against contingencies, convened 'elaborate ceremonies at various stages of a member's life' and 'regulated a person's life from apprenticeship to death' (Pinkard 2000: 6) – to a *moralische Harmonie*, a communitarianism based on intellectual effort.

Hegel's turn to philosophy for a solution to the ambivalence of modernity amounted to reading the transition to modernity as both necessary and progressive – the full detail of which he worked out in *Die Phänomenologie des Geistes* (published in 1807), where he provided what he hoped would be a 'plausible account of contemporary society as actualizing in its own way certain important human values and providing its own patterns of integration and community' (in Plant 1983: 78).

This text pivots on concepts central to understanding what the turn away from religious reformation to philosophy meant to Hegel – bifurcation, integration, dialectic, Spirit and teleology. To provide a philosophical response to the necessary fragmentation that is modernity now meant reading the development of society in terms of oppositions and bifurcations, which are systematically overcome in ever-higher degrees of integration (the dialectic) in the long march of history that will culminate (teleology) in the reunification of *Geist* (Spirit/Mind) with itself; Mind coming through its Senses, as it were. In Hegel's own words: 'The Absolute ever plays a moral tragedy with itself in which it ever gives birth to itself in the objective world, then in this form of itself gives itself over to suffering and death and then raises itself out of its ashes to glory' (in Plant 1983: 80).

Hegel's work became a noteworthy philosophy of modernity precisely because he gave up on the civil religion project and reconstituted (explained and embraced) fragmentation *as a necessary moment in the history of every individual and society*.

The idea of a dialectical process through which Mind is alienated in history – or *as* history – only to perpetually subsume that alienated state into higher forms of integration, culminating in the End of history, *that* was Hegel's 'proper' philosophical solution to the problem of the fragmentation of the individual and society, a problem that had been haunting him since he first grappled with it in the school essay he wrote at the age of eighteen.

The purpose of this short detour through Hegel's intellectual coming-of-age is twofold. In the first place, I have tried to demonstrate something of the generality of modernity conceived as the moment when belonging becomes a problem for thought. This generality was revealed through a temporary *epoché* of the colonised consciousness that revealed as analogous the transition from ubuntu to Ubuntu and *sinnliche* to *moralische Harmonie*. The second purpose is to highlight how important it was for Hegel to have turned away from religious reform to historiography-driven philosophical understanding. The former was always premised on a regressive view of history, while the turn towards philosophy proper was premised on its opposite, a generative view of history as purposeful, in the sense that pain and suffering were understood as necessary moments in a much bigger story, in which even 'the Passion and Crucifixion were necessary *developments* in the life of God' (Plant 1983: 80).

In this gesture of the later Hegel, we see him contest the historicity of temporality as a solution to the ambivalence of modernity. It is a crucial gesture for us because it goes to the heart of Mbembe's critique in 'African Modes of Self-Writing' (2002), namely that postcolonial Africanists tried to make sense of the trinity of slavery, apartheid and colonialism through a regressive *historicism*. We can be more specific now. The problem was not that Africanists adopted grand narratives to make sense of what had happened to Africa and how to postulate hope, but that they adopted specifically Hegelian (because teleological) grand narratives of redemption that posited/promised final liberation from colonial oppression in the complementary terms of an Afro-radical promise of liberation, pivoting on the seizure of the state and a Revolutionary nativist recovery of a lost self that would one day, again, recognise itself in the face of history.

But how do we unsettle the pivotal status of colonialism in these grand narratives without trivialising the immense suffering of the colonised? Perhaps the *epoché* allows us to make a different move, one that views colonialism not as pivotal moment that generates a redemptive myth of decolonisation, but instead views colonialism as a disruption. The idea of colonialism as a disruption or interruption is not new – as Ato Sekyi-Otu has argued:

For supposing colonialism and its archetype, apartheid, are, in a more ethically significant sense, not so much a matter of racial dispossession and injustice but rather an event of disruption? What then? That is certainly a textually defensible reading of Fanon's understanding of colonial history. In effect Fanon says in one and the same crucial paragraph in *The Wretched of the Earth* that colonialism effects not only a cultural dispossession but also a 'dislocation' of the moral grammar of the subjugated people (236). This formulation anticipates Wole Soyinka's account of the colonial condition as one of 'interrupted history.' Even more strikingly, Fanon's formulation foreshadows the Nigerian historian J. F. A. Ajayi's audacious claim made in an essay published more than thirty years ago to the effect that colonialism was an episode in African history (2003: 11).

Only an episode, perhaps, but still, as Sekyi-Otu himself acknowledges later in the same article, one 'hell of an episode'. Nonetheless, what we stand to gain from viewing colonialism not as pivotal, but as an interruption or episode, is a first step in the direction of avoiding the kind of historicism or teleological grand-narrative posturing that have produced two dominant dead ends in Ubuntu discourse: on the one hand, the patronising teleology of Afro-radicals, specifically of the historicist Cosmopolitan or scientific Marxist variety, for whom Ubuntu is merely a useless and outdated precapitalist momento of a moral grammar that has nothing left to say; on the other hand, the eschatological, redemptive historicism of the nativist Saviour, for whom a full recovery and repositing of that moral grammar is not only possible, but urgently needed by the whole world.

For the rest of this chapter, I want to deploy a distinction between *historicism* – as critiqued by Mbembe (2002) – and Hegel's recognition of the philosophical imperative to *historicise* modernity. That we should historicise our existence, both individual and collective, that we should tell stories that make sense of temporality and the flux of becoming is inescapable; we cannot help but do this. But we do not necessarily have to do it through any kind of histori*cism*; that is, through the identification of historical Laws, for which the existence of any particular human being is as trivial as the existence of a planet is to the law of gravity. The challenge, I argue, consists in denying the one Hegel, while embracing the other: we have to accept the Hegel who insisted that the proper philosophical response to modernity is one that historicises experience and bases understanding on a theory of history, but we have to deny the Hegel who responded to this challenge by producing a totalitarian – because dialectical *and* teleological – form of historicism, a coming-of-age story in which Africa appeared as no more than a footnote because it had nothing to offer Mind. What we need is a different philosophy of history.

In the remainder of this chapter, I do no more than sketch the outlines of such a philosophy of history, one that will, I believe, release a repressed (because politically incorrect) meaning of Ubuntu as an uncanny (un/familiar) reminder of an *archē* humanism. The last chapter builds on this meaning of Ubuntu by asking how such a meaning may assist us in reassessing the role Ubuntu *qua* critical humanism can play in relation to constitutionalism in general and the democratic project in particular.

Colonialism and the arrow of time

> In each instance the dominating civilisation posed itself to the dominated as no less than the future, hence the dilemmas of extinction or hybridisation.
> — Lewis Gordon, 'Justice Otherwise: Thoughts on Ubuntu'

Earlier in this report, I pointed out how Ubuntu is often defined by juxtaposing the dictum 'I am because we are' – which only as recently as 1993–95 became representative of its meaning (Gade 2011: 313) – with the Cartesian 'I think therefore I am'. A typical example reads as follows:

> Where Descartes said 'I think, therefore I am', the African would rather say, 'I am related, therefore, we are.' In African spirituality, the value of interdependence through relationships comes high above that of individualism and personal independence . . . the practice of cooperation is more relied upon than competition (Kalilombe in Tomaselli 2009: 584).

Let us start by pursuing the implications of this juxtapositioning with René Descartes in relation to what historically came *before* and *after* Descartes in the history of the West. In terms of what came *after* Descartes, the obvious question is: Why compare a contemporary Ubuntu conception of personhood with a Western, modernist notion of personhood that is 300 years old? Why legitimise the novelty and (always suggested) superiority of the Ubuntu notion of personhood with a Western conception of personhood that, as influential as it may have been for a long time, is no longer representative of how personhood is thought of in the West? Western thought about personhood has gone far beyond Descartes in a range of ways, articulating the self in relation to others and the world in ways that now bear very little resemblance to the sovereign *cogito* articulated by Descartes. In fact, certain post-Cartesian understandings of personhood, such as we find in Martin Heidegger's ontological hermeneutics and various forms of communitarianism, particularly feminist ethics of care, are not only indistinguishable from Ubuntu but, given the logic of retrodiction, often essential for the articulation of Ubuntu. Why, then, this historically disjunctive comparison?

I think the temporal disjunction has everything to do with the politics of identity and in many ways echoes the kind of historiographic moves made by African Socialists – which should not come as a surprise because the stakes are the same. The claim that the Ubuntu-based notion of personhood is unique and superior (one because of the other) has two objectives: first, to restore African dignity by demonstrating that Africans can make an original and worthwhile contribution to philosophy; second, to demonstrate the usefulness and relevance of this philosophy, by showing how it is capable of addressing not only parochial identity issues, but also global political ones. In other words, what the Ubuntu theorist has to (re)produce is nothing less than a *locally unique* but *globally relevant* philosophy. In order to simultaneously achieve these ends, Ubuntu has to be differentiated, not from Western communitarianism, but from the Cartesian tradition of the autonomous *cogito*. Only by conflating the West with the latter can the uniqueness and hence salvific promise of Ubuntu be sustained.

But if Ubuntu discourse has a problem with what came *after* Descartes in Western thought, it is even more uncomfortable with what came *before* Descartes – for very similar, although perhaps more dangerous reasons:

> Before the [West's] modern era, single large scale bodies like the Church subsumed social, cultural and political activity under a single organizational system. This system, before the Enlightenment at least, was similarly communitarian in practice, as are claims made for contemporary Africans. With the collapse of the great ecclesiastical polities during the Thirty Years' War (1618–1648), people began to develop new ways of organizing (Tomaselli 2009: 587).

Descartes is what he is and the European Enlightenment is what it is because both signal an important moment in Western history: when belonging became, first and foremost, a problem for thought – which, in Western history, refers to the moment when the individual became both the point of reference for the recognition of a lost belonging and the point of departure for the reinvention of a new way of thinking about belonging. Nothing marks this moment in Western modernity more clearly than the revival of the social contract as a methodological fiction, through which theorists of Western modernity attempted to think through what it meant to posit, as a real possibility and problem for thought, the recognition that 'the laws of society come neither from God nor from tradition but from human volition' (Todorov 2003: 23). Prior to this moment, most Western societies were characterised by a lived communitarian praxis of *sinnliche Harmonie* very similar to the world suggested by the ubuntu praxis of interdependence. It is very difficult to be more precise here about the differences and similarities between ubuntu and these premodern communitarian praxes and traditions, considered as political economies of obligation, because a combination of Western hegemony and African identity politics would trouble such a comparison with hints of a social developmentalism that was the sine qua non of colonialism. I am, of course, referring to the idea that all societies go through the same stages of development or that there is a blueprint for the social evolution of all human societies.

To imagine what such a blueprint may have looked like was a favourite pastime of Western scholars of modernity spanning the period from Thomas Hobbes, in the early seventeenth century, to the work of classical modernisation theorists, in the 1950s and beyond. Constitutive of all these grand narratives of social evolution were two elements: one, a division into *stages* of development and two, an account of the *mechanism* that drove societies from one stage to the next. The two most influential accounts were undoubtedly those of Karl Marx and developmental psychoanalysts, such as Stanley Hall and Sigmund Freud. According to Marx, all societies pass from communalism through feudalism to capitalism and beyond that to socialism. The mechanism that accounts for this perpetual transformation is the tension between the forces and relations of production, so that every next phase of development comes into existence as the solution to a tension generated between them. Feudalism is the solution to otherwise unresolvable tensions generated by advanced communalism; capitalism solves the tensions generated by feudalism, socialism those generated by late capitalism and so on. This explains the persistence of the belief that societies cannot somehow skip any stage of development: the stages are locked into one another as a linear chain of problem-solving solutions – hence Marx's oft-quoted statement, in which, to emphasise a mechanistic over an organistic reading of his thought (Rader 1979), a country that is more developed industrially only shows to one less developed the image of its own future. At the origin of this chain, we find the simplest, most rudimentary form of socio-economic arrangement (communalism) and at the End, the most sophisticated (socialism), in which humans have restored the sense of organic communality lost by the original transition from communalism to feudalism and beyond. History, then, is always about the recovery of a primal loss and the End is the moment when the loss recognises its recovery.

Working in a very different domain, developmental psychologists and psychoanalysts, such as Hall and Freud, produced an eschatological blueprint with a very similar linear trajectory. In this version of things, 'civilisation' came to mean something like 'social maturity', so that to proclaim a society 'civilised' was the same as proclaiming it 'mature'. The language was that of individual psychology and in the same way that individuals were thought to evolve from childhood through adolescence to maturity, collective entities, such as societies and civilisations, were thought to evolve towards their own maturity. In this version of things, the mechanism that accounts for the evolutionary drive is 'recapitulation' – an idea first put forward by Ernst Haeckel, who invented the terms 'ontogeny' and 'phylogeny' and combined them in what became known as the phylogeny-ontogeny hypothesis. According to this hypothesis, societies advanced toward maturation by re-enacting the stages of development that an individual goes through and vice versa. We can learn more about childhood by studying primitive, childlike societies and we can learn more about these societies by understanding that they essentially behave in the same way as individuals in early childhood do. In the United States, for instance, Hall studied childhood play as a re-enactment of the rituals, beliefs and conventions of their savage adult ancestors. 'The child,' he says, 'revels in savagery, and if its tribal, predatory, hunting, fishing, fighting, roving, idle playing proclivities could be indulged . . . they could . . . be far more humanistic and liberal than all the best modern schools could provide' (in Gould 1977: 142; see also Praeg 2010a). The individual child re-enacts the first stages of social development of so-called primitive societies and, in so doing, behaves in the childlike manner of those societies who, for their part, were merely re-enacting the initial stage of the development of all societies on their way to civilised maturity. Of course, it was admitted that Western societies had had the same humble origins, but it was held that they had since recapitulated further, more advanced stages of development; they had already gone through their adolescence and were fast approaching maturity. In short, then, the principle of recapitulation at the heart of the phylogeny-ontogeny hypothesis imagined every society to recapture or re-enact the same universal stages of development and societies were judged superior or inferior to the extent that they had managed, or not, to leave behind their savage and childlike Origin in order to approached the End of civilised maturity or, as Ferguson in *An Essay on the History of Civil Society* put it, had managed to advance 'from primitive simplicity to complicated refinement' (in Plant 1983: 21).

The *epoché* that allowed us to recognise the transition from ubuntu to Ubuntu as similar to *sinnliche* to *moralische Harmonie* seems to play straight into this kind of developmentalism. It seems to leave us with one of two equally undesirable choices: we either accept the developmentalist argument and embrace some version of the thesis that Africa is lagging 300 years behind in the modernity project, or we feign incredulity at the very suggestion of grand-narrative theorising and the kind of similarity revealed by the first *epoché*. I want to argue that there is a third alternative that would allow us to recognise the arrow of time and even admit to broad structural similarities in social evolution, while at the same time refusing the political implications of these classic, Western grand narratives of social evolution.

A broccoli theory of evolution

It seems to me that to compare the development of two societies in order to arrive at the conclusion that one is more advanced than, and therefore superior to, the other, we need to accept at least two assumptions about the framework in which the comparison is made. The first is that there is a Beginning and an End; the second is that societies race from the former to the latter in a straight line. This is essentially a Newtonian world view, in which space is absolute and time is linear. Grand narratives, such as those of Marx and Freud, were fundamentally indebted to the teleological structure of Hegel's historiography and, as such, secularised versions of Christian messianism. Only in a universe where there is the teleological anticipation of things coming to an End does it make any sense whatsoever to divide the world into societies that are superior (because closer to that End) and those that are inferior (because further away from it). In other words, although Western grand narratives never conceived of development in absolute terms, but always relatively; that is, societies relative to one another, the race itself was thought to unfold in absolute space, in an image of space demarcated by a Beginning and an End, with linear time connecting the two.[10]

---

10. For a concise and useful discussion of the impact of, first, Newtonian physics and, later, the new physics on the social sciences and humanities, see Mudimbe and Jewsiewicki (1996: 1–33).

In the grand narratives of Western modernity that gradually flattened the vertical Chain of Being into a horizontal and evolutionary Chain of Becoming (Praeg 2010a), the Beginning and End were conceived of in a variety of terms that, depending on the kind of narrative in question (economic, social, psychological) became more or less interchangeable: the Beginning was associated with being childlike, savage and communal; the End, with being mature, civilised and socialist. The overriding image of this conceptual framework is of a 100-metre dash, with its visible starting block and finish line. For all its simplicity, it presents us with nothing less than the ontological assumptions of colonialism. Is it any wonder that the description of Ubuntu as a typical premodern world view or as a mere function of a precapitalist subsistence economy would annoy Africanists, who sense in this description the politics of this colonialist ontology at work? And should we be at all surprised that in response to this patronising developmentalism, African Socialists tried to have their grand-narrative cake and eat it too, by declaring African communalism at once the Beginning and End of a new way of historicising the temporal dimension of social evolution?

But we no longer live in a world of absolute time and space. In a universe that is materially relativist and, in terms of ideas, non-teleological – a world of systems theory, complexity theory, fractal geometry and the like – things are very different. These theoretical developments allow for the possibility of retaining the idea that there may be structural generalities in social evolution, without yielding to the ideological gradation in terms of 'more advanced' and 'less advanced', 'superior' and 'inferior'. To get a sense of what such a non-teleological narrative of social evolution looks like, it is useful to return to the original meaning of the word 'evolution'.

The idea of recapitulation was introduced in a context when the word 'evolution' had none of its contemporary Darwinian connotations. In fact, evolution used to refer to the exact opposite of its contemporary meaning, namely *preformation*, which was a rival biological theory at the time. Preformationists such as Albrecht von Haller believed that 'all human bodies were created fully formed and folded up in the ovary of Eve and that these bodies are gradually distended by alimentary humour until they grow to the form and size of animals' (Gould 1977: 29). The word that was used to describe this pointless 'unfolding' of preformed creatures derived from the Latin *evolutio*, which denotes 'an unrolling of parts already existing in compact form, as in a scroll or the fiddlehead of a fern'. According to this meaning of the word, how a biological or social entity came to be what it was had nothing to do with environment or circumstance. Evolution simply referred to the process whereby organisms unfolded their preformed essence. Herbert Spencer would significantly alter this meaning of the word by insisting that evolution referred to changes of increasing complexity, as a result of an organism's interaction with its environment. This, in turn, set the stage for Haeckel's introduction of the phylogeny-ontogeny hypothesis and its appropriation by developmental theorists and psychoanalysis as a mechanism that accounted for the maturity of more complex societies, a maturity that in the teleological frame of Western modernity came to mean superiority.

It is the pointlessness of evolution as understood by Haller that I want to return to here, but with one caveat: it would be silly to accept the notion of preformation because such an emphasis on endogeny can no longer be taken seriously. The reason why I want to return to Haller is because his understanding of evolution was curiously non-teleological; that is, quite literally pointless or not relative to any End. Evolution as the 'unrolling of parts . . . as in a scroll or the fiddlehead of a fern' is a pointless evolution indeed. It is not a race from Beginning to End, but rather a process of increasing complexity in space-time. When we translate this vision of evolution into the language of a non-teleological narrative of social evolution, we arrive at something such as the process described by Patrick L. Baker, for whom social evolution, contrary to the teleological narratives of evolution typical of Western modernity, has essentially been

> a move from a few humans living in many small centres with weak centripheral and centrifugal forces, using low amounts of energy, and having a very limited entropic effect on their environments to many humans living in a few large centres with strong centripheral and centrifugal forces, using vast amounts of energy, and having an enormous entropic impact on their environments. There has been a movement, then, from low entropy to high entropy societies, from many to a few social centres, and from slowly changing to quickly changing social formations. The notions of centriphery and entropy can, therefore account for the pattern of human social evolution (1993: 140–1).

If we then translate this vision back into an organistic (as opposed to mechanistic) reading of the Marxist grand narrative of social evolution (see Rader 1979), we are presented with a somewhat similar picture:

> The development of towns and social classes is not simply an invention of the West imposed on Africa. Historically, the development of agriculture and increased productivity, either through increased fertility of the land ... or development of irrigation and other techniques, allowed for the creation of social surplus ... As long as there was no permanent social surplus the community remained basically rural, basically insecure, basically equal ... There is nothing uniquely 'African' about this (Babu 1981: 57).

Elsewhere I have commented on this new vision of social evolution derived from the new physics that 'there is no sense in maintaining that high entropy societies are superior to low entropy societies or even that higher entropy and/or increased complexity is a desirable state of affairs' (Praeg 2010a: 307). In the absence of an End, there can be no development, only change and difference of the fractal kind; that is, in the same sense we would talk about more and less developed broccoli florets, without suggesting that one is superior to the other for being bigger.

Probably the most powerful image of non-teleological evolution comes from Lewis Carroll's *Through the Looking-Glass and What Alice Found There*, in which the Red Queen comments, 'It takes all the running you can do, to keep in the same place' (1998: 46). Evolutionary theorist Leigh van Valen first appropriated this image in 'A New Evolutionary Law' (1973) in what he called the Red Queen hypothesis. He used it to describe the 'evolutionary arms race', which describes a situation in which, given the fact that all species are co-evolving, an improvement in one species will inevitably lead to improvements in other species, so that in the long run everything changes, while everything stays the same. Geerat J. Vermeij popularised this absurdity in his *Evolution and Escalation: An Ecological History of Life* (1987) to demonstrate the evolutionary arms race between predators and prey. The only way a fox can compensate for the fact that a new generation of rabbits is running faster than the previous generation is to learn to run faster than previous generations of foxes. In the end, both predator and prey run faster, without either having achieved an objective advantage. The implication is clear: a social welfare state in which people live to 110, however more complex or stratified it may be and however more entropic noise it generates, is not more advanced or superior to a traditional desert community in which people live to 110 anyway. Such is the exquisite pointlessness of progress and evolution.

What all this means is that it is really the patronising politics of earlier, teleological – mechanistic or Newtonian – grand narratives of development that makes it so objectionable to suggest that Ubuntu is a typically premodern phenomenon, ideally suited to societies at a communal or subsistence level of production or, more negatively, that the transition to capitalism should render (or has rendered) the political economy, of which it was a function, irrelevant and that even if it did retain any relevance, there is nothing uniquely African about it because we find similar forms of communitarianism in all subsistence-driven, premodern societies. On the other hand and in light of the new physics, we lose nothing by presenting ubuntu as a form of premodern communitarian praxis in a post-teleological, grand-narrative framework of social evolution.

The key notion here is 'asynchronicity'. Many societies (or 'civilisations', if you wish) all over the world have experienced and continue to experience evolution towards higher entropy (modernity), but *not all at the same time*. Had this been the case, modernity would have been a synchronous business; the evolution of societies all over the world would have been synchronised like a global collection of clocks. But they are not. Instead, the developmental clocks of societies respond to very different and highly specific (because contextual) combinations of endogenous and exogenous factors, with the result that the process described by Baker occurs in an *asynchronous* fashion. The important thing to bear in mind is that although this asynchronicity manifests a 'lag' or difference between various societies, outside of a teleological framework of Beginnings and Ends, *this difference means nothing*. As a result, it is entirely possible to present Ubuntu as premodern communitarian praxis – with all the implied advantages and limitations – without thereby positing Africa as an 'always already regressive, backward epistemological construct' (Farred 2003: 70). This post-teleological appreciation of the absurdity of co-evolution is the *ontological foundation of post-coloniality*, of what in Chapter 2, with reference to Mudimbe, I call the *relativist* a priori of postcoloniality, as opposed to the preceding *historicist* a priori of colonialism.[11]

Only in a world of asynchronous modernities is it possible for Ubuntu to have generated such a huge array of different, and often conflicting, conceptual personae as those mapped in Chapter 2. Ultimately, the logic of asynchronous modernities

---

11. What is frustrating about Mbeki's African Renaissance is its implicit reliance on the assumption of equality that is a function of a postcolonial relativist a priori, while explicitly undermining that relativism by nominating the moment in terms of the familiar 'Renaissance'. As I try to show here, an argument for the 'similarity of the modern moment' can be made in a way that does not render Africa 'epistemologically anachronistic' (Farred 2003: 69).

plays out in identity politics at a global scale and each persona implies a political stance, assumed on the basis of what this means: Are the global trends of the developed societies so dominant and hegemonic that the local cannot find any original expression (the Cosmopolitan and the Archivist)? Or can we somehow bracket or suspend the dominance of these traditions and the archive they have constructed on Africa, in order to liberate past values for our own (Revolutionary) or collective (Saviour) redemption? Alternatively, and in terms of the tension generated between Revolutionary fervour and Cosmopolitan déjà vu, we can ask: is Ubuntu *exceptional* or is it simply more of the same? The tension between these meanings generates a profound instability in Ubuntu discourse: between the need to be special and the fear of being backward, between the hope that Africa is leading the change and the fear that it is merely catching up. These tensions simmer under the surface of Ubuntu discourse, creating everywhere an instability that is nowhere explicitly addressed.

To conclude this chapter, I want to look at the political matrix within which claims to Ubuntu's exceptionalism plays out. I shall argue in the following and last chapter that there is a way of appropriating Ubuntu in a manner that falls prey to neither (identitarian) Revolutionary exceptionalism nor to more of the Cosmopolitan same: this meaning of Ubuntu is of the un/familiar or uncanny.

Ubuntu exceptionalism

> Nothing changes when society breaks the mirror of madness (abolishes asylums, gives speech back to the mad, etc.) nor when science seems to break the mirror of its objectivity (effacing itself before its object, as Castaneda does, etc.) and to bow down before 'differences.' Confinement is succeeded by an apparatus which assumes a countless and endlessly diffractable, multipliable form. As fast as ethnology in its classical institution collapses, it survives in an anti-ethnology whose task is to reinject fictional difference and Savagery everywhere, in order to conceal the fact that it is this world, our own, which in its way has become savage again, that is to say devastated by difference and death.
> — Jean Baudrillard, *Simulations*

The idea that, in the form of Ubuntu, we are presented with something unique, something exceptional to the point of being miraculous or salvific, the whole quasi-religious iconography of forgiveness and infinite humanism that has come to envelop the figure of Mandela as the embodiment of the very meaning of Ubuntu, is by and large articulated by two *imaginaires*: a global, racist *imaginaire* and a local, racialised *imaginaire* of cultural nationalism. In relation to Ubuntu, the global *imaginaire* plays a game of racialised exceptionalism that serves to naturalise both economic neoliberalism and its ideological constituent, neo-racism. At a conceptual level, the manner in which these two *imaginaires* interface with one another can best be understood with reference to Jean Baudrillard's *Simulations* (1983) and Jane Gordon and Lewis Gordon's analysis in *Of Divine Warning: Reading Disaster in the Modern Age* (2009).

Let me start with the simple counter-observation that, for the vast majority of black South Africans, there was never anything particularly exceptional about Mandela's behaviour after his release from prison. The fact that he insisted on a message of forgiveness and reconciliation, instead of demanding justice and/or retribution for apartheid crimes against humanity, came as a big surprise to the global *imaginaire* (in which I include the majority of white South Africans). For ordinary black South Africans, there was no difference between this and what so many of them would later do at the Truth and Reconciliation Commission hearings. The story of exceptionalism – first attached to Mandela and later to the country's transition, which reduced the miraculous nature of the latter to a function of the miraculous nature of the former – did not emerge from within a local African *imaginaire*, but from within the Western-centric discourses of a racist, global *imaginaire*. The function of a rhetoric of divine exceptionalism embodied by Mandela is more sinister than one might suspect. As Gordon and Gordon have argued, at first glance the celebration of exceptional black individuals, such as Mandela and Barack Obama, may be interpreted as a sign that racism has been overcome by an epiphany of recognition – and yes, on a superficial, mostly symbolic level, this is the case. But on another level, it is also the opposite, for as Gordon and Gordon argue:

> Contemporary racism requires a loved absence by which a hated presence is maintained. Put differently, in addition to the negative image of black people that many non-blacks may have is a sometimes secretly harboured, idealized image of the exception, of a perfect black individual whom they could love, admire, even idolize. In its structure, it props up the antiblack racist into the presumed standpoint of legitimate judgement of who, among all the black people in the world, counts as worthy (2009: 93).

The elevation of Mandela as exceptional was not only an elevation of Mandela the individual out of the category of ordinary individuals or statesmen, but also an elevation of Mandela the *black* individual out of the category of black people, so that this *imaginaire* could valorize him as an individual, *while retaining its racial prejudice in relation to ordinary black people* in general. This is the racist subtext of the quasi-theological discourse on South Africa's transition that in another sense really demonstrated the disappointment of Afro-pessimists. Gordon and Gordon comment:

> The power of the idealized exception is such that it stimulates devotion, even obsession, because of its symbolic potency: It is a function of its expected impossibility. Because once deemed impossible, because ideal, it arrives as a magical or divine force, for only magicians, gods, or G-d [or saints] can achieve the impossible (2009: 94).

The same logic applies to those instances where the philosophical exceptionalism of Ubuntu is commented on and celebrated. Once we have been alerted to the definitional circularity that constantly reproduces the uniqueness of Ubuntu and its salvific promise, the next question becomes: but why this fascination with Ubuntu? Why does this global *imaginaire* not take its own humanism or communitarianism seriously enough as political praxis? Why is it that in the philosophical and political discourses of this *imaginaire*, Western forms of communitarianism are only ever trivialised as 'unrealistic' or as 'nice to have in an ideal world', a mere theoretical, if naive, alternative to the putatively inescapable praxis of neoliberal individualism and political realism? My point is simple: In a global political economy where this is the standard response to communitarian thought and praxis, it makes perfect sense that an example of a working communitarian praxis elsewhere should not only be exceptionalised as 'miraculous', but also projected as being from 'over there', as something *Africans are good at*. To point to Africa as the locus of some naturalised communitarian praxis, to locate it geographically 'over there', is a gesture that fulfils a complex variety of conservative (and conserving) sociological and political functions. What these are can best be summarised with reference to Baudrillard's analysis of the way in which such pointing to the 'over there' functions in relation to the place and meaning of Disneyland in American culture:

> Disneyland is there to conceal the fact that it is the 'real' country, all of 'real' America, which *is* Disneyland (just as prisoners are there to conceal the fact that it is the social in its entirety, in its banal omnipresence, which is carceral). Disneyland is presented as imaginary in order to make us believe that the rest is real, when in fact all of Los Angeles and the America surrounding it are no longer real, but of the order of the hyperreal and of simulation. It is no longer a question of a false representation of reality (ideology), but of concealing the fact that the real is no longer real, and thus of saving the reality principle . . . [Disneyland] is meant to be an infantile world, in order to make us believe that the adults are elsewhere, in the 'real' world, and to conceal the fact that real childishness is everywhere . . . (1983: 25).

How does one conceal the fact that childishness is everywhere? By creating a space in which people can be childish 'over there'. Once we have succeeded in making ourselves and others believe that we must 'go there' to be childish, we will have forgotten, and assisted everyone else in forgetting, how childish all of us are 'over here'. This is the moral function of the geographical *dislocation*, of the gesture that *locates* communitarianism as viable political praxis 'over there' in Africa. Once the global *imaginaire* has succeeded in this dislocation, it has managed to secure for itself a double-confirmation in *space* and *time* of the inescapability of neoliberal individualism as political and economic praxis. In terms of its spatial dislocation, the gesture confirms that 'only Africans are capable of communitarian praxis because they have Ubuntu' and in terms of its temporal dislocation, 'Don't expect a communitarian praxis from us because it is a rare, miraculous thing'.

Of course, what is really annoying about such self-legitimising projections is that the global *imaginaire* uses this self-affirmation as a substitute act of recognition, which similarly leaves the racial matrix intact, by pretending to recognise the superiority of communitarian praxes over liberal alternatives – forgiveness over revenge, restorative justice over retribution and so on – often summarised in a melancholy statement such as, 'We have so much to learn from the Africans', which really only conceals how things work in the racialised matrix of the global *imaginaire*: it would rather pay Africans the play-play compliment of being ahead of the game than allow itself to be interrogated by the practical possibilities of its own communitarian traditions.

In this reified realm of collective projections, we find a happy marriage between a global and a certain nationalist, local *imaginaire*. For nothing suits the intellectual of this local *imaginaire* and its nationalist ideology better than the Revolutionary suggestion that Africa's communitarian praxis puts it streets ahead of the rest of the world. Nothing suits its own desire for exceptionalism better than the play-play compliment that it is the solution to the root of all individualist evils. In this win-win collusion, the West gets to naturalise its racist, neoliberal individualism, while Africa manifests for itself a dignified place in the world order on the back of its so-called exceptional communitarianism, a logic of binary displacement that, because of its conflation of Ubuntu with being African, renders Ubuntu *qua* humanism and therefore as a mode of critique, impotent as viable response to Africa's own Big Men.

Of course, to effect this exceptionalism, the racist global and racialised local *imaginaires* have to collude in an act of forgetfulness: of Western, communitarian subjectivity/praxes that came both before and after Descartes. Buried underneath this heady concoction of Western self-legitimation and African identity politics lies the simple fact of an *archē* violation: both the global hopes for an exception and the African need for authenticity amount to responses in bad faith to what all parties would agree is the simple message of Ubuntu, prior to its being politicised in the racialised dialectics of colonialism and liberation, as a statement about our shared humanity.

Conclusion

The first *epoché* in this chapter is premised on the axiomatic assumption that modernity is the moment when belonging becomes, first and foremost, a problem for thought. This axiomatic reduced – in order to comprehend – questions of spectacular complexity to a basic set of interactions that allows us to conclude with a very specific question, namely, what are the implications of this axiomatic for South Africa's postcolonial modernity, characterised as it is by a bifurcation between constitutionalism and a subaltern political economy of obligation? Perhaps the following:

- We may well want to respond to the fragmentation that is postcolonial modernity by reinventing the sacred or spiritualised belonging of premodern praxis – as what we may call a 'civic religion' or spiritualised humanism;
- doing so will be limited by two essential features of this reappropriation: one, the attempt at secularising the historical praxis of belonging will falter

by delegitimating what made the historical praxis most compelling and specific in the first instance: a transcendent God, the proximity of the living-dead and so on; and two, that any such reinvention will likely only address the existential fragmentation and not the socio-economic fragmentation, of which the former is a function;
- the reinvention of belonging needs to be accompanied – no, *founded* – on a different legitimation, not the kind found in appeals to the beyond, but the kind derived from a theory of history;
- a postmodern theory of history suggests the asynchronicity of modernities externally (relative to one another) *and* internally (as constitutive of the condition of postcoloniality as such). In other words, the premodern is no longer to be valued as 'backward' and 'problematic', something that should be left behind by the march of history. In the relativist a priori of the post-, the pre- continues *alongside* the project of (post)coloniality: no longer to be judged as lack, nor to be dialectically redeemed as necessary step along the way;[12]
- lastly, such asynchronicity suggests a place and a meaning – and along with this, a legitimacy derived from its historicity – of Ubuntu that we can perhaps best theorise in terms of that which is never to be forgotten, but never to be made wholly familiar either; that is, of Ubuntu as perpetually un/familiar or uncanny.

The notion of Ubuntu as the uncanny, then, becomes a very useful way of understanding essential features of the complex relationship between Ubuntu and modernity (both Western and postcolonial) – some of which feed back into the racialised matrix of exceptionalism.

What Descartes sacrificially excluded from the dictum '*Cogito ergo sum*' was not simply any reference to an Other, but the notion, fact or recognition of relationality itself, of the very idea that the self exists in relation to the world (hence the Idiot). The combined rationalism of Descartes and the historiography

---

12. This *alongside* suggests a position between, on the one hand, Lévi-Strauss's synchronic distinction between 'a science of the concrete' and a 'science of the abstract' and, on the other hand, Jack Goody's insistence on a diachronical historical process that accounts for the 'growth of knowledge'. For a more detailed discussion of this distinction, see Mudimbe (1988: 28–35).

of Hegel literally made relational existence the *unthought* of Western modernity, by declaring relationality rationally dispensable and historically irrelevant. By 'unthought', I mean to refer to that which first had to be *recognised – sinnliche Harmonie*, for Hegel and the relation that our senses establish between us and the external world, for Descartes – before it could get problematised and declared rationally suspicious and historically irrelevant. The logic of interdependence was twice transcended in order to become the unthought foundation of Western modernity.

But what we repress or leave behind never simply goes away. Instead, it re-emerges in a different form at another time in unsuspecting places. The unthought of relationality would return to haunt Western modernity in its confrontation with people who (still) profoundly believed in the relationality of existence. This encounter re-presented the West with nothing less than the potential threat of an *inexecution* of its founding, a potentially devastating *peripeteia* or reversal of fortune that would have forced the West to recognise something universal in its particular experience. But instead the West responded by *universalising its particular experience*. This assumed the form of elevating rationality as one possible mode of engagement with the world to the status of *the* primary mode of engagement with reality – which meant turning it into a universally applicable criterion for judging who is human and who is not.

As I argue in the conclusion to Chapter 1, I find it illuminating to think of scientific racism as a particular form of violence that only becomes possible as a response to this uncanny encounter with the original exclusion that made Western modernity possible. Racism is the violence that maintains the founding moment of Western modernity as inscrutable to itself, thereby enabling its perpetual execution. Racism is the violence par excellence that enabled the West to execute its modernity and the reason why we could think of its projection of the accompanying fear of inexecution as the historic a priori of colonialism. According to Max Horkheimer and Theodor Adorno in 'The Concept of Enlightenment', what I am referring to as the fear of *inexecution* can be presented in terms of two related fears that are a function of Western Enlightenment, viewed as a 'nominalist tendency' (2002: 17): on the one hand, the fear of the unknown, of there being 'an outside' beyond human control (11), which necessitated the reduction of *every*thing to some*thing*; on the other hand, a fear of any form of collectivism, abstract or concrete. In the words of Horkheimer and Adorno: 'Enlightenment finally devoured not only symbols but also their successors, universal concepts, and left nothing of metaphysics behind except *the abstract fear of the collective from which it had sprung*' (emphasis added).¹³

The model of asynchronous modernities proposed here allows us to understand better the full impact and some of the consequences of what it means to claim, as I did earlier, that what is most specific about hypermodernity is the spectre of a founding that will remain eternally exposed, visible to itself and therefore, *inexecuted*. From this ambivalence, from this founding that is not a founding, much follows. And if we are looking for a meaning and a place for Ubuntu in relation to this juridico-politically (un)founded, it is not to the quasi-transcendental or the Law of laws that we should turn, but rather to Ubuntu as un/familiar reminder of what South Africa's modernity failed to 'leave behind' and of what continues to haunt it in the form of a reminder of the original injustice that was sacrificially excluded from its founding, contractual axiomatic. But this exclusion is complex because it also represented the collective will of the liberated. This fact points us in the direction of another founding aporia – more precisely, an *aporia-archē*, the logic of which can only be revealed through a second *epoché*.

---

13. No doubt, placing this phrase in the context of my analysis stretches its intended meaning somewhat, but I think this is justified by Horkheimer and Adorno's description of 'Enlightenment as a nominalist *tendency*' (2002: 17, emphasis added). In addition, doing so certainly does not violate the spirit of what in many ways reads like a deconstruction *avant la lettre* of the concept of 'Enlightenment' – they first published this description in 1944.

CHAPTER 5

The Law
Second *Epoché*

> The mere fact that the tenets that underpin this philosophy are intensely expressed by Africans, do[es] not make those values exclusively African.
>
> — Joe Teffo, 'Botho/Ubuntu as a Way Forward for Contemporary South Africa'

> Thus we keep our objective thinking tied to a relational stake at the heart of caring.
>
> — Nel Noddings, *Caring*

The intention behind the *epoché* of the previous chapter was not to trivialise any claim about Ubuntu's particularity, but rather an attempt to frame such claims with reference to what seems to me most typical about the moment when societies come to think of themselves as modern. The specific insight that emerged from that *epoché* was that, in an important sense, it does not matter *how* or for what reasons a society arrives at the point where belonging becomes, first and foremost, a problem for thought – whether through internal revolutions or external influence (a difference of degree more than kind, anyway) – the net effect is familiar: the transition from a communitarian praxis of belonging, in which social relations are constitutively prior to any coherent concept of individual*ism*, to a world in which a conception of the priority of the individual, to some disputed extent, forms the point of departure for speculation about the very *possibility* of belonging and the social.

But what does it mean to say that modernity is the moment when belonging becomes a problem for thought? Much of this chapter is an attempt to elaborate on this meaning, in order to put it to work in a way that will hopefully shed some light on issues that are all complex in their own right and contribute to a picture of 'supercomplexity' (Barnett 2000) when considered together. In order to bring some clarity to this supercomplexity, let me articulate two axiomatics upon which the second *epoché* is premised.

In the first instance, there is an *ontological* axiomatic. From this follows the need for what I think of as the second, *political*, axiomatic: the institutions of modernity that exist for making, interpreting and enforcing the rules we live by have to reflect (and assist us in mediating) a fundamental tension or contradiction at the heart of the ontological axiomatic. Prior to modernity, the institutions of so-called premodernity made this tension bearable by keeping it invisible, by concealing it behind transcendental appeals to the Will of God or the matrix that regulated human relationships with the living-dead. From such an ontological grounding of belonging, everything else was deducted: morality, the law and an understanding of justice. However, once this deduction is denaturalised by the separation of church and state, or tradition and politics, what used to be a praxis (ubuntu/*sinnliche Harmonie*) becomes an abstract problem for thought (Ubuntu/*moralische Harmonie*). What now becomes visible and inescapable is a contradiction at the very heart of belonging that, although apprehended rationally, cannot be resolved through any appeal to rationality. No philosopher of Western modernity better understood this aporia than Immanuel Kant, who realised that with modernity or Enlightenment, rational thought became the foundation for thinking through a number of problems about human nature and existence that, by their very nature, exceeded rational thought. In his introduction to *Critique of Pure Reason*, he argues:

> Human reason has the peculiar fate in one species of its cognitions that it is burdened with questions which it cannot dismiss, since they are given to it as *problems* by the nature of reason itself, but which it also cannot answer, since they transcend every capacity of human reason (1998: 99, emphasis added).

In this light, we can elaborate the ontological axiomatic of modernity to read: (1) modernity is the moment when a tension at the heart of belonging becomes *visible* in a way that leaves it unredeemable by any appeals to something beyond the human domain; (2) as a problem that can, in future, only be *addressed by thinking* (and thinking about thinking), while accepting (3) that thinking can *never resolve* the tension or contradiction. In other words, modernity is the moment when belonging becomes, first and foremost, an *unresolvable* problem for thought.[1] When we accept this, we are positing thinking as a condition of the possibility of belonging, while implicitly acknowledging the limitations of thinking being *as belonging*. The recognition of the limits of thinking, the inability of rational thought truly to think what it means to belong, amounts to an implicit realisation that, in future, there will only ever be a praxis and a thought of belonging without legitimation or, rather, that the legitimation of belonging will be internal to or constitutive of a meta-reflective praxis of belonging. This sounds complex, but the idea is quite simple: I can never think that I belong (to a group or society of any kind); thinking at best affords me the relative assurance, 'I *think* I belong'. To *know* that I belong; that is, to feel that I belong, requires something that cannot be thought, something that happens beyond the limits of thinking – an exchange with others that, for as long as I remain open to it, may constitute being as belonging.

At this point, let us also replace the distinction between premodern/modern and traditional/modern with a distinction that derives from the logic of asynchronous modernities developed in the previous chapter. On the one hand, there is what we can describe as the *(post)modernised imaginaire* of those for whom belonging has been for some time, first and foremost, a problem for thought; on the other hand, there is the *modernising imaginaire* of those for whom belonging is in the process of becoming a problem for thought. For the former, institutions of modernity (such as the Constitution) derive their quasi-sacred status and legitimacy from the fact that they represent the last possible response to belonging as unresolvable problem for thought. For the modernising *imaginaire*, these same institutions have no such self-evident or internal legitimacy simply because, although belonging has increasingly become a problem for thought, it has not yet become *first and foremost* a problem for thought; that is, a problem that can *only* be resolved by accepting as irreversible the inversion, to a significant extent, of the historical priority of praxis over thought, common good over individual freedom, belonging over being and so on. For this latter *imaginaire*, there still exist sufficient residual

---

1. This terror of an unresolvable contradiction at the heart of the social perhaps explains Hannah Arendt's comment in *On Revolution*: 'Hence, in theory as in practice, we can hardy avoid the paradoxical fact that it was precisely the [modern] revolutions, their crisis and their emergency, which drove the very "enlightened" men of the eighteenth century to plead for some religious sanction at the very moment when they were about to emancipate the secular realm fully from the influences of the churches and to separate politics and religion once and for all' (1963: 186).

elements of a praxis of belonging, rooted in custom, tradition and religion, to conceal the fundamental contradiction at the heart of the human condition, in order to lend belonging a certain actionable givenness. In other words, belonging is still a viable praxis and the claims of institutions of modernity to derive their legitimacy from being the last bulwark against the inevitable fragmentation of the social, a danger that always simmers below the surface of the social as a result of our contradictory human nature, go begging, remain suspended or simply have no currency. In this *imaginaire* – a political economy of obligation, of which the ontological axiomatic has been supplemented, hence already relativised – there is a sense in which these institutions simply pose as solutions to non-existent problems (who needs all that paperwork if you can organise the same effect through the networks of belonging that mark the continuation of the now perverted, because relativised, political economy of obligation?) (see Chabal and Daloz 1999).

Of course, the claim is often made that South Africa is an exceptional African country because, unlike other African states, it 'underwent a true industrial revolution in the space of a century' (Bayart 1993: 35). This claim can be deceptive for suggesting the absence of a conflict between these two *imagainaires*, as if the post-apartheid state were not a series of complex gradations of these two hypothetical *imaginaires* – gradations that trace with varying intensity the fissures and fault lines that have resulted from lopsided development, urbanisation, selective industrialisation and racialised modernisation. Still, to insist on this gradation of *imaginaires*, to recognise this as a time of profound fragmentation, where there are no South Africans (yet) and in which we are presented with a profound challenge to think beyond that fragmentation to the very possibility of collectively imagined belonging, to recognise all of this is simply to recognise at a meta-reflective level and in a manner appropriate to the time and place of postcoloniality, that for the 'us' of the national *imaginaire* (which aspires to straddle the gradations of different *imaginaires*) belonging has become, first and foremost, a problem for thought.

What is the tension or contradiction that bifurcates the concept of belonging in this modern moment? Simply put, it is the fact of plurality: the fact that I want my freedom and you want yours; that I need you in order to conceive of my freedom, but you are also a threat to my freedom. Plurality in this modest philosophical representation resurfaces as the bad marriage of Andy Capp in his embattled existence with Flo: 'I can't live with her and I can't live without her.' There are many ways in which we can give more theoretical substance to this metaphor, but given the concern of this chapter with the question of Ubuntu in relation to the law, let me turn for a more philosophical articulation to the jurisprudence of Duncan Kennedy, from whom I have been borrowing the phrase 'fundamental contradiction' all along.

The fact that Kennedy articulated this contradiction in the institutional domain of law calls for some clarity on the relationship between the ontological and political axiomatics. The first refers to the fundamental contradiction that haunts human belonging, as such, while the second relates to the institutions of modernity devised to mediate this contradiction. The former reflects a tension between the desire to exercise my freedom and the inescapable limitation placed on this by the existence of others: I am driven by a constant tension between wanting to realise my interests *and* having to recognise our interdependence, both as a condition *for* and a limitation *on* the realisation of those interests. My assumption about the relationship between the ontological and political axiomatics is the following: if this tension is what is most specific about the modern condition, ideally, the political institutions of modernity exist not only to mediate the tension, but to do so in a way that recognises, thereby giving equal effect to, both aspects of the ontological contradiction; that is, the tension between wanting to realise my interests *and* having to recognise our interdependence. The tension that constitutes us ontologically should be reflected in the political institutions that exist to mediate this tension as a solution to what belonging means. Extended to the juridical as one kind of modern, political institution, this means accepting the need for the juridical to reflect a *balanced* engagement with what is essentially a superficial division between two different sets of assumptions – individualism and altruism – that shadow all modern legal cultures. As Johan van der Walt puts it, a post-apartheid law

> would indeed require that the liberal and conservative 'counterparts' to which Kennedy refers . . . would indeed be *counter-parts*. It would require that they not be so far *apart* that they cannot, when circumstances demand, take stances that deviate from their typical ideological positions, stances that are for this reason non-ideological (2005: 166).

That there should be a structural or isomorphic correspondence between the logic of the ontological axiomatic and the structure of the political axiomatic, in which the latter offers us an institutional representation of the contradiction constitutive of the former, is no more than an assumption or meta-axiomatic that I cannot defend here. Suffice it, as a last gesture in that direction, to quote Frank Michelman's assessment of the fundamental contradiction, that it represents one of the 'most important tensions of human existence . . . thereby [giving] life much of whatever it has of value and meaning' (in Van der Walt 2005: 170).

If the first *epoché* revealed modernity as the moment when belonging becomes a problem for thought, the second *epoché* will reveal that the tension between individualism and communitarianism, between the pursuit of self-interest and a recognition of the common good – in Kennedy's terms, the tension between individualism and altruism – is at the heart of what belonging is taken to mean in modern legal cultures. The same risk of universalising reductionism that haunted the first *epoché* applies here, except that what we stand to gain from taking this risk a second time is the important insight that the so-called tension between the contractual axiomatic of the Constitution and the communitarian axiomatic of Ubuntu (the so-called problem of conflicting Western and African ontologies) is *not* unique, not exceptional or even particularly problematic because it is principally a tension between individualist and altruist tendencies, constitutive of modern legal cultures. This is the generality that I seek to make visible through the second *epoché*.

After the second *epoché*, the subsequent movement of particularity then allows us to return to post-apartheid modernity, in order to illuminate the question about Ubuntu in relation to the law, by asking two more precise questions: first, what is most particular about post-apartheid modernity? Here the answer seems pretty straightforward: it is the radical asymmetry in the way that political institutions reflect the fundamental contradiction. This generates a second question: what role, if any, can Ubuntu-engaged adjudication play in the realisation of greater symmetry; that is, of a more just modernity, in which the ontological axiomatic is reflected in the political institutions tasked with mediation between the pursuit of individual interests and the recognition of others as condition for the possibility of that pursuit? Of course, in order to answer the second question, we have to posit a meaning of Ubuntu adequate to the task. The meaning I advance derives from the first *epoché* and posits Ubuntu as figure of the un/familiar or uncanny.

The first part of this chapter performs the second *epoché* of generality; the second part returns to the particularity of the Ubuntu question. Positing its meaning as uncanny, I restate the concern there as a question of how to understand the emancipatory potential of the uncanny in relation to our constitutional regime.

A second *epoché*

The most fundamental question that human societies have always had to grapple with is seemingly simple: How do we constitute one from the many? Plainly put, how do we move from the recognition that we are many individuals to the creation of one entity, a We? This is the problem of plurality or difference, how to constitute a We on the basis of the recognition that the individuals who potentially make up this We hold a plurality of different political beliefs, religious convictions and so on. The problem peculiar to the moment of modernity is one of thinking belonging without annihilating difference. Kennedy articulates this problem in all its ruthless, incisive simplicity as a *fundamental contradiction*.[2] The contradiction arises from the simple given that 'relations with others are both necessary to and incompatible with our freedom' (Kennedy 1979: 213). If I were alone in the world, I would be exactly that – *alone*. I would not be able to claim that I am 'free' in any meaningful sense of the word. I need others in order to entertain the possibility of being free. However, their presence also threatens that very freedom. As Van der Walt puts it:

> Your freedom is not my freedom. Your freedom threatens my freedom. Mine threatens yours. This may be disconcerting, but it at least implies that we recognise ourselves to be *more than one*. This recognition is the beginning of political life. Following Arendt, one could say it recognises the *conditio sine qua non* and *conditio per quam* of political life (2005: 150–1).

The realisation that there is plurality, of there being at least two, is both the *condition for* the possibility of the political, as well as the condition *through which* we conduct the political, both the condition *for* and *of* politics. It is the *archē* as principle that makes possible the political, as well as the rule through which the political proceeds. Plurality, in other words, is the perpetually constituting principle of politics. Small wonder that Kennedy considers the contradiction so basic that he thinks of 'the

---

2. In this summary I claim some freedom of interpretation and start with Kennedy's later publication – 'The Structure of Blackstone's Commentaries' (1979), to which I then pay no further attention – and work my way back to an earlier text that I look at in some detail, 'Form and Substance in Private Law Adjudication' (1976). The reason for this is because the fundamental contradiction articulated in the 'Commentaries' is, in a sense, no more than a phenomenological articulation of the deep political division described in 'Form and Substance'. Read in chronological order, the fundamental contradiction is a deepening of the description of that division. For reasons relating to the purpose of the second *epoché*, I do not pay attention to Kennedy's later 'Freedom and Constraint in Adjudication: A Critical Phenomenology' (1986). For a discussion of the latter, see Van der Walt (2005: 152–67).

history of legal thought *as* the history of the fundamental contradiction' (1979: 216, emphasis added).

The plurality described here, argues Van der Walt, presents us with an impasse that always threatens the destruction of plurality and therefore the very existence and possibility of the political:

> Your liberty and my liberty, to the extent that they really are two different liberties with implications of two distinct autonomies, give neither of us nor anyone else the liberty or power or right to decide what is to be one when the mutual threat between them becomes critical; when the threat turns into actual disputes (2005: 151).

In a very general sense, this is the problem of politics that Western philosophers, at least as far back as Plato, have grappled with: how to make society possible, through what kind of authority (if any at all) or agreement can the difference that is pluralism be mediated, in order to create the unity of civil society, without in the process destroying the very plurality that necessitated a mechanism to deal with plurality in the first instance? If we are to live together, it is exactly this impasse that needs to be negotiated. This intense and pervasive contradiction, although it permeates every aspect of our lives, both personal and social, is the fundamental contradiction that the law cannot bridge or resolve, but only find temporary mediations for. Judges do this when they are called upon to adjudicate between contesting claims. They have to recognise plurality and adjudicate on the tension that arises from it, without destroying the plurality that is the quintessence of the political in the process.

The word we use to describe this process of adjudication without destroying plurality is *just*. Always a tenuous negotiation, a judge cannot adjudicate in absolute freedom; s/he has to do so within the law (by applying legal rules) and where those do not suffice, by appealing to extrajuridical social norms or legal standards that will enable him/her to legitimise a certain judgment on the basis that one claim, more than another equally legitimate claim, is more consonant with the general aim or purpose of the law. For Kennedy, the history of understanding such extralegal justifications in relation to the law can be divided into three phases that, for clarity's sake, I want to call the religious, the sovereign and the modern:

1. *Religious*: An initial phase, during which it was held that the law can coincide with God's will – eighteenth-century Western common law in which 'positive law was of a piece with God's moral law as understood through reason and

revelation' (Kennedy 1976: 1725). Applying the law simply meant applying common law in a way that was consonant with Christian ethics – which explains the dominance of altruist over individualist applications of the law during this time.

2. *Sovereign*: A second phase, which Kennedy refers to as 'Classical Individualism', during which the law was considered a separate, sovereign or self-enclosed system of rules, a closed universe, in which judges did no more than apply the rules. It was thought possible to simply deduct a judgment from the classical concepts and rules that constituted the law – concepts such as liberty, free will, property, fault, proximate cause, the 'subject matter of the contract', title, cause of action, privity, necessary party, literal meaning, strictly private activity and a host of others (1731). This approach to law is associated with formal or formalist legal thought and its description as 'Classical Individualism' derives from the fact that it was premised on the 'fundamental idea that private law rules protect individual free will' (1730). A third phase came about as a result of the critical insight that such a sovereign understanding of the law as a closed and therefore perfectly just system of rules was not possible and that in fact 'the legal order . . . was shot through with discretion masquerading as the rule of law' (1749).

3. *Modern*: This third phase was marked by a combination of the death of God and the realisation that rules are not perfect, that *interpretation of the law is always, simply and interminably political*; the recognition that 'no issue of substance can be resolved merely by reference to one of the Classical concepts' (1731); that 'there simply was no deductive process by which one could derive the "right" legal answer from abstractions like freedom or property' (1748); that judicial law-making does not simply result from such a mystical deduction from concept to consequence, but also from 'the judge's moral, political and economic views and in the idiosyncracies of his understanding of the character of the fact situation' (1732).

The latter phase is what I have been referring to as modern legal culture. It is a culture in which the law is no longer understood as a sovereign entity closed in upon itself, but as a rule-governed domain that, even at the level of Constitutional Court judgments, interfaces with politics simply because judges inescapably bring their politics to bear on their interpretation of the law.

In modern democracies, there is supposedly a clear distinction between the three branches of government: the legislature makes the rules we live by, the courts interpret those rules and the executive implements them. In order to implement a rule, we need to be certain that it is a good rule and that we know what it does and does not mean. We expect the rules made by the legislature to be clear, but often they are not. In deciding what the rules mean and what they should be interpreted to mean, courts – in particular, judges – have considerable power, a power that shades off from interpretation of rules into the legislative domain of rule-making – so much so that Kennedy is quite right when he comments that 'as long as the judge has the power to formulate a new rule rather than applying an old one, it is clear that he or she has a measure of political or legislative power' (1976: 1752).[3]

For Kennedy, a deep division in adjudication in the United States becomes visible when we analyse the manner in which judges bring their politics to bear when they exercise this bounded freedom to (also) legislate. When judges cannot but allow their own politics to enter into how they interpret, change and amend laws – in short, when they make a new rule, instead of mindlessly applying an old rule – they bring a politics to bear on their bounded freedom that cannot always simply be represented in terms of coherent ideologies or personalities. We should not expect judges to consistently speak to one side of the division. Better to think of the division Kennedy has in mind, as – to borrow a phrase from Lewis Gordon – two *geographies of thought*, which represent two different ways of understanding what it means to make claims and to settle claims within the wider framework of an understanding of what the law is all about; two geographies that emerge as an emphasis, either on the priority of individual rights or on the importance of the common good – a division, as Kennedy puts it, between individualism or altruism. In United States law and politics, this translates into the familiar opposition between liberalism and conservatism. Comments Van der Walt:

---

3. A fluidity of the separation of powers that leaves us with, at best, the following: '*Some* kinds of complex factual questions are appropriate for the judiciary; others are not. *Some* social values or purposes are capable of reasoned elaboration by judges; others are not, and must be left to the legislature. On the formal level, there is eclecticism about when we should use rules and when standards. *Sometimes* it will be true that we can trust the judge to apply the purposes of the legal order directly to the particular facts, without worrying either about arbitrariness or about the inefficiencies generated by uncertainty. Sometimes, on the other hand, we will want him to distinguish clearly between his lawmaking and law-applying roles' (Kennedy 1976: 1764–5).

> The two ideologies self-evidently relate respectively to the two elements of law that derive from the fundamental contradiction of simultaneously being threatened by and dependent on the liberty of others . . . Liberalism endorses the altruistic or communitarian side of the law, the side of the law concerned with the plight of the *others* who for various reasons are less capable or incapable of looking after their own interests. Conservatism . . . is concerned with the promotion of self-reliance . . . of selves who . . . hardly need any promotion (2005: 163).

This polarity was articulated very clearly when former US president, Bill Clinton, speaking in support of Barack Obama's bid for a second presidential term, 'boiled the difference beteen Obama and Republican opponent Mitt Romney down to a simple, essential point. The choice he said, would be between voters who "wanted to be part of a *we're all in this together society* or a *winner takes all, you're on your own society*"' (*Guardian* Reporter 2012). But it is Kennedy's formulation of this division, not in terms of the ideological polarity of United States party politics, but as two general geographies of thought, which is relevant for this second *epoché* – as a rather lengthy quotation from 'Form and Substance in Private Law Adjudication' demonstrates:

> The 'freedom' of individualism is negative, alienated and arbitrary. It consists in the absence of restraint on the individual's choice of ends, and has no moral content whatever. When the group creates an order consisting of spheres of autonomy separated by (property) and linked by (contract) rules, each member declares her indifference to her neighbor's salvation – washes her hands off him the better to 'deal' with him. The altruist asserts that the staccato alternation of mechanical control and obliviousness is destructive of every value that makes freedom a thing to be desired. We can achieve real freedom only collectively, through *group* self-determination. We are simply too weak to realize ourselves in isolation. True, collective self-determination, short of utopia implies the use of force against the individual. But we experience and accept the use of physical and psychic coercion every day, in family life, education and culture. We experience it indirectly, often unconsciously in political and economic life. The problem is the conversion of force into moral force, in the fact of the experience of moral indeterminacy. A definition of freedom that ignores this problem is no more

than a rationalization of indifference, or the velvet glove for the hand of domination through rules (Kennedy 1976: 1774).

Altruistic adjudication makes arguments informed by the greater good, the reason why we have law at all, the greater purpose that the law is supposed to fulfil and so on. Individualists prefer to milk the contractarian axiomatic for what are essentially conserving ends: individual rights, free will and the protection of property. But, and here is the catch, both positions lack an ultimate justification or legitimation for their viewpoints. In the same way that altruists can no longer claim, as they used to during the religious phase of the law's relationship to society, that we have to institutionalise the recognition of our interdependence (conceived as altruism) because God says so, individualists can no longer coherently claim that any consequence in law deductively follows from the founding principles of individual free will and security of property – as they did when legal practitioners still believed in the sovereignty of the juridical. This mutual lack of meta-legitimation makes for a very specific kind of conflict: there is nothing *within* the law that allows for the resolution of the conflict generated by different interpretations *of* the law. No meta-appeal is possible to something outside the law that would enable us to arbitrate between differences in adjudication because the conflict or tension between the two geographies of adjudication is constitutive of the law itself. The reason for this lies in the status of the ontological contradiction as *archē* of the political, as the originating logic that contains within itself both the principle and the rules for the application of that principle. Simply put, once we have accepted that the fundamental contradiction itself is unresolvable, given the death of God and the imperfection of rules, individualism and altruism appear as no more than two shifting signifiers that mark the outer limits of possible answers we can come up with in response to the contradiction. I think it fair to surmise that in the context of the United States, within which Kennedy was writing, the conflict between individualism and altruism has three important features that are a function of this lack of meta-legitimation.

In the first instance, it is a *balanced* ideological conflict, in the sense that individualism and altruism represent two equally viable political and moral positions that find more or less equal representation in the opinions, judgments and, sometimes, in the judges themselves. It is also balanced in the sense that the two geographies of thought coincide or overlap to some indeterminate extent with the division between Democrats and Republicans.

Second, it is a *superficial* conflict, in the sense that no appeal to either first principles or transcendental grounds can solve or redeem the conflict. The tension has bottomed out. As Kennedy argues:

> At an elementary level, it makes it clear that it is futile to imagine that moral and practical conflict will yield to analysis in terms of higher level concepts. The meaning of contradiction at the level of abstraction is that there is no metasystem that would, if only we could find it, key us into one mode or the other as circumstances 'required' (1976: 1775).

This is what it means to refer to the conflict as *superficial*: the *archē* pluralism, which is both sine qua non and *conditio per quam* of the political as such and which the law exists to mediate through adjudication, is replicated within the politics of adjudication as a fundamental division or pluralism. In other words, the problem of pluralism is replicated in the plurality of solutions offered in response to the problem of pluralism. To recognise this fractal of pluralism is to recognise the founding nature of the modern political, the fact that plurality is the perpetually constituting principle of law considered a continuation of, and not simply the answer to, the political. As Van der Walt observes: 'The acute regard for the fundamental contradiction renders possible an understanding of *politics* in general and the *politics* of law in particular in terms of the *political* . . .' (2005: 165).

A third feature of the conflict between individualist and altruist tendencies in Kennedy's context of adjudication is a *paradox of self-negation*: neither individualist nor altruist can produce a principle that will prevent the consistent application of their respective interpretations of the law from undermining the law itself. Altruists admit 'they have no principles capable of logically determining where, short of total collectivism, they would stop the expansion of legally enforceable altruistic duty', while 'individualists no longer have any principles that determine where, short of the state of nature, *they* would stop the *contraction* of altruistic duty' (Kennedy 1976: 1733).[4]

---

4. For Kennedy, one of the three important issues where this conflict between altruism and individualism plays out in private law and modern legal thought is in the debate he denotes as centring on 'Community vs. Autonomy', where at issue is 'the extent to which one person should have to share or make sacrifices in the interest of another in the absence of agreement or other manifestation of intention' (1976: 1733).

The post-apartheid jurisprudence that Van der Walt outlines in his *Law and Sacrifice: Towards a Post-Apartheid Theory of Law* (2005) is much indebted to Kennedy's discussion of the fundamental conflict between individualism and altruism. For Van der Walt, the superficiality of the conflict characterises post-apartheid law par excellence, for it means that no decision should ever be considered final; nothing that is decided against cannot re-enter a future contemplation of a similar set of facts for renewed legitimation. A judge may express an individualist tendency by deciding for private property owners against shack-dwellers who occupy land illegally in one set of facts, but this decision does not nullify the shack-dwellers' claim forever, nor does it suggest that they had no case to start with, or that they were somehow 'wrong' to assume the right to contest individual private property rights, with an appeal to second-order, socio-economic rights. In another case and under different circumstances, the same judge or a different one may express an altruistic tendency, by acknowledging the shack-dwellers' claim instead. As Van der Walt comments:

> His or her temporary judgement in favour of some at the cost of others would not constitute a mere dismissal of the concerns of those against whom the judgement goes, but merely a momentary *setting aside* of these concerns, a *setting aside* that keeps these concerns in play, keeps them *alongside* those favoured for the moment, keeps them alongside so as to allow them 'to fight another day' (2005: 166).

The implication for post-apartheid jurisprudence is clear:

> This is why a post-apartheid theory of law would turn on an analysis of law as sacrifice and analyses of legal sacrifices. It insists on the necessity of keeping any suggested gain in meaning alongside the concomitant loss of meaning that could otherwise all too easily and too soon, be lost out of sight. It insists on always keeping the losers *alongside* the winners. This *alongside* . . . is the horizontal depth of space that a post-apartheid theory of law would seek to open (Van der Walt 2005: 171).

Unlike Van der Walt, I do not think there is a seamless translation into post-apartheid modernity of the idea that, through a combination of the death of God and the disappointment of formalism, a fault line between individualism and altruism has appeared that now runs through post-apartheid adjudication in a way that will remain unresolvable at a meta-level. Although the second *epoché* suggests that this is an important half of the truth, I think there is something particular about post-apartheid modernity that requires us to proceed more cautiously.

In the context of Kennedy's analysis in the United States, the conflict was said to be *balanced*, *superficial* and *paradoxical*, but in our post-apartheid context, the very assumption of this conflict as *balanced* or its reduction to 'mere tendencies in adjudication' is out of place. In the context of the United States, one may argue that the conflict represents a tension between two long-standing ideological positions, with their respective political expressions, ideologies, historical precedents, judgments, judges, party representation, lobbyists and so forth – in other words, the fault line between these two traditions *understood as tendencies* is *clear*, by which I mean one can, as Kennedy does in 'Form and Substance' (1976), give a more or less coherent description of each. This is not the case for us, or it is only so in a very problematic sense because (and to the extent that) it collapses in an identitarian representation of the two geographies in question as African communalism versus Western liberalism.

Of course, this racialising of the geographies of thought offered by the fundamental contradiction is to be expected, given the history of colonialism. Be that as it may, the problem with this racialisation is that it obscures, through a collapse into identity politics, what could be reproductive about the tension. Obscured in the process, but made visible by the second *epoché*, is the fact that modernity is constituted, first and foremost, as the tension between individualism and altruism, writ large at an institutional level. For us, then, the division between individualism and altruism described by Kennedy and which I take to be constitutive of modernity is, depending on one's politics, either problematically unclear or problematic because too clear. The second *epoché* suggests that the idea of a radical ontological incommensurability is exaggerated because, in a general sense, Ubuntu presents no more than a local, contextual language for the articulation of the altruist geography of adjudication, constitutive of the modern juridical. The fact that this exaggeration remains at play simply cannot be reduced to Ubuntu *qua* problem, but must also be acknowledged as a sign of race and racism. In a first, historical sense, there is the racialisation of the fundamental contradiction that tends to amount to dumping everything political and juridical that smacks of altruism into the politicised category of 'African culture'; second, there is a more contemporary racism in the form of a legal demand that a definitive description of Ubuntu should precede its invocation in law.[5] In Van der Walt's *Law and Sacrifice*, this demand becomes a self-fulfilling prophecy in the sense that, because no effort is made to interpret Ubuntu as an engagement with the fundamental contradiction, Ubuntu does not get to articulate the kind of definitional clarity that could eventually make it applicable in law.

As for the second criteria of Kennedy's description of the division, that it should be *superficial* because no appeal beyond either individualism or altruism/communalism can justify why either should constitute the ultimate principle of adjudication – this is indeed the case for post-apartheid modernity as well. Like any other modernity that is attempting to found an imagined We on a set of agreed-upon rules, we too must do so in the absence of any kind of appeal to gods or ancestors that marked the religious phase of the development of the law. There is no extrajuridical appeal possible that will, once and for all, settle the squabble between individualist and altruist assumptions of what belonging means. In this sense, we can say that while the manifestation of the division between individualism and altruism in post-apartheid jurisprudence is superficial, it is not, as in Kennedy's case, a *balanced* superficiality.

The playing field between individualist and altruistic tendencies is not level, but rather, as a direct result of colonialism, skewed in favour of individualism. Standards, histories, customs and habits; that is, *forms of life* that represent the altruistic, social or communitarian, are and continue to be fundamentally marginalised and instituted against. To say that in post-apartheid South Africa the conflict between individualism and altruism is asymmetrically skewed in favour of the former is to disagree with Van der Walt's easygoing adoption of Kennedy's theoretical framework: when a post-apartheid judge adjudicates, he or she is never simply entertaining the tension between the two geographies as a profoundly aporetic moment of sacrificial decision-making (Derrida 1992a), the outcome of which can simply be understood in terms of a temporary victory of the one over the anticipated return of the other, at a later stage. We have to start elsewhere, namely with recognising the asymmetrical or unbalanced representation of the

---

5. For a succinct critique of this criticism, based on Amartya Sen's critique of John Rawls in *The Idea of Justice* (published in 2009), see Furman (2012: 40).

fundamental contradiction at an institutional level. Van der Walt appropriates *the principle* that modern adjudication is balanced, superficial and paradoxical, but he does not acknowledge the de facto imbalance or radical assymetry that constitutes the juridical *as political praxis*. For Van der Walt:

> An acute regard for the fundamental contradiction is crucial to the post-apartheid theory of law ... for a post-apartheid law would indeed require that the liberal and conservative 'counterparts' to which Kennedy refers ... would indeed be *counter-parts*. It would require that they not be so far *apart* that they cannot, when circumstances demand, take stances that deviate from their typical ideological positions, stances that are for this reason non-ideological (2005: 166).

I interpret Van der Walt to be in agreement with Kennedy that adjudication in modern legal culture is paradoxical and superficial, but, still following Kennedy and this time uncritically so, he also assumes that in a post-apartheid modernity we are presented with a *balanced* superficiality between individualist and altruist geographies of adjudication, in which the spectre of injustice is simply a function of the hypothetical, and to be avoided, apart-ness of these two 'counterparts'. This is not the case, for the spectre of injustice is a function of the colonial legacy that plays itself out as the continued tendency to prioritise one over the other, individualism over altruism. If ever there were an argument for transformative constitutionalism that derived, not from the phantom of normative consensus, but that followed as articulation (*qua* rule) of the *archē* (*qua* principle), it is exactly this continued asymmetrical representation at an institutional level of the ontological axiomatic.

In light of this, the obvious question is: What kind of 'force' or logic will compel us towards greater equilibrium between the two geographies of thought constitutive of modernity? This question reveals the final failure of Van der Walt's neo-apartheid jurisprudence. For, what we are presented with is a theory in which the *raison d'être* of post-apartheid jurisprudence is argued to consist in a self-conscious justification of its sacrifices, yet, at the precise point where Ubuntu (as a contextual debate to think through the fundamental contradiction) should become the cornerstone of such a post-apartheid juridprudence, we find Ubuntu discourse specifically and African theorists in general excluded, without any justification or explanation – as if they have nothing to say, nothing to contribute to the manner in which we grapple with this contradiction.⁶ No effort is made to draw on the contextual theorising of the social standards that would otherwise articulate local, postcolonial understandings of the fundamental contradiction.⁷ The law is expected to be self-conscious about its sacrifices, but not the philosophy of law. A truly post-apartheid jurisprudence will think through the fundamental contradiction in local, historical terms; it will take cognisance of the fact that we have a young tradition that attempts to do just that by recognising Ubuntu, at the very least, as a signifier for one constitutive element of the modern juridical. This second *epoché* merely touched on what it would mean to interpret Ubuntu as such a signifier. Fascinating questions remain that cannot be explored here.⁸

---

6. This is all the more disappointing given Van der Walt's criticism of the way the late Arthur Chaskalson invoked Ubuntu in *S. v. Makwanyane*, with a 'frightening' 'lack of jurisprudential rigour': 'Chaskalson P founds his argument regarding *ubuntu* not with reference to African jurisprudence or African literature on the meaning of *ubuntu*; apart from invoking the postamble of the 1993 Constitution, he simply founds it with a reference to a phrase of Justice Brennan in *Furman v Georgia*. Compared with his extensive references to Western and international sources . . . he makes little or no effort to establish clearly what *ubuntu* means and what exactly it holds for a legal system' (2005: 109). I am not sure what I find more frightening: a Constitutional Court judgment that invokes Ubuntu with a lack of rigour or a jurisprudential critique of that judgment that ignores African theorists altogether.
7. A good starting point would be those texts that explicitly address as problematic the binary of Western individualism versus African communitarianism. In this regard, see Eze (2008) and Christians (2004).
8. Consider, for example, the following: Kennedy's 'Commentaries' (1979) marks a turn towards subjective existentialism, in which law becomes not part of the solution, but part of the problem, since, as Peter Gabel argues, it 'conceals and normalises the "traumatic absence of connectedness" between human beings in late capitalist culture by defining human relations in terms of imaginary ideas such as "rights" and "duties"' (in Van der Walt 2005: 157). This conclusion really leaves us with two options; one: to proceed down the road of critical legal theory in order to theorise against the legitimating function of the law or two, as Kennedy himself puts it, 'the development of a concrete disalienating social movement that would make imaginary forms of social cohesion unnecessary' (in Van der Walt 2005: 158). Ultimately, I have pursued neither of these options and perhaps the real challenge consists in embracing both the delegitimating politics of critical legal theory and the politics of transformation: the one relying on the law to effect changes, the other delegitimising the very possibility of the law to restore the intersubjectivity (Kennedy's 'intersubjective zap') that exists, prior to the fetishising of relations in abstraction, such as 'duties' and 'rights', 'community' or even 'Ubuntu'. Tantalising is the possibility that the distinction between ubuntu praxis and an Ubuntu retrodicted through law would allow us to do both.

Kennedy's identification of a fundamental division between individualist and altruist geographies of adjudication allows us to make two successive moves: first, to argue that the second *epoché* reveals this contradiction as typical, not of a racialised postcoloniality in particular, but of modernity as such. It allows us to frame, in more universal terms, the *general* contradictory nature of law-making at a time when neither a background consensus on the moral aims of the law nor a belief in the possibility of deducing right answers from first principles within the law exists. At such a time, 'every occasion of lawmaking will raise the fundamental conflict of individualism and altruism, on both a substantive and a formal level' (Kennedy 1976: 1766). But as much as the *epoché* allows us to appreciate this generality, it also compels us to travel in the opposite direction and to ask: What is specific about this tension in postcoloniality or, as I prefer to think of it, hypermodernity? This particularity resides in the radical asymmetry of the two geographies and leaves us with a question to be pursued in the rest of this chapter, namely: How do we think through the question of restoring balance or symmetry to this superficiality? What role, if any, can Ubuntu as racialised signifier of the altruistic play in emancipation so understood? These are questions that can only be addressed by returning to a particularity that is now hopefully illuminated from within by what was revealed through the second *epoché*.

A return to particularity

> Since the Russian Revolution, the growing consciousness of the oppressed masses, especially of the working classes, in the developing countries makes it impossible to subjugate the workers to the appalling conditions which were characteristic of the Japanese periods of 'primitive accumulation' and early capitalism. In our epoch the philosophy of prosperity before social justice has been replaced by a new philosophy which demands prosperity with social justice.
> — Abdulrahman Babu, *African Socialism or Socialist Africa?*

One of the most difficult things about conceiving the emancipatory potential of Ubuntu relates to questions of positioning; that is, on having clarity on three related issues. First, what do we mean by emancipation? Second, how do we *position* Ubuntu in such a discourse of emancipation? Third, once we have decided on its position, what *meaning* do we attribute Ubuntu, in order for it to contribute to the project of emancipation from the position attributed to it? In order to be very clear about what we can reasonably expect from this return to the particular question of Ubuntu in relation to the modern juridical, we need some preliminary clarity on these questions.

As a response to the first question, Sampie Terreblanche has argued that the necessary transformation of South Africa's colonialist and apartheid history demands that the patterns of unfree black labour he describes in *The History of Inequality in South Africa, 1652–2002* (2002), need to be broken or undone. More recently, in *Lost in Transformation: South Africa's Search for a New Future Since 1986* (2012), he has argued that the African National Congress (ANC) may have missed the opportunity to bring about this change, a pessimism that also resonates with Hein Marais's analysis in *South Africa Pushed to the Limit: The Political Economy of Change* (2011). Less pessimistically, we can say that the very necessary change these authors insist on, whether to be brought about by a second transition within the macro-economic frame of neoliberalism or whether Marikana will in retrospect become the Soweto uprising of the real revolution, the point is that when we talk about emancipation we refer, at a minimum, to correcting the lack of symmetry in the institutional representation of the fundamental contradiction. Now, whether we think of this emancipated future, this balanced or 'new' South Africa and the form of government it will assume as a social democracy or a socialist democracy is, for the purposes of this report, neither here nor there. What interests me is the fact that this vision points to the realisation of what is in many ways the *raison d'être* of critical humanism, namely the assumption of human beings as free and equal and that in realising this vision of 'free human beings living together in an ethical community' (Cornell 2014), there is a role for what the shackdwellers movement calls a 'revolutionary Ubuntu' (in Cornell 2014), radically incompatible with the logic of capitalism.

But what might this role be? It seems there are broadly two responses to this question. On the one hand, there is the activist ubuntu ethic of grassroots social movements, such as Abahlali baseMjondolo (see Gibson 2011: 201) and the Ubuntu Project, a subversive counter-hegemonic political and subaltern legality, 'which by its very combination of terms, challenges the conventional definition of legality in Anglo-American jurisprudence as a set of institutionised state structures that legitimise both coercive power and a recognisable system of rules and principles that can be known as law' (Cornell 2014). On the other hand, there is the Ubuntu of formal juridical discourse, in which the place and meaning of Ubuntu as a term, value, concept or philosophy has been contested ever since it was first incorporated in the post-amble of the 1993 Interim Constitution, dropped by the authors of the

1996 final Constitution, only to make its way back into constitutional jurisprudence via a number of landmark judgments that, with varying degrees of success and plausibility, invoked Ubuntu, either to give local flavour to well-known legal arguments or, more daringly, to prioritise the realisation of collective socio-economic rights (for example, housing) over individual rights (property ownership) – what, in terms of the second *epoché*, we now recognise as the prioritising of the altruist over the individualist geography of thought. Within jurisprudence, the validity of these invocations of Ubuntu has been hotly disputed for a variety of reasons, mainly rooted in two concerns: on the one hand, the putative irreconcilability of its communitarian axiomatic with that of a liberal regime of individual rights and, on the other hand, the problem of not being able to define exactly what we mean by Ubuntu. This is the discourse that I am interested in here. How do we position Ubuntu in relation to this juridical discourse and how do we respond to the challenge that we cannot invoke what we cannot define?

At this stage, it should be clear that if Ubuntu is to be considered a glocal phenomenon, the question of its precise articulation as demanded by law will, of necessity, remain moot. Given its glocality, the fact that Ubuntu retrodicts various meanings, depending on the global discourse it is interfacing with and the local demands it is responding to, I want to suggest that we change the question, away from an epistemological concern with its meaning (always incapacitated by the combination of identity politics and global interfaces) towards a pragmatic political concern with how to position this glocal Ubuntu in relation to the law. The second *epoché* has already left us with one suggestion. At the level of generality, Ubuntu can be understood and therefore positioned as the local name for the altruist geography constitutive of any modernist legal discourse. But as interesting and relevant as that may be as an overall, general framework, we need a more precise answer, suitable to the particular context of post-apartheid modernity, one that takes into account the historicity of context and the politics of law. To start working my way towards this question, a brief but necessary return to the condition of hypermodernity that I introduced in Chapter 3 is necessary.

Hypermodernity

It is often mistakenly assumed that postmodernism comes *after* modernism as some kind of next stage or phase of intellectual and cultural development. This is not the case, for as Jean-François Lyotard argued in '*Une note sur le post*', postmodernism is really modernism *becoming aware* of its own blind spots.

Postmodernism is modernism working out the 'initial forgetting' that made it possible (Lyotard in Kearney 1998: 21). The self-consciousness we associate with postmodernism is just that: modernism becoming conscious or aware of its blind spots, remembering that which needed to have remained forgotten in order for modernism to have executed or performed itself. What I have in mind with *hypermodernism* is a modernism that is, per definition, not afforded the benefit of this performative execution of modernism, the temporal dimension or passing of time between an initial or foundational forgetting and a later uncovering or un-forgetting of what made it possible. Hypermodernity is, from the start, or constitutively, self-consciously aware of the blind spots of modernism. The *hyper* in hypermodernism does not simply refer to the self-consciousness or meta-awareness of postmodernism, but very specifically to recognising modernity *as* modernity *at the moment of* modernity.[9] This inability to forget modernity in order for it to be executed, so that we may later return to it in order to grapple with its meaning, raises its own peculiar *problematique*, one that we can denote as the potential problem or danger or, less normatively, as the condition of *inexecution*. The meta-consciousness of hypermodernity often makes it difficult, even impossible, to 'make the moves' or execute certain political modes of being and belonging that we have come to associate with modernity – the sovereignty of the state, the autonomy of the individual, the myth of the nation and so on.[10] We now recognise these desires in advance as modernist, *as* myths and therefore, in some sense, as no longer executable. Unlike the nationalisms of Western modernity that managed to execute the myth of the nation successfully on the back of various transcendental legitimations, such as the Promethean myth or the notion of being God's Elect, the nationalisms of hypermodernity can never execute and consolidate such unity

---

9. It is, of course, more complex than this. All I can do to circumscribe this complexity is to offer, by way of juxtaposition, two statements. On the one hand: that as much as the founding text of Western modernity (from a novelist's perspective) – Miguel de Cervantes's *Don Quixote* – exemplifies hypermodernity, exactly what accounts for this hypermodernity (its irony and self-consciousness) had necessarily to be absent in the execution of Western modernity as a philosophical and political programme. On the other hand, as Milan Kundera has argued in *The Art of the Novel* (1988): the *raison d'être* of the novel is that it remembers everything that philosophy forgets.
10. 'Constructing something as modern as the nation in a post-modern context requires of us a double-thinking of our mimesis, of the fact that we are consciously imitating a well-worn form while [nonetheless] hoping that we would be subconsciously articulated by it – hence our hypermodernity' (Praeg 2012: 298).

because an appeal to a transcendental founding is no longer possible. The project of modernity will always and at many levels remain *inexecuted* – either because we look at ourselves from the outside in with a postmodern, nudge-nudge, wink-wink appreciation of the fatality of the desire for things natural and teleological or, less patronising but equally devastating, simply because we recognise *this* moment as *that* moment.

Hypermodernity, then, is a peculiarly postcolonial experience of modernity, a peculiar kind of self-consciousness that is a function of the asynchronicity described in the previous chapter. In this post-teleological asynchronicity, the premodern communitarian is not going to go away, find itself either returned or dialectically *aufgehoben* through the relentless march of a teleological history. Postcoloniality is not the end of history as much as the recognition that history is going nowhere and that, in fact, globalisation is in many ways nothing but the systematic generalisation of the postcolonial condition.[11] For me, the usefulness of the term 'hypermodernity' consists in the fact that it retains references to a condition that is at once general (modernity) and specific (hyper) – a duality that was the condition for the first and second *epoché* respectively. What is the position and meaning of Ubuntu in such a context of hypermodernity, when the questions of modernity and of what belonging means confronts a society that, unlike Western societies, never did and never will come to think of its historical praxis of belonging (ubuntu) simply as something that got left behind by the teleological march of history, dialectically sublimated through ever-increasing and superior ways of being?

The meaning of Ubuntu

The meaning Ubuntu acquires in a context of asynchronous modernities is that of the uncanny. Ubuntu fascinates not because of *what it is*, but because of the time in which it offers us an uncannily sublime reminder of the fundamental inter-

---

11. Hypermodernity reconfigures the relationship beteen the premodern and the modern in terms of a dialectic, without the promise of a sublimation or *Aufhebung*. The notion of asynchronous modernities – of which hypermodernity denotes its experience from a postcolonial perspective – describes a non-directional interaction, probably better captured in Walter Benjamin's post-Hegelian notion of a 'constellation' or configuration, of which we must hope that it will, one day, fall into place in a way that will make sense, without confusing this hope with the expectation that it will or, if/when it does, that it will make sense absolutely, finally or even in any way that we already anticipate, in terms of what 'making sense' does, will, may or must mean. See Benjamin (1977), Adorno (1977) and Bernstein (1991).

dependence, which modernity everywhere threatens to 'forget' (Lyotard), leave behind, sublimate or develop in the performance of what, in various modes of its executory violence, it calls modernity, progress, development, maturity or increased complexity. From the perspective of asynchronous modernities, premodernity in general and u/Ubuntu in particular coincide with and are carried forth alongside modernity.[12] But this 'alongside' generates two different kinds of experiences of asynchronous modernity for the local and global *imaginaires*.[13] In the local *imaginaire*, it gives rise to the condition I have described as hypermodernity. For the global *imaginaire* – which overlaps significantly with certain racial and class fault lines of the local *imaginaire* – it raises the question of an imperative to remember that was poignantly articulated by Jacques Derrida in an interview with Richard Kearney:

> My own conviction is that we must maintain two contradictory affirmations at the same time. On the one hand we affirm the existence of ruptures in history, and on the other hand we affirm that these ruptures produce gaps or faults (*failles*) in which the most hidden and forgotten archives can emerge and constantly recur and work through history. One must surmount the categorical oppositions of philosophical logic out of fidelity to these conflicting positions of historical discontinuity (rupture) and continuity (repetition), which are neither a pure break with the past nor a pure unfolding or explication of it (in Kearney 1984: 113).

For the global *imaginaire*, Ubuntu becomes visible because of the asynchronicity of modernities, in which a premodern, communitarian praxis re-emerges in order to recur, thereby reinventing itself as a critique of the very modernity that constructs u/Ubuntu as premodern communitarianism. Here the power of and fascination

---

12. '... the mutuality of communitarian practices deriving from the survival experience of subsistence agriculture and food sharing practices remains central to much African civic discourse and public justice' (Fackler in Tomaselli 2009: 586).
13. The binary implication of talk about 'alongside', namely that the premodern and modern coexist alongside each other as two clearly separate and identifiable logics is, of course, no more than a function of an analytical distinction made for the purposes of modelling a certain interaction. In real terms, postcoloniality does not conform to such a simplistic, Western modernist schemata.

with Ubuntu derive to a large extent from the fact that it ascended in a decidedly post-Cold War moment, when all other ideological alternatives to capitalism that, *alongside* capitalism, used to remind us of our fundamental interdependence, seem to have lost ideological momentum. In the global *imaginaire*, Ubuntu steps into this tired place in order to remind us of our shared humanity. That it would do so with a fair amount of comical clumsiness is to be expected, as for example, when Bill Clinton told a Labour conference in the United Kingdom: 'Society is important because of Ubuntu' (in Coughlan 2006) – a delightful incoherence, possibly only rivalled by John F. Kennedy's infamous '*Ich bin ein Berliner*'.

But this is a very ambivalent position for Ubuntu to occupy because it can only play this role of positing past realities as future possibilities through a perpetual deconstruction of two essential building blocks of Western modernity: a linear conception of time and the binary separation of self and other, being and belonging. As I argue below, the fact that Ubuntu interrogates these two basic assumptions of Western modernity accounts for the fact that *coming from Africa*, it will always invoke in the Western imagination one of two extreme responses: that of the salvific (*qua* critique of Western modernity) or that of the irrationally racist (*qua* threat of the inexecution of Western modernity). This ambivalence is what I seek to capture with the notion of Ubuntu as un/familiar or uncanny.

Nobody did more than Sigmund Freud to convert the uncanny into a useful philosophical concept. For his discussion on the topic – '*Das Unheimliche*', translated as 'The Uncanny' (1973 [1919]) – he drew on a couple of fundamental insights derived from a combination of etymology and the previous work of Ernst Jentsch and Friedrich Schelling. From the etymology of the word, he gathered that it referred to what was frightening – even, as in the cases of Arabic and Hebrew, to what is daemonic or gruesome. Jentsch, realising that not all things frightening invoke in us a sense of the uncanny, narrowed the experience of the uncanny down to what is frightening *because unfamiliar*. But the conceptual problem persisted, for not all things unfamiliar invoke in us a sense of the uncanny. And here an insight by Schelling proved decisive to Freud's theorising of the concept. For Schelling, the uncanny is 'the name for everything that ought to have remained . . . secret and hidden but has come to light' (in Freud 1973 [1919]: 225). In other words, the uncanny presents something that is frightening because unfamiliar and it is unfamiliar, not simply because it is unknown, but exactly because it used to be known, but has subsequently become unknown or forgotten (because repressed, forgotten, *aufgehoben* or sublimated). The coming to light of this un/familiar, its resurfacing in a time and place where it no longer belongs, unsettles us and makes us feel *unheimlich* (unhomely). This eventually led Freud to his own definition of the uncanny as 'that class of the frightening which leads back to what is known of old and long familiar' (220).

Freud's fundamental insight was that the uncanny pertains to phenomena that we would like to consider historical, but which have nonetheless, somehow, found their way back into the present. More precisely, this historical phenomenon is one that we believe we have actively overcome or 'surmounted' (Freud 1973 [1919]: 236). The latter concept is central to Freud's understanding because it suggests that somewhere in our past, we had a 'friendly' or natural relationship with some projection of our imagination or some way of being, but we have subsequently 'matured' and 'left that way of being behind'. For instance, at one stage in our social development, Freud writes, we may have understood the evil actions of individuals in terms of their ability to channel the evil intention of spirits or transcendental forces. But in light of the phylogeny-ontogeny hypothesis, we can say that as modern people, we have outgrown or 'surmounted' this belief because we now recognise in evil actions just that: the actions of a morally depraved individual. This said, in exceptional circumstances – such as instances of extreme evil or cases in which somebody explicitly claims to act on behalf of special spirits – our historically familiar association of evil with the supernatural may return to unsettle our secular, modern way of being. Our finding such thoughts about the return of a historical way of being in the world somewhat plausible would be accompanied by a sense of the uncanny; we would be unsettled or made to feel unhomely in the present because the present moment would have reconstituted itself in terms of a logic which, until then, we were convinced had become something of the past. As Freud puts it:

> We – or our primitive forefathers – once believed that these possibilities [supernatural manifestations of evil] were realities, and were convinced that they actually happened. Nowadays we no longer believe in them, we have *surmounted* these modes of thought; but we do not feel quite sure of our new beliefs, and the old ones still exist within us ready to seize upon any confirmation. As soon as something *actually happens* in our lives which seems to confirm the old, discarded beliefs we get a feeling of the uncanny (1973 [1919]: 247–8).

The historical state of being or belief has now returned, only to leave us with an unsettling experience of ambivalence that has both a cognitive and temporal dimension. Cognitively, we find ourselves facing something that is at once familiar and unfamiliar; familiar because we used to be like that or believe in that sort of thing; unfamiliar, because having moved on, we no longer quite recognise it. The unhomely or uncanny is the experience of the un/familiar.

Much of this experience is a result of the temporal dimension of the ambivalence. Encountering the uncanny, we find ourselves in the present without being present – worse, of strangely occupying more than one temporal zone simultaneously. This suggests that the vertigo that accompanies our experience of the uncanny is the result of an atavistic belief in the linearity of time itself. The notion of a haunting return of the repressed/sublimated is a function of a conception of time in which we live from point A to point B, all the while getting further away from A and closer to B. The experience of the uncanny reveals something quite different, which, given the centrality of time in our conceptions of being and belonging, we find quite terrifying: time is not a linear, horizontal affair, but one of layered verticality. We are terrified by the implication that we are always simultaneously capable of more than one mode of being and belonging and that how we are and how we think of belonging in the world is a function of context, past decisions and so on – however much we would like to persuade ourselves that they represent historical stages of development in the lives of individuals and societies. Freud writes: 'The uncanny effect of epilepsy and of madness has the same origin. The layman sees in them the working of forces hitherto unsuspected in his fellow-men, but at the same time he is dimly aware of them in remote corners of his own being' (1973 [1919]: 243). At its core, the experience of the uncanny is a function of repetition – so much so that 'this factor of involuntary repetition which surrounds what would otherwise be innocent enough with an uncanny atmosphere . . . forces upon us the idea of something fateful and inescapable' (237).

As illuminating as Freud's essay on the nature of the uncanny may be, aside from a couple of references to works of fiction, he has very little to say about how people are likely to respond in a face-to-face encounter with what elicits an experience of the uncanny. This should not come as a surprise because his psychoanalytic interest was primarily diagnostic. However, the ambivalence of the uncanny, deriving as it does from a profound cognitive and temporal disjunction, encourages us to speculate on at least two kinds of responses. Instead of explaining them in the abstract, I will do so in a manner that will stay close to our concern with Ubuntu.

In Western, teleological grand narratives of evolution, what connected individual and social evolution was the phylogeny-ontogeny hypothesis, according to which each individual repeats or recaptures the grand narrative of social evolution. Modernity generally came to refer to that precarious middle phase when the individual has left behind the innocence of assumed belonging (ubuntu/*sinnliche Harmonie*), but has not yet fully worked out the nature of and the conditions for the maturity of contemplated belonging (Ubuntu/*moralische Harmonie*). From this we can conclude at least two things: first, that Western individuals who understand themselves as living this rather simplistic, linear story will experience an encounter with a premodern praxis of belonging, such as Ubuntu, as uncanny; that is, as a confrontation *in the present* with a way of being and belonging that, so the story goes, belong *to the past*, which they believe they have surmounted – essentially a confrontation with the un/familiar 'collectivism' that preceded individualism. By bringing the past back to life or by manifesting the past in the present, the uncanny causes a fissure in the individual's experience of what is foundational to Western modernity: a linear, horizontal *conception* of time is threatened by the vertical *experience* of time. In effect, the uncanny *threatens to obliterate difference itself* – either the difference that one society imagines to exist between itself (as civilised and mature because individualist) and another (as uncivilised and immature because communal) or the difference that an individual imagines to exist between a past self and his/her present, individuated self.

When individuals and societies find themselves confronted by this threat, they typically resort to violence because violence, as René Girard reminds us in *Violence and the Sacred* (1988), is the most reliable way of putting an individual or society 'back in their place', of reconstituting a difference that ought to exist because it reflects an assumed natural (here, linear) state of affairs. Is it any coincidence that scientific racism, as we know it today, emerged as a phenomenon of Western modernity, of the watershed moment in Western social evolution when individual*ism* became accepted as a given and belonging became first and foremost a problem for thought? Should it come as a surprise that communalism is the unthought of individualism – and by 'unthought', I mean that Other upon which individual*ism* depended for its very invention, but which had to become unthought – that is, at worst forgotten and unfamiliar and at best reminiscent of a past, primitive way of being? Is racism not an experience of the uncanny return of what had become unthought – a return that threatened with obliteration (and therefore inexecution) the very difference that had become constitutive of the Western understanding of itself? And was colonialism not simply *the violence that (re)made that difference*? Is racism not ultimately rooted in the fear so precisely articulated by Max Horkheimer and Theodor Adorno when they comment that the 'Enlightenment finally devoured not only symbols but also their successors, universal concepts, and left nothing of metaphysics behind except *the abstract fear of the collective from which it had sprung*'? (2002: 11, emphasis added).

Racism will appear wherever difference is threatened with collapse because racism is the strategy par excellence that societies and individuals have always deployed to propel themselves down a mythical path of linear development. It is the hatred that (re)makes a difference. It is also the reason why Ubuntu – as shorthand for the communal – could *never* have been celebrated as a positive phenomenon in the context of a colonial historicist a priori: any such celebration would have threatened the founding of Western modernity with *in-difference*, de-differentiation (per Girard); that is, with inexecution.

But the postcolonial a priori of relativism is a very different order of things: Western individualism has become the default state of being for a globalising neoliberalism that has forgotten about belonging; in fact, it is only because it has forgotten about belonging that we have become so acutely aware of Ubuntu. Individualism is being shadowed by the unthought of its invention. This is why, in the global *imaginaire*, the meaning of Ubuntu oscillates between being a sign of the salvific and a figure of the primitive and why responses to it oscillate between violent dismissal (where it threatens Western modernity with de-differentiation) and salvific exceptionalism (where it signals a redemptive return to what modernity violated in its execution). Ubuntu is suspended between its embrace as sign of the salvific and its dismissal as a backward sign of what was thought to have been surmounted.

The reappropriation of Ubuntu-as-uncanny suggested here is not entirely novel. In fact, to name it as such really only articulates a familiar, if subdued, theme in Ubuntu discourse. If these references have not yet been thematised or named in the manner suggested here, it is possibly because of the inherent dangers of an implicit colonialist developmentalism. In the space opened up by a post-teleological historiography of social development, however, there is no such danger. Quite the contrary, Ubuntu now appears with all the ambivalence of a return of the forgotten that is a critique of the present. Here are some examples of this uncanny thematic:

> Even in issues like conservation, tribal peoples have shared what is now considered as an extremely advanced First World way of thinking. They saw themselves as custodians, realising that if they destroyed the environment they could not survive. It appears that as we grow in wisdom in the First World, so we learn to respect the wisdom of the ancients. This wisdom still lives in tribal societies (Murove 2009a: 327).

Of course, the reference to 'tribalism' marks the locus of a simultaneous gain and loss: a gain because we can leverage Ubuntu as a critique of the entropic forces of modernity, but also a loss because its description in terms of the colonialist invention of 'tribalism' reinserts that very potential into the kind of developmentalist grand narrative we are trying to avoid. More cautious is Barbara Nussbaum, who writes: 'Could soul force be a beautiful quality deeply inherent in all human beings that, through the forces of time, urbanisation, industrialisation and concomitant alienation, tends to be denied, suppressed and temporarily forgotten' (2009b: 104)? Peter Senge similarly remarks about the emotional poverty of industrialised societies: 'We really have no idea what we have lost in the industrial age. I think that the profound unhappiness of the industrial age is invisible to us. When you spend time with people in Africa, there is a different energy' (in Nussbaum 2009a: 245). Luke L. Pato, too, recognises Ubuntu as a 'cultural ethos, a spirituality, which is not necessarily better, or superior, or for that matter inferior to those of other people, but from which others can learn and improve their understanding of one another' (in Munyaka and Motlhabi 2009: 68). M. Munyaka and M. Motlhabi elaborate: 'This is how it should be understood by those people who see nothing uniquely African in *Ubuntu*. When considering community as a constitutive element of *Ubuntu*, the importance of a person *will be seen again* as a moral, social, relational and compassionate being' (emphasis added).

Ubuntu statements such as these become not expressions of a unique philosophy, but rather the recognition of a unique temporality in which Ubuntu functions as an uncompromising mnemonic:

> I have always known that deep down in every human heart, there is mercy and generosity. No one is born hating another person because of the color of his skin, or his background, or his religion . . . Man's goodness is a flame that can be hidden but never extinguished (Mandela in Nussbaum 2009b: 105).

If Ubuntu's uniqueness resides not in *what* it is, but in *when* it becomes visible as a communitarian praxis that uncannily reminds us of our interdependence, it follows that the salvific status attributed to it derives not from the fact that it brings the West something that it does not know, but from the fact that it reminds the West of something it has forgotten, something we all always already have and which has now again become visible, only because of the asynchronicity of modernities.

This is what we may refer to as the general position of Ubuntu in contemporary discourses, both local and global. Closer to home, the more specific function of Ubuntu as uncanny consists in the fact that it haunts the juridico-political structure with a question as simple as it is profound: Is the vision of justice projected by the constitutional order a just vision? Is the justice it promises, a just justice? This is not a question that we can address or even make sense of from within the constitutional order itself, for the simple reason that the question emerges from an enunciative space beyond what is imaginable in terms of the contractarian axiomatic of the Constitution. Let me say something about this space because it is only from an understanding of this space that we can achieve our end, not arguing for a normative consensus on why we *should* invoke Ubuntu in adjudication, but rather a maximal understanding of the context of adjudication in which it would be legitimate and meaningful to do so.

Positioning the uncanny: The justice of justice

To position Ubuntu in relation to the law means situating or contextualising its signification as uncanny historically and contingently, with reference to the *über*-sign of South Africa's modernity, its impressive Constitution. In exploring how to position it in relation to the law, I proceed on the basis of the following mixed bag of assumptions and arguments already made in this report:

1. South Africa's modernity is constituted through a double negation of Africa: first, through the embrace of the constitutional democratic nation-state as a political form and, second, by committing itself to a reinvention of traditional values in line with constitutional values – effectively a circumcision of phallo-primocentrism in line with constitutionalism.
2. This double negation is a function of the arrow of time and therefore irreversible.
3. Because of the logic of asynchronous modernities and the spectre of inexecution that continues to haunt it, our modernity has generated a

vertical, double structure of justice – vertical in the sense that the Constitution, posited as hegemonic law, remains shadowed by a subaltern conception of justice that is a function of a political economy of obligation. The idea of a vertical, double structure of justice posits a Western political conception of the equality of rights-bearing individuals before the law, which conceives of justice as the prudent balancing of (sometimes conflicting) rights. In the South African Constitution, dignity is one such right, guaranteed by the state conventionally conceived as *executor* of the people's will, with an *executive* mandated to exercise the most fundamental right associated with its monopoly on the means of violence, namely to *execute* individuals who pose a fundamental threat to its existence. The subaltern conception of the political, grounded in the logic of a political economy of obligation, does not recognise the individual in these abstract terms as rights-bearing (see Ramose 1999: 102–28). In terms of this logic:

> Individuals belong to a state. They also belong to tribes, religious groups, regions, age groups, economic networks, without any monocausality. So powerful individuals will try to use the state for the group's benefit (and also for their own personal benefit), and groups perceived rightly or wrongly as powerful will try to instrumentalize one another and together will try to instrumentalize the state (Chabal 2009: 361).

Here, as Gérard Prunier puts it, 'the state is always *somebody's* state, never *the State* in the legal abstract form beloved of Western constitutional law. It is the Museveni distatorship for the Acholi, the Arab state for the southern Sudanese, the *mestiço* state for UNITA, or the Tutsi state for the Hutu' (2009: 361). From the perspective of a constitutional filter, this is the down side. But from the perspective of contemporary Africanists, the up side is a Revolutionary understanding of justice in which equality imports both dignity and equity or justice (Shivji 2014). The Cosmopolitan option here consists in exploring the possibility of liberating this Revolutionary unity of justice, equality and dignity under the unifying phrase of 'Ubuntu in relation to the law'. As such, it is the enunciative space of the question regarding the justice of justice.

4. Any attempt to explore this enunciative space encounters a problem in the history of a racialised culture that reduces this expansive, subaltern understanding of justice to an 'African communitarianism', irreconcilable with a Western, contractarian Law of law.
5. The resulting 'conundrum' is a clear example of what Kroeze (2002), with different intent, criticises as legal formalism: the process through which a political phenomenon is reduced to the logic of the law, in such a way that it cannot but appear as problematic in terms of the law.
6. Beyond this formalism and contrary to its reductive logic, Ubuntu can be understood in at least two additional senses: one, as already partly compatible with the law in those instances where it retrodicts in the language of human rights; two, where there is a residue that exceeds this retrodiction, the excess can be understood as and appropriated by an altruistic interpretation of the law, of which Ubuntu may (never *has to*) function as sign.
7. Allowing altruism to speak the language of Ubuntu may counter what Achille Mbembe refers to as the 'accelerated turn to an *everyday politics of expediency* rather than a demanding, *disciplined politics of principle*' (2011: 10) because it will address both the alienation from the law evident in claims that the Constitution is a Western imposition *and* allow us to conceive of dealing with socio-economic rights in a substantive, rather than a narrow, procedural manner.[14]

All this leaves us with the question to be addressed here: what legitimation do we imagine for the invocation of Ubuntu, beyond the generality of altruism suggested by the second *epoché*? In the section that follows, my suggestion is to rethink what we mean by legitimation. What if we can root the imperative to invoke Ubuntu *qua* contextual, political sign of the altruistic wholly within the structure of the founding of the law itself? What if the act of adjudication can be demonstrated to derive whatever legitimacy it needs to invoke Ubuntu from the fact that every act

---

14. See Brand (2003). We can achieve more substance in at least three ways: legally, by articulating a substantive duty for the provision of a basic minimum as the basis for a judgment (48); juridico-morally, through normative consensus on the *telos* (purpose) or Law of law; philosophically, by countering this 'flight from substance' (Flemming in Brand 2003: 51) by articulating a maximal understanding of the context in which it occurs.

of adjudication is a reiteration of the South African Constitution's founding aporia, more specifically the *aporia-archē* of the Constitution that leaves both the Constitution and its re-enactment in adjudication indeterminate in relation to an original injustice? Let us consider the essential features of this hyphenated founding by sketching the essential features of each term in turn.

The aporetic founding

The facts seem deceptively simple: the Constitution represents the culmination of Western political and intellectual development and, in this sense, is inextricably part of or a continuation of – and because of its lasting status, the most enduring monument to – colonialism. This said, the a priori of rights-bearing individualism that infoms the Constitution was also embraced by the liberation struggle as a sine qua non of liberty, so that the final Constitution of 1996 marks both the culmination of the struggle *against* colonialism (the 'birth certificate' of the new nation, with all its attendant implications of a final execution [Ebrahim 2011]), as well as the culmination of colonialism, understood as the triumphant grafting onto Africa of a Western political form. In other words, the Constitution is at once the most lasting trace *of* colonialism and the culmination of the struggle *against* colonialism. As such, its founding marks, not only the *gain* or the beloved 'bridge' of much constitutional jurisprudence of the late 1990s, but also the simultaneous *loss* of the very possibility of ever restoring the original injustice that Mogobe B. Ramose so often reminds us of.

The implication of this contradictory status of the founding is equally simple: the fact that the Constitution was born of an original injustice means that the question of what it means to be just, of what it means to do the right thing, will always exceed the juridical mechanisms that exist to address it. While the fact of an original injustice and the memory of that fact are both real, the range of constitutional arrangements devised to address it – mechanisms that pivot on a capitalist market economy with limited, if any, capacity to recognise an injustice committed regarding a people or a 'race' – can never restore that injustice absolutely, it can merely *address* it. As a result, true justice will always exceed the grasp of the juridical – in a different, additional way to which it does so anyway, according to Derrida (1992a).[15]

---

15. And in a different way, Derrida understands this excess as 'aneconomic'.

This excess is not the kind of excess we can address simply by multiplying the number of juridical measures to deal with it. The reason for this, as Lyotard so clearly argued in *The Differend: Phrases in Dispute* (1988), is that we are not only dealing with two *different* conceptions of justice, but something closer to a *differend*: in order to argue for restitution, those who suffered the original injustice would have to adopt the language of Western, colonialist law of private property, thereby multiplying (by becoming complicit in) the original violation or injustice. The law can only compute contesting claims to land in terms of the logic of its Law of law: contractual exchanges premised on an individualist a priori, which translates into contesting claims about *ownership* of entities with abstract exchange value. To argue for redress of the original injustice in such terms is to become complicit in the injustice itself because what was most specific about the precolonial African relationship to land was exactly that it could not conceive of land in terms of abstract exchange value. Rather, it was conceived in terms of usufruct, the metaphysical meaning of which derived from an understanding of belonging in terms of origin, locality and so on. When I argue that the original injustice *exceeds* the grasp of the law, I mean *exceed* in the sense that, with the adoption of the Constitution, the excess is constituted as irrecuperable *differend* that henceforth persists only in the form of or *as* a question about the (im)possibility of the justice of justice.

Another way to describe this contradictory status of the Constitution is to say that it pivots on a profound and unresolvable paradox (aporia): on the one hand, its very existence constantly recalls the original injustice of colonialism, of which it is now the most lasting trace, an imposition over a topography irreducible to the logic it represents. On the other hand and, given the arrow of time, the Constitution is also the only mechanism that can respond to this memory by addressing the original injustice it recalls. This means the Constitution is founded on the context-specific aporia of *a legal order premised, in part, on an original injustice that can only be addressed by the legal order itself*. Formulated differently, the Constitution's founding principle (*archē*) is that of the aporia: more precisely, the aporia *as archē* or first principle. The fact of the irrecuperable or excessive nature of the original injustice and the anticipation, now messianic, of an absolute justice, a just justice anticipated as an adequate response to the original injustice, the fact that the Constitution exists to mediate between what is irrecuperably lost and the realistic anticipation of a justice that will recognise this loss, this founding *aporia-archē* means that in a context of asynchronous modernities, the founding of the South

African state (conventionally understood) will, in principle, always remain inexecutable. Alternatively, it will find that it can only pursue the promise of execution through a proportional increase in force.

In terms of the generality suggested by the second *epoché*, described earlier in this chapter, there is nothing particular about recognising the founding moment of the law as an aporetic tension between the necessary injustice (because invariably violent) of its founding and the promise of justice held out to the We represented in, thereby constituted by, the preamble. The founding of juridico-political orders is always aporetic, in the sense that their promise of justice is premised on the injustice that was necessary for the consolidation of the right to violence. What is particular beyond the *epoché* is how hypermodernity complicates this logic because the injustice of the founding continues alongside the juridico-political as the impossibility of the collective amnesia that otherwise would, *in the long run*, forget about the founding injustice. The violence that is the subject of the question generated by the aporia of every founding – when will they forget the violence of the origin? – will never go away or become sublimated or forgotten, so that the collective may one day again find itself confronted with an expanded understanding of justice, either to be accepted as a salvific reminder of what their amnesia exists to conceal or to be dismissed as the normative fumblings of the evolutionary immature. To say that the founding of the hypermodern postcolonial state will remain inexecuted is to acknowledge the impossibility of this trajectory of collective amnesia and to accept, in a spirit of responsibility, the question about the justice of justice as a lasting expression of the constitutive origin (*archē*) of the juridical.

We will have to find a different way of negotiating this impasse. A clue lies perhaps in saying that as problematic and inadequate as these constitutional gestures that exist to address the excess may be, once we accept the arrow of time, the original injustice, while forever remaining irrecuperable will and does nonetheless provide us with a *horizon of justice*, perhaps even a *geography of justice*, within which to frame our engagement with the question regarding the *justice of justice*. In other words, yes, with democracy, 'injustice came to be constitutionalized' (Ramose 2002b: 470), but only the Constitution can bear witness to, remind us of and respond to this original injustice, within the limits of the paradox (or aporia) of what it means for a sovereign state to be premised on the forever visible and articulated interrogation of its own claim to juridical sovereignty.

Legal, constitutional justice, then, becomes an aporetic pivot, in the sense that its very existence marks the loss of original justice, while holding out the

Constitution as the only viable way of beginning to think about what it means to interrogate the justice of justice. It is a hyphenated founding, pivoting on an *aporia-archē* that I think we should look to when we consider the question of Ubuntu in relation to the law. What we may gain in the process is another change in the question we ask: not 'how do we legitimise the invocation of Ubuntu?' but rather, 'can invoking Ubuntu amount to a meaningful response to the obligation of the law to address the question of the *justice of justice*?' – a question that now derives wholly from within the very structure of the founding of the law itself.

It may be argued that such an appeal to the justice of justice smacks of a modernist desire to escape the *superficiality* of the modern juridical, that it is only another way of making a meta-argument one way or the other. No and yes. No, in that as long as we think of meta-justification in terms of a spatial metaphor that sees two conflicting claims being adjudicated by a third, higher or meta-position uncontaminated by the logic of either two: God uncontaminated by legal rules and rules uncontaminated by God. Modern legal culture is what it is because we realise that neither of these two positions is possible anymore – hence the superficiality of the division between individualism and altruism. Yes, if we think of meta-justification as embedded in one of the imperatives itself, one that temporarily allows us to prioritise (or meta-justify) the altruistic or communal over the individualist. In effect, what is articulated here is a third way of understanding the relationship between Ubuntu and the law: neither as quasi-transcendental nor as Law of laws, but as a very specific, contextual reminder of a concern with the original injustice that derives internally from the logic of the founding of the law itself. What would be the implications of such a claim for the act of adjudication? To answer this question, we need to look more closely at the second term in the hyphenated founding, the aporia as *archē*.

Archē: Adjudication as the praxis of the uncanny

I emphasise the *act* of adjudication as a form of doing because I think that in the relevant literature there is a general lack of appreciation for the distinction between what we *say* when we invoke Ubuntu (what we *mean* by the concept) and what we *do* when we invoke it. What we say has been a constant bone of contention, resulting in the oft-repeated criticism that we cannot invoke what we cannot define. I return to this criticism below. For now, let me focus on the performative dimension of what we *do* when we invoke Ubuntu in adjudication.

The term *archē* is usually understood to refer to the beginning or the origin of things and that is indeed its etymological meaning in Greek: beginning, origin or first cause. But in *On Revolution*, Hannah Arendt reminds us that *archē* has the double etymological sense of origin *and* rule, of an original principle that contains within it the rules for its future application. An example may clarify. According to Arendt, the American War of Independence and its resulting Constitution were both unique – a uniqueness that would last 'until the breakdown of the European colonial system and the emergence of new nations in our own century' (1963: 213). This consisted in the recognition that it is futile to search for an Absolute to appeal to in order to break the vicious circle in which all beginnings are invariably caught, namely that of seeking an Immortal Legislator or God to legitimise the beginning. What made modern revolutions modern was the fact that they were founded on the belief that this 'absolute' lies *in the very act of the beginning itself* (205). Until then – including the fiasco that was the French Revolution in many ways – it was thought that a new beginning that was not legitimated from outside the beginning itself would not last because it would not be legitimate. The beginning would remain arbitrary and therefore inexecutable. Only some appeal to an external Legislator could prevent this from happening. The American War of Independence managed to do what the French Revolution failed to, namely to begin by staring the fundamental contradiction squarely in the face, without any appeal to an external mediator to ease the fact of its unresolvable nature. Instead, Americans contracted among themselves to put in place institutions that, drawing their strength and legitimacy from the contract and nothing but the contract, would assist them in a perpetual mediation of the contradiction. Here, the *archē* or *beginning* is that of a contract. But the contract also functions as a *principle* to be carried forth into the future as a *rule* that will determine future action as iterated contract-making. Arendt succinctly summarises this relationship between origin and rule as follows:

> What saves the act of beginning from its own arbitrariness is that it carries its own principle within itself, or, to be more precise, that beginning and principle, *principium* and principle, are not only related to each other, but are coeval. The absolute from which the beginning is to derive its own validity and which must save it, as it were, from its inherent arbitrariness is the principle which, together with it, makes its appearance in the world (1963: 214).

What saves the beginning from collapsing under the weight of its own arbitrariness is the fact that along with the beginning (as contract), a principle or rule is given for future actions, which effectively means that every contract made and entered into amounts to a re-enactment of the origin as contract (which explains why the United States is such a litigious society, as well as what may otherwise appear as the fetishisation of the prohibition against lying and not keeping promises).

The relevance for us of what it means to think about *archē* as origin (beginning) and rule (principle) relates to the meaning of the phrase 'constitutional democracy'. On the face of it, the judiciary, by virtue of the fact that it possesses neither Force (like the executive) nor Will (like the legislative), may appear to be the weakest of the three branches of government. In South Africa, this relative weakness, in principle, is not in fact quite true, since given the weakness of the official opposition party, the Constitutional Court is often said to effectively function as the unofficial opposition. But the idea of a relative weakness is also untrue in a general sense. For, as Arendt argues, it is exactly its lack of power and the relative permanence of its judges that in another sense make it the supreme seat of authority. This authority derives from the status of Constitutional Court judgments as a perpetual reiteration of the Constitution, 'a kind of continuous constitution-making' (1963: 201). In the words of Woodrow Wilson, the Constitutional Court is 'a kind of Constitutional Assembly in continuous sessions' (in Arendt 1963: 201). Formulated differently and in terms of the *archē* as origin and rule, in a post-Absolutist or modernist time, the Constitution is the new beginning (contract) that carries with it the rule for contract-making, which the Constitutional Court re-enacts *as* and *in* principle every time it adjudicates. For final clarity of what this means, we have to turn to Arendt, not the philosopher, but the teacher who, following Plato, explains:

> The way the beginner starts whatever he intends to do lays down the law of action for those who have joined him in order to partake in the enterprise and to bring about its accomplishments. As such, the principle inspires the deeds that are to follow and remains apparent as long as the action lasts (1963: 214).[16]

---

16. 'For the Greek word for beginning is [*archē*] and [*archē*] means both beginning and principle. No later poet or philosopher has expressed the innermost meaning of this coincidence more beautifully and more succinctly than Plato when, at the end of his life he remarked almost casually [translated from the Greek: the beginning is more than half of the whole]' (1963: 316, note 55).

The relevance of these two insights – the coeval nature of origin and rule and the Constitutional Court as locus for the perpetual re-enactment of the principle that constituted the beginning – is of extreme relevance to us. I have argued that the *archē* or first principle of the South African Constitution is that of *aporia as archē*, or *aporia-archē* – a principle that, defying the logic of first principles, according to which there should be only One at the origin, actually appears as two principles, conjoined in irredeemable tension. Considered as a beginning, what Arendt's analysis suggests is that every act of constitutional adjudication is also a re-enactment in and as rule, of this beginning as *aporia-archē*. Every act of constitutional adjudication is always already given to us, a priori, as a reiteration of the founding *aporia-archē*.

We do not need a normative argument for why the law should be open, or how to open the law *to*, the original injustice, the understanding of subjectivity (being-as-belonging) or its implicit understanding of justice because the law is *constitutively* open to the original injustice, so that every act of adjudication, *qua* reiteration of the *aporia-archē*, is a priori open to that subjectivity and the negation of its historical conception of justice, which was never excluded from the Constitution at the founding moment. The founding openness to the original injustice that made the law possible opens it in principle to the need to account for itself, to give an account of itself, not only in terms of justice, but also in terms of the justice of justice. Formulated differently, every act of adjudication should be understood to be both constituted *as* and reconstituting *of* a response to the question, 'Is the justice being dispensed a just justice?' – a question that always already suspends the idea that justice dispensed in terms of the contractual axiomatic alone could be just.

Demonstrated here is the fundamental political nature of the law – not as the institution that adjudicates on the political, but one in which adjudication is, in a very real sense, a continuation of the political. Small wonder, then, that the contestation over the deployment of Ubuntu in adjudication should be so highly charged and emotive. Any argument for or against doing so will imply a conception of the political, of *thinking* and *being* in relation to the law, its openness to the political, the nature of justice and the possibility of the law to recoup the original injustice that it in part represents. It should also come as no surprise, then, that these political stances represent the conceptual personae mapped in Chapter 2 of this report.

The conceptual personae of constitutional jurisprudence

In 'The Emerging Role of *Ubuntu-Botho* in Developing a Consensual South African Legal Culture', Helen Keep and Robert Midgley state the following juridical bottom line for the incorporation of Ubuntu into the law:

> It should be remembered, however, that *ubuntu-botho* is not a foundational value expressly mentioned in the Constitution. If it is to be treated as core, or to have any effect on our jurisprudence, then this can only be done in one of two ways: by treating it as embodying the spirit, purport and objects of the Constitution and so allowing it to permeate the law in an indirect way; or to give it more direct influence by interpreting one of the core values, dignity, as embracing *ubuntu-botho*. These are not mutually-exclusive options, however. In the *Makwanyane* and *Port Elizabeth Municipality* cases, for example, *ubuntu-botho* was used to promote the 'spirit, purport and objects' of the Constitution, yet *ubuntu-botho* also finds a natural home in the value of respect for human dignity, as courts have found on various occasions (2007: 34).[17]

The standard responses to legal scholars who have proceeded in either of these two ways reveal certain recurring thematics of Ubuntu discourse in general. What most of them have in common is the problem of definition; that is, the criticism that we cannot invoke what we cannot define. As a rule, this undefinability of Ubuntu is explained or accounted for in a number of ways, of which the following seem to be the most salient:

1. As *inherently unknowable* or not articulable: This often assumes the form of an argument that maintains that those who try to define Ubuntu are trapped in an alien, Western mode of thinking. As Freddy Mnyongani puts it: 'For lawyers trained within the Western paradigm of defining and categorising concepts, *ubuntu* is a very frustrating concept to deal with. This is so because *ubuntu* defies categories' (2010: 135; see also Bohler-Muller 2005). In the words of Yvonne Mokgoro, '*Ubuntu* it seems, is one of those things that you recognise when you see it' (1998: 15). Here we

---

17. Keep and Midgley's note: 'See, for example, *Dikoko v Mokhatla* par 68 and *City of Johannesburg v Rand Properties (Pty) Ltd and Others* 2006 (6) BCLR 728 (W) pars 63–64'.

can distinguish between two forms of violence at work in any attempt to define Ubuntu: first and in its universality, what Derrida (1981) calls 'transcendental violence' – the necessary violation of the particularity of a thing, in order to speak about it at all, a violent negation that is nonetheless a condition of the possibility of any conversation and, by deduction, of the political; second, a particular violence resulting from the fact that Western knowledge constructions proceed through a kind of epistemological genocide of things African (see, for example, Ramose 1999: 41–66 and Bennett 2011). The particular dilemma here is, of course, that through retrodiction the second form of violence doubles as a further example of the first.

2. *Extrapolated approximation*: Despite this sense of an irrecuperable loss, a movement of extrapolation nonetheless: Ubuntu is *equated with* 'a culture' that emphasises communality (Langa, par. 224, *Makwanyane*); it is considered to *translate into* humanness (Mokgoro, par. 308, *Makwanyane*) or *expresses* an 'ethos' of love (Mahomed, par. 263, *Makwanyane*). To say that Ubuntu equates this or that, that it translates as X or expresses Y, is to say nothing about Ubuntu itself and, in this sense, any extrapolated approximation is but a restatement of the inherent undefinability of the concept.

3. The *fate of a loan/lone word*: The undefinability results, not from the specificity of colonialism and Western epistemic domination, nor from inappropriate abstract modes of knowing, but is a matter of language in translation. As C.J.E. Ball reminds us, ubuntu is a loan word and is therefore 'highly susceptible to change, not only because it is novel, but also because it is isolated. Its links with the language from which it was borrowed are broken, and it has no semantic connections with other words in the language into which it has been absorbed' (in Bennett 2011: 31). Here a fractal self-similarity between form and content in the debate emerges: the word 'ubuntu' has individuated into the abstract and lost the meaning that would otherwise derive from a sense of belonging. This loss of meaning should not come as a surprise because, after all, a word is a word through other words.

4. *Rhetorical strategies*: Possibly the most sympathetically insightful response has come from Irma Kroeze (2002), who argues that *S. v. Makwanyane* put an end to any future invocations of Ubuntu in adjudication because of the rhetorical strategies employed by the six concurring judgments that

invoked Ubuntu. Kroeze explains this problem as one of legal formalism in constitutional adjudication (260). In terms of this formalism, three standard rhetorical moves were made in *S. v. Makwanyane* that, while seeking to incorporate Ubuntu, actually militate against future invocation. According to a first Cosmopolitan move, it was argued that 'the values of *ubuntu* are no different from those found in any other civilised society or legal system'. Kroeze argues: 'Whether this is true or not is not actually the point. The point is that, once you regard *ubuntu* as just a local example of a universal phenomenon, it is no longer a separate concept that needs to be articulated and applied.' The second rhetorical move entails the use of concepts in the definition of Ubuntu that are so general, abstract or vague that the 'concept simply collapses under the weight of the expectations'. She continues: '*Ubuntu* is said to include the following values: communality, respect, dignity, value, acceptance, sharing, co-responsibility, humaneness, social justice, joy, love' and the problem with these concepts is that they are by and large empty (260). But it is the third rhetorical move that Kroeze considers the most devastating:

> In most cases it quickly becomes clear that *ubuntu* is presented in such a way that it is clearly an alternative to liberalism: if liberalism is individualistic, *ubuntu* must be communitarian; if liberalism emphasises individual rights, *ubuntu* must stress group rights; competition v compassion; confrontation v conciliation; and so on. But this keeps the debate stuck in the liberalist dichotomies and hierarchies. It limits the choices to either liberalism or communitarianism. It is forced into the politics of form prescribed by *liberal* formalism. And that denies the idea of *ubuntu* any transformative potential (2002: 261).

I would argue – in fact, much of this report has been the argument – that the three rhetorical moves identified by Kroeze – to *equivocate*, *generalise* and *juxtapose* – haunt the debate on Ubuntu as such and are not specific to legal formalism. Each of the three rhetorical strategies circumscribes one of the many ways in which the logic of retrodiction is concealed by the demands of identity politics. As such, they represent political stances that should by now be familiar: the first two Cosmopolitan strategies of equivocation and generalisation see in Ubuntu nothing specific and, because of this lack of identitarian specificity, nothing worth being interrogated by. The second, *generalisation*, is particularly worrying because its vacuity and sentimentality are achieved through the exclusion of everything substantial from Ubuntu, including its constitutive violence and counter-hegemonic (and therefore conflictual, revolutionary, confrontational or violent) insistence on an expanded understanding of justice that could enable us, under certain conditions and in certain circumstances, to prioritise collective good over individual rights. The third, *juxtapositioning*, manifests the Conformist reduction of anything social or altruistic to a problematic African axiomatic, irreconcilable with a liberal regime of rights.

That juridical discourse should reflect the various conceptual personae as an embodiment of a particular political stance on what it means to conjoin being African and thinking Africa simply points to the fact that the interpretation of laws, including the Constitution, is political and that the politics at play in adjudication, as well as the critical reception of Ubuntu-engaged adjudication in constitutional jurisprudence, will reveal the political fault lines of greater Ubuntu discourse. To consider all the acts of adjudication and to show how they reveal these personae at work would require a separate study. I can only offer the most general sense of the personae we find in adjudication and jurisprudence respectively. Given my interest in the emancipatory potential of Ubuntu, my main concern is providing a more sympathetic interpretative frame for the revolutionary adjudication of former Constitutional Court justices Sachs and Mokgoro.

Given the nature of the question about Ubuntu in relation to the law, we can expect to find the following divide: adjudication will per definition manifest only two of the conceptual personae, the Prophetic (the Revolutionary and, possibly although unlikely, the Saviour) and the Cosmopolitan. Adjudication is not the place to argue whether or not Ubuntu should be invoked. Judges either do or they do not. They do because they are open to meta-questions about Africanity and justice or they do not because they are inhibited by the values associated with Ubuntu (Conformist) and/or its lack of definition (Archivist). As far as its conceptual personae are concerned, Ubuntu-engaged adjudication will per definition be *empathetic*. These judgments either limit their concern with Ubuntu's emancipatory potential to South Africa (Revolutionary), or they may explicitly or implicitly go so far as to hold Ubuntu up as a universalising solution to some of the contradictions generated by liberal democratic regimes everywhere (Saviour). Alternatively, in what appears as a 'mere' instance of the generalising rhetoric critiqued by Kroeze, a legal scholar or judge may reflect a broader and more universal concern with the possibility of reinvigorating humanism as a political category (Cosmopolitan).[18]

In jurisprudence, on the other hand, we may well expect to find the entire array of conceptual personae, including the antipathetic personae of the Conformist and Archivist because, unlike judges, legal scholars can invoke Ubuntu in order to argue why it should not be invoked. I want to conclude by splicing the Revolutionary conceptual persona into the argument of this and the preceding chapter in order to motivate, not why Ubuntu *should* be invoked in adjudication, but why it is very meaningful to do so.

The Prophetic persona: Conceptual geography of a revolution

The Revolutionary image of thought is one of *recollection* and the mode of being, *spectral*. The *locus classicus* of this persona in adjudication – a status deriving from its founding nature – was AZAPO *v. President of the Republic of South Africa* (1996). Steve Biko's wife was among the applicants who challenged the constitutionality of the Act that established the Truth and Reconciliation Commission on the grounds that section 27 of the Act, which granted conditional amnesty to applicants, denied them the right to trial, guaranteed by section 22 of the Interim Constitution. Legally, the question was whether amnesty violated the constitutionally guaranteed right to justice. Mohamed D.P. ruled that this was not the case because the Constitution itself 'permitted or authorised such violation' (*AZAPO*, par. 10) in the form of an epilogue that should be interpreted as the kind of provision, allowed for in section 33(2), which may under certain circumstances be invoked to suspend fundamental rights. The fact that this judgment constitutionalised the epilogue (see Cornell and Muvangua 2011: 103) is relevant here because the epilogue stated a preference for 'understanding to vengeance, reparation over retaliation, *ubuntu* over victimisation'. That the judgment only invoked Ubuntu indirectly is not the point. What matters is Mohamed D.P.'s explanation of why the Constitution-makers (in conceiving the epilogue) and Parliament (in passing the Act) allowed for this temporary suspension of the cornerstone of the individual right to justice. The answer is simple: only the guarantee of amnesty to perpetrators could conceivably set in motion a process that would give reality to past suffering and afford the victims of apartheid the 'collective recognition of a new nation' (*AZAPO*, par. 16).

---

18. See, for instance, Cornell and Panfilio (2010).

At stake here was the problem that haunts the founding of all juridico-political orders: how to turn the still *spectral* We of the preamble into the *substantial* We of the nationalist imagination? Nothing better captures the spectral nature of the We at this particular point than the epilogue's reflection on the Constitution as a 'historic bridge' that both victim and perpetrator had to cross to enter 'the new society . . . which is the vision that informs the epilogue' (*AZAPO*, par. 18) – a crossing that would be jeopardised if law-makers did not temporarily suspend the individual right to justice. Simply put, the judgment suspended an individual right to justice for the sake of the creation of a We, as a condition of the possibility for the future exercise of individual rights (par. 50). Mediating between the spectral nature of fragmented, past selves and an anticipated, future national self is an image of thought as recollection: that we can and, as a matter of urgency must, uncover and recollect (our) u/Ubuntu.

What remained undeveloped in Mohamed D.P.'s judgment was the relationship it posited between, on the one hand, an understanding of justice that exceeded the contractual axiomatic (in the sense that it temporarily invoked a communitarian imperative as a future guarantor of the contract) and, on the other hand, the justification of this suspension of individual rights, with an appeal to the improvement in socio-economic conditions this would afford:

> Those negotiators of the Constitution . . . could have chosen to direct that the limited resources of the State be spent by giving preference to the formidable delictual claims of those who had suffered from acts of murder, torture or assault perpetrated by servants of the State, diverting to that extent, desperately needed funds in the crucial areas of education, housing and primary health care (*AZAPO*, par. 44).

At work here is a conception of justice that not only briefly exceeded the contractual axiomatic, but did so *substantially* by recognising in justice the inseparable unity of dignity, community and material conditions.

Of course, this temporary suspension of the contractual axiomatic was very carefully circumscribed by constitutional provisions and in that sense not to be repeated (bar under conditions stipulated in article 37). We can read this temporary suspension, this founding of the new South Africa on a constitutional exception, in one of two ways: either as typical of the aporia that characterises the founding of all new juridico-political orders, an aporia according to which 'every new order announces itself through the violation of what it stands for' (Praeg 2008b: 218) or we can argue that, given the condition of hypermodernity, the political order founded on this aporia is never going to be *executed* through the collective amnesia that necessarily must follow it, in order to enable this execution; that this is not simply a founding aporia, but an *aporia-archē*, the aporia as an origin, a beginning or principle that carries itself forth as the rule of its future applications.

As I argued above, hypermodernity suggests a modernity that will remain inexecuted, by virtue of the fact that the origin cannot be left behind because there is no teleology of history possible and because postcoloniality is that condition in which, because of that impossibility, the premodern will continue alongside the project of modernity, in the form of an original injustice that can be neither forgotten nor rectified. I also argued that every act of adjudication is an iteration of the *archē*, the application of the rule that was given in the beginning. We can state all of this more precisely now: every act of adjudication is *both* the reconstitutionalisation of the original injustice and a recognition *of* and an address *to* that original injustice. The fact that constitutional provisions very carefully sealed *AZAPO v. President* off from future iterations of the suspension of the contractual axiomatic does not protect the constitutional order from the very logic to which it opened itself *in that founding moment*. The 'agonising, balancing act between the need for justice to victims of past abuse and the need for reconciliation and rapid transition to a new future' (*AZAPO*, par. 21), *that* toss-up, was the articulation of the *aporia-archē*, the founding of a constitutional order that, because of its hypermodernity and its constitutive and future openness to the original injustice, will always remain unfounded, haunted by an origin it cannot forget or leave behind, a haunting that will always present itself as the question: Is the justice being dispensed here just? That former justices Sachs and Mokgoro, among others, were and have been willing to address this question head-on, that they adjudicate(d) from the perspective of this meta-question, not by pushing the limits as much as by thinking of the limits as a Möbius strip, an ever-revolving interface between the un/founded, accounts for their ambivalent status as well-loved and controversial, but always *empathetic*, Revolutionaries.[19] The responses of their critics have pivoted around two main issues – the question of values and the problem of definition. Both are premised on

---

19. For a very useful introduction, summary and discussion of their and other Ubuntu-engaged judgments, see Cornell and Muvangua (2011). For an example of empathy in relation to these figures, see Peté (2010).

an *image of thought* and a *mode of being* that we now recognise as the Conformist and Archivist respectively.

The Conformist conceptual persona

As argued in Chapter 2, this is an *antipathetic* persona because, while it recognises in ubuntu the reality of an endogenous practice, it sees no future for a reappropriated Ubuntu as an emancipatory praxis. The reason for this is an acute, but exaggerated emphasis on either the phallo-primocentric values, of which ubuntu historically was a function, or on the dangers of conformism represented by Ubuntu *qua* communitarianism. Exemplary of this approach is the work of Ilze Keevy who, in a series of articles (2009a, 2009b and 2009c), has essentially argued for the incompatability of Ubuntu with constitutional values. Of course, these are very real concerns and issues that need to be addressed. However, such a critique needs to be balanced, recognising Ubuntu as a living, evolving tradition, a profound example of the manner in which past traditions reinvent themselves in the present, *as* the present. We need to acknowledge that this reinvention is a messy business and Ubuntu cannot be held hostage to a past political economy of obligation and its associated values. Reinvention is a paradoxical affair, in which the best of Western modernity can be invoked to critique those values and the best of Ubuntu can be invoked to critique the limitations of Western modernity – a reciprocity evident in, for example, the fact that while dignity informs our reinvention of Ubuntu, the memory of ubuntu also informs our reinvention of dignity. In the absence of a recognition of this complexity, a critique that merely exaggerates the twin dangers of outdated values and conformism may leave one feeling held hostage by tradition, in a way that some may be forgiven for interpreting as a passive-aggressive form of racism.[20]

The Archivist conceptual persona

The Archivist, another antipathetic persona, conjoins *curating* as image of thought with a mode of being that is ghostly or *spectral*. As a political stance, it becomes evident in relation to three kinds of claims made about Ubuntu: one, an exaggerated

---

20. A psycho-sexual drama of Fanonian proportions is evidenced by Keevy's conclusion in 'The Constitutional Court and Ubuntu's Inseparable Trinity' that to privilege Ubuntu *qua* religious world view over other value systems in Constitutional Court judgments amounts, not only to a violation of the freedom of religion guaranteed in section 15(1), but indeed 'constitutes the rape of constitutionalism and the rule of law' (2009a: 85).

reductionism, according to which we will never really understand Ubuntu because it is so fundamentally inscribed in the Western epistemolgical archive as to be reducible to it; two, that to the extent that we can access the past, there is nothing there because Ubuntu amounts to little more than a 'superstitious communitarianism little concerned with the value of individual life, but significantly so with the wealth represented by cattle and the hierarchical superiority of a feudal nobility' (Van der Walt 2005: 112); third, to the extent that there may be something in Ubuntu, there is nothing 'specific and singular' about it that would do more than 'add a local, indigenous and communitarian touch to the Christian, Kantian or Millsian respect for the individual that informs Western jurisprudence' (111).[21]

The issues raised here represent some of the very real difficulties involved in thinking through the question of Ubuntu: as a way of thinking within *and* against tradition; a communitarianism that underestimates its own constitutive violence; a glocal phenomenon inextricably dependent on global discourses for its articulation and so on. But as with the Conformist, what disappoints about the way this persona conjoins the meaning of thinking (as curating) with a certain mode of being (as spectral) is not the nature of the questions raised – for they must be raised – but the simplistic reduction of Ubuntu to ubuntu, a reluctance to grapple with the question of Ubuntu, a refusal to think about thinking as becoming, to be interrogated by the question of Ubuntu, to be summoned by 'a certain type of eschatology' (Derrida in Kearney 1984: 119).

Conclusion

The critical movement of the conceptual personae in this report should have made it clear by now that it does not generate a simplistic question of right or wrong.[22] All personae take as a point of departure, as their most fundamental conceptual

---

21. In fairness, Van der Walt offers this reading as the subtext of Justice Sachs's interpretation of ubuntu in his concurring judgment in *S. v. Makwanyane*. However, it is clear that this is (also) the subtext of his own evaluation of the future potential of Ubuntu in adjudication (see 2005: 109–15).
22. What would complicate the reconstitution of an analysis of conceptual personae in terms of a discourse on ethics is the fact that one does not choose a persona, but is chosen by it. As Gilles Deleuze and Félix Guattari put it: 'The conceptual persona is not the philosopher's representative but, rather, the reverse: the philosopher is only the envelope of his principle conceptual persona ... the philosopher's name is the simple pseudonym of his persona' (1994: 64).

category, 'the human' – the *thinking*, *being* human. What the personae represent is nothing more than how the category of the human must necessarily and perpetually fail into politics, in order to actualise various forms of the political. In this sense, to critique a persona is not to judge it, but rather to make explicit how it conjoins assumptions about thinking and being, to demonstrate how these assumptions make any persona possible and how, in so doing, they always already articulate the limitations of a persona and what it can tell us about thinking and being. In terms of Ubuntu discourse, the tension between an original injustice and legal justice – this double structure of justice – gives credence to, in the sense of making possible, every conceptual persona that articulates what it means to address that tension; at the same time and for the same reason, the tension also makes it impossible to simply adjudicate, in the sense of judging as right or wrong, between such personae. Rather than adjudicating between them (thus no doubt replicating one of the personae in the judgement itself), we will come to realise that the Prophet – in his/her political capacity as Revolutionary and/or beyond, in his/her quasi-religious commitment to being a Saviour – speaks *from* the eternal imperative to redress the original justice, while the Conformist, the Archivist and the Cosmopolitan personae speak *to* the historical impossibility of doing so.

Very little has been said in this report about the work of those authors who represent the conceptual persona of the Text Worker or Construction Worker.[23] In these texts, thinking is *becoming* and the mode of being is *migratory*. Here, there is no tension between acknowledging the archival dimension of the discourse on Africa and arguing for its reinvention as counter-philosophical anthropology, aimed at emancipatory praxis. They present a view of reinvention marked by neither historical resignation nor Revolutionary fervour. Authenticity is conceived, not in terms of a 'lost and found', but in terms of a perpetual commitment to becoming, a perpetual reconstruction. In terms of the geo-political tensions between North and South or global and local, Ubuntu is embraced as an autopoetic phenomenon that emerges interstitially in the spaces where the global and local intersect. This invokes an emotional response that is neither sympathetic nor antipathetic, but perhaps *dyspathetic* – leaving us with an Ubuntu as dyspathetic, glocal phenomenon reproduced by and for subjects who participate in its reproduction and have loyalties that exceed the local, although they have a vested interest in promoting the local,

---

23. An example of a text in this mode is Gade (2011).

while fully appreciating it as both a function *of* and a solution *to* the forces of the global. Here, writing is committed to the hard work of labouring towards authenticity, not in the Revolutionary belief that the self can coincide with itself or that its authenticity is the absolution of the rest of the world (Saviour) or that the self is not possible because it is only an invention (Archivist). To write towards authenticity as an anticipatory attitude – 'self-writing', as we understand it from Mbembe (2002) – is not to be understood as a practice of writing of or about a preconstituted self, but about reconstituting the self through the practice of writing. Neither at its beginning nor at its end can/will the self be immanent in the process of writing. The act of writing is endless manual labour, not in a Sisyphean sense, but endless because authenticity is a function of perpetual writing, of becoming as the eternally deferred promise of being. The major concern of the Text or Construction Worker, then, is not with recovering ubuntu, but with claiming and tracing it, paying attention to where it does not fit into discourse and deploying it manually *to do things*. In this emphasis on *doing*, there is at work a certain type of eschatology that holds out the promise of a future reunification of ubuntu with Ubuntu. Perhaps the mode of thinking implicit in this persona is also reflected, at a meta-level, in the way this report has attempted to represent the sympathetic dimensions of the other personae in all their balanced superficiality: in the introduction, the Cosmopolitan; in Chapter 2, the Archivist; in Chapter 3, the Conformist; and in this final chapter, the Revolutionary.

CODA

In Itself

> But when a belief vanishes, there survives it – more and more vigorously so as to cloak the absence of the power, now lost to us, of imparting reality to new things – a fetishistic attachment to the old things which it did once animate, as if it was in them and not in ourselves that the divine spark resided, and as if our present incredulity had a contingent cause – the death of the gods.
> — Marcel Proust, *Remembrance of Things Past*

Sidestepping the idea that we can somehow arrive at normative consensus on why Ubuntu should be invoked in adjudication, I attempted in the last two chapters of this report to argue that there is nonetheless, to coin an awkward phrase, an 'immanent meta-legitimation' at work in juridical discourse that motivates in favour of altruistic adjudication. I also suggested that adjudication interpreted as the iteration of the *archē* may be conceived as the locus of a reunification of ubuntu with Ubuntu: the place where, following Giorgio Agamben (1999), belonging is recognised as having no grounding or foundation beyond the praxis of communication and its capacity to create a sense of belonging.

Agamben's essay '*Se: Hegel's Absolute and Heidegger's Ereignis*' is a reading of the history of Western metaphysics as essentially the history of our desire to name that which exists in and of itself – that which, because of its self-enclosed definition, can function as ground or *archē* of everything else. There are still traces of this desire in our languages: in English *in itself*, in Afrikaans *insigself* and in German *an sich*. This metaphysics persists in the demand for a definition of Ubuntu *in itself* as a condition for the possibility of articulating and building community upon that self-enclosed recognition. The result can at best be an antipathetic Revolutionary persona – antipathetic because, unlike the Archivist and Conformist, it recognises in Ubuntu a profound emancipatory force but, like the Conformist and Archivist, cannot accept its invocation until it is adequately defined. If the problem is that '*ubuntu* was linked *not on its own terms* but on the terms of the

Western-influenced legal system which had for many years relegated it to the margins' (Mnyongani 2010: 144, emphasis added), an antipathetic response to that dilemma is, as Freddy Mnyongani argues, that we should somehow 'de-link' Ubuntu from philosophical and jurisprudential discourse, in order for Ubuntu to be 'assessed, analysed and understood in its proper African worldview context' because 'only then would its importance be realised and valued for *what it is*' (emphasis added). This is nothing but undercover metaphysics or metaphysics masquerading as identity politics. Definitions do not ground us; the act or praxis of language, of shared communication does – that is, to the extent that we can still meaningfully talk about groundless grounding as a grounding at all. But this is how I read Agamben's conclusion in '*Se':

> That man – the animal who has language – is as such the ungrounded, that his only foundation is in his own action, his own giving himself grounds, is a truth so ancient that it lies at the basis of humanity's most ancient religious practice: sacrifice. However one interprets the sacrificial function, in every case what is essential is that the activity of human community is grounded in another one of its activities – that, as we learn from etymology, all *facere* is *sacrum facere*. At the centre of sacrifice simply lies a determinate *activity* that is as such separated and excluded, becoming *sacer* and hence invested with a series of ritual prohibitions and prescriptions. Once it is marked with sacredness, an activity is not, however, simply excluded; rather, it is henceforth accessible only through certain persons and determinate rules. It thus furnishes society and its unfounded legislation with the fiction of a beginning; *what is excluded from a community is in truth what founds the whole life of community, being taken up by a community as an immemorial past* [emphasis added]. Every beginning [*inizio*] is, in truth, initiation; every *conditum* is an *ab-sconditum* (1999: 135).

In actualising this groundless belonging through Ubuntu-engaged adjudication, in this unification of Ubuntu as, yet again, or perhaps the continuation of a now-expanded ubuntu praxis, we have some principles to draw on: the undefinability of Ubuntu is not a problem to be overcome but, considered as a glocal phenomenon, the sine qua non of its invocation in emancipatory praxis; following the logic of the second *epoché* the locus of its invocation, specifically in relation to the law, is in communicating altruistic adjudication in a modern juridical, where the tension between individual rights and social commitment is entirely *superficial*; in a context where this superficiality is radically asymmetrical, the legitimation for invoking Ubuntu does not derive from any point, logic or argument beyond the law, but from the *aporia-archē* of its founding; this Ubuntu – a function of modernity as much as a critique of it – is a sign, of both an original in/justice that cannot be recovered and an excessive justice that must be possible; Ubuntu-engaged adjudications amount to both a universal articulation of the altruistic and a particular, contextual engagement with this immemorial past that haunts us as the question about the justice of justice – a sign of hypermodernity that will perpetually shadow our liberal democratic project with necessary incompleteness.

SELECT BIBLIOGRAPHY

Adorno, T.W. 1977. 'The Actuality of Philosophy'. *Telos* 31: 120–33.
Agamben, G. 1998. *Homo Sacer: Sovereign Power and Bare Life*. Trans. D. Heller-Roazen. Stanford: Stanford University Press.
———. 1999. *Potentialities: Collected Essays in Philosophy*. Stanford: Stanford University Press.
Appiah, K.A. 1997. 'Cosmopolitan Patriots'. *Chicago Journals* 23(3): 617–39.
Arendt, H. 1963. *On Revolution*. London: Faber and Faber.
———. 1994. *Essays in Understanding, 1930–1954: Formation, Exile and Totalitarianism*. New York: Schocken Books.
Babu, A.R.M. 1981. *African Socialism or Socialist Africa?* London: Zed Books.
Bailie. G. 1995. *Violence Unveiled: Humanity at the Crossroads*. New York: Crossroad.
Baker, P.L. 1993. 'Chaos, Order and Sociological Theory'. *Sociological Inquiry* 63(2): 123–49.
Barnett, R. 2000. *Realizing the University in an Age of Supercomplexity*. Buckingham and Philadelphia: SRHE and Open University Press.
Barrett, P. 2008. 'The Quest for *Ubuntu* in a Coming-of-Age South Africa: Questions Arising from Dietrich Bonhoeffer's Latter Ideas'. *Religion & Theology* 15: 8–27.
Bateson, G. 1972. *Steps to an Ecology of Mind*. New York: Ballantine Books.
Baudrillard, J. 1983. *Simulations*. New York: Semiotext(e), Columbia University.
Bayart, J-F. 1993. *The State in Africa: The Politics of the Belly*. London: Longman.
Beets, P. and L. le Grange. 2005. ' "Africanising" Assessment Practices: Does the Notion of Ubuntu Hold Any Promise?' *South African Journal of Higher Education* 19: 1197–207.
Benégas, R. 2006. 'Côte d'Ivoire: Patriotism, Ethnonationalism and Other African Modes of Self-Writing'. *African Affairs* 105(421): 535–52.
Benjamin, W. 1977. *The Origin of German Tragic Drama*. London: Verso.
Bennett, T.W. 2011. 'Ubuntu: An African Equity'. *Potchefstroom Electronic Law Journal* 14(4): 29–61.
Berlin, I. 1969. 'Historical Inevitability'. In *Four Essays on Liberty*, 41–118. Oxford: Oxford University Press.
Bernstein, R.J. 1991. *The New Constellation: The Ethical-Political Horizons of Modernity/Postmodernity*. Cambridge: Polity Press.
Bewaji, J.A.I. 2003. 'Beyond Ethno-Philosophical Myopia: Critical Comments on Mogobe B. Ramose's *African Philosophy through Ubuntu*'. *South African Journal of Philosophy* 22(4): 378–415.
Bewaji, J.A.I. and M.B. Ramose. 2003. 'The Bewaji, Van Binsbergen and Ramose Debate on *Ubuntu*'. *South African Journal of Philosophy* 22(4): 378–414.
Birmingham, P. 2006. *Hannah Arendt and Human Rights: The Predicament of Common Responsibility*. Bloomington: Indiana University Press.

Bloom, H. 2003. 'Introduction: Don Quixote, Sancho Panza, and Miguel de Cervantes Saavedra'. In *Don Quixote*, Miguel de Cervantes; trans. Edíth Grossman, xxi–xxxv. New York: HarperCollins.

Bohler-Muller, N. 2005. 'The Story of an African Value'. *SA Publiekreg/SA Public Law* 20(2): 266–80.

Bongmba, E.K. 2004. 'Reflections on Thabo Mbeki's African Renaissance'. *Journal of Southern African Studies* 30(2): 291–316.

Bonn, M. 2007. 'Children's Understanding of "Ubuntu"'. *Early Child Development and Care* 177(8): 863–73.

Brand, D. 2003. 'The Preceduralisation of South African Socio-Economic Rights Jurisprudence, or "What are Socio-Economic Rights for?"' In *Rights and Democracy in a Transformative Constitution*, ed. H. Botha, A. van der Walt and J. van der Walt, 33–57. Stellenbosch: SUN Press.

Carroll, Lewis. 1998. *Through the Looking-Glass and What Alice Found There*. New York: The New American Library.

Cavarero, A. 2000. *Relating Narrative: Storytelling and Selfhood*. New York: Routledge.

Chabal, P. 2009. *Africa: The Politics of Suffering and Smiling*. London: Zed Books.

Chabal, P. and J-P. Daloz. 1999. *Africa Works: Disorder as Political Instrument*. Oxford and Bloomington: International African Institute with James Currey and Indiana University Press.

Chitando, E. 2008. 'Religious Ethics, HIV and AIDS and Masculinities in Southern Africa'. In *Persons in Community: African Ethics in a Global Culture*, ed. R. Nicolson, 45–65. Pietermaritzburg: University of KwaZulu-Natal Press.

Christians, C.G. 2004. 'Ubuntu and Communitarianism in Media Ethics'. *Ecquid Novi* 25(2): 235–56.

Coertze, R.D. 2001. 'Ubuntu and Nation Building in South Africa'. *South African Journal of Ethnology* 24(4): 113–18.

Cornell, D. 2004. 'A Call for a Nuanced Constitutional Jurisprudence: Ubuntu, Dignity, and Reconciliation'. *SA Publiekreg/SA Public Law* (special edition, *Public Law in Transformation*) 3(19): 666–75.

———. 2014. 'Ubuntu and Subaltern Legality'. In *Ubuntu: Curating the Archive*, ed. L. Praeg and S. Magadla. Pietermaritzburg: University of KwaZulu-Natal Press.

Cornell, D. and N. Muvangua. 2011. *Ubuntu and the Law: African Ideals and Postapartheid Jurisprudence*. New York: Fordham University Press.

Cornell, D. and K.M. Panfilio. 2010. 'Conclusion'. In *Symbolic Forms for a New Humanity: Cultural and Racial Reconfigurations of Critical Theory*, 151–77. New York: Fordham University Press.

Coughlan, S. 2006. 'All You Need is Ubuntu'. *BBC News Magazine*, 28 September. Available at http://news.bbc.co.uk/2/hi/uk_news/magazine/5388182.stm.

Dandala, M.H. 2009. 'Cows Never Die: Embracing African Cosmology in the Process of Economic Growth'. In *African Ethics: An Anthology of Comparative and Applied Ethics*, ed. M.F. Murove, 259–79. Pietermaritzburg: University of KwaZulu-Natal Press.

Deleuze, G. and F. Guattari. 1994. *What is Philosophy?* London: Verso.

———. 2004. *Anti-Oedipus: Capitalism and Schizophrenia*. London: Continuum.

De Maria, W. 2009. 'Does African Corruption Exist?' In *African Ethics: An Anthology of Comparative and Applied Ethics*, ed. M.F. Murove, 357–75. Pietermaritzburg: University of KwaZulu-Natal Press.

Derrida, J. 1981. *Writing and Difference*. London: Routledge & Kegan Paul.

———. 1992a. 'Force of Law: The "Mystical Foundation of Authority"'. In *Deconstruction and the Possibility of Justice*, ed. D. Cornell, M. Rosenfeld and D. Carlson, 3–68. New York: Routledge.

———. 1992b. 'Mochlos; or: The Conflict of the Faculties'. In *Logomachia: The Conflict of the Faculties*, ed. Richard Rand, 1–35. Lincoln: University of Nebraska Press.

———. 2001. *On Cosmopolitanism and Forgiveness*. London: Routledge.

Diagne, S.B. 2002. 'Keeping Africanity Open'. *Public Culture* 14(3): 621–3.

Dirlik, A. 2002. 'Historical Colonialism in Contemporary Perspective'. *Public Culture* 14(3): 611–15.

Dostoyevsky, F. 1988. *The Idiot*. London: Penguin.

Douglas, H. 2010. 'Difficult Liberation: Reading Levinas in Africa'. *The Johannesburg Salon* 3. Available at http://jwtc.org.za/the_salon/volume_3.htm.

Du Toit, L. 2008. 'Old Wives' Tales and Philosophical Delusions: On "the Problem of Women and African Philosophy"'. *South African Journal of Philosophy* 27(4): 413–28.

Ebrahim, H. 2011. 'The South African Constitution: Birth Certificate of a Nation'. Paper presented at the Constitution-Making Forum: A Government of Sudan Consultation, 24–25 May, Khartoum, Sudan. Available at http://unmis.unmissions.org/Portals/UNMIS/Constitution-making%20Symposium/2011-05_Ebrahim_South%20Africa.pdf.

Ekeh, P. 1975. 'Colonialism and the Two Publics in Africa: A Theoretical Statement'. *Comparative Studies in Society and History* 17(1): 92–112.

Enslin, P. and K. Horsthemke. 2004. 'Can Ubuntu Provide a Model for Citizenship Education in African Democracies?' *Comparative Education* 40(4): 545–58.

Eze, M.O. 2008. 'What is African Communitarianism? Against Consensus as a Regulative Ideal'. *South African Journal of Philosophy* 27(4): 386–99.

Fanon, F. 1969. *Toward the African Revolution: Political Essays*. New York: Grove Press.

———. 1980. 'Algeria Unveiled'. In *A Dying Colonialism*, 13–42. London: Writers and Readers Cooperation.

Farber, M. 1963. 'First Philosophy and the Problem of the World'. *Philosophy and Phenomenological Research* 23(3): 315–34.

Farred, G. 2003. 'Repressions of the Modernist Unconscious: A Critique of the "African Renaissance"'. In *Postmodernism, Postcoloniality, and African Studies*, ed. A. Magubane, 61–81. Trenton: Africa World Press.

Foucault, M. 1982. *The Archaeology of Knowledge*. New York: Pantheon.

Freud, S. 1973 [1919]. 'The Uncanny'. In *The Standard Edition of the Complete Psychological Works of Sigmund Freud*, Vol. 17, 217–53. London: The Hogarth Press.

Friedland, W.H. and and C.G. Rosberg. 1964. *African Socialism*. London: Oxford University Press.

Friedman, M. 1989. 'Feminism and Modern Friendship: Dislocating the Community'. *Ethics* 99(2): 275–90.

Furman, K. 2012. 'Exploring the Possibility of an Ubuntu-Based Political Philosophy'. MA thesis, Rhodes University, Grahamstown.
Gade, C.B.N. 2011. 'The Historical Development of the Written Discourses on Ubuntu'. *South African Journal of Philosophy* 30(3): 303–29.
Galgut, D. 2003. *The Good Doctor*. New York: Grove Press.
Gasa, N. 2012. '"Designed to Suit the Psychology of the Natives"?' *Mail & Guardian*, 24 May. Available at http://mg.co.za/article/2012-05-24-designed-to-suit-the-psychology-of-the-natives.
Gibson, N.C. 2011. *Fanonian Practices in South Africa: From Steve Biko to Abahlali baseMjondolo*. Pietermaritzburg: University of KwaZulu-Natal Press.
Girard, René. 1988. *Violence and the Sacred*. London: The Athlone Press.
Gordon J.A and L.R Gordon. 2009. *Of Divine Warning: Reading Disaster in the Modern Age*. Boulder: Paradigm Publishers.
Gordon, L.R. 2007. 'Problematic People and Epistemic Decolonization: Toward the Postcolonial in Africana Political Thought'. In *Postcolonialism and Political Theory*, ed. N. Persram, 121–41. Lanham: Lexington Books.
———. 2008. *An Introduction to Africana Philosophy*. Cambridge: Cambridge University Press.
———. 2014. 'Justice Otherwise: Thoughts on Ubuntu'. In *Ubuntu: Curating the Archive*, ed. L. Praeg and S. Magadla. Pietermaritzburg: University of KwaZulu-Natal Press.
Gould, S.J. 1977. *Ontogeny and Phylogeny*. Cambridge: Harvard University Press.
Greene, Graham. 1961. *A Burnt-Out Case*. London: William Heinemann and Bodley Head.
Guardian Reporter. 2012. 'The Clintons: The Real Winners of the 2012 Election'. *Mail & Guardian*, 30 September. Available at http://mg.co.za/article/2012-09-30-the-clintons-the-real-winners-of-the-2012-election.
Gyekye, K. 2002. 'Person and Community in African Thought'. In *Philosophy from Africa: A Text with Readings*, ed. P.H. Coetzee and A.P.J. Roux, 297–313. Oxford: Oxford University Press.
Hegel, G.W.F. 1988. *The Difference between Fichte's and Schelling's System of Philosophy*. New York: State University of New York Press.
Heidegger, Martin. 2008. *Being and Time*. Trans. John Macquarrie and Edward Robinson. New York: HarperPerennial.
Horkheimer, M. and T. Adorno. 2002. *Dialectic of Enlightenment: Philosophical Fragments*. Stanford: Stanford University Press.
Hountondji, P.J. 1983. *African Philosophy: Myth and Reality*. Trans. H. Evans, with collaboration of J. Ree. London: Hutchinson University Library for Africa.
———. 1996. *African Philosophy: Myth & Reality*. Bloomington: Indiana University Press.
Hurst, A. 2004. 'Derrida's Quasi-Transcendental Thinking'. *South African Journal of Philosophy* 23(3): 244–66.
Jucevièienë, P. and R. Vaitkus. 2007. 'The Development of Higher Education for the Knowledge Society and the Knowledge Economy'. In *Higher Education and National Development: Universities and Societies in Transition*, ed. D. Bridges, P. Jucevièienë, R. Jucevièius, T. McLaughlin and J. Stankevièiûtë, 43–55. London: Routledge.
Jules-Rosette, B. 2002. 'Afro-Pessimism's Many Guises'. *Public Culture* 14(3): 603–5.
Kant, I. 1970. 'Perpetual Peace: A Philosophical Sketch'. In *Kant's Political Writings*, ed. H. Reiss, 93–131. Cambridge: Cambridge University Press.

———.1998. *Critique of Pure Reason*. Ed. P. Guyer and A. Wood. Cambridge: Cambridge University Press.
Kearney, R. 1984. *Dialogues with Contemporary Continental Thinkers: The Phenomenological Heritage*. Manchester: Manchester University Press.
———. 1998. *The Wake of Imagination: Toward a Postmodern Culture*. Minneapolis: University of Minnesota Press.
Keep, H. and R. Midgley. 2007. 'The Emerging Role of *Ubuntu-Botho* in Developing a Consensual South African Legal Culture'. In *Explorations in Legal Cultures*, ed. F. Bruinsma and D. Nelken, 29–57. Den Haag: Reed Business.
Keevy, I. 2009a. 'The Constitutional Court and Ubuntu's Inseparable Trinity'. *Journal for Juridical Science* 1: 61–88.
———. 2009b. 'Ubuntu: Ethnophilosophy and Core Consitutional Values'. In *Ubuntu, Good Faith and Equity: Flexible Legal Principles in Developing a Contemporary Jurisprudence*, ed. F. Diedrich, 24–49. Cape Town: Juta.
———. 2009c. 'Ubuntu Versus the Core Values of the South African Constitution'. *Journal for Juridical Science* 2: 19–58.
Kemahlioglu, O. 2011. 'Jobs in Politicians' Backyards: Party Leadership Competition and Patronage'. *Journal of Theoretical Politics* 23(4): 480–509.
Kennedy, D. 1976. 'Form and Substance in Private Law Adjudication'. *Harvard Law Review* 89(8): 1685–788.
———. 1979. 'The Structure of Blackstone's Commentaries'. *Buffalo Law Review* 28(2): 205–383.
———. 1986. 'Freedom and Constraint in Adjudication: A Critical Phenomenology'. *Journal of Legal Education* 36(4): 518–62.
Kochalumchuvattil, T. 2010. 'The Crisis of Identity in Africa: A Call for Subjectivity'. *Kritike* 4(1): 108–22.
Kompridis, N. 2006. *Critique and Disclosure: Critical Theory between Past and Future*. Cambridge: MIT Press.
Kopytoff, I. 1964. 'Socialism and Traditional African Societies'. In *African Socialism*, ed. W.H. Friedland and C.G. Rosberg Jr, 53–63. Oxford: Oxford University Press.
Kroeze, I.J. 2002. 'Doing Things with Values II: The Case of *Ubuntu*'. *Stellenbosch Law Review* 2: 252–64.
Kuhn, L. 2007. 'Why Utilize Complexity Principles in Special Enquiry?' *World Futures* 63: 156–75.
Kundera, M. 1988. *The Art of the Novel*. London: Faber and Faber.
Kymlicka, W. 2002. *Contemporary Political Philosophy: An Introduction*. Oxford: Oxford University Press.
Letseka, M. 2012. 'In Defence of Ubuntu'. *Studies in Philosophy and Education* 31(1): 47–60.
Lyotard, J-F. 1988. *The Differend: Phrases in Dispute*. Minneapolis: University of Minnesota Press.
MacIntyre, A. 1982. *After Virtue: A Study in Moral Theory*. London: Duckworth.
Mamdani, M. 2002. *When Victims Become Killers: Colonialism, Nativism and the Genocide of Rwanda*. Princeton: Princeton University Press.
Mann C. 2013. 'Village Thinking at a National Level'. *Mail & Guardian*, 8–14 February. Available at http://mg.co.za/article/2013-02-08-00-south-africa-village-thinking-at-a-national-level.

Marais, H. 2011. *South Africa Pushed to the Limit: The Political Economy of Change*. Cape Town: University of Cape Town Press.

Marx, C. 2002. 'Ubu and Ubuntu: On the Dialectics of Apartheid and Nation Building'. *Politikon* 29(1): 49–69.

Masoga, M.A. 1999. 'Towards Sacrificial-Cleansing Ritual in South Africa: An Indigenous African View of Truth and Reconciliation'. *Alternation* 6(1): 213–24.

Mazrui, A.A. 2009. 'Africa's Wisdom Has Two Parents and One Guardian'. In *African Ethics: An Anthology of Comparative and Applied Ethics*, ed. M.F. Murove, 33–61. Pietermaritzburg: University of KwaZulu-Natal Press.

Mbembe, A. 2002. 'African Modes of Self-Writing'. Trans. S. Rendall. *Public Culture* 14(1): 239–73.

———. 2009. 'Postcolonial Thought Explained to the French: An Interview with Achille Mbembe'. *The Johannesburg Salon* 1. Available at http://www.jwtc.org.za/the_salon/volume_1/achille_mbembe.htm.

———. 2011. 'Democracy as a Community of Life'. *The Johannesburg Salon* 4. Available at http://www.jwtc.org.za/volume_4/achille_mbembe.htm.

McDonald, D.A. 2010. '*Ubuntu* Bashing: The Marketisation of "African Values" in South Africa'. *Review of African Political Economy* 37(124): 139–52.

Mdluli, P. 1987. 'Ubuntu-Botho: Inkatha's "People's Education"'. *Transformation* 5: 60–77.

Menkiti, I.F. 1984. 'Person and Community in African Traditional Thought'. In *African Philosophy: An Introduction*, ed. R.A Wright, 171–80. Lanham: University Press of America.

Metz, T. 2007. 'Toward an African Moral Theory'. *The Journal of Political Philosophy* 15(3): 321–41.

———. 2009. 'African Moral Theory and Public Governance: Nepotism, Preferential Hiring and Other Partiality'. In *African Ethics: An Anthology of Comparative and Applied Ethics*, ed. M.F. Murove, 335–57. Pietermaritzburg: University of KwaZulu-Natal Press.

Mgqolozana, T. 2009. *A Man Who is Not a Man*. Pietermaritzburg: University of KwaZulu-Natal Press.

Mnyaka, M. 2003. 'Xenophobia as a Response to Foreigners in Post-Apartheid South Africa and Post-Exilic Israel: A Comparative Critique in the Light of the Gospel and Ubuntu Ethical Principles'. Ph.D. dissertation, University of South Africa. Available at http://uir.unisa.ac.za/handle/10500/1176.

Mnyongani, F. 2010. 'De-linking Ubuntu: Towards a Unique South African Jurisprudence'. *Obiter* 31(1): 134–45.

Mohiddin, A. 1981. *African Socialism in Two Countries*. Kent: Croom Helm.

Mokgoro, Y. 1998. 'Ubuntu and the Law in South Africa'. *Buffalo Human Rights Law Review* 4: 15–25.

Molele, C. 2011. 'Ben Turok: "Criticism Not the Issue, But the Way it's Done"'. *Mail & Guardian Online*. Available at http://mg.co.za/article/2011-09-09-ben-turok-criticism-not-the-issue-but-way-its-done.

Mudimbe, V-Y. 1988. *The Invention of Africa: Gnosis, Philosophy, and the Order of Knowledge*. Indiana: Indiana University Press.

———. 1991a. 'Revelation as a Political Performance'. In *Parables and Fables: Exegesis, Textuality, and Politics in Central Africa*, 3–32. Madison: University of Wisconsin Press.

———. 1991b. 'Philosophy and Theology as Political Practices'. In *Parables and Fables: Exegesis, Textuality, and Politics in Central Africa*, 32–68. Madison: University of Wisconsim Press.

Mudimbe, V-Y and B. Jewsiewicki (eds). 1996. *Open the Social Sciences: Report of the Gulbenkian Commission on the Restructuring of the Social Sciences*. Stanford: Stanford University Press.

Munyaka, M. and M. Motlhabi. 2009. 'Ubuntu and its Socio-Moral Significance'. In *African Ethics: An Anthology of Comparative and Applied Ethics*, ed. M.F. Murove, 63–85. Pietermaritzburg: University of KwaZulu-Natal Press.

Murithi, T. 2009. 'An African Perspective on Peace Education: Ubuntu Lessons in Reconciliation'. *International Review of Education* 55: 221–33.

Murove, M.F. 2009a. 'An African Environmental Ethic Based on the Concepts of *Ukama* and *Ubuntu*'. In *African Ethics: An Anthology of Comparative and Applied Ethics*, edited by M.F Murove, 315–33. Pietermaritzburg: University of KwaZulu-Natal Press.

———. 2009b. 'Beyond the Savage Evidence Ethic'. In *African Ethics: An Anthology of Comparative and Applied Ethics*, ed. M.F Murove, 14–33. Pietermaritzburg: University of KwaZulu-Natal Press.

———. 2009c. 'Introduction'. In *African Ethics: An Anthology of Comparative and Applied Ethics*, ed. M.F Murove, xiv–xvi. Pietermaritzburg: University of KwaZulu-Natal Press.

Murove, M.F. (ed.) 2009. *African Ethics: An Anthology of Comparative and Applied Ethics*. Pietermaritzburg: University of KwaZulu-Natal Press.

Ngoenha, S.E. 2006. 'Ubuntu: A New Model of Global Justice?' *Indilinga: African Journal of Indigenous Knowledge Systems* 5(2): 125–34.

Nkasawe, M. 2012. 'Traditional Leadership is Part of Us'. *Mail & Guardian*, 25–31 May. Available at http://mg.co.za/article/2012-05-24-traditional-leadership-is-part-of-us.

Noddings, N. 1986. *Caring: A Feminine Approach to Ethics and Moral Education*. Berkeley: University of California Press.

Nussbaum, B. 2003. 'African Culture and Ubuntu: Reflections of a South African in America'. *Perspectives* 17(1): 1–12.

———. 2009a. 'Ubuntu and Business: Reflections and Questions'. In *African Ethics: An Anthology of Comparative and Applied Ethics*, ed. M.F Murove, 238–59. Pietermaritzburg: University of KwaZulu-Natal Press.

———. 2009b. 'Ubuntu: Reflections of a South African on Our Common Humanity'. In *African Ethics: An Anthology of Comparative and Applied Ethics*, ed. M.F Murove, 100–11. Pietermaritzburg: University of KwaZulu-Natal Press.

Nyerere, J.K. 1967a. *The Arusha Declaration*. Available at http://www.marxists.org/subject/africa/nyerere/1967/arusha-declaration.htm.

———. 1967b. *Freedom and Unity*. Oxford: Oxford University Press.

Onuoha, B. 1965. *The Elements of African Socialism*. London: Deutsch.

Peté S. 2010. 'South Africa's Quixotic Hero and His Noble Quest: Constitutional Court Justice Albie Sachs and the Dream of a Rainbow Nation'. *Obiter*: 1–15.

Pinkard, T.P. 2000. *Hegel: A Biography*. Cambridge: Cambridge University Press.

Plant, R. 1983. *Hegel: An Introduction*. Oxford: Basil Blackwell.

Praeg, L. 2000. *African Philosophy and the Quest for Autonomy: A Philosophical Investigation*. Amsterdam: Rodopi.

———. 2007. *The Geometry of Violence: Girard, Africa, Modernity*. Stellenbosch: SUN Press.

———. 2008a. 'An Answer to the Question: "What is [Ubuntu]?".' *South African Journal of Philosophy* 27(4): 367–85. Reprinted in *Au-delà des lignes: Fabien Eboussi Boulaga, une pratique philosophique*, ed. L. Procesi and K. Kavwahirehi, 347–74. Munich: LINCOM Europa, 2012.

———. 2008b. 'The Aporia of Collective Violence'. *Law Critique* 19: 192–223.

———. 2010a. 'Africa: Globalisation and the Ethical'. In *Complexity, Difference and Identity*, ed. P. Cilliers and R. Preiser, 287–316. Dordrecht: Springer.

———. 2010b. 'Teaching, and Teaching (as) Transformation'. *South African Journal of Philosophy* 29(4): 1–17.

———. 2012. 'The Condition of Hyper-Modernity: Sarah Bartmann's Funeral'. In *Donga*, ed. A. Finlay and P. Wessels, 298–9. Johannesburg: BLeKSEM.

———. Forthcoming. 'Rethinking Girardian Reconciliation: The Myth of the Exception'. In *Creative Reconciliation: Conceptual and Practical Challenges from a Girardin Perspective*, ed. V.N. Redekop and T. Ryba. Lanham: Lexington Books.

Praeg, L. and S. Magadla (eds.). 2014. *Ubuntu: Curating the Archive*. Pietermaritzburg: University of KwaZulu-Natal Press.

Proust, M. 1985. *Remembrance of Things Past*. Vol. 1. London: Penguin.

Prozesky, M.H. 2009. 'Cinderella, Survivor and Saviour: African Ethics and the Quest for a Global Ethic'. In *African Ethics: An Anthology of Comparative and Applied Ethics*, ed. M.F Murove, 3–14. Pietermaritzburg: University of KwaZulu-Natal Press.

Prunier, G. 2009. *Africa's World War: Congo, the Rwandan Genocide, and the Making of a Continental Catastrophe*. Oxford: Oxford University Press.

Quayson, A. 2002. 'Obverse Denominations: Africa?' *Public Culture* 14(3): 585–8.

Rader, M. 1979. *Marx's Interpretation of History*. New York: Oxford University Press.

Ramose, M.B. 1999. *African Philosophy through Ubuntu*. Harare: Mond Press.

———. 2002a. 'Historic Titles in Law'. In *Philosophy from Africa: A Text with Readings*, ed. P.H. Coetzee and A.P.J. Roux, 461–3. Oxford: Oxford University Press.

———. 2002b. 'I Conquer Therefore I am the Sovereign: Reflections upon Sovereignty, Constitutionalism, and Democracy in Zimbabwe and South Africa'. In *Philosophy from Africa: A Text with Readings*, ed. P.H. Coetzee and A.P.J. Roux, 463–500. Oxford: Oxford University Press.

Readings, B. 1996. *The University in Ruins*. Cambridge: Harvard University Press.

Renan, E. 1990. 'What is a Nation?' In *Nation and Narration*, ed. H.K. Bhabha, 8–23. London: Routledge.

Richardson, N. 2009. 'Can Christian Ethics Find its Way and Itself in Africa?' In *African Ethics: An Anthology of Comparative and Applied Ethics*, ed. M.F Murove, 129–55. Pietermaritzburg: University of KwaZulu-Natal Press.

Ryan, A. 1996. 'Hobbes's Political Philosophy'. In *The Cambridge Companion to Hobbes*, ed. T. Sorell, 208–45. Cambridge: Cambridge University Press.

Said, E.W. 1986. 'An Ideology of Difference'. In *'Race,' Writing and Difference*, ed. H.L Gates, 38–58. Chicago: University of Chicago Press.

Sekyi-Otu, A. 2003. 'Fanon and the Possibility of a Postcolonial Critical Imagination'. Paper prepared for the CODESRIA Symposium on Canonical Works and Continuing Innovations in African Arts and Humanities, University of Ghana, Legon, Accra, 17–19 September.

Shivji, I.G. 1973. *The Silent Class Struggle*. Dar es Salaam: Tanzania Publishing House.
———. 1976. *Class Struggles in Tanzania*. Dar es Salaam, New York and London: Tanzania Publishing House, Monthly Review Press and Heinemann.
———. 2006a. *Let the People Speak: Tanzania Down the Road to Neo-Liberalism*. Dakar: CODESRIA.
———. 2006b. 'Rule of Law and Ujamaa in the Ideological Formation of Tanzania'. *Social and Legal Studies* 4(2): 147–74.
———. 2008. *Pan-Africanism or Pragmatism: Lessons of Tanganyika-Zanzibar Union*. Dar es Salaam: Mkuki na Nyota.
———. 2009. *Where is Uhuru? Reflections on the Struggle for Democracy in Africa*. Oxford: Fahamu Books.
———. 2014. 'Utu, Usawa, Uhuru: Building Blocks of Nyerere's Political Philosophy'. In *Ubuntu: Curating the Archive*, ed. L. Praeg and S. Magadla. Pietermaritzburg: University of KwaZulu-Natal Press.
Shoba, S. 2011. 'Court Ruling on Hate Speech Deals New Blow to Malema'. *Business Day Online*. Available at http://www.bdlive.co.za/articles/2011/09/13/court-ruling-on-hate-speech-deals-new-blow-to-malema.
Shutte, A. 1993. *Philosophy for Africa*. Cape Town: University of Cape Town Press.
———. 2001. *Ubuntu: An Ethic for a New South Africa*. Pietermaritzburg: Cluster Publications.
———. 2009. 'Ubuntu as the African Ethical Vision'. In *African Ethics: An Anthology of Comparative and Applied Ethics*, ed. M.F Murove, 85–100. Pietermaritzburg: University of KwaZulu-Natal Press.
Sieyès, E.J. 1963 [1789]. *What is the Third Estate?* London: Pall Mall Press.
Sprinzak, E. 1973. 'African Traditional Socialism: A Semantic Analysis of Political Ideology'. *The Journal of Modern African Studies* 11(4): 629–47.
Stace, W.T. 1962. *A Critical History of Greek Philosophy*. London: Macmillan.
Swartz, S. 2006. 'A Long Walk to Citizenship: Morality, Justice and Faith in the Aftermath of Apartheid'. *Journal of Moral Education* 35(4): 551–70.
Teffo, J. 1998. 'Botho/Ubuntu as a Way Forward for Contemporary South Africa'. *Word and Action* 38(365): 3–5.
Tempels, P. 1969. *Bantu Philosophy*. Paris: Présence Africaine.
Terreblanche, S. 2002. *The History of Inequality in South Africa, 1652–2002*. Pietermaritzburg: University of Natal Press.
———. 2012. *Lost in Transformation: South Africa's Search for a New Future Since 1986*. Johannesburg: KMM Review Publishing Company.
Thomas, C.G. 2008. '*Ubuntu*: The Missing Link in the Rights Discourse in Post-Apartheid Transformation in South Africa'. *International Journal of African Renaissance Studies* 3(2): 39–62.
Todorov, T. 2003. *Hope and Memory: Lessons from the Twentieth Century*. Trans. D. Bellos. Princeton: University of Princeton Press.
Tomaselli, K.G. 2009. '(Afri)Ethics, Communitarianism and Libertarianism'. *International Communication Gazette* 71(7): 577–94.
Tshoose, C.I. 2009. 'The Emerging Role of the Constitutional Value of *Ubuntu* for Informal Social Security in South Africa'. *African Journal of Legal Studies* 3: 12–19.

Tshwaku, K. 2010. 'The Right to Write What is Right'. *Grocott's Mail*, 17 September. Available at http://www.grocotts.co.za/content/right-write-what-right-17-09-2010.

Vale, P. 2010. 'What Has Happened to the Humanities?' Schonland Lecture delivered at Rhodes University, 28 September.

Van Binsbergen, W. 2001. '*Ubuntu* and the Globalisation of Southern African Thought and Society'. *Quest* 15(1–2): 54–89.

Van der Walt, J. 2005. *Law and Sacrifice: Towards a Post-Apartheid Theory of Law*. London: Birkbeck Law Press.

Van Niekerk, G.J. 2000. 'A Common Law for Southern Africa: Roman Law or Indigenous African Law?' In *Roman Law at the Crossroads*, ed. W.J. Kamba and M.O. Hinz, 83–103. Cape Town: Juta.

———. 2005. 'Succession, Living Indigenous Law and *Ubuntu* in the Constitutional Court'. *Obiter* 26(3): 478–87.

Van Valen, L. 1973. 'A New Evolutionary Law'. *Evolutionary Theory* 1: 1–30.

Van Vuuren, H. 2010. 'Cloud of Secrecy Hides the Rot'. *Mail & Guardian*, 3–9 September. Available at http://www.mg.co.za/article/2010-09-13-cloud-of-secrecy-hides-the-rot.

Venter, E. 2004. 'The Notion of Ubuntu and Communialism in African Educational Discourse'. *Studies in Philosophy and Education* 23: 149–60.

Vermeij, G.J. 1987. *Evolution and Escalation: An Ecological History of Life*. Princeton: Princeton University Press.

Vervliet, C. 2009. *The Human Person, African Ubuntu, and the Dialogue of Civilizations*. London: Adonis and Abbey.

Vogler, C. 2002. 'Social Imaginary, Ethics, and Methdological Individualism'. *Public Culture* 14(3): 625–7.

Von Freyhold, M. 1979. *Ujamaa Villages in Tanzania*. New York: Monthly Review Press.

White, H. 1973. *Metahistory: The Historical Imagination in Nineteenth-Century Europe*. Baltimore: Johns Hopkins University Press.

Wiredu, K. 2002. 'The Moral Foundations of an African Culture'. In *Philosophy from Africa: A Text with Readings*, ed. P.H. Coetzee and A.P.J. Roux, 287–97. Oxford: Oxford University Press.

———. 2008. 'Social Philosophy in Postcolonial Africa: Some Preliminaries Concerning Communalism and Communitarianism'. *South African Journal of Philosophy* 27(4): 332–8.

Woods, J. M. 2003. 'Rights as Slogans: A Theory of Human Rights Based on African Humanism'. *National Black Law Journal* (17)1: 52–66.

Zolberg, A. 1964 . 'The Dakar Colloquium: The Search for a Doctrine'. In *African Socialism*, ed. W.H. Friedland and C.G Rosberg Jr, 113–27. Stanford: Stanford University Press.

INDEX

accountability 2
accounting 2
adjudication 233–5, 239, 263, 267, 270, 275
   altruistic 235, 275, 276–7
   deployment of Ubuntu in 263
   as praxis of the uncanny 260
   Ubuntu-engaged 276
Adorno, Theodor (with Horkheimer, Max) 222–3, 252
   'The Concept of Enlightenment' 222
Africa
   history 102–3
   and the law relationship 183–7
   radical inequality 146
African academic project 105
'Africanising' 182–3
African modes of being 96–7
   characters and personae 97–100
   matrix of classification 100–19
African National Congress (ANC) x, 65–6, 68, 179, 243
African Renaissance 67, 194
African Socialism 12, 23, 24, 46, 67, 137–75, 138–54, 174–5
   doctrinal clarity on meaning 150
   postcolonial Tanzania 163–4
African Socialists 25, 139, 142–6, 174
Afri-Forum and Another v. Malema and Others 18

Afrikaner nationalism 83
   rebellions against British colonial rule 83–4
Afro-pessimists 18
Afro-radicals 86, 87, 206
Afro-Shirazi Party 140
Agamben, Giorgio 168
   Homo Sacer 168
age 40–1
altruism 228, 229, 233, 235, 237–42, 256, 260
American War of Independence 261
ANC Youth League 17, 179–80
Anglo-Europeans 190
   tradition of political thought 189
anthropology
   empirical 35
   philosophical 21–9, 33, 35, 36, 41, 60
anti-apartheid struggle 51–2, 65
anti-colonial violence 17
anticommunitarian spirit 199
apartheid 8, 118
   to democracy transition 182
   struggle against 190
aporia-archē 270
   founding of Ubuntu 277
   logic 223, 260
   of South African politico-juridical order 178
aporia of the untimely 146
   between memory and possibility 147–8

Appiah, Anthony   107
  'Cosmopolitan Patriots'   107
Arab state for the southern Sudanese   255
archē   230, 270, 275
  beginning, origin or first cause   260–1
  as contract   261–3
  humanism   198
  as origin (beginning) and rule (principle)   262
  pluralism   236
  point of origin   121–2
  of the political   235
  'reconciliation'   40
  violation   220
Archivist   22, 95, 96, 102, 104–6, 109, 112, 131, 216, 267, 268, 273, 274
  conceptual persona   271–2
Arendt, Hannah   13, 34, 262–3
  'Concern with Politics in Recent European Philosophical Thought'   13
  On Revolution   149, 261
  'On the Nature of Totalitarianism'   85–6, 169
Aristotelian virtue ethic   12, 13
articulation (*qua* rule) of the *archē* (*qua* principle)   240
association   42
  contractual understanding of   43
asymmetry
  external   11
  internal   11
asynchronicity   215
  post-teleological   246
asynchronous modernities   215–16, 226, 247, 258–9
  model   223
authority as function of loyalty   41

autochthony/being from here   88
  value of   91
auto-nomination   45
autonomy   86–7, 148
  future (Revolutionary)   96
auto-violation   123
axiomatic
  ontological   225, 228
  political   225, 228
  see also meta-axiomatic
AZAPO v. President of the Republic of South Africa   268, 270

Baudrillard, Jean   216
  Disneyland in American culture   218–19
  Simulations   216–17
being (individual)   35–36, 41, 44
  analysis of   42
  identity   37, 38–40
  locality   37, 40–6
  origin   37–8
being-as-belonging praxis   75, 107
belief systems   38
belonging (community)   34, 35–6, 41, 44–5, 79, 198, 204, 205, 220, 224, 252, 265
  absence of transcendental legitimation   204
  betrayal of   175
  meta-reflective praxis   226
  ontological grounding   225
  possibility of   224–5, 226
  reinvention   221
  residual elements of a praxis   226–7
  ritualised process   60–1
  sacred sense of   197
  social   41
  unresolvable problem for thought   226
Benjamin, Walter   167

Berlin, Isaiah   85
  'Historical Inevitability'   85
bifurcation   204
Biko, Steve   176–8
  legacy as human rights activist   177
  political and intellectual Revolutionary   176
Bill of Rights   185
Black Consciousness   56–7, 176
Blixen-Finecke, Karen von (pseudonym Isak Dinesen)   119, 131–2
  Out of Africa   119
'blooming of African uniqueness'   87
Blut und Boden myth   113
Boesak, Allan   72, 73–4
Britain
  administration   160–2
  capitalist economy   162
  Report of the Royal Commission   162
  values through education   161

capitalism   68, 136–7, 143, 243, 248
  monopolistic   168
capitalist economy   162
  before colonialism   161–2
capitalist individualism   143, 166
  ban on   167–8
Carroll, Lewis   214
  Through the Looking-Glass and What Alice Found There   214
Cartesian
  Idiot   122
  'I think therefore I am'   207
Cavarero, Adriana   119–20
  unity, the Other, the gift   120
Cervantes, Miguel de   151
  Don Quixote   151

Chabal, Patrick   33, 35–9, 40–5, 60, 227, 255
  Africa: The Politics of Suffering and Smiling   21, 103–4
Chain
  of Becoming, horizontal and evolutionary   212
  of Being, vertical   212
childishness   219
Christianised UbunTutu   39, 76
Christianity   34, 37, 52, 80, 232
  Abrahamic tradition   188
  as example of objective religion   199
  and human rights   53
  modern reinvention of the sacred   200–1
  nature of faith   199
  rise of as a subjective religion   201
Christian messianism, secularised versions of   211
  ubuntufied   76
  of the West   188
circumcision   59, 60
Civilisation of the Universal   111, 115, 121, 124–5
class differences   107
Clinton, Bill   234, 248
coercion
  benevolent communitarian   181
  principle   165, 175
  ritualised   175
  violence of   178
cogito (solipsistic Idiot)   112
Cold War ideological binary   136–7
collective good over individual rights   267
Colloquium on Policies of Development and African Approaches to Socialism, Dakar   137

colonialism   39, 49, 51, 61, 152, 205
   and arrow of time   182–3, 207–11
   suspension or *epochē* of narrative   198
colonisation, struggle against   190
common good   233
   over individual freedom   226
communal harmony   185
communalism   154–5, 239
   African   82, 142
   Beginning and End   146, 148, 211–12
   post-colonial, as African Socialism   23
communality
   onto-triadic   186
   premodern forms   197, 221
   and Ubuntu   265
communal or social society   164–5
communication
   praxis   275
   shared   276
communion of souls   156–7
communitarian axiomatic of Ubuntu   229
communitarian or altruistic logic   27
communitarianism   22–3, 43, 85, 89, 93, 208, 272
   African   12, 22, 23, 46, 256
   African, versus Western individualism   54
   Africa's praxis   220
   Conformist   96
   consensus   60–1
   history of thought and praxis   102
   naturalised praxis   218
   precolonial (ubuntu praxis)   25
   racialised   111
   subsistance-driven, premodern societies   215
   visible as political choice   177–8
   Western   208

communitarian thought, pre- and post-Cartesian Western traditions   89–90
communitarian tradition   110–11
community   196
concept of the sacred   187–8
conceptual personae in report   272–3
conflict
   balanced ideological   235, 238
   paradoxical   238
   superficial   236, 238
Conformist   22, 100, 110, 131, 267, 268, 272, 273, 274
   conceptual persona   271
conformity   175
Constitution   *see* South African Constitution
Constitutional Court   75, 232, 262–3
constitutional jurisprudence, conceptual personae of   264–8
Construction Worker   96, 100, 273, 274
contemporary discourses of Ubuntu   254
contemporary philosophical practices   45
contemporary reinvention of traditional ethics   89
contraction of altruistic duty   236
contribution   115, 116, 125
'conversion principle'   191–2
Cosmopolitan   22, 100, 106, 124, 131, 187, 206, 216, 267–8, 274
   image of thought as comparison   106
   persona   108, 109
   strategies of equivocation and generalisation   266–7
cosmopolitanism
   contemporary, non-historicist variety   106
   historicist   106–7
critical humanism   10–12
   mode of critique   20, 21
cultural authenticity   180

cultural praxis (habitus)   165
culture   138
   African   238–9
   modern legal   194
   and reproduction of tradition   165–6
   Ubuntu equated with   265
curating   103

decolonisation   17, 87, 88, 184, 205
definition, question of   135–6
Deism of contemporary Enlightened Europe   197
dependence   62, 131
Derrida, Jacques   1–3, 25, 247
   Force of Law   149
   'Mochlos; or: The Conflict of the Faculties'   1–2
Descartes, René   98–9, 207–9, 221–2
   '*Cogito ergo sum*'   221
de-territorialised ubuntu   47
development, lopsided   227
dialectic   204
difference
   expressed as ideology   166–7
   as master trope   43–4
   or sameness   91
differentiation paradox   92–3
dignity scholarship   136
Dinesen, Isak   *see* Blixen-Finecke, Karen von
Diop, Cheikh Anta   55
dispute resolution   185
dogmatism   53
Du Bois, W.E.B.   56
due process   181

East African Community   140
East African Institute of Social and Cultural Affairs, Nairobi   150–1

economy of obligation   85
   traditional political   182
Egypt   87–8
emancipation
   discourse   242–3
   project   147, 188
emancipatory force of Ubuntu   275–6
emancipatory ideology   135
emancipatory praxis, Ubuntu as   21–9, 271
Enlightenment   97, 225, 252
   project of autonomy and freedom   88
epistemology   99, 100, 103, 181
   knowing and writing about Africa   85
   knowing the world   98
   questions   6–7
epochē (suspension of judgement)   27, 28–9
   first   194–207
   second   229–42, 244
equality   45, 155, 176, 179, 181
   political   138–9
   Western-dominated modernist discourse   148
Equality Court   15–16, 17
ethical codes   40
ethics   78, 147
   Christian   232
   virtue   85
ethnicity   39
ethnic morality   64, 78
ethnophilosophers   55, 180
ethnophilosophy   13, 94
'ethos' of love and Ubuntu   265
Eurocentric developmentalist narratives   111
European Enlightenment   73, 208–9
evolution
   broccoli theory   211–16
   individual and social   251

preformation biological theory 212, 213
   Western, teleological grand narratives 251
exceptionalism 92
   salvific 252
existential alienation (loss of self) 86
exploratory attitude 96
extralegal justifications in relation to law
   modern 231, 232
   religious 231–2
   sovereign 231, 232
extrapolated approximation 265

Fanon, Frantz 14, 17–18, 56–7, 74–5, 115, 129, 147
   'Algeria Unveiled' 56–7
federalism 184
feminist ethics of care 208
Ferguson, Adam 196
   An Essay on the History of Civil Society 196, 211
feudalism 209–10
filtering 166
   theoretical 166
First Philosophy 6, 9–10, 22, 145
   political as 12–18
First World War 160
forgiveness and reconciliation 14, 17, 80, 85, 180, 217
   belonging 80
   Christianised or spiritualised understanding 24
   quasi-sacred notion of dignity 80
Foucault, Michel 48
fragmentation 227
fraternity 176, 181
fratricide and civil war threats 166
freedom 87–8, 100, 131, 176, 228, 230
   indivisible 116

free will 235
French Revolution 261
Freud, Sigmund 209–10, 211, 248
   'Das Unheimliche' ('The Uncanny') 248–50
   see also uncanny
fundamental contradiction 228, 230

gender and age 41
geographical dislocation 219
geographies of thought 233
Germany 160, 194–5
   folk religion 197
   Stürmer und Dränger thinkers 195
ghost as mode of being 112
Girard, René 251
   Violence and the Sacred 251–2
global
   archivist and cosmopolitan 101–9
   and local a prioris 81, 101
globalisation 11, 37, 101, 114, 190
glocal phenomenon 11, 34, 101
glocal Ubuntu 61, 81
   in relation to the law 244
God's Elect, notion of being 245
Goethe, Johann Wolfgang von 195
Gordon, Jane 217
   Of Divine Warning: Reading Disaster in the Modern Age 217
Gordon, Lewis 12, 17, 19, 21, 22, 55, 84, 135, 217, 233
government branches
   courts 233
   executive 233
   legislature 233
grace, dirty work of 127–31
grassroots social movements
   Abahlali baseMjondolo 243

Ubuntu Project   243
greater good   235
Greece, Ancient   195–6
Greek
    and Athenian society   196
    decline of folk religion   201
    religious experience   199

Haeckel, Ernst   210
Hall, Stanley   209–10
Hamitic hypothesis   39
Hegel, G.W.F.   27, 195–207
    Das Leben Jesu   200
    Die Phänomenologie des Geistes   204
    Die Positivität der christlichen Religion   201
    historiography   211, 221–2
    moralische Harmonie   204, 205, 251
    Phenomenology of Spirit   27
    philosophy of modernity   204–5
    problem of modernity   201–2
    reunification of *Geist* (Spirit/Mind) with itself   204
    sinnliche Harmonie   204, 205, 209, 222, 251
    sinnliche to *moralische Harmonie*   211
Heidegger, Martin   7
    ontological hermeneutics   208
historical praxis   61–2
historical racism and contemporary identity politics   91
historicism   206–7
    of Afro-radicalism and nativism   106
    epistemological   86
    ontological   86
historicists   196, 197
    a priori   48–9, 106, 145
historicity   221

historiography   197
    philosophical understanding   205
    of sorcery   87
history
    philosophy of   197
    postmodern theory   221
    writing   84
Hobbs, Thomas   209
Hölderlin, Friedrich   195
Holomisa, Chief Phathekile   185
Holy Roman Empire   196
home in the world, at (*Heimlichkeit*)   198
homelessness (*Unheimlichkeit*)   198
Horkheimer, Max (with Adorno, Theodor)   222–3, 252
    'The Concept of Enlightenment'   222
human
    collectivities   164
    communality   163
    condition (sameness)   91
    evolution as equal participants of history   145
    relationships with the living-dead   225
    thinking, being   273
humanism   11–12, 85, 93, 115, 130, 189
    African   19, 46, 94, 132
    critical   10, 243
    failure of   132
    and humanising   20
    interstitial   117
    as mode of critique   19–20
    necessary failure   126–7
    quasi-transcendental understanding   188
    secular   55
    spiritualised   220
    transcendental   75, 130–1
    universal (critical)   189

Western forms   89
Zambian   50–1
humanist force of reconciliation and mediation   130
humanity
   intersubjective   189
   shared   67, 79, 93, 181–2, 189
humanness and Ubuntu   265
human rights   34, 37, 85, 256
   Christianity   53
   liberal discourse of individuals   52
hypermodernity   25, 92–3, 151, 179–80, 244–6, 270, 277
   and (im)possibility of the founding   148–51
   inexecution   150, 152
   meta-consciousness   245
   power of the as-if   151–3

identity   37, 38–40, 185, 186
   African politics   209
   ethnic   38
   idealist question   137
   politics   14, 53, 136, 276
   postcolonial   136
   tribal   38
ideological conflict, balanced   235
ideology   118–19, 158
   African Socialism   36
Idols of the Mind   193
image of thought   98, 271
imaginaires   44, 95, 115–16, 218
   local, racialised of cultural nationalism   11, 217, 220, 247
   global, racist   11, 217, 218, 219, 220, 247–8, 252
   modernising   226
   (post)modernised   226

imayibuye, return of Africa to Africa(ns)   182
'immanent meta-legitimation' in juridical discourse   275
independence   87, 131, 136, 179
   or cultural sovereignty   91
individualism   82, 102, 111, 114, 155, 198, 224, 228, 229, 232, 233, 235, 237–42, 252, 260
   and altruism tension   28
   ideological representation   165
   neoliberal   219
individualist a priori   44
individuality   198
individual psychology   210
individual rights   176, 181, 182, 233, 235, 277
   suspension of   269
individuated individual   190, 192
industrialisation   51
   selective   227
inherently unknowable or not articulable   264–5
initiation   59
injustice   29
   original   184, 258
integration   204
interdependence
   conceived as altruism   235
   empathetic and antipathetic manifestations   63–4
   familial   175
   logic of   44–5, 48, 49, 55, 62, 66, 89, 132, 166, 228
   precolonial logic   135, 137
   shared humanity   91
   Western philosophies   89
Interim Constitution   177, 185, 243–4, 268
iteration, problematic conception of   112

Jewsiewicki, Bogumil   180
juridico-political orders   4, 75–6, 269
justice   64, 69–70, 186, 189, 225, 263
   different conceptions or *differend*   258
   double structure   186–7, 273
   geography of   259
   horizon of   259
   individual right to   268
   of justice   255, 259, 260
   legal, constitutional   259–60
   and the *stokvel*   63

Kant, Immanuel   69, 73, 199, 225
   Critique of Pure Reason   225
Kantian individual, philosophical anthropology of   196
Kennedy, Duncan   8, 27–8, 228, 231, 233, 236, 239–42
   'Form and Substance in Private Law Adjudication'   178, 234–5, 238
Kennedy, John F.   248
   '*Ich bin ein Berliner*'   248
Kenya   144, 162
   Swynnerton Plan   162
Kenyatta, Jomo   141
kin (reciprocity)   41–2
Kingdom of Fraternal Unity   165
kinship-based unity   43–4
knowledge-construction, racialised   179
knowledge-production   2, 3, 36, 105
Kopytoff, Igor   153–4
Kuti, Fela   35
   'Shuffering and Shmiling' song   35

land   37–8
   communal ownership   155
   communal system of tenure   162
   principles governing ownership   162

Land Ordinance of 1923   162
language, act or praxis of   276
law   28–9, 136, 225
   African   187, 190
   altruistic tradition of interpreting   28
   call to 'Africanise the law'   182–3
   customary   190
   incorporation of Ubuntu   264
   in defence of   73–4
   founding principle and purpose   191
   as guarantor of equality of all   62
   indigenous African   185, 190
   or justices   28
   as normative critique   192
   in relation to politics   183
   Roman-Dutch   185
   rule of   74
   teleological purpose   192
   and Ubuntu   186–7, 227–8
Law   256
   of law   49, 190–1
   subversions in name of solidarity   71
   and Ubuntu   186
leadership
   hereditary and democratic   186
   traditional   186
legal formalism   256
legal pluralism   185
Lévinas, Emmanual   7–8
liberal constitutionalism   9
liberal democratic order   75
liberal-democratic retrodiction of tradition   183–4
   sovereign, pluralist, cosmopolitan options   183–4
   see also retrodiction
liberalism   22–3, 102
   and conservatism   233–4

liberation
    fighters 94
    as self-recognition 56
    struggle 87, 182
    from Western modernity 90
liberty 181
living-dead 38, 42
local: conformist and prophet 110–14
locality 37, 40–6
    and community 40
    origin and identity 40
logic
    of coercion 33
    of interdependence 36, 47, 50
Lyotard, Jean-François 244
    The Differend: Phrases in Dispute 258
    'Une note sur le post' 244–5

Malema, Julius 15
    singing of *Dubul' ibhunu* 15, 17–18
Mandela, Nelson 16–17, 72, 115, 127, 128, 179, 217–18
Manheim, Karl 34
    Ideology and Utopia 34
manual labour 274
Marais, Hein 243
    South Africa Pushed to the Limit: The Political Economy of Change 243
Marikana strike x, xii, 243
Marx, Karl 144, 209, 211
    The German Ideology 158
Marxism 143–4, 206
Marxist and nationalist categories 86
Marxist historical grand narrative 143
Marxist-motivated improvement in material conditions 147
Mazrui, Ali 116
material exploitation (loss of resources) 86

Mbeki, Thabo 194
Mbembe, Achille 21, 83, 101, 102, 106, 107, 111, 121, 147, 179, 181, 256, 274
    'African Modes of Self-Writing' 85, 87, 88, 205
mestiço state for UNITA 255
meta-axiomatic 228
meta-critique
    of reason 21–9, 82, 84
    of Ubuntu 131
Michelman, Frank 228–9
migrant thinking a prioris 47–8
    first global a priori: colonialism 48–9
    first local a priori: urbanisation 50–4
    second local a priori: constitutionalism as 'liberation' 58–64
    second global a priori: dialectic of recognition 55–7
Mitchell, Sir Philip, governor of Kenya 144
mode of being 99, 271
    migratory 273
modernity 26, 27, 34, 198, 203, 220, 224–5, 229, 238, 245
    condition of personal and social fragmentation 200
    European 152, 197–8
    historical statement of 89
    imperative to historicise 206
    ontological axiomatic 225–6
    postcolonial 27, 138, 220
    racist, Western 87
    see also Western modernity
modern legal cultures 229, 232–3, 260
modes
    of being 98, 112, 268
    of thinking 83
    see also African modes of being
Montaigne, Michel de 151

moral code of cultures   97, 181
   and moral aspirations   97–8
moral-economic justice   63
morality   225
   and ethics distinction   77–8
Mudimbe, V-Y   101–2, 105, 117, 180
   The Invention of Africa: Gnosis, Philosophy, and the Order of Knowledge   101, 103
Museveni dictatorship for the Acholi   255
'*Muthu u bebelwa munwe*' (a person is born for the other)   51
'myth of primitive unanimity'   154

narratives
   nativist   86–7
   teleologial   86
National Houses of Traditional Leadership   185
nationalisation   172
nationalism   75, 179
nationalist social engineering   172
nativist meta-narratives   93
nativist optimism   105
necklace murders   65, 66, 175, 181
négritude   129
   and Ubuntu   121
neo-apartheid jurisprudence   240
neoliberal economics   9
neoliberalism   68
neo-racism   217
Newtonian world view   211
Nguni languages   50
   abelungu or *makgowa* (white people)   50
Nietzsche, Friedrich   99–100
Nkrumah, Kwame   19, 111
nomos, spirit of Law   x–xi, 54, 114, 115, 181, 182

non-teleological evolution   214
Nyerere, Julius   19, 25, 26, 67, 69, 112, 121, 127–31, 135–76
   African Socialist project   175
   'Freedom and Socialism'   172
   Freedom and Unity   163
   'The African and Democracy'   154
   Ujamaa project   23–4, 88, 116, 135, 140, 142
   'Ujamaa: The Basis of African Socialism'   167

Obama, Barack   217, 234
obligations   42–3, 107
   political economy of   45
   regime   54
ontogeny   210
ontological reduction of reality to textuality   103
ontology   99, 100
   being in the world   98
   modes of being postcolonial African   85
opinion, differences in ontological terms   175
oppression   88
oral genres   65
Organisation of African Unity (OAU)   137
origin   37–8, 39
   marker of community   37–8
Other, the   122
Other-violation   123–4
ownership
   contesting claims of   258
   entities with abstract exchange value   258

Pan-Africanism   90–1
parochialism   94
particularity   242–4
pathêtikos, based on *pathos*, suffering   127

performativity of the founding   151, 180
personae
　antipathetic   100
　sympathetic   100
personal and social fragmentation   197
personal autonomy   180
personhood
　African conceptions   80
　as gift from other persons   123
　and humanness   59
　post-Cartesian understandings   208
　Ubuntu-based notion   208
　understanding of   58
　Western thought   207–8
phallo-primocentric values   185, 271
phenomenologies   89
philosophers, Western   231
philosophical conversation   6–9
philosophy
　African   4–5, 12
　Africana   5
　emancipatory   94
　of an *ethnos*   9
　glocal (modern, contemporary)   37
　locally unique but globally relevant   208
　political   13
　translation or codification   61
　Western   5
phylogeny-ontogeny hypothesis   210, 213, 251
Plato   231, 262
Pliny, the Elder   117
　Historia Naturalis (Natural History)   117
pluralism   236
plurality   227, 230–1
poeticists   195–6, 197
political, the   6–10, 15, 181

as archē of intellectual traditions   105
　order   147
　questions   8–9
political capital   130–1
political economy
　of commodity capitalism   143–4
　contemporary or future of individual freedom   62
　global   218
　of obligation   33, 35, 47, 61–2, 186, 227, 255, 271
　of ubuntu   21–2
political tribalism   39
political truth   180–1
politico-juridical
　domain   41
　system   4
politico-religious analysis   200
politics   3
　of the gift   131
　sovereign, identity   181–2
post-apartheid South Africa   4, 43, 68
　imagined community   190
　jurisprudence   237, 239, 241
　modernity   229, 237–9
postcolonial Africa   86
　development ideology   94
　and ethnic neo-medievalism   184
　relativist a priori   145
　societies   38
postcolonial a priori of relativism   252
postcolonial historicism   179
postcoloniality   43, 113–14
　ontological foundation   215
　and self-determination   56
postcolony *qua* politico-juridico-economic system   64
postmodernism   113–14, 244–5

post-Second World War era 143
poverty 107, 118
    war on 172
power 13–15, 41, 117, 129, 186
    asymmetrical relations 180
    of traditional leaders 185
precapitalist, ujamaa praxis 163
premodernity 225, 247
premodern/modern and traditional/modern 226
principle of repetition (tradition) 91
problematique, general and particular 26
Promethean myth 245
property, protection of 235
Prophet 100, 111, 127, 131
Prophetic persona 22, 111, 267
    conceptual geography of a revolution 268–71
psychological humiliation (loss of dignity) 86

quasi-spiritual humanism 39
quasi-transcendental 187–9

race 180
racialisation as 'fundamental contradiction' 27
racialised modernisation 227
racial prejudice to black people 218
racism 252
    and exoticism 46
    mutations 92
    reactionary 105–6
    scientific 222
radical ontological incommensurability 238
radical pluralism 10
rationality 222
reality, study of 48
recapitulation idea 212–13

reciprocity 107
recollection 112, 116
    revolutionary image of thought 111
reconciliation 40, 79, 176
    Christian notions 85
    ideological notions 85
    philosophical notions 85
re-creating the world in its own image 116
redemptive re-configuration 125
reductionism 229, 272
refraction 64, 77–81
reification 64–81
relativist a priori 48, 49
religion 38, 39, 227
    civic 220
    contemporary folk 200, 201
    conversion to different 39
    fluidity as identity marker 9
    objective 199
    premodern 197
    or spirituality 197
religion-based societies 157
republican constitutionalism 62
resources, shared 67
responsibility 1–6
    principles 3–4
re-territorialised (reinserted) ubuntu 47
retrodiction 11, 64, 77–81, 139
    call to Africanise Christianity 81
    logic of 266
    opposite of prediction 81
    see also justice; solidarity; violence
Revolutionaries, empathetic 270–1
Revolutionary 22, 100, 110, 111, 127, 164, 267, 273, 274
    antipathetic persona 275
    commitment to emancipation 114
    conceptual persona 113, 174

discourse on Ubuntu   112–13
French pursuit (freedom, equality, fraternity)   176
mode of being   112, 268
nationalist   128
political   176
recollection   116, 268
redemption   216
spectral   268
'revolutionary Ubuntu'   243
rhetorical strategies   265–6
rights   45, 269
   avant la lettre   54
   collective and sovereignty   184
   regime   54
   universal   183
Royal Commonwealth Society Journal   130
Rwanda genocide   38–9

sacred as civic religion reinvention   199
sacredness of human life   188
Saviour   22, 95, 110, 114–19, 124, 127, 164, 267, 274
   collective redemption   216
   gift-bearing persona   123
   meets Idiot   119–27
   persona   115, 125
   redemptive   116
'scheme of identification'   39
Schelling, Friedrich   196–7, 248–9
Schiller, Friedrich   195, 196, 199–200
scientific socialists   142, 144–6
Scottish Enlightenment thinkers   196
secularisation of ubuntu praxis   51–2
self-consciousness   203
self-determination   49, 148
self-interest   4, 166
   and Other-care tension   193–4

self-negation paradox   236
self-sufficiency (autonomy, sovereignty)   123
self-writing, African modes of   85–95, 274
Senghor, Léopold Sédar   55, 96, 137, 139, 156, 167–8
   universalist nativism   121
service delivery arguments   186
'shared humanity' idea   118
Sieyès, Emmanuel Joseph   149
   What is the Third Estate?   149
social cohesion   168
social commitment   277
social contract   10, 189–90
   as methodological fiction   209
social democracy   243
social evolution   212, 213, 215
   Marxist grand narrative   213–14
   Western grand narratives   211
social fragmentation   199
social fraternity   156
socialism   89, 136–7, 143
   avant la lettre   19, 25, 139, 145
   democratic   168
   memory or utopian possibility question   142–6
   as psycho-juridical regime   170
   as state of mind   156
   see also African Socialism; African Socialists
socialist *avant la lettre*   159
socialist democracy   243
social morality   199
social ontology   143
social relations of workforce   68
social sacred and sacred social   199–200
socio-economic development   144
socio-political domain   41
socio-political landscape of Rome   201

socio-religious reform to philosophical comprehension   202
solidarity   64, 70–7
   antipathetic   71–4
   empathetic subversions   70–1
   rhetoric   175
   transcendent   74–6
South Africa
   founding of state   258–9
   industrial revolution   51
   intellectual isolation   94
   post-industrial revolution   43
   transition to democracy   118
South African Communist Party (SACP)   68
South African Constitution   27, 49, 61, 62, 73, 149, 185, 186, 189, 191, 226, 229, 244, 254, 257–60, 267, 269
   aporia as *archē* or *aporia-archē*   263
   archē or first principle   263
   founding *aporia-archē*   29, 257–9
South African Constitutional Court jurisprudence   264
sovereignty   86–7, 90–2, 148, 179, 185
   cultural   181
   political   180
Soweto uprising   243
Spirit   204
spirit of ubuntu   40
Sprinzak, Ehud   153–9
Stalin, Joseph   23
Steuart, Sir James   196
   An Inquiry into the Principles of Political Economy   202
   necessary process of progressive social evolution   203
   theory of socio-economic evolution   202–3
stratification   155

subjectivity
   being-as-belonging   263
   human   187, 188
super-personal entities or forces   87
S. v. AZAPO   176–8
S. v. Makwanyane and S. v. AZAPO   265–6

Tanganyika   160–3
   cash-crop farmers   162
   freehold as foreign, unAfrican concept   168–9
   independence   127, 129–31
   League of Nations, British mandate   160
Tanganyika African National Union (TANU)   140, 162
Tanzania   137–40, 158–9, 167
   Arusha Declaration   140, 160, 167
   colonised by Germany   160
   Kigoma Operation   172
   means of production in hands of elite   174
   Operation Dodoma   172
   postcolonial class struggle   173
   Ujamaa/Ubuntu villages   171–3
   Villages and Ujaama Villages Act   172–3
   Wagogo people   172
   working class   142
teleological Afro-radical narrative   90
teleological meta-narratives   93
teleology   204
   Aristotelian understanding of   125
Tempels, Placide   43
   Bantu Philosophy   159
   summary of premodern African thought   199
Terreblanche, Sampie   243
   Lost in Transformation: South Africa's Search for a New Future Since 1986   243

The History of Inequality in South Africa, 1652–2002   243
Text Worker   96, 100, 273, 274
theology
   civil   199
   social   199
thinker, private   99
thinking
   is becoming   273
   and being in relation to the law   263
   limits of   226
   meaning of   98, 99
   as recollection   111
   about thinking   225
Todorov, Tzvetan   19
   Hope and Memory: Lessons from the Twentieth Century   19–20
Touré, Sékou   156
tradition   227, 272
   reinvention of   197
Traditional Courts Bill   185
traditional courts, rural   186
Traditional Leadership and Governance Framework Act   186
transatlantic slave trade   87, 152
transformation   64–81
   implicit legitimacy   49
   of traditional leadership   186
transformative constitutionalisation   183
transformative constitutionalism   183, 240
transition from *sinnliche* to *morarische Harmonie*   194
trans-personal entities or forces   87
tribalism   253
trust or vote of confidence   155–6
Truth and Reconciliation Commission (TRC)   64, 74, 75, 79, 118, 176, 217
   amnesty to perpetrators   268

Tutsi state for the Hutu   255

ubuntu   40, 60
   conversion of into Ubuntu   66, 71
   as cultural praxis   45–6
   as ethnic morality   78–9
   ontic orientation   60
   philosophy   50
   praxis and abstract Ubuntu   76, 79–80
   praxis into Ubuntu philosophy   175–6
   qua glocal   54
   re-presentation of as Ubuntu   137
   sinnliche Harmonie   225
   transition to Ubuntu   194
   as Ubuntu   36–7, 84, 138, 141, 198, 205
   unity of idealist and materialist dimensions   33–4
Ubuntu
   as abstract ethic   78–9
   as African communitarianism   89
   as African humanism   89
   as African philosophy   4–5
   as African Socialism   89
   as authentic ethic with emancipatory potential   101
   contemporary abstract ethic   64
   dyspathetic, glocal phenomenon   273–4
   equivocate, generalise, juxtapose in debate on   266
   exceptionalism   216–21
   'I am because we are'   9, 52, 89, 122, 138, 207
   'I exist *because* of others'   42
   as Law of law   187–94
   logic of *qua* Law of laws   191, 192
   meaning of   246–54
   moralische Harmonie   225
   nationalism   138

as philosophical practice   45–6, 138
qua communitarianism   271
as quasi-transcendental status   187–94
question of modernity   194, 221
raison d'être   90, 123
as redemptive communalism   154
as Redemptive Gift   124–5
as revolutionary force   101
texts   104–5
as uncanny   252–3
unification   276
univocity and plurivocity   76–7
Ubuntu/botho   50, 52
ubuntufied Christianity
reconciliation and forgiveness   138
see also Christianised UbunTutu
ujamaa
as African Socialism   140–1
as political economy of obligation   137–8, 159
praxis of familyhood   140, 165
as Ujamaa   140, 141
Ujamaa   141
ban strategy   153–60
filter, ban, coerce   166
ideology   138, 142
ideology of Familyhood   162
national familyhood   140
project   150
supplement strategy   160–71
ujamaa/ubuntu
analogy   136–42
love, sharing, labour   164–5
love, sharing, work   69, 163, 165
ujamaa/Ujamaa   138
uncanny   248–50
the justice of justice   254–7
unheimlich (unhomely)   249

United Kingdom Labour conference   248
United Nations   129
General Assembly   127, 128
United States   238
adjudication   233–5
Democrats and Republicans   235
law and politics   233
party politics   234
United States of Africa   151–2
unity
dignity, community, material conditions   269
logic of   44
priority of   42
value of   4
universal phenomenon (Cosmopolitan)   96
urban constitutionalism   186
urbanisation   51, 80, 227

values
African communality and solidarity   176
historical   45
see also phallo-primocentric values
Van der Walt, Johan   228, 230–1, 233–4, 236, 239–40
Law and Sacrifice: Towards a Post-Apartheid Theory of Law   237, 239–41
Van Valen, Leigh   214
'A New Evolutionary Law'   214
Red Queen hypothesis   214
Vermeij, Geerat J.   214
Evolution and Escalation: An Ecological History of Life   214
victimisation neurosis   88
xenophobic, racist, negative, circular   88
victimology   87
violence   64, 69–70, 79, 135, 171–3, 222, 251–2

constitutive   22, 25, 33, 50, 65, 272
converting into a moral force   178
and the just   65–70
phallo-logocentric, the West   182
phallo-primocentric, precolonial African societies   182
as political choice   26
of sovereignty   116–17
translation of praxis into ideology   156
of ubuntu   178
visibility   177
on Western Other and African self   57

We
attempt to found an imagined   239
and the plurality or difference problem   230
spectral nature   269
substantial nature   269
wealth (development)   136–7
Weber, Max   65, 154–5
Western, contractarian Law of law   256
Western epistemological archive   272
Western hegemony   209
Western individualism versus African Communalism   193
Western individualist   23
Western modernity   64, 81–2, 124, 145, 179, 182, 209, 213, 222, 245, 251
    de-differentiation   252
    in-difference   252
    inexecution   252
    qua critique of   248
    racist   5
Western philosophical conception   13
Western social evolution   251
'wish image' (state yet to come)   167

World-Disclosing Humility   116, 124, 128, 129
world-historical developments   113–14
World-Redeeming Saviour   128

Yengeni, Tony   72–3

Zambian humanism   50–1
Zimbabwe   184
    Lancaster Agreement   184